DEATH BY DEFAULT

A Policy of Fatal Neglect
in China's State Orphanages

Human Rights Watch/Asia

Human Rights Watch
New York • Washington • Los Angeles • London • Brussels

ISBN 1-56432-163-0
Library of Congress Catalog Card Number 95-81738

HUMAN RIGHTS WATCH

Human Rights Watch conducts regular, systematic investigations of human rights abuses in some seventy countries around the world. It addresses the human rights practices of governments of all political stripes, of all geopolitical alignments, and of all ethnic and religious persuasions. In internal wars it documents violations by both governments and rebel groups. Human Rights Watch defends freedom of thought and expression, due process and equal protection of the law; it documents and denounces murders, disappearances, torture, arbitrary imprisonment, exile, censorship and other abuses of internationally recognized human rights.

Human Rights Watch began in 1978 with the founding of its Helsinki division. Today, it includes five divisions covering Africa, the Americas, Asia, the Middle East, as well as the signatories of the Helsinki accords. It also includes five collaborative projects on arms transfers, children's rights, free expression, prison conditions, and women's rights. It maintains offices in New York, Washington, Los Angeles, London, Brussels, Moscow, Dushanbe, Rio de Janeiro, and Hong Kong. Human Rights Watch is an independent, nongovernmental organization, supported by contributions from private individuals and foundations worldwide. It accepts no government funds, directly or indirectly.

The staff includes Kenneth Roth, executive director; Cynthia Brown, program director; Holly J. Burkhalter, advocacy director; Robert Kimzey, publications director; Jeri Laber, special advisor; Gara LaMarche, associate director; Lotte Leicht, Brussels office director; Juan Méndez, general counsel; Susan Osnos, communications director; Jemera Rone, counsel; Joanna Weschler, United Nations representative; and Derrick Wong, finance and administration director.

The regional directors of Human Rights Watch are Peter Takirambudde, Africa; José Miguel Vivanco, Americas; Sidney Jones, Asia; Holly Cartner, Helsinki; and Christopher E. George, Middle East. The project directors are Joost R. Hiltermann, Arms Project; Lois Whitman, Children's Rights Project; Gara LaMarche, Free Expression Project; and Dorothy Q. Thomas, Women's Rights Project.

The members of the board of directors are Robert L. Bernstein, chair; Adrian W. DeWind, vice chair; Roland Algrant, Lisa Anderson, Alice L. Brown, William Carmichael, Dorothy Cullman, Irene Diamond, Edith Everett, Jonathan Fanton, James C. Goodale, Jack Greenberg, Alice H. Henkin, Harold Hongju Koh, Jeh Johnson, Stephen L. Kass, Marina Pinto Kaufman, Alexander MacGregor, Josh Mailman, Andrew Nathan, Jane Olson, Peter Osnos, Kathleen Peratis, Bruce Rabb, Orville Schell, Sid Sheinberg, Gary G. Sick, Malcolm Smith, Nahid Toubia, Maureen White, and Rosalind C. Whitehead.

Addresses for Human Rights Watch
485 Fifth Avenue, New York, NY 10017-6104
Tel: (212) 972-8400, Fax: (212) 972-0905, E-mail: hrwnyc@hrw.org

1522 K Street, N.W., #910, Washington, DC 20005-1202
Tel: (202) 371-6592, Fax: (202) 371-0124, E-mail: hrwdc@hrw.org

10951 West Pico Blvd., #203, Los Angeles, CA 90064-2126
Tel: (310) 475-3070, Fax: (310) 475-5613, E-mail: hrwatchla@igc.apc.org

33 Islington High Street, N1 9LH London, UK
Tel: (171) 713-1995, Fax: (171) 713-1800, E-mail: hrwatchuk@gn.apc.org

15 Rue Van Campenhout, 1040 Brussels, Belgium
Tel: (2) 732-2009, Fax: (2) 732-0471, E-mail: hrwatcheu@gn.apc.org

Gopher Address://gopher.humanrights.org:port5000

"States Parties recognize that every child has the inherent right to life..."

U.N. Convention on the Rights of the Child (ratified by China in 1991)

"A physician shall owe his patient complete loyalty and all the resources of his science."

International Code of Medical Ethics, World Medical Association, 1949

"Sie ruh'n, sie ruh'n, als wie in der Mutter Haus" ("They rest, they rest, as if in their mother's house")

From *Kindertotenlieder* (Songs on the Death of Children), by Gustav Mahler

ACKNOWLEDGMENTS

This report was researched and written by Robin Munro, China researcher and director of the Hong Kong office of Human Rights Watch/Asia, and Jeff Rigsby, a consultant to Human Rights Watch/Asia and formerly a freelance journalist based in Shanghai. Robin Munro was the primary researcher for source materials cited in the text, compiled the mortality data and the individual medical histories, and wrote Chapter 4. Jeff Rigsby provided invaluable research assistance, translated published materials, and wrote the remainder of the text. The authors collaborated closely during the nine-month-long project and are jointly responsible for the final report. Human Rights Watch/Asia gratefully acknowledges the extensive assistance provided by staff of the Boston-based organization Physicians For Human Rights, who assembled an expert team of U.S. physicians to help us evaluate the medical data from Shanghai. We also extend our sincere thanks to the numerous people in China and elsewhere who contributed vital information but who, for various reasons, must remain anonymous. The report was edited by Cynthia Brown, program director of Human Rights Watch; Susan Osnos, the organization's communications director; and Juan Méndez, its general counsel; production assistance was provided by Paul Lall, an associate of Human Rights Watch/Asia. We are also grateful to Rick Schwab for his contribution of time and expertise in producing the photographs used in this report.

Our main debt is to Dr. Zhang Shuyun, formerly a senior staff member of the Shanghai Children's Welfare Institute. Beginning in 1989, Dr. Zhang led an unsuccessful four-year campaign to expose the abusive conditions prevailing at the Shanghai orphanage, an effort which ended her professional career. At much personal risk, Dr. Zhang left China in March 1995 to take her case to the international community. The painstaking compilation by her and many of her former colleagues of an extensive archive of primary documentation on the lives and deaths of Shanghai's orphaned and abandoned children provided the indispensable basis for this report. Major credit is also due to the numerous other residents of Shanghai who supported Dr. Zhang's efforts to protect the lives and dignity of the city's orphans. These included public officials, lawyers, doctors, journalists and ordinary citizens, all of whom in various ways helped, without realizing it, to prepare the ground for this report. While we must stress that they are in no way responsible for the content or conclusions of the report, we hope that they may take some satisfaction, three years after the defeat by local authorities of their own efforts to expose abuses against Chinese orphans, in its publication.

The majority of China's abandoned and orphaned infants die in total obscurity. Our acknowledgements would be incomplete without mentioning one notable survivor of the orphanage system, a person destined for a very different and still uncertain future. Ai Ming, who spent the first twenty years of his life at the Shanghai Children's Welfare Institute, escaped from China in June 1995, after recording crucial photographic evidence of the needless deaths at the Shanghai orphanage. This report is dedicated to him, in the hope of his eventual safe return to China.

CONTENTS

TABLES

I. SUMMARY AND RECOMMENDATIONS

China's Orphans and Human Rights

In response to widespread criticism of its human rights record, the Chinese government has frequently argued that the international community places too much emphasis on civil and political rights, while neglecting the more basic rights to food, shelter, and subsistence–rights which China claims to have secured for its citizens more effectively than some democratic countries. In accordance with the country's post-1949 political tradition, China's leaders assert that economic well-being forms the basis for the enjoyment of all other rights, and that the protection of economic rights can therefore justify restrictions on civil liberties.

In some important respects, China's record in protecting social and economic rights may serve as a model for the rest of the developing world. Levels of well-being, as measured by social indicators such as literacy and life expectancy, are considerably higher in China than in other countries at comparable stages of development, and in some cases higher than those in much wealthier nations.

But China's claim to guarantee the "right to subsistence" conceals a secret world of starvation, disease, and unnatural death–a world into which thousands of Chinese citizens disappear each year. The victims are neither the political activists nor the religious dissidents who dominate the international debate over human rights in the People's Republic; they are orphans and abandoned children in custodial institutions run by China's Ministry of Civil Affairs. This report documents the pattern of cruelty, abuse, and malign neglect which has dominated child welfare work in China since the early 1950s, and which now constitutes one of the country's gravest human rights problems.

Human Rights Watch/Asia has now pieced together at least a fragmentary picture of conditions for abandoned children throughout China, including staggering mortality rates for infants in state institutions and the persistent failure of official statistics to track the vast majority of orphans, whose whereabouts and status are unknown

The evidence–largely official documents cited in detail below–indicates that the likelihood of survival beyond one year, for a newly admitted orphan in China's welfare institutions nationwide, was less than 50 percent in 1989. The documents also show that overall annual mortality at many of China's orphanages is far higher than that documented in any other country. In Romania in December 1989, for example, when foreigners first visited the grim state orphanages housing abandoned and handicapped children and were outraged by what they found there, a representative of the France-based humanitarian group Médecins du Monde stated that the 1989 death rate from infectious disease and neglect was 40 percent, in one home that was

1

particularly abusive. In the Chinese provinces of Fujian, Shaanxi, Guangxi and Henan, overall annual mortality among institutionalized orphans that year ranged from 59.2 percent to 72.5 percent.

When sustained over an extended period, moreover, any of the above annual rates means far higher actual mortality. We estimate that in China's best-known and most prestigious orphanage, the Shanghai Children's Welfare Institute, total mortality in the late 1980s and early 1990s was probably running as high as 90 percent; even official figures put the annual deaths-to-admissions ratio at an appalling 77.6 percent in 1991, and partial figures indicate an increase in 1992. Neither institutional welfare policy nor the size of the orphanage system have changed notably since then, while the crisis of abandoned children continues unabated, due in part to China's one-child policy. In the case of Shanghai, there have been cosmetic improvements at the orphanage itself since 1993, designed to encourage foreign adoption, but there is evidence that many disabled infants and children are now simply transferred to a facility outside the city, where access for outsiders is extremely rare and where, according to numerous reports received by Human Rights Watch/Asia, the children are grossly mistreated.

Unlike their Romanian counterparts, the management and staff of China's orphanages cannot claim that their shortcomings result from a lack of funding or from inadequately paid employees. Dispelling a misconception reflected in nearly all Western media coverage of the issue to date, Human Rights Watch/Asia's research confirms that many Chinese orphanages, including some recording death rates among the worst in the country, appear to enjoy more than sufficient budgets, including adequate wages, bonuses, and other personnel-related costs. Expenses for children's food, clothing, and other necessities, however, are extremely low in institutions throughout the country.

The crisis, both nationwide and in Shanghai, is known to the top leadership of China's Ministry of Civil Affairs. Conditions at the Shanghai orphanage are well known to the local political elite and by members of the Politburo. But the government reaction has been to maintain a facade of normalcy, to punish dissenters who have sought to expose abuses and, in certain crucial cases, to promote those responsible for the abuses.

A Nationwide Crisis

Abandonment of children surged in China during the 1980s, in part due to the one-child population control policy and in part due to policies restricting adoption by Chinese couples who are not childless. The national statistics on mortality cited in this report do not contain a gender breakdown, but anecdotal and journalistic reporting on orphanages nationwide reveals that the vast majority of children in orphanages are, and consistently have been during the past decade, healthy infant girls; that is, children without serious disabilities who are abandoned because of traditional attitudes that value boy children more highly. The financial and social problems that these children are perceived to constitute are made more acute by the fact that Chinese couples are not permitted to adopt them, for the most part.

Reports of inhumane conditions in Chinese orphanages have attracted growing international concern in recent years, prompted chiefly by the country's greater openness to foreign press coverage and charitable work financed from abroad, as well as a dramatic increase in overseas adoptions from the People's Republic. Although some scattered allegations have succeeded in bringing to light grave abuses against China's orphans, there has been virtually no effort to place these charges in context through systematic research on the country's institutional welfare system.

The Chinese government's own statistics reveal a situation worse than even the most alarming Western media reports have suggested. In 1989, the most recent year for which nationwide figures are available, the majority of abandoned children admitted to China's orphanages were dying in institutional care. Many institutions, including some in major cities, appeared to be operating as little more than assembly lines for the elimination of unwanted orphans, with an annual turnover of admissions and deaths far exceeding the number of beds available.

In any case, the majority of abandoned children in China never reach the dubious security of a state-run orphanage. Many are sent instead to general-purpose state institutions, where they are confined indiscriminately with retarded, disabled, elderly, and mentally disturbed adults. Although the statistical evidence is unclear, the limited eyewitness information available suggests that death rates among children held in these facilities may be even higher than in China's specialized orphanages.

In addition, Chinese official records fail to account for most of the country's abandoned infants and children, only a small proportion of whom are in any form of acknowledged state care. The most recent figure provided by the government for the country's orphan population, 100,000 seems implausibly low for a country with a total population of 1.2 billion. Even if it were accurate, however, the whereabouts of the great majority of China's orphans would still be a complete mystery, leaving crucial questions about the country's child welfare system unanswered and suggesting that the real scope of the catastrophe that has befallen China's unwanted children may be far larger than the evidence in this report documents.

Evidence From Shanghai

In addition to nationwide statistics on the condition of China's institutionalized children, Human Rights Watch/Asia has recently obtained a large quantity of internal documentation from one of the most prominent specialized orphanages in the country, the Shanghai Children's Welfare Institute. Based on these documents, which include medical records and other official files recording the deaths of hundreds of children, and on the testimony of direct witnesses who left China in 1995, Human Rights Watch/Asia has concluded that conditions at the Shanghai orphanage before 1993 were comparable to those at some of the worst children's institutions in China, several of which have already been exposed in journalistic accounts in the West. Since 1993, a program of cosmetic "reforms" has transformed the Shanghai Children's Welfare Institute into an international showcase for China's social policies, while an administrative reorganization of the city's welfare system has largely concealed the continuing abuse of infants and children.

Ironically, the Chinese government has praised Shanghai's municipal orphanage extensively as a national model for the care of abandoned and disabled children. In addition to frequent flattering coverage in China's official media, the Shanghai Children's Welfare Institute receives considerable financial support from Chinese and international charities and hosts a steady stream of private and official visitors. Behind the institution's glossy official image, however, lies a pattern of horrifying abuse. The brutal treatment of orphans in Shanghai, which included deliberate starvation, torture, and sexual assault, continued over a period of many years and led to the unnatural deaths of well over 1,000 children between 1986 and 1992 alone. This campaign of elimination could be kept secret through the complicity of both higher- and lower-level staff, and because the city's Bureau of Civil Affairs, responsible for the orphanage, also runs the crematoria, where starved children's corpses were disposed of with minimum oversight, often even before a death certificate had been filled out by the attending physician. In addition, officials of various Shanghai municipal agencies knowingly suppressed evidence of child abuse at the orphanage, persistently ignored the institute's high monthly death figures, and in 1992, quashed an investigation into orphanage practices.

Conditions in the Shanghai orphanage came close to being publicly exposed in the early 1990s as a result of pressure by concerned orphanage employees, local journalists and sympathetic Shanghai officials. By 1993, however, virtually all the critical staff members were forced out of their positions and silenced. The orphanage leadership was assisted in its efforts to cover up the truth by three of the city's top leaders: Wu Bangguo, Shanghai's Communist Party secretary; Huang Ju, the city's mayor; and Xie Lijuan, deputy mayor for health, education, and social welfare. Wu, Huang, and Xie were fully informed of the abuses occurring at the Children's Welfare Institute, but took no action to halt them or to punish those responsible, acting instead to shield senior management at the orphanage and to prevent news of the abuses from reaching the public. Meanwhile, Wu Bangguo and Huang Ju have risen to positions of national prominence in China's ruling Politburo.

The cosmetic changes at the Shanghai orphanage since 1993 have been engineered by Han Weicheng, its former director. Although he was a major perpetrator of abuses there, Han was promoted to an even more senior position within the municipal welfare bureaucracy. At about the same time, the orphanage was opened to visitors and large numbers of children from the city's orphanage began to be transferred to another custodial institution, the Shanghai No. 2 Social Welfare Institute. Located on Chongming Island, a remote rural area north of Shanghai, the No. 2 Social Welfare Institute, which is ostensibly a home for severely retarded adults, has been transformed since 1993 into a virtual dumping ground for abandoned infants delivered to the orphanage. While the city government has aggressively promoted the adoption of healthy or mildly disabled orphans by visiting foreigners, reports from visitors to the orphanage in 1995 indicate that infants with more serious handicaps are generally diverted to the Chongming Island institution within weeks or months of their arrival. Human Rights Watch/Asia has not been able to ascertain the mortality rates of children at the No. 2 Social Welfare Institute, but has collected credible reports of severe mistreatment and of staff impunity. Extreme secrecy surrounds the functioning of the Chongming Island institution, raising serious suspicions and fears as to the likely fate of children transferred there.

Perversion of Medical Ethics

Some Western observers have charged that the phenomenally high death rates among China's abandoned children result from neglect and lack of medical training on the part of orphanage employees. Anecdotal evidence from foreign charity workers and adoptive parents has painted a grim picture of decrepit and poorly financed institutions run by demoralized and unskilled nursing staff.

However, medical records and testimony obtained by Human Rights Watch/Asia show that deaths at the Shanghai orphanage were in many cases deliberate and cruel. Child-care workers reportedly selected unwanted infants and children for death by intentional deprivation of food and water—a process known among the workers as the "summary resolution" of childrens' alleged medical problems. When an orphan chosen in this manner was visibly on the point of death from starvation or medical neglect, orphanage doctors were then asked to perform medical "consultations" which served as a ritual marking the child for subsequent termination of care, nutrition, and other life-saving intervention. Deaths from acute malnutrition were then, in many cases, falsely recorded as having resulted from other causes, often entirely spurious or irrelevant conditions such as "mental deficiency" and "cleft palate."

The vast majority of children's deaths recorded at the Shanghai orphanage thus resulted not from lack of access to medical care but from something far more sinister: an apparently systematic program of child elimination in which senior medical staff played a central role. By making unfounded diagnoses of mental retardation and other disorders, these doctors have helped to disseminate the widespread belief–which appears to be quite inaccurate–that virtually all of China's abandoned children are physically or mentally handicapped. Worse, the Shanghai orphanage's medical staff then used these supposed disabilities as a justification for eliminating unwanted infants through starvation and medical neglect. Such unconscionable behavior by doctors in China's most advanced and cosmopolitan city points to an ethical crisis of immense proportions in the country's medical profession.

This corruption of medical ethics reflects broader trends in Chinese law and health policy, including recent debates in the National People's Congress, the country's nominal legislature, on legalizing euthanasia for the incapacitated elderly. Official press reports indicate that the Chinese government may also have given serious consideration to allowing euthanasia for handicapped children, but has declined to do so for fear of the international repercussions. The medical evidence suggests, however, that just such pseudo-eugenic practices may have been carried out at the Shanghai Children's Welfare Institute. At the very least, the city's abandoned infants, even when not genuinely disabled, became the victims of a policy of deliberate and fatal neglect resulting in their wholesale death by default.

Reports from the Shanghai orphanage also indicate that medical staff there misused their authority in other ways. In several cases, children who were accused of misbehavior or were in a position to expose abuses at the orphanage were falsely diagnosed as "mentally ill" and transferred to psychiatric hospitals against their will; in one case, a teenage girl named Chou Hui was imprisoned for four months to prevent her from testifying that she had been raped by orphanage director Han Weicheng. Many other children were given powerful drugs without any apparent medical justification, in order to control their behavior. Human Rights Watch/Asia calls on the leaders of the Chinese medical profession to denounce these gross ethical violations and to take urgent steps to improve standards of medical ethics in China.

The Need For A Worldwide Response

The enormous loss of life occurring in China's orphanages and other children's institutions calls for immediate action by the international community. The United Nations and its specialized agencies must take the lead in investigating conditions in China's child welfare system and in bringing these abuses to an end. Governments throughout the world must make the treatment of China's abandoned children one of their highest priorities as they continue to press for improvements in the country's human rights record.

The People's Republic of China ratified the United Nations Convention on the Rights of the Child in December 1991, and submitted its first implementation report to the U.N. Committee on the Rights of the Child in 1994. The Chinese government has thus submitted itself voluntarily to international monitoring on the treatment of its minor citizens. Nevertheless, the evidence compiled in this report shows that China's policies towards abandoned infants and children are in clear violation of many articles of the convention. Human Rights Watch/Asia urges the Committee on the Rights of the Child to place conditions in the Chinese child welfare system at the top of its agenda for the coming year. Specialized agencies working on children's issues in China, such as the United Nations Children's Fund (UNICEF) and the World Health Organization, should also make a thorough reform of the country's orphanage system their highest priority. We further call for an immediate investigation into abuses against institutionalized children in China by the Special Rapporteur on Extrajudicial Executions, who investigates patterns of deliberate state action resulting in death.

Action by the United Nations and its agencies must be accompanied by a strong response from national governments. Bilateral pressure on China to ensure the rights of abandoned infants and children should be given at least as high a priority as demands to free political and religious detainees or to end torture and ill-treatment in the country's prisons. Protecting the lives of China's orphans must remain at the top of the agenda in any future human rights dialogue with the Chinese authorities.

Despite the Chinese government's generally hostile attitude towards Western human rights organizations, Human Rights Watch/Asia believes that many government and Communist Party officials will recognize the need for immediate action to resolve this humanitarian crisis. Other branches of the Chinese government must hold the Ministry of Civil Affairs and its officials fully accountable for the atrocities being committed against China's orphans. Human Rights Watch/Asia calls on the authorities to take immediate steps to bring an end to these abuses and offers its full cooperation to the Chinese authorities in formulating the necessary reforms. A list of the organization's recommendations follows.

Ending Impunity in Shanghai

Most Chinese citizens familiar only with official media reports on the Shanghai Children's Welfare Institute accept the authorities' claim that conditions for the city's orphans are exemplary. This report shows that the fate of most abandoned children in Shanghai is, in fact, much the same as elsewhere in China. Until 1993, the majority of infants brought to the institute died there within a few months of arrival, and the minority who survived to older childhood were subject to brutal abuse and neglect.

Indeed, the only genuinely unique feature of the Shanghai orphanage appears to be its success since 1993 at generating revenue for the municipal Civil Affairs Bureau. The city's newly reorganized child welfare system now presents the municipal orphanage as its acceptable public face, serving as an advertisement for both charitable giving and profitable foreign adoptions, and a ban on negative media coverage of the Children's Welfare Institute has been in force since 1992.

Human Rights Watch/Asia believes that the spectacular financial success of the Shanghai policies is the real motive behind official praise of the city's child welfare system as a national model. We fear that efforts to duplicate the Shanghai experience elsewhere in China are likely to further worsen conditions for the country's abandoned children, and to strengthen the vested interest of the Ministry of Civil Affairs in obstructing genuine reforms.

Any attempt to improve the treatment of Chinese orphans must therefore begin by reopening the official investigation into misconduct within the Shanghai Civil Affairs Bureau, launched in 1991 and abruptly terminated the following year. Above all, such an inquiry would seek the widest possible publicity for any evidence of wrongdoing uncovered and would pursue appropriate legal sanctions against bureau employees found responsible for abusing children and causing avoidable deaths.

Such an inquiry will confront the fact that a number of people associated directly or indirectly with abuses at the Shanghai orphanage continue to hold positions of authority, and many have since been promoted or otherwise risen in status. The beneficiaries of this apparent impunity range from ordinary staff members such as the child-care worker Xu Shanzhen, certified as a "model worker" in early 1995 despite her brutal abuse of a retarded child, to the former Communist Party secretary of Shanghai, Wu Bangguo, who reportedly ordered media coverage of the scandal suppressed and has since been appointed vice-premier of China.

However, these obstacles make it all the more imperative that swift action be taken at the most senior levels to break the cycle of impunity. Human Rights Watch/Asia urges the Chinese authorities to take the following immediate steps:

1) The highest government and Communist Party officials in the country should publicly state their determination to investigate unnatural deaths and abuse of children in welfare institutions run by the Shanghai Civil Affairs Bureau.

To demonstrate this commitment, the authorities should immediately reopen the 1991 inquiry into conditions at the Shanghai Children's Welfare Institute. The leadership of the new investigation should be entirely independent of both the Shanghai municipal government and the Ministry of Civil Affairs. Such an inquiry could be led by a specially appointed committee of delegates to the National People's Congress or the Chinese People's Political Consultative Conference. Members of the committee should include medical and legal professionals and should be drawn from throughout the country.

Pending the outcome of the investigation, all management personnel at the institution should be suspended from their positions and replaced by an independent leadership group, preferably including a number of qualified medical doctors, which would aid the authorities in gathering evidence about conditions at the orphanage. Administrative authority over the city's custodial welfare system should be temporarily transferred from the Shanghai Civil Affairs Bureau to another government department, possibly the Shanghai Public Health Bureau.

2) The authorities should emphasize that institute staff members implicated in criminal offenses against children, including murder, rape, assault, sexual abuse, and financial corruption, will be tried and punished according to Chinese law. Criminal penalties should be applied as well to those responsible for administrative violations, such as falsification of medical records and unlawful disposal of corpses, which constitute, among others, the crime of "dereliction of duty" (*duzhi zui*) under China's Criminal Code.

In reopening the investigation, the authorities should place particular emphasis on the practices of "summary resolution" before 1993, whereby children were intentionally killed through deprivation of food and medical care. Public statements by senior officials should stress that all such incidents, where they can be verified, will be prosecuted to the full extent under Chinese law.

3) The scope of the investigation should be extended beyond the original terms of the inquiry launched in 1991, and should examine evidence of complicity by senior Shanghai officials in shielding the management of the Children's Welfare Institute. Criminal charges of "dereliction of duty" should be brought against present and former city officials who appear to have knowingly suppressed evidence of child abuse at the orphanage. Among the officials so implicated, in official documents cited in this report, are Wu Bangguo, the former Communist Party secretary of Shanghai; Huang Ju, Shanghai's former mayor; Xie Lijuan, the city's deputy mayor; and Sun Jinfu, director of the Shanghai Civil Affairs Bureau.

4) The investigation should also examine the legal culpability of other official bodies in Shanghai which helped to conceal misconduct within the Civil Affairs Bureau, in the process implicating their own officials in possible criminal acts. At a minimum, these include:

- the Shanghai Public Security Bureau, for allowing the Children's Welfare Institute to disobey regulations governing the reporting of unnatural deaths; for unlawfully detaining and intimidating Chou

Hui, the plaintiff in a rape case against the then-director of the orphanage, Han Weicheng; and for failing to investigate the orphanage employees accused of assaulting Chen Dongxian, a driver at the Shanghai orphanage;

- the Shanghai Public Health Bureau, for failing to investigate the extremely high monthly death figures reported from the Children's Welfare Institute over a period of years;

- the Shanghai Supervision Bureau, for suppressing evidence obtained during an eight-month-long inquiry that it carried out into conditions at the Children's Welfare Institute in 1991 and 1992.

5) The investigation should urgently examine the present situation at the Shanghai No.2 Social Welfare Institute, including evidence of unlawful practices such as the detention of mentally normal adults against their will; and, the use of disciplinary measures constituting torture or ill-treatment. Special attention should also be paid to conditions for infants and young children secretly transferred to the Chongming Island institute since 1993, and should seek to determine whether the killing of infants through "summary resolution" or other similar methods is presently occurring there. A criminal investigation should be opened into the alleged rape and murder of a twenty-nine-year-old woman, named Guang Zi, at the facility in August 1991.

6) The municipal Propaganda Department should lift its present ban on critical coverage of events at the Children's Welfare Institute, and invite journalists familiar with conditions at the orphanage to publish any information which might assist the authorities in their investigation. The progress of the official inquiry, including any resulting criminal prosecutions, should be publicized without restraint by local and national media.

Public Accountability

Despite the urgent need to resolve these outstanding problems in Shanghai, the above measures represent only the first stage of what should be a nationwide campaign to improve conditions for children in China's welfare institutes. A critical factor in the success of any such effort will be the Chinese government's willingness to expose these institutions to intensive public scrutiny, not only from concerned foreigners but, even more importantly, from China's own citizens. The deceptive policy of "openness" introduced by the Shanghai Children's Welfare Institute in 1993 must be replaced by genuine transparency in order to prevent future abuses from going undetected.

Human Rights Watch/Asia believes the following measures are likely to produce immediate and substantial improvements in the quality of care for children in state custody, even without fundamental reforms in management and law:

1)   The Ministry of Civil Affairs should immediately publish comprehensive statistics on the scale of China's child abandonment problem. These should give detailed figures on the number of abandoned infants and children discovered in each Chinese province in recent years, as well as the number of such children offered up for legal adoption, fostered with private families, and placed in institutional care.

The ministry should also publish a list of all custodial institutions in China which care for unsupported minors, including specialized orphanages, urban "social welfare institutes," and collectively run "respecting-the-aged homes" in rural areas. The list should include the location of each institution and its population on a specified date, as well as all available statistics on child intake and mortality rates in recent years. In future, such basic population statistics for each institution should be published on an annual basis.

Since most abandoned infants and children in China are delivered to the civil affairs authorities by local police departments and hospitals, the Ministry of Public Security and the Ministry of Public Health should begin compiling and publishing regular statistics on child abandonment, including the sex and estimated age of each child discovered. This will provide an independent check on the accuracy of intake figures submitted to the Ministry of Civil Affairs by individual institutions, and will prevent the under-reporting of intakes which allegedly took place in Shanghai during the 1980s.

2)   The Ministry of Civil Affairs should make public its policy on "fostering" orphans and abandoned children in private family care, including details of the screening process, if any, for prospective foster parents, and of monitoring procedures aimed at ensuring that fostered children are treated humanely.

3)   The propaganda organs of the Communist Party should publicize the severe problems in Shanghai's child welfare system, and instruct the state-controlled media throughout China to investigate conditions for children in welfare institutions within their own area of coverage. The Ministry of Civil

Affairs should ensure that journalists participating in these investigations receive full cooperation from institute staff, including unrestricted access to all children in each institution. Any abusive or negligent conditions uncovered during the course of journalists' inquiries should be publicly exposed and promptly remedied. Objective reporting on conditions in China's child welfare system should remain a priority indefinitely.

4)   Welfare institutes should permit unscheduled visits by local residents, including both Chinese and foreign nationals. Local civil affairs authorities should encourage public involvement in the care of orphans, particularly by qualified medical personnel.

5)   The United Nations Children's Fund (UNICEF) and established private children's charities from overseas should be granted access on a regular basis to all welfare institutions holding minors.

Management Reforms

Although the steps outlined above are likely to bring about a sharp reduction in some of the worst abuses within the child welfare system, basic changes in institutional management are equally important in order to guarantee that these initial improvements last. These include administrative measures to strengthen the outside monitoring of children's treatment, as well as improvements in the selection, training and discipline of institute staff. Human Rights Watch/Asia recommends that the Chinese authorities undertake the following reforms:

1)   The leadership of the Ministry of Civil Affairs should publicly state its commitment to improving conditions for institutionalized children, and should emphasize that the directors of welfare institutes and other management-level staff will be evaluated primarily on their success in reducing children's death rates to an absolute minimum. The directors of welfare institutes where child mortality rates appear to be higher than expected, given normal levels of care, should be subject to investigation and dismissed if mismanagement is shown to be a contributing factor.

2)   The Ministry of Civil Affairs should immediately begin reorganizing its custodial welfare system to ensure that minors and adults are kept in separate institutions. The use of all-purpose "social welfare institutes" to warehouse orphans and other incapacitated persons should be ended as soon as practically possible.

3) The Ministry of Civil Affairs should cooperate with the Ministry of Public Health and the Ministry of Public Security to ensure that staff of welfare institutions strictly follow all rules and other legal requirements regarding the reporting of inmates' deaths. All deaths of minors in institutional care should be treated as potentially unnatural, and hence subject to reporting, investigation and documentation requirements of the Public Security Bureau, as well as independent autopsies by qualified medical personnel affiliated with the Bureau of Public Health. Local health bureaus which are notified of a significant number of children's deaths in welfare institutions within their jurisdiction should immediately call for an investigation by local authorities.

4) The Ministry of Civil Affairs should promulgate strict rules prohibiting the abuse of children in welfare institutions, such as excessive corporal punishment, tying of children's limbs, medically unjustified use of drugs to control children's behavior, and all forms of paid or unpaid child labor. The ministry should also promulgate a formal disciplinary policy to be applied by institute management in cases of misconduct by junior staff.

5) All staff at custodial welfare institutes should undertake a period of formal training, aimed at impressing on newly assigned employees that the protection of inmates' well-being is of paramount importance. Ordinary child-care workers should be trained in basic first-aid techniques, particularly to respond to cases of choking and accidental injuries, and in appropriate feeding methods for infants and small children, especially those with disabilities.

6) Welfare institutes should be staffed with, or (where personnel shortages cannot be resolved) be provided with full and regular outside consultancy services by, an adequate number of fully qualified medical professionals, including specialists in pediatrics. Doctors whose medical educations were interrupted, for example during the Cultural Revolution, should not be employed as institute medical staff unless they have completed the necessary remedial coursework.

7) The surgical repair of harelips, cleft palates and other correctable birth defects should be one of the highest medical priorities for welfare institutes and cooperating local hospitals. Abandoned infants requiring these relatively inexpensive procedures should receive them as soon as medically advisable, and should be given individual attention in the meantime to ensure that they remain adequately nourished.

8)   Infants and small children should not be classified as "mentally retarded" until they are old enough to undergo appropriate psychological tests. Training programs for child-care workers should emphasize the importance of individual care, attention and stimulation for infants' normal mental development.

Legislative Reforms

The phenomenon of child abandonment is not unique to China, and many of the factors which lead parents to abandon their children are beyond the government's power to remedy, at least in the short term. Rural poverty, prejudice against the disabled, traditional attitudes towards female children, and the pressures generated by the country's stringent population policy all contribute to the problem. It must be stressed, however, that whatever the reasons for the orphanhood or abandonment, once such children are accepted into state care, the government has an unshirkable duty to provide them with adequate care and protection.

For the foreseeable future, China will need to maintain a system of state-run foster care for some orphans, particularly the severely disabled. However, Human Rights Watch/Asia believes that relatively minor legislative changes would enable most children now living in welfare institutions to be placed for adoption with Chinese families. An effective domestic adoption program would eliminate the need for institutional care for virtually all of China's abandoned children.

Human Rights Watch/Asia urges the Chinese authorities to take the following steps:

1)   China's "Adoption Law" and its implementing regulations should be amended to abolish the legal distinction between "orphans" and "abandoned infants." The provisions of the adoption law which prohibit adults under age thirty-five and couples with children from adopting abandoned infants without handicaps, and which prohibit foster parents from adopting more than one abandoned child, should be repealed.

2)   The State Commission for Family Planning should issue instructions to local family planning authorities, expressly prohibiting any interference in the adoption of children from welfare institutions.

3)   The propaganda organs of the Communist Party should publicize changes in the country's adoption policy through the official media. Both the media and the State Commission for Family Planning should actively promote the adoption of orphans as an alternative for couples seeking larger families than China's population policies allow.

II. SOCIAL WELFARE IN MODERN CHINA

Organized programs of foster care for orphans and abandoned children have existed in China since long before the founding of the People's Republic. In certain parts of the country, mainly the south, such welfare work was traditionally carried out by "benevolent associations" established by clans or extended families, often financed by endowments of farmland. Elsewhere, charitable institutions funded by wealthy individuals and groups provided similar assistance on a more limited scale. Beginning in the nineteenth century, humanitarian work by foreigners, organized almost exclusively by the country's growing number of Catholic and Protestant missions, expanded dramatically and began to play a primary role in caring for Chinese orphans, particularly in the major cities.

After the 1949 revolution, China's privately financed charities were rapidly deprived of their economic basis, as land reform destroyed the financial power of the rural clans and the nationalization of urban business eliminated the old middle class. The new government's religious policies banned proselytizing by foreign nationals and forced China's Christian churches to sever their overseas links, leading to the departure of all Western missionaries by the early 1950s. Even so, the unraveling of this often woefully inadequate system of private charity must have been viewed with little regret, or even as being a step forward, by many observers at the time. A new political system held out the hope of eradicating many of the social evils which earlier reformers had hoped merely to alleviate: hunger, unemployment, prostitution, drug addiction, and vagrancy.

Nearly five decades later, proof of widespread atrocities in the country's state-run orphanages, including the routine murder of children by deliberate starvation, calls for a fundamental reevaluation of China's record on protecting the civil and political rights of its citizens, to address these and other severe abuses which result, directly or indirectly, from government policies in the realm of social and economic rights. This chapter surveys the transformation of China's social welfare system since 1949, and identifies the historical and political roots of the crisis now devastating the country's abandoned children. On the basis of documents published by the Chinese authorities themselves, Human Rights Watch/Asia has established that the People's Republic has not, at any time since its foundation, attempted to provide adequate care for orphans and other dependent groups, such as the handicapped, the destitute elderly, and the mentally disabled. Instead, the interests of the needy have been consistently subordinated to those of powerful political interest groups, particularly the Communist Party and military establishments, and to the goals of a series of political campaigns. For the majority of abandoned children in China today, the state's policy of malign neglect means an early and lingering death.

15

China's Civil Affairs Bureaucracy: Welfare State Or Police State?

A New Order

The concept of "social work" has always had an ambiguous significance in the People's Republic of China. Although the term is often used in roughly the Western sense, to describe the state's humanitarian and protective responsibilities towards the disadvantaged, it can also convey the very different meaning of "social control," directed at elements of society considered dangerous. The so-called "Social Department" (*Shehuibu*) of the Communist Party's Central Committee, for example, was responsible for promulgating comprehensive prison regulations shortly before the party seized power in 1949.[1] In the first years of the new government, both the humanitarian and coercive elements of "social work" played a crucial role in consolidating Party authority.

The Communist victory saw a dramatic reduction in the number of people in need of charitable relief, as the end of more than a decade of almost continuous warfare restored basic public order and the normal functioning of the economy. But China's leaders also expected that the establishment of a new economic system would virtually eliminate the need for *ad hoc* assistance in the future. Indeed, the entire concept of allowing "social work" to continue in a socialist society was ideologically suspect, since it called into question the state's promise to eradicate the old evils of poverty and social marginalization. One representative official text on the subject takes special pains to distinguish between "capitalist" and "socialist" forms of social work:

> In line with the development of the capitalist economy, some capitalist countries use the slogans of the "welfare state" and "social service" to undertake broad social work encompassing many aspects of social life. But their set of social insurance and welfare measures and social relief policies is mainly for harmonizing disputes between labor and capital, moderating class contradictions, and satisfying the needs of the monopoly capitalist class. They reflect the reformism of the bourgeoisie and are a manifestation of unbalanced capitalist development.[2]

---

[1] "Prison Regulations of the Social Department of the Communist Party Central Committee" (1948), reprinted in *Contemporary Prisons of Hubei (Hubei Jindai Jianyu)*, Hubeisheng Xinwen Chubanju, December 1987, pp.256-257.

[2] "Social Work and Social Welfare in Chinese Socialism," in Lu Mouhua, *Specialized Topics in Civil Affairs Work (Minzheng Gongzuo Zhuanlun)* (Nanchang: Jiangxi Renmin Chubanshe, April 1988), p.4.

In accordance with this doctrine, China's earlier programs of charitable relief, whether financed by the Nationalist government or by private donors, were uniformly dismissed as part of a strategy of "welfarism" (*fulizhuyi*) aimed at diffusing working-class resentment and undermining opposition to the capitalist system. But the Communist authorities recognized that major social problems still remained to be dealt with:

> In a socialist society, the production of poverty by class exploitation and class oppression has been wiped out, and the social-class origins of the series of problems produced by poverty have already been rooted out. But in the final analysis, a change in the social system cannot result in the life of the society being totally discontinued and reconstructed, and the problems of poverty handed down from the old society cannot be eradicated and cleaned up in a brief historical period.[3]

The task of "cleaning up" these problems in a socialist society was therefore characterized as a limited project, one which might take some time but would nevertheless end when the residual effects of the "old society" had fully passed away. Just as importantly, such work represented a clean break from the reformist policies of the recent past:

> It is not the compassionate favor of some philanthropist, nor is it a tool for moderating class contradictions under the cruel exploitation and violent oppression of the bourgeoisie. In essence, the task of social relief and welfare work under socialism is an indispensable part of constructing socialist material and spiritual civilization. This is the basic nature and content of socialist social work.[4]

The historical evidence, however, tells a different story. Both the scope and the priorities of Chinese social policy during the socialist period have been far more explicitly "welfarist" than at any time in recent history. The primary function of social work since 1949 has been to maintain support for the authorities among politically influential sections of the population, including China's military and Communist Party

---

[3] *Ibid.*, p.4.

[4] *Ibid.*, p.4.

elites. At the same time, the strong ideological pressure to demonstrate that the need for "social work" is indeed being gradually eliminated has led to wholesale denial of China's very real difficulties, including the problem of child abandonment. The politically driven aim of minimizing such problems has consistently led to an extreme form of tokenism, in which only symbolic efforts are made to address a massive humanitarian challenge.

The Dual Function of the Civil Affairs Authorities

The Communists' use of "social work" as a tool of political control constitutes part of a broader strategy, initiated immediately after the 1949 revolution, of eliminating all potential challenges to Party authority by turning China's citizens into wards of the state. During the early years of the new government, urban joblessness was virtually eliminated by a system of lifetime employment and comprehensive social benefits for workers in state enterprises, while collective agriculture was expected to provide for the basic material needs of the peasantry. For a sizeable number of young peasants, enlistment in the armed forces offered one of the few legitimate paths of social mobility, as well as incomes that were sometimes higher than those available on the rural communes. This comprehensive system of guaranteed employment often failed to assure minimum levels of subsistence, particularly in rural areas, but it did succeed in transforming nearly the entire population into direct or indirect dependents of the Communist government.

The authorities recognized, however, that the combination of state employment in the cities, communal agriculture in the countryside, and a massive military and bureaucratic establishment would fail to include a small minority of Chinese citizens, who for various reasons could not participate effectively in production. These included demobilized and disabled soldiers and their dependents; villagers affected by natural disasters; elderly peasants without family members to rely on for support; and those requiring institutionalization, including orphans and abandoned children as well as the mentally ill, the handicapped, and the severely retarded.

Responsibility for the care and management of these groups was originally assigned to the "civil affairs departments" (*minzheng bumen*) of China's Interior Ministry.[5] During the Cultural Revolution, the Interior Ministry was abolished and its various duties parceled out to other agencies, with the tasks of its civil affairs departments eventually transferred, in 1978, to a newly established Ministry of Civil Affairs.

---

[5] This term was in use long before the establishment of the People's Republic. Official departments dealing with "civil affairs" existed in China even during the imperial period.

The public face of "civil affairs work" includes an assortment of social responsibilities, which are officially divided into four broad categories:

- paying cash benefits to military personnel, veterans, "revolutionary martyrs" and their dependents ("preferential care work");

- placing demobilized military personnel in civilian employment ("settlement work");

- supplying aid to disaster areas, regions of chronic food shortage, and individuals and families in distress ("social relief work");

- operating sheltered workshops for the handicapped and institutions for custodial care, including orphanages, old-age homes, and psychiatric hospitals ("social welfare work").

The civil affairs bureacracy thus purports to fill the unavoidable gaps in a socialist welfare system which is otherwise very extensive.[6] But it also performs a much wider range of less publicized functions, many of which serve to enforce social control rather than guarantee social welfare. Some of these administrative duties, such as the demarcation of boundaries between administrative jurisdictions, are relatively uncontroversial.[7] In other cases, however, an ostensibly neutral function serves a hidden authoritarian purpose. All marriages in China, for example, must be registered with local bureaus of the Ministry of Civil Affairs, a requirement which allows the ministry's staff to prohibit early marriages and to screen couples for their supposed "eugenic" compatibility.[8] Chinese citizens seeking to establish nongovernmental organizations (NGOs) or other private associations are also required to register first with the Ministry of Civil Affairs, thus assigning the ministry frontline responsibility for the suppression of independent social and political activity in China. Notable

---

[6] With the recent shift to market economic policies in urban China, the Ministry of Civil Affairs has begun to assume additional tasks similar to those of welfare bureaucracies in the West, such as paying unemployment benefits to workers laid off from state enterprises.

[7] The recent experiments with "direct village elections" in China's rural areas, sometimes described as a step towards further political liberalization, are also administered by the Ministry of Civil Affairs.

[8] The civil affairs departments play a major role in enforcing the eugenic provisions of China's newly-enacted "Law on Maternal and Infant Health Care," as well as provincial family-planning regulations which are sometimes even more draconian.

victims of this policy (which has been in effect since the 1950s, though only recently codified in legislation) include the Beijing-based dissident Tong Zeng, who applied unsuccessfully to register an organization to campaign for the payment of war reparations to Chinese citizens by the government of Japan; and also members of the Shanghai-based "China Human Rights Association," who attempted repeatedly but fruitlessly prior to 1994 to register their organization with the civil affairs authorities, and most of whom subsequently received three-year jail terms for their efforts.

The civil affairs departments often combine social welfare and law enforcement aims in the same policies. For example, the legal distinction between urban and rural residents, which has traditionally formed the basis for guaranteed employment in China's cities, is maintained only by a strict policy of forcibly returning unauthorized rural migrants to their places of origin. Such returns are administered and carried out by the Ministry of Civil Affairs, which operates special urban "deportation stations" for this purpose. The ministry also shares responsibility with the Ministry of Public Security for the management of compulsory drug-rehabilitation centers.

In some cases, the functions of "civil affairs work" are even more explicitly punitive. The Ministry of Civil Affairs controls the so-called "work-study schools" (*bangong bandu* or *gong-du xuexiao*), which are youth reformatories authorized to detain juvenile offenders without trial. It is also one of three departments (together with the Ministry of Public Security and the Ministry of Labor, which administer China's system of "labor re-education," in which adult alleged offenders can be held in custody without trial for up to three years.

The Elite Priority: "Preferential Care" and "Settlement"

With its hodgepodge of charitable, administrative, and coercive duties, the Ministry of Civil Affairs is a distinctly odd candidate for managing orphanages and other custodial-care institutions. Moreover, the distorted set of priorities imposed on the ministry from above has virtually guaranteed that these tasks would be neglected or ignored altogether. Thus, the introduction to one of the few official English-language texts on civil affairs work summarized the ministry's social responsibilities in the late 1980s as follows:

> The work of the civil affairs departments includes: handling social welfare service, giving relief to people in disaster areas and in poverty; [and] providing benefits for disabled servicemen and families of martyrs and servicemen .... In China, there is a total of about 200 million people receiving social insurance provided by the civil affairs departments. They include childless older people, disabled people, orphans, poor families, families of martyrs and

servicemen, disabled servicemen, demobilized servicemen, retired army officers and Red Army veterans.[9]

This rather sketchy description of the ministry's functions gives no indication of how many of the 200 million beneficiaries of social assistance fall into each of the categories listed. Perhaps unintentionally, however, the authors also reveal that institutional homes run by the ministry house "407,000 childless older people, disabled people, and orphans," and that "in recent years, over 11.8 million poverty-stricken households have received government aid" from the ministry. The implications of the arithmetic are clear.

The Ministry of Civil Affairs is, in fact, almost exclusively an adjunct of the Chinese military and official bureaucracies. Its primary function is to guarantee the livelihoods of government cadres, military and police personnel, "revolutionary martyrs"[10] and their immediate families, by paying pensions and other benefits and by assisting demobilized soldiers in finding employment. Nearly all Chinese-language commentaries on civil affairs work identify the functions of "preferential care work" (youfu gongzuo) and "settlement work" (anzhi gongzuo) for these groups as the ministry's most basic responsibilities. One official text, covering the entire range of Chinese social insurance policy, defines these tasks as "presently the major component of China's social guarantee work."[11]

The responsibility of the civil affairs authorities for "settlement work" doubly hampers their effectiveness in providing welfare services to civilians. "Settlement," in principle, means assigning productive civilian employment to demobilized soldiers

---

[9] Civil Affairs Work in China, ed. Xu Chengqi (Beijing: Ministry of Civil Affairs of the People's Republic of China, January 1987), p.3.

[10] The designation "revolutionary martyr" (geming lieshi) refers not only to those Communists who died before the success of the 1949 revolution, but also to any cadre or uniformed officer who dies or is seriously injured in an official capacity. For example, one directive issued jointly by the Interior Ministry and the Ministry of Forestry on September 18, 1966, deals with the problem of "compensatory treatment for forestry police personnel who sacrifice their lives, are disabled, or die of illness" while on duty. (Notes and Comments on Civil Affairs in China [Zhongguo Minzheng Cidian], edited by Cui Naifu [Shanghai Cishu Chubanshe, December 1990], p.460.)

[11] Overview of China's System of Social Guarantees (Zhongguo Shehui Baozhang Zhidu Zonglan), ed. "Overview of China's System of Social Guarantees" Compilation Committee (Shahe Municipality, Hebei Province: Zhongguo Minzhu Fazhi Chubanshe, June 1995), p.1,161.

and army officers. In many cases, however, the Ministry of Civil Affairs is unable to arrange such work, and instead offers staff positions within its own bureaucracy. Although no statistics are available, it is reported that a large proportion of the ministry's senior staff are retired officers of the People's Liberation Army.

The ministry's task thus consists largely of administering a system of "social welfare for the elite," aimed at purchasing the allegiance of those groups whose dissatisfaction might threaten Communist Party authority. Along with the dominant military influence within the civil affairs bureaucracy itself, this underlying goal has ensured that the care of indigent civilians is consistently given the lowest priority among the aims of civil affairs work. This has been a matter of established policy at least since the mid-1950s, as one official commentary dated June 1959 indicates:

> In accordance with the goals of the [Communist] Party Central Committee and the State Council, the Third National Conference on Civil Affairs Work in 1955 established the main tasks of the civil affairs departments as preferential care, settlement of demobilized soldiers, disaster relief and social relief work .... [There] are still a small number of dependents of martyrs and soldiers, disabled soldiers, and [members of] the masses who are partly or entirely lacking in the ability to labor, who suffer difficulties in such areas as livelihood and medical care, and who need preferential treatment or relief.[12]

The Interior Ministry's "priorities" in civil affairs work are almost invariably ranked in the same order as that given here: services to military personnel and government officials figure most prominently, followed by civilian disaster relief, which if not carried out effectively poses the threat of civil unrest in rural areas. Aid to poor families and individuals ("social relief work") ranks last among the "main tasks of the civil affairs departments," while "social welfare work" for the institutionalized, who pose no conceivable threat to established authority, is ignored altogether.

Not surprisingly, the overwhelming emphasis on assisting targets of "preferential treatment" at the expense of the "masses" has left most Chinese civilians, including orphans, virtually unprotected in the face of adversity. Lacking both the mandate and the institutional capability to perform their assigned humanitarian functions, the branches of the civil affairs bureaucracy dealing with social welfare have

---

[12] *Compilation of Statistical and Historical Reference Materials on Civil Affairs (Minzheng Tongji Lishi Ziliao Huibian)*, ed. Ministry of Civil Affairs Planning and Finance Department (Beijing: Zhongguo Shehui Chubanshe, October 1993), p.593.

played a largely symbolic role. The historical record clearly shows that the Chinese authorities have consistently made only token efforts at sheltering those in need of institutional care. Far more attention has been devoted to the punitive and coercive functions of civil affairs work, including political and ideological indoctrination for those receiving social assistance. The chaotic and often violent political campaigns of the past five decades have also exerted an especially destructive influence on civil affairs work, possibly because of its low priority in the eyes of China's leadership.

The history which follows is derived from published records of the Ministry of Civil Affairs in Beijing and of local civil affairs authorities throughout the country. Two especially detailed sets of official records, which chronicle civil affairs work in Harbin municipality and the Guangxi Zhuang Autonomous Region, provide the basis for extended case studies.

Institutional Care in the People's Republic: A Nationwide Chronology

The Communist Period to 1956: "Production and Rehabilitation"

With the foundation of the People's Republic of China in 1949, the new Communist authorities immediately faced severe social problems in the urban areas where they had only recently seized power. Civil war and the economic mismanagement of the former Nationalist government had dislocated millions of people and generated severe poverty and unemployment in most Chinese cities. As the government recognized, the resulting underclass of vagrants, prostitutes, drug addicts, and petty criminals was both a major source of hardship and a potential threat to Party authority.

Over the next few years, social order in urban China was quickly restored. This was achieved partly by new controls on rural migration to the cities, but also by the ruthless eradication of those elements considered dangerous to the state. For a minority of serious offenders, such as the leaders of criminal gangs and "secret societies," this meant summary execution at the hands of the new police authorities. The civil affairs branches of the Interior Ministry played an equally critical role in this campaign, however, taking huge numbers of urban social deviants into custody for "rehabilitation." Although the ministry's role was essentially one of law enforcement, the process of "rehabilitation" was also intended, at least in principle, to train prostitutes and other marginal groups for legitimate employment and represented the socialist state's first attempt to deal with urban poverty. In what was to become a familiar pattern, the welfare and punitive functions of the civil affairs departments were effectively fused, leaving many officials themselves unclear about the appropriate dividing line between the two.

One official history of civil affairs work describes the immediate aftermath of the revolution as follows:

In the early days of the state's establishment, the civil affairs departments were responsible for many important tasks, in order to thoroughly complete the democratic revolution, to stabilize social order, to establish and solidify the newborn political power, and to restore the processes of the people's economy .... In order to shelter the vagrants, beggars, prostitutes and so forth left over from the old society, all major cities established rehabilitation institutes (*jiaoyangyuan*) as a matter of priority. At this time, the disabled, the elderly, and children being sheltered were mixed together with the vagrants in what were known collectively as "production-and-rehabilitation organs" (*shengchan jiaoyang jigou*).[13]

The policy of mixing vagrants and petty criminals with the young, the old, and the disabled in these general-purpose institutions (commonly called *shengchan jiaoyangyuan*, "production-and-rehabilitation institutes") was established largely as a matter of convenience. The civil affairs authorities had recently assumed control of a large number of private religious and other charitable institutions which were already sheltering orphans and other destitute persons. Although new centers for the "rehabilitation" of minor offenders were established after 1949, many of these older charitable facilities were simultaneously put to use for the same purpose–a clear indication of the new government's priorities in urban social work. In some cases, orphanages and foundling homes were used specifically for housing street children and juvenile delinquents, generally referred to in the historical records as "incorrigible children."[14]

The state's need for ideological self-legitimation also played a key role in the decision to destroy the humanitarian functions of the old charities. Official hostility to Christian mission work, as the most conspicuously "welfarist" component (in the pejorative sense mentioned above) of Western intervention in Chinese society, dominates many of the local histories of Chinese civil affairs work. For example, the

---

[13] Meng Zhaohua and Wang Minghuan, *Historical Manuscripts on Civil Affairs in China (Zhongguo Minzheng Shigao)* (Harbin: Heilongjiang Renmin Chubanshe, January 1987), pp.299-300. The Chinese term *jiaoyang*, "rehabilitation," normally carries a punitive implication, and is more often translated as "re-education" in certain contexts (for example, *laodong jiaoyang*, "labor reeducation"). At present, China's civil affairs authorities generally use the term *kangfu* ("recovery, restoration to health") to signify "rehabilitation" in a purely medical sense, as when referring to treatment for disabled children.

[14] Literally *wanlie ertong*, "stubborn and evil children."

annals of Baoding Municipality, Hebei Province, describe the pre-revolutionary welfare system in the following terms:

> During the Ming, Qing, and Republican periods, the Baoding authorities and charitable groups in society established foundling homes (*yuyingtang*), "halls of integrity" [for widows] (*quanjietang*), child-rearing centers (*yuyousuo*), relief institutes (*jiujiyuan*), and so forth, for the care of destitute infants and children, solitary widows, and disabled old people .... Foreign churches also established institutions to care for the old, the disabled, and infants and children. The Catholic Church's Gongjiao Foundling Home, on the pretexts of religion and universal love, took in female infants who had been abandoned by their parents, [but] in reality many innocent baby girls were horribly abused and killed there.
>
> After the liberation of Baoding on November 22, 1948, the municipal people's government took over and reorganized the Baoding Relief Institute,[15] and on May 1, 1949, turned it into the city-run Production-and-Rehabilitation Institute (later renamed the "Social Relief Institute," and then the "Social Welfare Institute"). On September 13, 1952, the municipal people's government decided to have the city's Civil Affairs Bureau take over the Catholic Gongjiao Foundling Home, which was turned into the No.2 Production-and-Rehabilitation Institute. From Baoding's liberation until 1956, the city's production-and-rehabilitation institutes sheltered, deported, and settled large numbers of beggars, vagrants, disaster victims, street children (*liulang'er*) and runaway troops from the former Nationalists. Those who were ill were given treatment, production was organized for those who could work, and segregated rehabilitation (*fenlei jiaoyang*) was achieved.[16]

---

[15] The "relief institutes" were workhouses for the destitute poor, run by the former Nationalist government.

[16] *Baoding Municipal Civil Affairs Annals (Baodingshi Minzhengzhi)*, ed. "Baoding Municipal Civil Affairs Annals" Compilation Committee (Beijing: Xinhua Chubanshe, September 1990), p.225.

This record of early socialist welfare policy in one northern Chinese city shows two characteristics which recur in local civil affairs annals from elsewhere in China. One is the ideological fervor of most of these official histories, aimed explicitly at discrediting the pre-revolutionary system of social welfare, particularly those elements administered by foreign churches.[17] The other, not coincidentally, is the new government's indifference to the welfare of orphans and other charity recipients, despite its claim to have ended alleged Christian atrocities against Chinese children. In Baoding, as elsewhere, local governments commandeered orphanages and foundling homes as detention centers for members of the urban population categorized as anti-social.[18]

The dual function of the new "production-and-rehabilitation" centers apparently caused some confusion within the civil affairs departments about the essential "nature" (*xingzhi*) of these institutions. The concerns of the bureaucracy appear to have been largely philosophical, however, and there is no evidence of any substantive objections to the policy of confining children together with adults, much less with criminals and socially deviants. Four years after the revolution, these theoretical dilemmas were briskly resolved by the following metaphysical proclamation from Beijing:

> At the Third National Conference on Urban Relief in 1953, it was proposed and stipulated that "production-and-rehabilitation bodies are relief and welfare organizations for the disabled, the elderly, and orphans, and at the same time they are also labor reform organizations for certain vagrants."[19]

---

[17] Although relations had been very tense since around 1952, the final schism between the Chinese Catholic church and the Vatican came during 1957–58, when the former was forced to repudiate Vatican authority after the Communist Party asserted the right to appoint all Catholic bishops in the country. Perhaps because of continuing tension between the People's Republic and the Vatican, which continues to maintain diplomatic relations with Taiwan, official attacks on Christian charities in pre-1949 China have focused almost exclusively on Catholic institutions.

[18] Since most private orphanages were probably operating at full capacity in the conditions following the civil war, the results for infants and children already being reared in these institutions were almost certainly catastrophic, despite the state's rhetorical commitment to "segregated rehabilitation."

[19] *Historical Manuscripts on Civil Affairs in China*, pp.300-301. The term "labor reform" (*laodong gaizao*, or *laogai* for short) invariably carries a punitive connotation in Chinese. At present, in fact, the term refers to China's vast network of penal camps for

By this time, however, the Interior Ministry's role in rehabilitating those "left over from the old society" was rapidly coming to an end. The flow of surplus labor from the countryside had been suppressed and most unattached rural migrants sent back to their home villages, largely eliminating urban unemployment. As a result, the "production-and-rehabilitation institutes" gradually shed some of their punitive functions in the early 1950s, and official records indicate that "the number of orphans, old people, disabled people, and infants being sheltered was expanded" after 1953.[20]

The records remain silent, however, on how these groups were supported in the early 1950s, before additional space became available, or whether large numbers of people were displaced by the conversion of former charitable institutions into detention centers for the urban underclass. This gap in the official history represents the first evidence of "missing" or "disappeared" orphans within the Communist welfare system–a problem which was to worsen dramatically over the following decades.

Nor do the national civil affairs histories discuss one of the most bizarre aspects of social welfare policy during this period: the new government's wholesale closure and dissolution of hundreds of established custodial welfare institutions, including orphanages and foundling homes. Statistics from the central Chinese province of Henan, to choose a representative example, illustrate the extent to which China's existing system of institutional care was dismantled. According to official records, Henan Province possessed no fewer than 122 custodial welfare institutions in 1946, shortly before the Communist takeover. Eighty-three of these were "relief institutes" (jiujiyuan) established by the Nationalist authorities at provincial or county level, which served both as workhouses for the destitute poor and as homes for orphans and abandoned children. In 1946, these cared for a total of 7,232 children, as well as more than 8,000 adults. Another twelve provincial-level "children's relief bodies" (yuyou jiuji jigou) served as specialized child welfare institutes, caring for an additional 4,400 children. Finally, Henan possessed twenty-seven privately-run orphanages caring for 2,550 children. The province's population of institutionalized minors thus totalled 14,182.[21]

By 1985, this huge institutional system had shrunk to a fraction of its former size. The whole of Henan Province in this year acknowledged a total of no more than 1,458 persons in formal institutional care, of whom just 288 were infants and children.

---

convicted offenders.

[20] *Ibid.*, p.301.

[21] *Henan Provincial Annals (Henansheng Zhi)*, ed. Henan Province Local Annals Compilation Committee (Zhengzhou: Henan Renmin Chubanshe, October 1993), pp.247-254.

The largest of the sixty "social welfare institutes" remaining in the province in 1985, the Zhengzhou Municipal Social Welfare Institute, contained just 178 inmates in all categories.[22] Given that the Provincial Foundling Home, in 1946 the largest custodial institution in Henan, at that time contained some 1,200 children, the contraction of the province's social infrastructure during nearly four decades of ostensibly socialist rule is truly astonishing.

This pattern was replicated at the national level. The Communists had assumed control of well over a thousand such bodies, including more than 400 Christian or Western-managed orphanages, more than 600 private "halls of benevolence," and hundreds of workhouses established by the former Nationalist regime. While some of these may not have offered custodial care, the statistics nevertheless show a huge drop in the number of residential institutions. By 1965, after what is officially described as a long process of constructing new facilities, a total of only 819 "social welfare institutions," including orphanages, existed throughout the country.[23] Clearly, many private charitable homes did not continue operating under state control after the revolution, as in Baoding, but were instead abolished shortly after being taken over by the Communist state. Although the national records are silent on this point, some local civil affairs documents describe the new authorities' dismantling of China's pre-1949 network of social relief in great detail. (See below, case studies on Harbin and Guangxi.)

The Reforms of 1956-1957: "Segregated Management"

Official policy towards China's custodial welfare institutions was substantially revised after 1956. By this time, the new government's control over Chinese society had been solidly established and the punitive function of the "production-and-rehabilitation institutes" was largely complete, so that emphasis could be shifted to their secondary (and, in many cases, original) role as centers for humanitarian relief.[24] This required a doctrinal reassessment of the "nature" of these institutions, as well as an effort to increase their number:

> In 1956 it was decided to readjust and reorganize "production and rehabilitation," to divide up the disabled people, old people, and children inside, to establish other rehabilitation institutes for

---

[22] *Ibid.*, pp.260-264.

[23] *Historical Manuscripts on Civil Affairs in China*, p.300.

[24] China's other systems of punitive detention camps (for "labor reform" and "labor re-education") were, of course, expanding dramatically during the same period.

disabled and old people and for children, and to make it clear that
these were social welfare organs (*shehui fuli jigou*).[25]

This change of policy marks the first official commitment at a national level
to "segregated rehabilitation" for the institutionalized–the most elementary
requirement of any humane system of care for orphans, mental patients, the elderly,
and the physically disabled.

However, this new policy was inadequately realized in practice. In Baoding,
for example, a center for "child rehabilitation," later renamed the Baoding Children's
Welfare Institute, was established in August 1956 to take in school-age children from
institutions throughout Hebei Province for what was described as a program of "work-
study" (*bangong-bandu*).[26] This indicates that institutionalized children and adults in
Hebei began to be held separately only after the establishment of the new children's
institute, four years after the conversion of Baoding's original orphanage to an all-
purpose center for "production and rehabilitation."

It is unclear how much "segregation" actually prevailed at the new
orphanage, since it was located on the grounds of an existing institution for the elderly
and disabled. More significantly, it should be noted that the term *bangong-bandu
xuexiao*, "work-study schools," refers to juvenile reformatories run by the Ministry of
Civil Affairs for offenders under the age of fourteen. This indicates that orphans in
Hebei were confined together with so-called "incorrigible children" even after the
segregating reforms of 1956. Indeed, the construction of a single province-wide center
for all such children suggests that concerns for administrative efficiency were driving
the civil affairs bureaus in the opposite direction, towards greater concentration of the
institutionalized.

Shortly afterwards, however, a different and far more sinister form of
"segregated management" emerged, based on exclusively ideological criteria. During
the Anti-Rightist Campaign of 1957, the residents of some urban welfare institutes,
which by then housed a largely disabled and elderly population as well as a significant
number of children, were systematically assessed by civil affairs staff to identify their
pre-revolutionary "class backgrounds." Separate departments with sharply contrasting
management policies were then established for residents of proletarian and bourgeois
origin. As official records from Baoding, for example, relate:

---

[25] *Historical Manuscripts on Civil Affairs in China*, p.301.

[26] *Baoding Municipal Civil Affairs Annals*, p.225.

In 1957, the production-and-rehabilitation institutes were reorganized. Disabled and elderly inmates with class backgrounds not of the laboring masses were placed in rehabilitation institutes for the disabled and elderly (*canlao jiaoyangyuan*), while unsupported old people with class backgrounds from the laboring masses were placed in old-age homes (*yanglaoyuan*), and these were separately managed.[27]

In some areas, this policy was carried to even more ludicrous extremes. A national-level memorandum, the 1959 "Draft Report on Problems in Civil Affairs Work," spells out Beijing's policy in this area in greater detail, apparently in an attempt to mitigate local excesses:

> Old-age homes should make care their priority, organize appropriate labor and recreational activities, and undertake necessary ideological education. In undertaking the task of caring for the old, they should also keep them healthy in body and mind and happy in their later years. Old people from middle [class] backgrounds or from the exploiting classes, or those with historical crimes who presently appear to be bad elements, should be held in a separate group, and their political and ideological education should be strengthened.[28]

Despite its endorsement of compulsory "ideological education" programs for the elderly, this passage represents a relatively moderate viewpoint, as it stresses that retirement homes should operate on the basic principle of "making care the priority" (*yi yang wei zhu*), with only a subordinate role for political indoctrination. The principle that welfare institutions were primarily centers for "care" was not as self-evident as it might seem. In certain parts of China, this principle was expressly repudiated during the 1957 campaign. (See below, case study on Guangxi.)

The contrast between the two forms of "segregated management" introduced during the late 1950s–one implemented only halfheartedly, the other with excessive zeal–indicates the clear priority of ideology over humanitarian considerations in civil affairs work. Although the Anti-Rightist Campaign was one of the first recorded

---

[27] *Ibid.*, p.233.

[28] *Compilation of Statistical and Historical Reference Materials on Civil Affairs*, p.600.

intrusions of China's complex political campaigns into the internal management of custodial welfare homes, it was not to be the last.

The Great Leap Forward: Hubris and Collapse

The Anti-Rightist Campaign was quickly overshadowed for most ordinary Chinese by Mao Zedong's proclamation in 1958 of a "great leap forward" in socialist industry and agriculture. The general history of the Great Leap is well known outside China: the collectivization of the country's rural economy was drastically accelerated, with most villages establishing communal dining halls to distribute free and unrationed meals; labor was diverted from agriculture in a heroic effort to develop heavy industry in the countryside, particularly steel production; and unorthodox farming methods were introduced throughout the country in an attempt to increase crop yields. The extreme pressure placed on local officials to report success in these areas produced an almost complete breakdown of accurate statistical reporting (the so-called "wind of untruthfulness"), and the resulting chaos in Chinese agriculture quickly led to three years of severe nationwide famine between 1959 and 1961, claiming an estimated twenty-seven million lives.[29]

Virtually nothing has been published outside China on the effects of the Great Leap Forward and its aftermath on civil affairs work, despite the obvious relevance of such tasks as social welfare and disaster relief during this period. The influence of the movement appears to have begun with the Fourth National Conference on Civil Affairs, which convened in 1958. Although the conference approved several proposals aimed at broadening the scope of the departments' welfare work, its most important

---

[29] A multi-volume, province-by-province set of population statistics studies published by the Chinese authorities since 1990 has for the first time provided hard empirical evidence for the scale of the early 1960s famine. According to the *Washington Post*, Judith Bannister, a demographer at the U.S. Census Bureau, has calculated the death toll for this period as being around thirty million. Chen Yizi, a former senior Chinese official who was forced into exile after the June 1989 crackdown on the Chinese prodemocracy movement and who now lives in Princeton, New Jersey, arrived, on the basis of a county-by-county review of deaths which he conducted in China prior to 1989, at a total figure of forty-three million deaths for the period of the famine. A research center in Shanghai, moreover, recently reached the same figure for the number of famine deaths. (Valerie Strauss and Dan Southerland, "How Many Died?", *Washington Post*, July 7, 1994.) The figure of twenty-seven million is the one generally agreed upon by demographers who have based their calculations on the officially released population data. For further information on the period in question, see *The Great Leap Forward Famine* (provisional title), by Jasper Becker, to be published by John Murray (London) later in 1996.

outcome was a dramatic increase in the number of small rural institutions for the care of the elderly, known as "respecting-the-aged homes" (*jinglaoyuan*).[30]

The construction of the "respecting-the-aged homes" represented a broadening of existing civil affairs work in the field of social relief. The civil affairs authorities in rural areas have traditionally been responsible for supporting households in extreme poverty (the so-called *wubaohu* or "five-guarantee households"), most of whom are elderly peasants without close relatives.[31] During most of the Communist period, this support has taken the form of direct subsidies for poor individuals and families by the rural commune authorities, who would assign them "work points," redeemable in grain and other goods, in excess of their actual earnings from labor on the commune.

However, some form of institutional care in village-run retirement homes has generally also been available for those among the elderly poor who are unable to care for themselves. At the start of the Great Leap Forward, the establishment of such homes quickly became the overriding aim of the rural civil affairs bureaus. Statistics from local annals indicate that these institutions were set up in huge numbers during 1958, only to disappear almost completely over the next two years. The construction of new "respecting-the-aged homes" was essentially a coercive project, as it represented a new policy of collectivizing social assistance by requiring all the destitute elderly, not merely the infirm, to take up residence in group institutions in order to qualify for relief. The civil affairs annals of Baoding city describe this shift as follows:

> In 1958, during the people's communization movement, there began to be collective forms of support [for the elderly]. The suburbs and urban districts established village old-age homes, and the "five-guarantee" old people were admitted into the homes.[32]

---

[30] Also known as "old-age homes" (*yanglaoyuan*).

[31] The "five guarantees" are of adequate food, clothing, medical care, housing, and burial expenses, as well as schooling for orphans.

[32] *Baoding Municipal Civil Affairs Annals*, pp.215-216.

A more detailed record of the same process appears in the annals of Red River Prefecture, Yunnan Province,[33] which describe the rise and fall of the rural retirement homes over a three-year period:

> During the high tide of people's communization in 1958, all areas of Red River Prefecture set up "respecting-the-aged homes." Gejiu Municipality established sixty-five [homes] containing 1,156 persons; Mile County established 101 [homes] containing 1,213 persons; Shiping County established seventy-eight [homes] containing 735 persons; Yuanyang County established sixty-three [homes] containing 1,107 persons; Hekou County established twelve [homes] containing eighty-nine persons....The important characteristic of these [homes] was "eating without payment."[34]

These ambitious arrangements quickly collapsed in the wake of the ensuing famine, however. The 1959 "Draft Report on Problems in Civil Affairs Work," published as food shortages were rapidly intensifying, tacitly acknowledged that the wild ambitions of the previous year had produced chaos within the Interior Ministry's bureaucracy. Some ministry officials, apparently convinced that China was on the verge of "full communism," had drawn the conclusion that the functions of the civil affairs departments were now historically obsolete.[35] By now, of course, it was clear that effective relief programs were more necessary than ever, but the collapse of the economy left considerable doubt about the state's capacity to handle the task. During the famine, in fact, the civil affairs departments saw their most urgent problem as one of paring back the country's welfare infrastructure to a sustainable level, after the massive overextension of the Great Leap. The "Draft Report" therefore called on local authorities to "consolidate, strengthen, and improve the work of the 'respecting-the-aged homes'" by making the rural elderly as nearly self-sufficient as possible:

---

[33] Red River Prefecture, which borders on Vietnam, is a designated "minority autonomous region" for the Hani and Yi nationalities. Gejiu Municipality is the prefecture's major urban area.

[34] *Red River Prefecture Civil Affairs Annals (Honghezhou Minzhengzhi)*, ed. Red River Prefecture Civil Affairs Bureau (Kunming: Yunnan Daxue Chubanshe, February 1993), p.222.

[35] *Compilation of Statistical and Historical Reference Materials on Civil Affairs*, p.593.

The targets of shelter of the "respecting-the-aged homes" should generally be limited to "five-guarantee" old people. Some "five-guarantee" old people who are still relatively robust, are willing to participate in production outside the homes, and are not willing to enter the homes, may be allowed to volunteer [for work]. "Respecting-the-aged homes" should not be lightly dissolved.[36]

Despite this recommendation, nearly all these institutions were, in fact, abolished in 1959 and 1960, however, a move presumably welcomed by those old peasants recorded as "not willing to enter the homes." The very small number of such homes left intact in 1960 indicates, however, that even the unsupported elderly who were genuinely incapacitated were left without access to custodial care during the famine.[37]

The Baoding municipal annals describe the effects of the famine on the rural elderly and other impoverished households somewhat euphemistically:

From 1959 to 1961, during the three-year period of economic difficulty, some communes and production teams were unable to implement work-point assessment subsidies for the "five-guarantee households," and gave them only basic rations (*jiben kouliang*).[38]

This account gives no indication of the fate of Baoding's earlier policy of providing elderly peasants with "collective forms of support." Records from other areas, however, indicate that the welfare policies of the Great Leap were dismantled with astonishing speed. In Red River Prefecture, for example, the rural retirement homes disappeared almost as quickly as they had been established:

In line with the disbanding of the communal dining halls of the village "people's communes," these "respecting-the-aged homes" and "happiness homes" were also swiftly reduced in number. According to statistics from the end of 1959, the entire prefecture still had sixty-two "respecting-the-aged homes," containing 970

---

[36] *Ibid.*, p.600.

[37] This was perhaps a moot point. The unwillingness of some elderly people to enter the "respecting-the-aged homes" during a period of mass starvation suggests that the homes had no food to offer.

[38] *Baoding Municipal Civil Affairs Annals*, p.216.

persons. By 1960, the whole prefecture had only seventeen "respecting-the-aged homes," containing 285 persons. Soon after the village "respecting-the-aged homes" had one after another been abolished or had naturally disbanded (*ziran jiesan*), the "respecting-the-aged homes" in the cities and towns were turned into rehabilitation or welfare institutes[39] for the disabled and elderly.[40]

Not surprisingly, this account is equally reticent about the actual effects of the famine, which ranks as one of the deadliest man-made disasters in human history. From the discreet reference to those rural retirement homes which "naturally disbanded," however, it can be safely assumed that many of these institutions were completely depopulated by the famine, which hit hardest at the very young and the very old. In an unexpected fashion, the results of the Great Leap Forward had largely eliminated the problem of caring for the destitute elderly in rural areas.

The Early 1960s: From Utopianism to Tokenism
Even as this task of the civil affairs bureaus was approaching its final solution, the authorities faced a new challenge: a wave of orphans and displaced children driven from their families by starvation. Although the youngest infants were generally the first to succumb to the famine, older children and teenagers in rural areas frequently migrated long distances in search of food, sometimes following the deaths of their parents.

Large numbers of rural adults also began gravitating towards China's cities and county towns around this time, and the Interior Ministry, which then administered civil affairs work, eventually issued a set of regulations (in cooperation with the Ministry of Public Security) to deal with what had become, by 1961, a serious problem of public order. The regulations specified that most peasant migrants should be summarily returned to their home villages, but made the following special provisions:

> Children, the old, the weak, the sick, and the disabled, who have no
> homes to go back to, should be returned to their original communes

---

[39] *Jiaoyang[yuan], fuliyuan.* The first term is also translatable as "re-education institutes" (see above, note 13), and the semantic distinction between these and the "welfare institutes" may in fact reflect a continuation of the class-based policies of the Anti-Rightist Campaign.

[40] *Red River Prefecture Civil Affairs Annals*, p.222.

or production teams for appropriate settlement and entrusted to the care of relatives and friends. Those who have absolutely no one to depend on should be appropriately settled by the civil affairs departments. A small number of incorrigible children may be sent for work-study.[41]

The number of older children with "absolutely no one to depend on" quickly increased, and a new wave of institutional development began, motivated this time not by the optimism of the Great Leap but by desperation. The Red River Prefecture annals, for example, indicate that almost immediately after the closure of the rural "respecting-the-aged homes," the civil affairs authorities began to set up large numbers of orphanages throughout the prefecture to accomodate children orphaned or displaced by the famine:

> According to separate and incomplete county and city statistics from 1961, Red River Prefecture had 1,956 orphans altogether, of whom 504 were in Shiping County, 400 in Mile County, 302 in Yuanyang County, 241 in Jianshui County, 312 in Honghe County, 105 in Jinping County, seventy in Lüchun County, twenty in Gejiu Municipality, and two in Hekou County. The great majority of these [places] separately established child rehabilitation institutes and centers in the early 1960s.[42]

Most of the areas listed above did, in fact, set up small orphanages during 1961, the last year of the famine. More detailed figures from one county, Shiping, indicate that most orphans taken into care during this period were boys between the ages of eight and sixteen.[43] But the most striking feature of these records is the sheer

---

[41] From "Excerpted Report of the Party Organizations of the Public Security and Interior Ministries On Resolutely Prohibiting Uncontrolled Movements of People," promulgated October 7, 1961. (Internal government document held in archive collection of Human Rights Watch/Asia, no publication details available.)

[42] *Red River Prefecture Civil Affairs Annals*, p.228.

[43] The Shiping County orphanage took in 64 children at its establishment in December 1961, of whom forty-four were male. Forty-four of these children were between the ages of eight and twelve, and twenty between the ages of thirteen and sixteen. Presumably this was because older sons often received preferential treatment within the family during periods of severe food shortage, and therefore outlived their parents, sisters, and younger brothers.

inadequacy of the official response to the disaster. The fact that fewer than 2,000 orphans for the entire prefecture were officially identified towards the end of the famine suggests that these estimates excluded most rural areas, with the prefecture's "incomplete statistics" based chiefly on reports from Gejiu Municipality and the county towns. The small number of orphans reported in Gejiu, which would have attracted large numbers of rural migrants in search of food, also implies that most vagrant children were quickly deported to their home villages in accordance with national policy.

In any case, population statistics from the local orphanages show that institutional care was unavailable even for most of those orphans located by county governments. The shortfall in Shiping County, whose orphanage took in only sixty-four of 504 orphans known to the authorities in 1961, is particularly conspicuous, but not atypical. The prefectural annals state, for example, that the Yuanyang County orphanage "sheltered 150 orphans" at its foundation in 1961, fewer than half the county total. Figures for other counties cover a period of several years, generally terminating in 1965 when several orphanages were closed or amalgamated.[44] Thus, the Mile County orphanage is recorded as having held "altogether 233 orphans and incorrigible children," while the Jianshui County orphanage "altogether sheltered eighty-nine orphans" and the Honghe County orphanage "altogether sheltered forty-five orphans."[45] The annals give no indication of what happened to the remaining orphans in each county, but the most plausible explanation is that they were among those rural migrants forcibly returned from the county towns to their original communes, regardless of the availability of food there.

The relatively larger population of the Mile County institution, which held a combined population of orphans and "incorrigible children," suggests that even during this period of extreme hardship, law enforcement remained the main goal of child welfare work in the prefecture. The existence of other large mixed-purpose institutions in Gejiu Municipality (which sheltered 122 children during the early 1960s) and Luxi County (which held 460 children during the same period) also indicates that delinquent children, rather than those in the greatest need, were the main targets of institutionalization during the famine.

Ironically, this may well have left the "incorrigible children" better protected than other displaced minors, most of whom received no such care. The fate of the latter group is largely unknown, however, as those not institutionalized simply vanish from

---

[44] By this time, many of their inmates would have been old enough to live independently.

[45] *Red River Prefecture Civil Affairs Annals*, p.229.

the prefectural records after 1961. Clearly, the statistical problem of "missing" orphans, which had arisen a decade earlier during the transformation of China's old charitable institutions, had re-emerged on an even larger scale after the famine.

This grossly inadequate response to the orphan crisis of the early 1960s is mirrored in other aspects of civil affairs work during the same period. Indeed, the state's effort during the Great Leap Forward to expand the system of rural old-age homes, despite the fantastic extremes to which it was carried, seems to have been China's last serious attempt to develop, expand, or improve facilities for institutional care. Since then, the history of China's social welfare policy has been one of virtually unmitigated neglect, accompanied by largely symbolic efforts to deal with the plight of the institutionalized.

The fate of repeated efforts to promote "segregated management" in welfare institutions illustrates the largely rhetorical nature of the civil affairs bureaus' humanitarianism since 1959. The records show that central authorities originally had high hopes for progress in this area. In an effort to extend the reforms of 1956, and in line with the general raising of expectations at the start of the Great Leap Forward, the Fourth National Conference on Civil Affairs Work in 1958 had added psychiatric care for destitute mental patients to the responsibilities of the Interior Ministry, and had called on local civil affairs bureaus to set up special units "to shelter those mentally ill people who had no homes to return to, no one to depend on, and no means of support (*wu jia ke gui, wu yi wu kao, wu shenghuo laiyuan*)."[46]

Later histories acknowledge, however, that this proposal was not widely adopted. Most areas of the country continued to lack specialized welfare facilities, either for mental patients or for other groups of institutionalized people with particular needs, including orphans. In light of the desperate economic conditions of the time, it seems highly unlikely that much progress was made in promoting "segregated management" during the early 1960s.

In fact, even the relatively small number of psychiatric institutions set up in accordance with the new directive failed in their stated mission of caring for the destitute mentally ill. Under an experimental policy launched in the late 1950s, these units were authorized to supplement their budgets by admitting "self-paying" patients (*zifei renyuan*) whose fees were paid by their employers or families, possibly in recognition of the state's inability to fund the new institutions. While the question of how to fund institutional care is clearly a matter for Chinese policy makers to decide, the result in this case has been that mental hospitals run by the civil affairs authorities

---

[46] *Historical Manuscripts on Civil Affairs in China*, p.301. In official statistics this term for indigent patients, including orphans, is generally abbreviated to *shehui san-wu*, "social three-nones."

have been occupied largely by paying patients since their establishment, leaving most of the Chinese population entirely without access to specialized psychiatric care.[47]

Despite this official inertia on the question of segregated treatment, the management of China's surviving welfare institutes did change dramatically in one respect during the post-Great Leap period. In the wake of an economic disaster created by policies of extreme egalitarianism, a group of moderate leaders in the central government, led by Deng Xiaoping and Liu Shaoqi,[48] promulgated new policies based on the principle of "distribution according to work." For most of the population, this meant a return to the system of household agriculture which had prevailed in the early 1950s. For the institutionalized, however, it entailed a drastic shift towards self-sufficiency and curtailment of state support.

Like the policy of segregating the destitute elderly by class background, this move towards self-financing (which often meant establishing handicraft workshops or other "sideline production" to employ the institutionalized) was carried to extremes in some parts of China, and the authors of the 1959 "Draft Report" felt it necessary to add a warning against overzealous implementation of the new system:

> Those who participate in production while in social welfare organizational units are those who, because of a lack of ability to labor, need to be looked after (*shenghuo xuyao zhaogu*). For this reason, the distribution system should differ from that of ordinary production units. Most old people, children, mental patients, lepers, and people with chronic illnesses or serious physical disabilities should not be expected to be self-supporting through their production....[It] is not necessary to completely implement the principle of "distribution according to work," so as to avoid spurring them to increase the intensity of their labor and affecting their physical health.[49]

---

[47] Presently, the majority of China's mental hospitals are run by the Ministry of Public Health, rather than the Ministry of Civil Affairs. The institutions run by the public health departments, however, are reserved exclusively for paying patients, generally those supported by their work units.

[48] At the time, Deng Xiaoping was General Secretary of the Communist Party and Liu Shaoqi was State President.

[49] *Compilation of Statistical and Historical Reference Materials on Civil Affairs*, p.600.

A separate comment on orphanage management indicates that excessive emphasis on "distribution according to work" was interfering with orphans' schooling and leading to the exploitation of child labor:

> Children's welfare institutes should obtain the assistance of the education departments, and should lay stress on doing cultural and educational work well. In thoroughly [implementing] the policy of "integrating education and productive labor," the goal is to educate children even better through appropriate productive labor. For this reason, hours of labor should not be unreasonably long.[50]

Given the conditions of the time, the new policy of self-reliance may have been unavoidable, despite occasional excesses. But along with the experimental admission of self-paying inmates to the civil affairs bureaus' newly established mental hospitals, this endorsement of more market-oriented social welfare policies by the Deng Xiaoping-Liu Shaoqi leadership faction established a precedent which was to be revived two decades later under very different circumstances.

Apparently oblivious to the impending famine, the authors of the 1959 "Draft Report" also called for a more thorough implementation of other plans approved by the Fourth National Conference, and proposed further dramatic improvements in institutional welfare policy:

> With respect to the problem of caring for old people and children without families, we must achieve segregation in management and discrimination in treatment. At present, old people, children, mentally ill persons, and adults with disabilities are still being jumbled together (*hunza zai yiqi*) in production-and-rehabilitation units in quite a few places. Not only does this make management difficult, but the welfare policies cannot be carried out very well. All regions should strive to set up segregated, specialized municipal or county-level units as soon as possible...[51]

Along with plans to "strengthen and improve" the rural old-age homes, announced shortly before their utter collapse, this is one of several proposals in the "Draft Report" which appear slightly surreal in retrospect. In any case, it may have

---

[50] *Ibid.*, p.600.

[51] *Ibid.*

been understood even at the time as a purely rhetorical device, since the report goes on, incomprehensibly, to endorse indiscriminate warehousing of the institutionalized only a few sentences later. Effective "welfare policies" are here subordinated to convenience in administration, with only a passing reference to the principle of segregation:

> With respect to shelter and management work for unsupported old people, children, mental patients and disabled people, there are presently some areas which, on the basis of segregated shelter and management, have established bodies under unified leadership: social welfare institutes (*shehui fuliyuan*). With this form it is easy to strengthen unified leadership and to lighten the management unit's multitude of duties. It may be tried out where conditions are appropriate.[52]

Another official source makes a valiant effort to reconcile these flatly contradictory proposals, noting confusingly that "after 1959, most provinces had begun establishing sanatoriums for the mentally ill, [while] some provinces and regions established general-purpose social welfare institutes in counties and cities."[53]

In practice, the rapid spread of general-purpose welfare institutions, once these had received the imprimatur of central authority, marked the end of any serious attempt to promote segregated care for China's institutionalized population. As the Baoding municipal annals indicate, these "social welfare institutes" were often simply rechristened facilities of the former "production-and-rehabilitation institutes," stripped of their punitive functions but continuing to warehouse an assortment of elderly, orphaned, disabled, and mentally ill inmates. Such institutions have since become the dominant form of custodial care provided by China's civil affairs authorities, housing the majority of those institutionalized in urban areas. Even today, fewer than half of all orphans in Chinese cities benefit from the most basic form of "segregated management," care in institutions exclusively reserved for minors. Dedicated orphanages, like dedicated psychiatric hospitals, are today extremely scarce and in some provinces nonexistent. (See Chapter 3).

The economy measures of the post-Great Leap period, and particularly the promotion of the "social welfare institutes" as inexpensive vehicles for institutional care, often reversed the tentative progress made towards specialization a few years

---

[52] *Ibid.*

[53] *Historical Manuscripts on Civil Affairs in China*, p.301.

earlier during the reforms of the late 1950s. In Baoding, for example, the orphanage founded in 1956, which had been established to shelter orphans from all of Hebei Province, was amalgamated in May 1961 with the Xiguan Rehabilitation Center for the Disabled and Elderly, on the grounds of which it was already located, to form a single "Municipal Social Welfare Institute." The next four years saw further repeated deterioration in the quality of custodial care for Hebei's orphans. In November 1962, the Baoding municipal bureaus of the interior, public security, and education jointly established a "work-study school" whose stated purpose was "primarily the shelter and reform of incorrigible children." In March 1963, all orphans still institutionalized in the Baoding Social Welfare Institute were transferred to this juvenile reformatory, a change of policy described, apparently seriously, as "in accordance with [the principle of] separate management and different treatment for [cases] of different natures." In 1965, however, the "work-study school" was re-amalgamated into the Baoding Municipal Social Welfare Institute and its inmates assigned to a "work-study class" (*gong-du ban*) within the institution.[54]

The Cultural Revolution: "Obstruction and Sabotage"

The early 1960s appear to have been an era of consolidation in Chinese civil affairs work under relatively moderate leadership.[55] Had these conditions continued, it is possible that China's custodial welfare system might have gradually recovered from the damage inflicted by the political campaigns of 1957 and 1958. The more abusive practices of the immediate post-famine period, such as the confinement of most inmates in amalgamated "social welfare institutes" and the excessive emphasis on self-reliance for those in institutional care, might have gradually diminished as economic conditions in China improved.

In the end, however, the civil affairs departments were held hostage to their administrative position within the Chinese government and their close association with duties of law enforcement. As one of China's most powerful bureaucracies, the Interior Ministry in Beijing quickly became a target of Mao Zedong's Cultural Revolution, launched in 1966 as an explicit attempt to destroy the autonomy of most existing structures of authority, including the government and Communist Party. Along with other agencies handling law-enforcement duties, including the procuracy, the courts, and the public security bureaus (police), the ministry was abolished in December 1968 and its staff in Beijing ignominiously banished to the remote

---

[54] *Baoding Municipal Civil Affairs Annals*, pp.235-236.

[55] Zeng Shan, an appointee of China's then president, Liu Shaoqi, served as Interior Minister from November 1960 until the ministry's abolition in 1968.

countryside. One official chronology of civil affairs work records the incidental irony of the ministry's final dissolution:

> *December 11, 1968*: The military representatives of the Supreme People's Procuracy, Supreme People's Court and Interior Ministry, together with the leadership group of the Ministry of Public Security, jointly sent to Chairman Mao, Premier Zhou, the Central Committee of the Chinese Communist Party and the Central Committee's Cultural Revolution [Leadership Group][56] a "Request for Instructions Submitted By a Small Number of Persons Still Remaining at the Ministry of Public Security and the Supreme People's Court [Recommending] the Abolition of the Supreme People's Procuracy, the Interior Ministry and the Three Units Run by the Office of the Interior," and, upon receiving Chairman Mao's written consent [to this proposal], they proceeded accordingly. Following the Interior Ministry's abolition, all comrades [from the ministry], apart from the few who remained to look after its offices in the capital, were transferred to perform manual labor at Cenhe Farm in Shashi Municipality, Hubei [Province].[57]

The same chronology's sole entry for 1969, and the last for nearly a decade, reports that "after the abolition of the Interior Ministry, responsibility for the various tasks formerly handled by the Interior Ministry was divided among relevant departments such as the Ministry of Finance, the Ministry of Public Security, and the State Planning Commission."[58]

At the local level, where the collapse of established authority had ushered in a phase of complex and violent political struggle, events were far more disorganized. Responsibility for the management of welfare institutions run by the civil affairs departments, including centers for custodial care as well as "welfare production units" (sheltered workshops employing the disabled) generally passed to municipal or county-level "Revolutionary Committees" (*Geming Weiyuanhui*) composed of leaders

---

[56] The "Cultural Revolution Leadership Group" (*Wen-Ge Xiaozu*), the body which directed and oversaw the entire course of the Cultural Revolution, was dominated by Mao Zedong, Jiang Qing, Kang Sheng and other top "ultra-Leftist" members of the Chinese leadership; Zhou Enlai was also a core member of the group.

[57] *Notes and Comments on Civil Affairs in China*, p.461.

[58] *Ibid.*, p.461.

of whichever faction held power at the time. Often, civil affairs work was taken over by multi-purpose "security-defense" organs under the control of the Revolutionary Committees.

The results of this power shift varied from place to place and are not always clear from the available historical records. Since the fall of the "Gang of Four" in 1976, such official histories have tended either to denounce the entire Cultural Revolution in lurid terms, as in the immediate post-Mao period, or else to skim over it as lightly as possible, the preferred approach in recent years. In neither case are the records generally forthcoming about the actual events of 1966-1976, but the scraps of available evidence suggest that their effect on Chinese civil affairs was at least as destructive as that of the Great Leap Forward.

As during the Great Leap, the attacks launched against civil affairs work during this period appear to have been purely ideological, representing an extreme version of the belief that such work should be unnecessary in a genuinely socialist society. An official report on the events of this period prepared by Cheng Zihua, the first Minister of Civil Affairs appointed after the Cultural Revolution, described the radicals' political motives and contrasted them with the more orthodox views of the post-Mao Party leadership:

> The Gang of Four...attacked social welfare work as "engaging in welfarism" and "imitating old-fashioned philanthropic work." The social welfare institutions and welfare production units play an important role in alleviating the living difficulties of the blind, the deaf, orphans, old people, disabled people, and infants, and are also a manifestation of the superiority of the socialist system. This is fundamentally different from the welfarism and old-fashioned philanthropic work which whitewashed the capitalist system and paralyzed the fighting will of the working people...[59]

Unfortunately for later historians, Cheng soon reached his limit of allowable candor. After reaffirming the ideological legitimacy of civil affairs work for the first time in over a decade, he referred to the damage caused by earlier "leftist" policies only in vague and general terms:

> The obstruction and sabotage of civil affairs work by Lin Biao and the "Gang of Four" produced extremely evil results....The supplies

---

[59] *Compilation of Statistical and Historical Reference Materials on Civil Affairs,* p.615.

to "five-guarantee households" and subsidies and relief for households in difficulties were cancelled, and a large number of social welfare institutions and welfare production units were disbanded. Tragic incidents such as migrations induced by famine, selling of children and women, and deaths by suicide even occurred.[60]

Local civil affairs records describe these events in only slightly greater detail, but individual cases are often revealing nevertheless. Many regional authorities seem to have performed a form of triage in response to the chaotic political situation affecting their work, focusing their efforts on accomplishing those tasks they considered most critical. The Baoding city annals, for example, record that "during the ten years of the Cultural Revolution, civil affairs work suffered severe interference and sabotage, and only preferential care work and relief work were able to be carried out."[61] However, the single reference to "relief work" in Baoding after 1966 states only that "during the Cultural Revolution, the 'five-guarantee' work of the communes and production teams in the suburbs and urban districts was still able to continue,"[62] suggesting that even this task was carried out rather ineffectually under the authority of the new Revolutionary Committees.

The more explicit records of Yunnan Province's Red River Prefecture tend to confirm this, noting:

> During the period of the Cultural Revolution, the collective-support system for the five-guarantee households suffered a distinct adverse influence, and the standards of collective supply and state relief declined. But the work of collective support did not cease, and gradually returned to normal after 1972.[63]

By contrast, the two tasks of civil affairs work traditionally given highest priority–the provision of social benefits to the ruling elite and the control of dangerous social elements–appear to have continued unabated throughout the Cultural

---

[60] *Ibid.*, pp.615-616.

[61] *Baoding Municipal Civil Affairs Annals*, p.2.

[62] *Ibid.*, p.216.

[63] *Red River Prefecture Civil Affairs Annals*, p.203.

Revolution. These tasks took a strikingly different form during this bizarre period, however. In the late 1960s, the civil affairs authorities played a major role in one of the most disastrous and thoroughly discredited policies of the time: the massive program of "sending down" (*xiafang*) city residents to the countryside, sometimes referred to in English as "rustication." This was a complex policy, aimed both at "re-educating" urbanites through agricultural labor and at protecting the population from an anticipated Soviet or U.S. attack.[64] The actual transfer of population to rural areas combined voluntary movement (especially of students and young people) with a large measure of coercion, and the civil affairs departments, which had long been responsible for expelling rural residents from China's cities, were therefore a natural choice for carrying out the compulsory relocations associated with the campaign.

In Yunnan Province, for example, the provincial Revolutionary Committee issued a series of directives on the implementation of the new national policy, and the Revolutionary Committee of Red River Prefecture promulgated more detailed regulations on September 10, 1969. These targeted three categories of urbanites for relocation:

> The first are targets of "going down to the villages and up to the mountains" (*xiaxiang-shangshan duixiang*). These are mainly unemployed idlers (*xiansan renyuan*) in urban areas, rural villagers blindly wandering in the cities, the dependents of [urban] employees who are not employed and who have homes to return to in the villages, and casual laborers (*zizhao-luangu renyuan*) in [administrative] organs, schools, factories, mines, and other units.

> The second are targets of evacuation (*shusan duixiang*). These are mainly the dependents lacking ability to labor of working cadres and staff members; the dependents lacking ability to labor of cadres and staff members who have retired, been martyred, or died of illness; and cadres and staff members in evacuated units and their dependents who lack ability to labor.

> The third are targets of deportation (*qiansong duixiang*). These are mainly landlords, rich peasants, counterrevolutionaries, bad

---

[64] The new policy of "evacuating and sending down the urban population" (*shusan xiafang chengzhen renkou*) was initiated by the so-called "August 23 order" of the Communist Party's Central Committee, which called on the country to "prepare to fight, avoid surprise attack by imperialism, preserve effective strength, and avoid unnecessary sacrifice."

elements and rightists who have not reformed themselves well; diehard elements from reactionary political parties and cliques or from reactionary secret sects and societies whose show of repentance has been poor; capitalists who have persisted in their reactionary stance; and the family dependents of counter-revolutionary elements who have been executed, imprisoned, or placed under police control who continue to uphold [their parents'] reactionary standpoint.[65]

The pattern of previous decades clearly reasserts itself here: the main "targets" of civil affairs work include both those singled out for favored treatment and those considered social and political threats. The aims of "preferential care" and social control were thus combined in a single policy.[66]

Burdened by this new responsibility and by continuing administrative disorder, many local civil affairs bureaus predictably failed to carry out their other duties, such as disaster relief, with even minimal effectiveness, leading to the "migrations induced by famine" later acknowledged by Cheng Zihua. As the policy of "sending down" urban residents was ·itself extremely unpopular and provoked considerable resistance, chaotic movements of people often resulted.

Evidence from Jiading County, a suburban area of greater Shanghai, hints at the scale of the social dislocation which followed. Since Shanghai is a traditional target of rural migrants, especially during periods of natural disaster, the county's civil affairs authorities bear much of the responsibility for controlling illegal migration in the surrounding region. Statistics on the number of persons "sheltered and deported" during the Cultural Revolution show massive increases in such migration between 1967 and 1969, exceeding even those which followed the post-Great Leap famine. The county's civil affairs annals explain the increase as follows:

In 1967, a large group of peasants affected by natural disasters in Jiangsu, Anhui, Henan, Shandong, and elsewhere, as well as other "blind wanderers" (*mangliu renyuan*), migrated to Shanghai. In

---

[65] *Red River Prefecture Civil Affairs Annals*, p.159.

[66] Since the expected air raids against Chinese cities never materialized, however, the "targets of evacuation" may not have found their status a particular privilege in this case.

addition, idle residents from the county's urban areas who had gone
to Luohu, in Anhui, came back in successive groups.[67]

The county eventually established an additional "deportation center" to deal
with this massive influx. Ironically, the coercive functions of Jiading's civil affairs
authorities served in this case to "solve" a problem created by the failure of civil
affairs bureaus elsewhere in eastern China to provide effective disaster assistance, and
by widespread resistance to the misguided policy of forcible "rustication."[68]

Inevitably, "social welfare work" received even less attention during the
Cultural Revolution than "social relief work," whose beneficiaries were far more
numerous and potentially more dangerous as well. The institutionalized, including
orphans and abandoned children, continued to rank lowest among the various "targets
of civil affairs work," even as the political persecutions of the period generated
uncounted thousands of additional orphans in need of care. As in the early 1960s,
institutionalized children often began to disappear altogether from the published
record.

The authors of the Baoding civil affairs annals, for example, concede that
institutional care in the city was devastated by the political winds of the period: "social
welfare work suffered great sabotage, and many tasks could not be accomplished
normally."[69] However, the effect of this "sabotage" on the city's orphans and juvenile
offenders, who in the mid-1960s were held in a "work-study class" within the Baoding
Municipal Social Welfare Institute, is unknown. The annals record only that "during
the Cultural Revolution, the work-study class was abolished,"[70] without describing the
results of this change for the children affected. In a more detailed history of this
institution, the period is obscured altogether in a haze of changing nomenclature:

On February 23, 1965, the Social Welfare Institute changed its
name to the Social Relief Institute, and established a separate

---

[67] *Jiading County Civil Affairs Annals (Jiadingxian Minzhengzhi)*, ed. Jiading
County Civil Affairs Bureau (Shanghai: Shanghai Shehui Kexueyuan Chubanshe, August
1991), pp.123-124.

[68] The collapse of China's system of disaster relief presumably worsened several
regional famines which occurred during the Cultural Revolution and led to sizeable refugee
flows.

[69] *Baoding Municipal Civil Affairs Annals*, p.226.

[70] *Ibid.*, p.236.

center for sheltering mental patients (*jingshen bingren shourongsuo*) and a department for infants and children (*you'erbu*). In January 1978, the name of the Social Relief Institute was changed back to the Social Welfare Institute....[71]

Other local annals show that virtually all custodial institutions for orphans, the elderly, and the disabled were closed during the Cultural Revolution, but give no further details. In the Guangxi Zhuang Autonomous Region, for example, it is recorded only that

> by the end of 1965, there were thirty-three orphanages altogether, holding 2,456 children. During the period of the Cultural Revolution, the orphanages suffered severe sabotage. By 1978, the entire region had two orphanages left, and in addition to the children's departments and infants' wards in fourteen social welfare institutes in the region, these sheltered 245 children and 130 infants altogether.[72]

Likewise, the annals of Red River Prefecture report that the local institutions established a few years earlier to absorb a handful of the region's displaced orphans vanished during the early years of the movement: "Between 1969 and 1970, child rehabilitation institutes in all areas of Red River Prefecture were abolished one after the other."[73]

The few remaining "respecting-the-aged homes" in the prefecture's rural areas which had survived the austerity measures of the early 1960s suffered the same fate: "One after the other, these...were abolished or naturally disbanded during the period of the Cultural Revolution."[74]

Only in one instance is the subsequent treatment of those institutionalized in these units recorded. After the abolition in 1969 of the Jijie Child Rehabilitation Institute in Gejiu city, according to the annals,

---

[71] *Ibid.*, p.237.

[72] *Ins and Outs of Civil Affairs (Minzheng Zongheng)*, ed. Wang Yujian (Nanning: Guangxi Renmin Chubanshe, April 1992), pp.69-70.

[73] *Red River Prefecture Civil Affairs Annals*, pp.229-230.

[74] *Ibid.*, p.222.

Apart from a portion [of the children] who were of age and who
were arranged to be sent down to the countryside to labor, the
remaining twenty-odd under-age orphans were [sent] for combined
settlement at the Gejiu Municipal Rehabilitation Center for the
Elderly and Disabled, [which] became the Gejiu Municipal
Rehabilitation Center for the Elderly, Disabled, and Children.[75]

The policy of "sending down" older orphans was probably widespread
during the early years of the Cultural Revolution, when secondary education was
largely suspended and other urban children of the same age were leaving home in
large numbers to travel and "exchange experiences." The fate of most infants and
younger children in the same institutions is left entirely unexplained, however. Very
few can have enjoyed the dubious benefits of "combined settlement" offered to those
at the Jijie orphanage, since most institutions for dependent adults were also closed
during this period. During the late 1960s, for the third time in China's postrevolutionary history, orphans thus "disappeared" in large numbers from the records
of the civil affairs bureaus.

Although published records become even more fragmentary for the later
years of the Cultural Revolution, it appears that welfare work in most parts of China
gradually resumed after 1972, when the local civil affairs departments were
reconstituted. For the next six years, however, these bodies operated in the absence of
any specialized central authority responsible for civil affairs policy. As later histories
admit, the result was a complete breakdown of discipline in many areas, leading to a
huge upsurge in cases of corruption and financial mismanagement. These included
what was probably the largest single embezzlement case in the history of Maoist
China, involving the theft of over 160 million yuan in disaster relief funds supplied to
Henan Province after devastating floods in August 1975.[76] As Cheng Zihua frankly
noted in a commentary on the period:

In recent years, under the poisonous [influence] of the "Gang of
Four," some people have developed capitalist thinking, and the
phenomena of corruption, embezzlement, and squandering of civil

---

[75] *Ibid.*, p.227.

[76] The floods were caused by the failure of the structurally unsound Banqiao and
Shimantan dams. This disaster, which was entirely unknown outside China until early 1995, is
believed to have been the deadliest dam collapse in human history. For an account of the
disastrous incident, see *The Three Gorges Dam in China: Forced Resettlement, Suppression
of Dissent, and Labor Rights Concerns*, Human Rights Watch/Asia, February 1995.

affairs funds have become very common. Corruption and waste are major crimes, and the misappropriation and waste of relief funds are crimes of an especially serious nature...[77]

The Era of Reform: "Self-Payment" and "Socialization"

Such brutal honesty had become possible only after the Third Plenum of the Eleventh Party Congress in 1978, at which Deng Xiaoping had fully consolidated his authority over the Chinese Communist Party and taken steps to liberalize the political climate. For the "targets" of China's civil affairs work, the earliest effects of Deng's ascendancy were dramatically beneficial, as the extremist policies of the Cultural Revolution were dismantled. In February 1978, a separate Ministry of Civil Affairs was established to assume the civil affairs functions of the former Interior Ministry. Under the leadership of Cheng Zihua, who served as Minister of Civil Affairs until May 1982, the ministry reasserted the legitimate role of welfare work in a still avowedly "socialist" China, and began gradually rebuilding the network of custodial institutions which had been all but destroyed over the previous decade.

Overcoming the political legacy of the Cultural Revolution was only the first of Deng Xiaoping's tasks, however. Deng's plans for the Chinese economy were to incorporate a large dose of the same "capitalist thinking" denounced in Cheng Zihua's 1978 speech. The new economic system achieved remarkable success in many areas, but for inmates of China's custodial welfare institutions, the effects of Deng's market-oriented policies were far more ambiguous.

The changes in China's productive economy after 1978 were based on a handful of relatively simple principles. One of the most important was the so-called "responsibility system," introduced first in agriculture and later (to a more limited extent) in state-owned industry. This entailed a decentralization of economic authority, allowing peasant families and state enterprise managers greater leeway in making production decisions. The same policy of increased local autonomy was applied to Chinese work units generally, in the belief that giving more power to individual managers would produce better results than continued bureaucratic control from above.

At the same time, China's new leadership called for a renewed emphasis on economic self-sufficiency for individual work units, similar to that promoted by Deng during his previous ascendancy in the early 1960s. For ordinary industrial enterprises, this often led to increased production efficiency as state subsidies were reduced. A less desirable side effect of this policy was intense pressure to commercialize the activities

---

[77] *Compilation of Statistical and Historical Reference Materials on Civil Affairs*, p.616. Cheng Zihua was Minister of Civil Affairs from 1978 to 1982.

of other units, such as hospitals and universities, whose basic functions were not directly productive.

Finally, Deng's development plans entailed a gradual opening of Chinese society towards the outside world, after decades of self-imposed isolation. The most immediate tangible results of the new policy came in the form of increased trade and investment, but longer-term payoffs for China were expected to include greater access to foreign expertise and technology, as well as the benefits of closer Chinese integration into the international community.

The effects of the reforms on civil affairs work have often mirrored their impact on Chinese society generally, but not always with equally happy results. Indeed, given the absence of legally enforceable rights for institutionalized patients in China and the almost complete lack of supervision with which custodial institutions are permitted to operate, the predictable effect of the new policies has been a dramatic increase in irresponsibility, neglect, and corruption on the part of the welfare institutes' management and staff. This trend is most clearly illustrated by changes in social welfare policy in Shanghai since 1993, which followed an unsuccessful four-year campaign to expose grave abuses at the city's main orphanage. Recent events in the Shanghai social welfare system will be examined in later chapters, but reports from elsewhere in China indicate that similar problems are likely to emerge throughout the country as the process of "reform and opening" continues.

Early plans to introduce the "responsibility system" to China's custodial welfare homes were clearly well-intentioned, reflecting a new frankness about the severe problems affecting these institutions and a willingness to try new management techniques. In an address to a 1985 colloquium on the "reform and restructuring" of the ministry's urban social welfare units, a senior Ministry of Civil Affairs official, Tang Yizhi, spoke bluntly about the scale of the problem. After a nod to the supposedly high quality of care in most such units, which he predictably cited as "a demonstration of the superior nature of our country's socialist system," Tang went on to acknowledge the institutions' real weaknesses:

> [We] must recognize that, speaking of the country as a whole, the development of the urban social welfare units is still very uneven, and that in relation to the needs of society and the expectations of the people, their shortcomings are still very great. In some places, there is inadequate understanding of the important status and function of social welfare work in the new period, not enough attention is paid to it, and its backward aspects have not changed for a long time .... In an extremely small number of social welfare units, the leadership groups are feeble and slack, management work is chaotic, and unlawful and undisciplined behavior [such as]

beating and abusing inmates has occurred. There have even been seriously unlawful and undisciplined incidents of inmates being injured or killed through beatings and persecution. The civil affairs departments at all levels must urgently implement effective measures to resolve these problems.[78]

Tang made several recommendations to remedy this situation, the first of which was to "simplify administration, expand authority, and institute the director responsibility system" (*jianzheng-fangquan, shixing yuanzhang fuzezhi*). As outlined by Tang, this policy entailed giving institute directors wider discretion over personnel management, including the right to hire and fire mid-level cadres; to discipline staff members for negligence or "indiscipline"; and to recruit specialized technical staff and contract workers on a temporary basis. Control over institute finances, including revenues from "self-paying" inmates and from inmates' productive labor, would also be decentralized to individual directors. Tang cited three units as having already taken the lead in improving the quality of care through such management reforms: the Ziyuan Psychiatric Institute in Sichuan Province; the Fuzhou Municipal Social Welfare Institute in Fujian Province, and the Shanghai No.2 Social Welfare Institute.[79]

During the mid-1980s, the Ministry of Civil Affairs also sought to promote greater financial self-sufficiency for the welfare institutes, chiefly by encouraging them to recruit more paying patients. The main "social welfare institute" in Baoding city, for example, began accepting such patients as early as 1984.[80] It seems that not all areas were equally enthusiastic about this particular policy, however. In the section of Tang Yizhi's 1985 address calling on the institutes to "expand the work of caring for the self-paying," he acknowledged that efforts to do so were already causing controversy within the lower levels of the civil affairs bureaucracy:

> Comrades have reported that there are presently major problems in the work of caring for the self-paying (*zifei shouyang gongzuo*). One is that some comrades are trapped in the old framework of

---

[78] *Selected Compilation of Documents on Civil Affairs Work (Minzheng Gongzuo Wenjian Xuanbian)*, ed. Ministry of Civil Affairs Policy Research Office (Beijing: Huaxia Chubanshe: December 1986), p.339.

[79] The Shanghai No.2 Social Welfare Institute, located on Chongming Island in the Yangtze River delta, is ostensibly a home for mentally disabled adults. Conditions at this institution are discussed in Chapter 7.

[80] *Baoding Municipal Civil Affairs Annals*, p.226.

[caring for] the "three-nones" targets,[81] are satisfied with the status quo, and do not dare to break new ground, [so that] the task of expanding care for the self-paying lacks enthusiasm. Another is that the standard of care is generally rather low and state subsidies are inadequate, [so that if] the self-paying [were to be admitted] in the near future, the rules would be relaxed (*dingze jianmian*).[82]

In fact, accepting "self-paying inmates" had been standard practice for some twenty years in one area of the ministry's social welfare work, namely the specialized "psychiatric welfare institutes." As noted earlier, these institutions cater almost exclusively to paying patients, thus forgoing any significant role in offering mental health care to the indigent. Since the effects of this policy were clearly visible by the 1980s, it is not difficult to imagine the fears of staff members in the specialized orphanages and general-purpose "social welfare institutes," some of whom were apparently resisting a similar commercialization of their own work.

In recent years, in fact, there is evidence that the push towards "self-payment" has indeed led to a worsening of conditions for the destitute inmates who were formerly the main targets of institutional care. In some parts of China, the shift towards recruitment of "self-paying" inmates has deprived many destitute patients of needed places. Official statistics from Beijing Municipality, for example, show that the city's general-purpose "social welfare institutes" held 932 patients at the end of 1989, of whom 588 were so-called "social three-nones." By 1993, however, the total institutional population in these units had increased to 958, but the number of destitute patients had fallen to just 370, while the number of paying inmates had increased from 307 to 530 over the same period. Less dramatically, the total population of the "social welfare institutes" in Shanghai Municipality rose from 2,012 to 2,554 over the same period, while the number of "social three-nones" decreased from 1,097 to 1,013 and the number of "self-paying" inmates rose from 910 to 1,530.[83]

---

[81] See note 46, above.

[82] *Selected Compilation of Documents on Civil Affairs Work* (1986), p.343.

[83] Figures from *China Civil Affairs Statistical Yearbook (Zhongguo Minzheng Tongji Nianjian)*, 1990 edition ed. Ministry of Civil Affairs General Planning Office, Zhongguo Shehui Chubanshe, December 1990, pp.94-95; 1994 edition ed. Ministry of Civil Affairs Planning and Finance Department, Zhongguo Shehui Chubanshe, April 1994, p.108. In both cities, a small number of institutionalized patients fell into a third category known as "targets of preferential care." For details on the policy of "preferential care" as it applies to custodial welfare institutes, see Chapter 3.

For local authorities seeking to cut the cost of supporting the indigent, various other options became available after 1978. One was to shift financial responsibility for their care to the private and "collective" sectors–a practice referred to, somewhat misleadingly, as "mobilizing social forces" (*fadong shehui liliang*). In some cases, this was a highly effective policy: the countless thousands of small workshops set up during the 1980s by district governments and urban "residents' committees," which were generally quite successful in exploiting new market opportunities in light industry and handicrafts, allowed many handicapped and unemployed adults to become self-supporting for the first time.

Those who were genuinely unable to work, however, were often expected to rely on local support as well. A report submitted in April 1983 to the Eighth National Conference on Civil Affairs by Cui Naifu, Minister of Civil Affairs from May 1982 until March 1993, made this clear in a section titled "Making Use of Various Channels to Do Social Relief and Social Welfare Work Well":

> [The work of] fostering and settlement should also make use of various channels. Apart from those undergoing fostering and settlement in social welfare units run by the civil affairs departments, [we] also want to rely on mobilizing the social forces of the grassroots and of organizations to run various types of small-scale social welfare units.[84]

In practice, this has meant that many indigent people, chiefly the elderly poor, have begun to receive custodial care in small, "collectively run" welfare institutions established in townships and villages, which are generally subsidized by profitable collective enterprises.[85] However, these institutions have apparently not played a major role in providing care to other groups, such as orphans and the mentally ill.

The welfare system's increased reliance on "social forces" has also meant a substantially larger role for private charitable donations, which China's civil affairs departments have pursued with increasing enthusiasm in recent years. Publicity surrounding the ministry's work with orphans and abandoned children has proved to

---

[84] *Compilation of Statistical and Historical Reference Materials on Civil Affairs*, p.627.

[85] The shift away from direct Ministry of Civil Affairs responsibility for funding these units reflects fiscal trends in China as a whole during the 1980s. As economic reforms have undermined the solvency of the central government, the cost of meeting social needs has been shifted to regional and local governments, themselves increasingly strapped for funds.

be a particularly effective fundraising technique, and has succeeded in bringing in substantial funding and in-kind donations from concerned Chinese citizens.

The rapid internationalization of Chinese society, one of the most important social trends in the country as a whole during the past fifteen years, has been relatively slow to affect the work of the civil affairs departments. Nevertheless, there are signs that a long and careful process of accumulating overseas connections, pioneered by Cui Naifu during his tenure as Minister of Civil Affairs, has finally begun to pay off for ministry officials.

Systematic cooperation between China's Ministry of Civil Affairs and the international community began more than a decade ago. Since 1982, the ministry has been operating a program for the "community rehabilitation of disabled children" in cooperation with the United Nations Children's Fund (UNICEF), aimed at training parents and medical workers in caring for disabled children.[86] The ministry's overseas contacts did not begin developing rapidly until 1985, however. In April of that year, a senior UNICEF official was invited to China on a "friendly visit" arranged by the ministry, and similar visits by official Swedish and Canadian delegations followed later the same year. In May 1985, the ministry launched a long-term project, in cooperation with the Austrian charity Kinderdorf International, to set up privately funded foster homes for orphans and abandoned children, known as "SOS Children's Villages."[87] Since then, UNICEF has provided various forms of financial and technical support to the Chinese state orphanage system, including donations of equipment and funding for staff training overseas. Participation by private charities based in Hong Kong and the West has also expanded substantially in recent years.

An additional source of funding for many child welfare institutes has come from placing children for overseas adoptions. Before 1991, this was apparently a rather haphazard process, with many individual orphanages effectively "selling" orphans to prospective parents for whatever amount they could negotiate. Since late 1991, however, a nationwide "Adoption Law" has attempted to standardize the foreign adoption process, but the new legislation continues to permit welfare institutes to

---

[86] *Addendum* to the *Report* submitted by the People's Republic of China to the United Nations Committee on the Rights of the Child (March 27, 1995), paragraph 135.

[87] *Notes and Comments on Civil Affairs in China*, p.477. The SOS program began with the establishment of two institutions in the northern cities of Yantai (Shandong Province) and Tianjin. More recently, new villages have been founded in Qiqihar (Heilongjiang Province) and elsewhere in China.

charge fees ranging from US$3,000 to US$5,000 for each child supplied.[88] In principle, the levying of such fees is unobjectionable, especially if it ensures that adoptions can proceed through properly constituted channels. Although the stated purpose of these fees is to recoup the cost of raising each child prior to its adoption, however, in practice they far exceed the actual sums spent on child care by these institutions (see Chapter 3). Foreign adoptions have thus become a major profit center for many of China's urban welfare institutes.[89]

Perhaps because of previous criticism in this area, the Chinese authorities have been particularly concerned to demonstrate to the outside world that China treats its disabled citizens, including inmates of welfare institutions, as humanely as possible. Given China's determination to excel in international athletic competition, it is not surprising that the Ministry of Civil Affairs has vigorously promoted China's participation in international sporting events for the handicapped. This process began in June 1985, with the establishment of the China Disabled Persons Athletic Association and of a Chinese branch of the International Special Olympics. The first organized participation by disabled Chinese athletes in overseas competition took place at the Fourth Fespic Games, a sports festival for disabled athletes from the Asia-Pacific region, held in Jakarta in August 1986: the ministry's records note meticulously that the Chinese participants "altogether won sixty-four gold medals, twenty-one silver medals, and three bronze medals, bringing honor to the motherland."[90]

An incident which occurred in 1992, however, suggests that the enthusiasm shown by certain of the ministry's officials toward the Special Olympics movement may be inspired more by personal greed than by patriotism. According to Dr. Zhang Shuyun, a former employee of the Shanghai Children's Welfare Institute, an orphaned girl named Luo Zhan competed as part of the orphanage's team of disabled athletes in the table tennis event at the Madrid Paralympics that year, and won three gold

---

[88] Shu Zhang, "Adoption Made Easier For Foreign Nationals," *Window* (Hong Kong), August 4, 1995, p.25.

[89] Reportedly, some conservative bureaucrats within the Ministry of Civil Affairs are uneasy with the promotion of foreign adoptions as a source of revenue, seeing this as a loss of face for China. According to the German magazine *Der Spiegel*, one senior ministry official has commented offhandedly that she "would rather have seen all the children die in our country than have them destroy our image abroad." (See Appendix P.)

[90] *Notes and Comments on Civil Affairs in China*, p.480. For a brief report on the Fourth Fespic Games, see "Games Tourney For Disabled Opens August 31 On Java," *Central News Agency* (Taiwan), August 31, 1986.

medals (one solo, two shared) together with a considerable sum in prize money. Most of this money, reportedly, was subsequently taken away from Luo by Han Weicheng, the orphanage director, and was never officially accounted for thereafter.

The ministry's exploitation of the International Special Olympics represents perhaps the most dramatic abuse of its new strategy of drawing support from "social forces" at home and abroad. More generally, however, Human Rights Watch/Asia believes that international financial support and assistance for China's state orphanages, including the recent expansion of the overseas adoption program, has in many cases provided virtually no benefit to the country's abandoned children. As foreign press reports have revealed, much of this international aid has been diverted to the benefit of the civil affairs bureaus' management and employees, sometimes leaving orphans and other institutional patients even worse off than previously.[91]

The effects of the radical "reforms" implemented in Chinese civil affairs work in recent years are best illustrated by the example of Shanghai, where Human Rights Watch/Asia has obtained detailed eyewitness testimony, photographic evidence, and extensive internal documentation on conditions in the city's child welfare system. These demonstrate gross violations of fundamental human rights, including the deliberate killing of children by starvation. The situation in Shanghai will be examined in greater detail in subsequent chapters.

Regional Case Studies

The following case studies, based on official records of civil affairs work in Harbin Municipality and the Guangxi Zhuang Autonomous Region, illustrate many of the same patterns observed for social welfare work in China as a whole since 1949. In both locations, the pre-revolutionary system of institutional care was systematically demolished after the Communist takeover, never to recover its former capacity. The political campaigns of the 1950s and 1960s inflicted further damage on an already weakened system, leaving virtually no custodial institutions intact by the late 1970s. Although the reforms of the Deng Xiaoping era appear to have reversed some of the most radical policies of the Cultural Revolution, eyewitness evidence from both localities shows that grave abuses of children's rights have continued into the 1990s.

---

[91] The U.S. State Department apparently shares this skepticism about the value of foreign financial support, noting that although cash payments for adoption have sometimes improved conditions for children remaining in institutional care, "we have heard some reports of misuse of funds for vehicles, travel, and entertainment....One orphanage director in Suzhou reportedly now drives a late-model Lexus." (Passage taken from unclassified State Department cable SHC1117, August 1995.) For a report on the disappearance of donations at the Nanning Social Welfare Institute, Guangxi Province, see boxed item: "Condemned To Die–For Being a Girl," below.

Harbin Municipality

Civil affairs annals from the city of Harbin, capital of the northeastern province of Heilongjiang, provide important insights into the development of China's social welfare policies since the Communist revolution. Harbin's history is unique in several respects which make it an especially illuminating example. For the first half of the twentieth century, the city was home to a large foreign community and boasted an unusually extensive network of private charities. China's northeastern provinces (the area formerly known as "Manchuria") were the first to come under Japanese occupation in the 1930s, and later among the first to be "liberated" by the advancing Communist forces after 1945. The present status of civil affairs work in Harbin, which has been under continuous Communist rule since 1946, thus shows the influence of the city's pre-revolutionary welfare system, of national policy since 1949, and of the brief intervening period when the municipal Communist leaders governed without central control from higher authorities in Beijing.

Harbin was a relatively cosmopolitan city before the revolution. Foreign nationals, chiefly White Russians, Japanese, and stateless persons (including a large number of European Jews), made up sixteen percent of its 1934 population of just over half a million.[92] The expatriate community had by then established some seventeen charitable institutions, including a number of orphanages and shelters for the destitute. The majority of these were set up in the 1920s, although a few date back to the earliest years of the century. Most catered to a specific ethnic or national group and were supported by funds raised within the same community, often by churches and synagogues. The institutions varied greatly in size: one of the smallest, the Jewish Retirement Home, held twenty-four elderly inmates in 1934, while the largest, the Franco-Russian Orphanage, cared for more than 160 orphaned girls.

Local Chinese charities were less numerous but often much larger, and tended to provide relief rather than custodial care. One of the most comprehensive was the Harbin branch of the World Red Swastika Society, a Taoist religious group which offered services ranging from a free outpatient clinic to a charitable school enrolling over 800 poor children. Facilities for Chinese orphans were more limited than those financed within the foreign communities, although at least two private institutions, the Foundling Relief Center and the Harbin Charitable Association, fostered orphans and abandoned infants during the 1930s.

---

[92] *Harbin Civil Affairs Annals (Haerbin Minzhengzhi)*, ed. Harbin Municipal Civil Affairs Annals Compilation Committee (Harbin: Heilongjiang Renmin Chubanshe, March 1991), pp.173-174. The authors of the annals have drawn heavily on the 1934 *Harbin Special Municipality Second Almanac on Municipal Conditions (Haerbin Tebieshi Di'erci Shishi Nianjian)* for statistics and other information on pre-revolutionary social work.

The succession of city governments which ruled Harbin under various regimes before 1946 also played a gradually expanding role in providing foster care for the very young, operating two state-financed homes for orphans. The Municipal Charitable Relief Center, founded in 1927 to assist "poor laborers," changed its function two years later to become a "shelter for the disabled elderly." At the same time, apparently, it began taking in children as well: the annals report that "during the Manchukuo era [the period of Japanese rule] ... [the center] sheltered 202 unsupported disabled elderly people and orphans." Likewise, the institution which later became Harbin's "Municipal Foundling Home" was originally established in 1909, shortly before the fall of the Qing dynasty, as a shelter for the poor. After a series of name changes, it assumed its final role as an orphanage only in 1933, by which time the city was already under Japanese occupation. In 1934 it held 230 Chinese and Russian orphans.

The regulations governing the Municipal Foundling Home, promulgated in 1933 by the Harbin Civil Affairs Bureau, listed seven categories of children eligible for shelter at the home, including "those for whom there is clear evidence of unjustified abuse by the head of household, stepmother, or guardian," as well as "those unbearably abused as foster children or child slaves." Under current policy in China, by contrast, cases of domestic child abuse are handled almost exclusively through mediation and there is no systematic provision made for children to be removed into care from abusive homes.[93]

Communist troops seized Harbin on April 28, 1946, eight months after the Japanese surrender. The new municipal authorities then enjoyed more than three years of relative autonomy before Mao Zedong proclaimed the establishment of the People's Republic of China in October 1949. The victory had an initially negative effect on welfare work in Harbin, as the charities' sources of funds in the private sector dried up:

> At that time, the local government's main task was to mobilize and organize the city's entire population to support the liberation war, and social relief work had not yet been taken in hand. Some of the directors and philanthropists of the old charitable groups, due to their not understanding the policies of the Communist Party,

---

[93] Other clauses in the 1933 Harbin regulations, however, have more sinister implications: children who entered the Foundling Home were barred from all contact with their natural parents, and the home was authorized to arrange marriages for orphan girls reaching adulthood, though only with their consent. This suggests that the Foundling Home may have been established as an experimental center for "re-education," designed to bring up its inmates as loyal subjects of the Japanese empire.

assumed a wait-and-see attitude. The financial support for all of these groups decreased day by day, with the result that all types of social relief work which they had previously engaged in came to a partial halt (*ban tingdun zhuangtai*).[94]

After some initial mistrust, however, a relatively successful working relationship developed between the new authorities and the directors of the philanthropic associations. In September 1948, the city government established a Harbin Municipal Social Affairs Association (*Haerbinshi Shehui Shiye Xiehui*), whose members consisted mainly of prominent leaders of the largest Chinese charities, including the World Red Swastika Society and the Harbin Charitable Association.[95]

The Social Affairs Association assumed responsibility for many of the new government's relief functions and immediately set up three new residential welfare institutions: a Relief Center for the Disabled and Elderly, a Relief Center for Women and Children, and a new municipal orphanage, all established in 1948.[96]

The first of these was designated as "a social welfare unit especially for sheltering disabled and elderly persons who are destitute and homeless (*liulishi*)," and originally took in sixty-seven inmates. The following year, however, the institution took on the different and possibly coercive responsibility of controlling the city's general vagrant population:

> In cooperation with the Harbin Municipal Committee on Dealing With Beggars (*Haerbinshi Qigai Chuli Weiyuanhui*), it sheltered 265 disabled and elderly beggars, and organized those among them who were able to work to participate in labor and production at the institute.[97]

---

[94] *Harbin Civil Affairs Annals*, p.181.

[95] The annals give no explanation of what happened to the city's existing Western-run charities. Presumably, most of their inmates and staff left Harbin around the time of the Communist takeover. (One exception was the Harbin Expatriate Old-Age Home, which had at least one surviving resident as recently as 1995.) The facilities of the foreign orphanages appear to have been closed or converted to other purposes, however, rather than made available for the care of Chinese children.

[96] It also took over various other tasks in civil affairs work, founding a municipal crematorium and several daycare centers for infants and toddlers.

[97] *Harbin Civil Affairs Annals*, p.182.

The function of the other institutes remained exclusively humanitarian, however. The second center, which offered shelter to abandoned children and to women with no means of support, was relatively small, holding at its peak no more than sixty women and sixteen minors. Most of its adult inmates were reportedly given "appropriate settlement" within a few years of its establishment. The new orphanage, founded in September 1948, began by assuming responsibility for more than 130 orphans previously cared for at a primary school run by the Harbin Charitable Association; in addition, in 1949 it took in more than 170 homeless children. Some fourteen of these later found outside employment and another forty-five were reclaimed by family members, leaving the orphanage population in 1951 at over 240 inmates.

By the early 1950s, Communist rule had been established throughout China's territory, and civil affairs work in Harbin came firmly under the control of nationwide policy. The results of this shift first became apparent in 1951, when responsibility for "vagrant reform" (*youmin gaizao*) was transferred from the city's Public Security Bureau to the Civil Affairs Bureau.[98] In September 1952, the Harbin Municipal Production-and-Rehabilitation Institute (*Haerbinshi Shengchan Jiaoyangyuan*) was established to implement this policy.

In line with the pattern observed throughout China around this time, the city authorities then immediately abandoned all efforts at providing segregated institutional care. The Relief Center for the Disabled and Elderly was shut down in 1952, and its inmates transferred to the Production-and-Rehabilitation Institute. Likewise, the Relief Center for Women and Children, whose adult inmates had already been successfully "settled," closed in the same year, and the orphans living there were sent for "alternative care" at the Production-and-Rehabilitation Institute. It is possible, but not certain, that the children held at the main Harbin orphanage suffered the same fate, as references to this institution in the municipal annals end after 1951. At least one local institution for children, the Acheng Orphanage, was also closed and amalgamated in 1952 (see below).

The early 1950s also saw the complete suppression of any institutional autonomy on the part of the city's former philanthropic leaders. The Harbin Municipal Social Affairs Association was reorganized, in November 1953, as a local branch of the state-controlled Chinese People's Relief Association, which assumed control of its assets and personnel. In May 1955, the new organization was amalgamated into the municipal Civil Affairs Bureau.

---

[98] *Ibid.*, p.184. The order to transfer this law enforcement function to the civil affairs authorities was issued by the Northeastern [China] People's Government. Heilongjiang Province had not yet been established as a separate jurisdiction in 1951.

Harbin also followed the national trend in seeking to reestablish "segregated management" a few years later, after the facilities at the Production-and-Rehabilitation Institute became "insufficient." With the foundation of the Harbin Municipal Psychiatric Care Institute (*Haerbinshi Jingshenbing Liaoyangyuan*) in 1956, the Harbin Municipal Old-Age Home (*Haerbinshi Yanglaoyuan*) in 1957, and the Harbin Municipal Institute for the Disabled and Elderly (*Haerbinshi Canlaoyuan*) in 1958, a modicum of specialized care was restored for at least some of the city's institutionalized population.[99] By the end of this period, as those in need of care were transferred elsewhere, the Production-and-Rehabilitation Institute had become exclusively a punitive institution for "vagrant reform."

However, a specialized orphanage was not among the new units set up during this period, and the annals give no indication of where the city's orphans were held in the late 1950s, although they acknowledge that a number of children had been held at the Production-and-Rehabilitation Institute after 1952. The annals do note that the institute established a children's section in 1959, which sheltered 170 "incorrigible children" that year, but there is no evidence that this section held orphans as well. Since the institute's non-penal functions had already been eliminated after 1958, it seems clear that abandoned children had been moved out by then. The national pattern of orphan "disappearances" here emerges at the local level in Harbin, not for the last time.[100]

The official records are equally silent on the fate of Harbin's orphans during the Great Leap Forward. Their account of "social relief work" in the same period, however, offers a telling commentary on the motives of the civil affairs authorities in 1958 and 1959. Characteristically, the municipal annals describe such relief work as a temporary measure, made necessary only by the persistent effects of the pre-Communist social system–and needed as much for maintaining social order as for alleviating hardship:

> Due to the fact that Harbin long suffered from the cruel domination
> and oppression of reactionary warlords, Tsarist Russia, and the
> Japanese aggressors, the people's lives were extremely
> impoverished. After Harbin's liberation in 1946, large numbers of
> unemployed workers, disaster victims, the urban poor, orphans, the

---

[99] *Ibid.*, pp.186-190. The new psychiatric institute began accepting self-paying patients as early as May 1958.

[100] As China's civil affairs annals are generally quite comprehensive, major gaps in the record can usually be interpreted to mean that the relevant functions of the department ceased altogether.

elderly, the disabled, infants, and vagrant beggars were loitering (*youdang*) in society, and society was extremely unstable.[101]

Although Harbin's social conditions were far more orderly after well over a decade of stable government, the continuing existence of urban poverty became an acute embarassment to local authorities on the eve of the Great Leap, when most Chinese believed the country was poised to achieve material abundance for all. By delegitimating the idea that social problems might persist even under socialist rule, China's leaders effectively made relief work itself ideologically impossible after 1958. Measures considered "welfarist," such as the provision of cash relief to needy families, had to be abandoned for ideological reasons, in favor of creating employment for the poor in units sponsored by the Civil Affairs Bureau. The bureau thus embarked on a strategy of "establishing social welfare production [units] in great numbers, and achieving a city without poor people" (*da ban shehui fuli shengchan, shixian chengshi wu pinmin*).

As the annals concede, this approach was an unqualified disaster. District civil affairs authorities in Harbin apparently struck large numbers of people from the relief rolls in 1958, but failed to establish enough new enterprises to employ them:

> In this year's work of massively establishing social welfare production [units], there arose a serious wind of untruthfulness (*fukua feng*). Some districts and neighborhoods one-sidedly pursued the target of a so-called "city without poor people." Without making appropriate arrangements for production, they wilfully abolished relief, and in this way achieved the "annihilation" (*xiaomie*) of relief households. [For example,] in July, Daoli District's Anjing Subdivision had formerly thirty-three relief households, including ninety-three persons, in the entire neighborhood. By August, this had been abruptly reduced to six households, including twenty-eight persons.[102]

Citing one case in which an elderly woman was reduced to eating garbage to survive, the annals conclude mildly that "the formulations of 'achieving a city

---

[101] *Ibid.*, p.143. It is especially striking that even "orphans, the elderly, the disabled, and infants" (*gu-lao-can-you*) are here characterized as a threat to public order.

[102] *Harbin Civil Affairs Annals*, pp.145-146.

without poor people' and 'annihilating relief households' were obviously impractical, as well as unscientific."

The shortfall in the city's relief services grew even more extreme in the following three years, however. By 1961, the annals record only that "the number of relief households had increased to 1,200, containing 4,200 people." Since this figure constituted less than one percent of Harbin's population during a period of acute famine, the civil affairs authorities had clearly abrogated all but a nominal role in mitigating the disaster. Indeed, the number of households receiving relief stayed constant at 1,200 until 1966, despite the economic recovery of the previous four years, suggesting that this figure represented a quota or set limit to be maintained for symbolic reasons, regardless of actual conditions in the city.

For Harbin's less visible institutionalized population, the official response to the famine was equally insignificant. After the reorganization of the Production-and-Rehabilitation Institute in the late 1950s, the annals' earliest reference to orphans appears only in 1960, when a "children's welfare institute" was established inside the Harbin Municipal Old-Age Home to care for "abandoned infants and orphans with no one to support them." As elsewhere in China, however, the role of this institution in sheltering the city's famine orphans was clearly marginal: the records show that it admitted only forty to fifty children each year until its closure in 1964. Those orphans with disabilities were then transferred to the city's Institute for the Disabled and Elderly, with the rest sent to another local institution, the Suihua Orphanage.[103]

After the mid-1960s, however, it becomes virtually impossible to trace the inmates of Harbin's welfare institutions, suggesting that the effects of the Cultural Revolution have been deliberately expunged from the historical records. All references to the Suihua Orphanage, for example, end after 1964. The Institute for the Disabled and Elderly was relocated in 1965 to the site of the city's main Production-and-Rehabilitation Institute, which had closed earlier the same year.[104] In October 1966, mysteriously, the unit was renamed the Municipal *Rehabilitation* Institute for the Disabled; it then promptly vanished from the historical records for fifteen years, reappearing only in 1981 as the newly christened "Municipal Social Welfare Institute." Although this is presently the main institution caring for abandoned children in Harbin, it is not clear whether it performed the same function during the Cultural Revolution, or even whether it continued to operate between 1966 and 1981.

---

[103] *Ibid.*, p.191.

[104] *Ibid.*, p.190. The vagrant inmates of the Production-and-Rehabilitation Institute were transferred in 1965 to the state-run Kedong Farm, presumably for permanent agricultural work.

The history of a smaller local institution, the Acheng Production-and-Rehabilitation Institute, is even more suggestive. This unit was formed in 1952 through the merger of the Acheng Orphanage and the Acheng Institute for the Disabled and Elderly, during the amalgamating administrative "reforms" of the period. According to the municipal annals,

> In 1954, in accordance with the goals of the provincial Civil Affairs Bureau, [the institute] took in eighty-three unsupported old and disabled people and eighteen orphans and child brides (*tongyangxi*) from eight counties, including Bin, Hulan, and Bayan. In 1956, it became the Acheng Old-Age Home, and in 1957 it was renamed the Acheng Rehabilitation Institute for the Elderly and Disabled. In 1972 it was [again] renamed the Acheng Old-Age Home, and in 1981 took in 240 old and disabled people from eleven counties in the Songhuajiang region. In July 1985 it was renamed the Acheng Social Welfare Institute, and was sheltering 216 old people.[105]

The Acheng institute's repeated name changes may seem farcical, but the functional transformations they appear to represent are in fact quite sinister. At some time during the period described, probably either in 1956 or 1972, the institute ceased to function as a home for abandoned children. There is no indication of the further whereabouts of those orphans in the unit at the time of the shift, however; they join the ranks of the children vanishing from the main Municipal Production-and-Rehabilitation Institute after 1956.[106]

The annals are considerably more forthcoming for the reformist period after 1978. Although the process of "socialization," in which funding responsibilities for welfare institutes are shifted to the private sector, seems now to be somewhat less advanced in Harbin than elsewhere in China, the city's Civil Affairs Bureau nevertheless claims to have made tremendous progress in social welfare work under Deng Xiaoping's rule. In some cases this is largely a matter of symbolism: most of the city's welfare institutes have now been awarded the honorary designation of "civilized

---

[105] *Ibid.*, p.191.

[106] The overwhelming importance attached to institutional name changes is a bizarre and inexplicable feature of many local civil affairs annals. The renaming of the Acheng institute in 1972, for example, is one of the few events of any kind which are recorded as having occurred in Harbin during the Cultural Revolution. This may, indeed, represent an extreme form of the tokenism affecting Chinese civil affairs work generally.

unit" (*wenming danwei*). Other improvements are apparently more substantive, reflecting the general increase in living standards in recent years: the annals claim that the "quality of food, clothing, and housing ... [had] shown a rather large improvement" by 1985.[107] These gains accompanied a shift towards more self-paying inmates in the city's welfare institutions, supplementing their traditional emphasis on care for the destitute and providing an additional source of revenue.

Nevertheless, some elements of the "reformed" welfare system cast doubt on the benefits these changes supposedly brought to the institutional population. Evidence from the municipal annals shows that the phenomenon of "missing" orphans persisted in Harbin long after the end of the Cultural Revolution. In Harbin's suburban areas (as distinct from the city proper) statistics from 1985 indicate that 838 persons, or roughly 0.3 percent of the suburbs' total population, qualified as members of "five-guarantee households" in need of relief. Although this total consisted primarily of the elderly, it also included sixty-three orphans and abandoned children.

A more detailed breakdown of these statistics fails to account for nearly half these children, however. Of the sixty-three suburban orphans recorded as receiving "five-guarantee" relief, some sixteen are listed as resident in collectively-run "respecting-the-aged homes," and another twenty as receiving foster care in private homes (a practice officially referred to as *fensan gongyang*, "dispersed support"). The remaining twenty-seven children, however, cannot be located in either category. They apparently represent a tiny fraction of the hundreds of thousands of abandoned children in China who are missing from the official statistics of recent years.[108]

The whereabouts of Harbin's urban orphans are more easily confirmed: since Harbin has no dedicated orphanage, most of them are presently held at the Harbin Municipal Social Welfare Institute. A journalist from the German magazine *Der Spiegel* visited this institution in June 1995 and described it as a "children's gulag."

---

[107] *Harbin Civil Affairs Annals*, p.173. The specific examples offered are somewhat less inspiring, however. Since the Harbin Municipal Psychiatric Care Institute shifted to the responsibility system, for example, it is recorded that "the quality of service has constantly improved, and under the painstaking nursing care [of the staff], patients confined to bed for long periods no longer develop bedsores, lice have been eradicated for several years now, and in recent years there have been no unnatural deaths of patients" (p.188).

[108] *Ibid.*, pp.159-161.

"The Children's Gulag of Harbin"[109]

The overseer rapidly barricades the entrance door behind the foreigner and thrusts her pointed chin forward: "Over there, there they all are." She quickly stamps into the care-room. Her boyfriend is visiting today. Who doesn't want to have his rest? In her absence Guo Ying is to look after the proprieties.

Guo Ying is fourteen years old. At least that's what it says on the yellowed slip of paper attached to her bed. She's just four feet two inches tall and thin as a rake. Her father is a drunkard, and her mother landed in an insane asylum. That brought her the stigma of mental illness. She has never attended a school; she can only leave the orphanage with the consent of her parents. But where are they? Guo Ying shrugs her shoulders. She has a life sentence. Yet of all people, this half-grown girl is the "Mother of the Station." Running past, she takes from the autistic boy the sticky cornbread he has just soaked in the waste water from the toilet. She takes out of the hands of an eight-year-old boy the tin bowl with which he is hammering a handicapped girl on the skull.

Then, where the care-worker had pointed with her arrogant movement, Guo Ying goes along a long hall. The plaster is crumbling from the wall. In a dim room, as big as a dance hall, babies and small children are lying–no, they are not lying, they are laid out, in cribs: handicapped small bodies, some just skin and bones.

Kicking and thrashing, they doze in their own urine, some naked, some dressed in a dirty little jacket. About thirty infants and small children are here, together with twenty mostly mongoloid women, shut off from the outside world....This room that's grave-cool even in summer is a madhouse and dying wing at the same time...

Under a bed in the next room: a small bundle of rags. "Dead," says the graceful Guo Ying, motionless. Last night, the infant, whose name no one knows, died. "While feeding, he couldn't take in any more air." He apparently suffocated, she guesses, shrugging her shoulders. The older children have wrapped the body in a couple of dirty cloths, which serve as a shroud. Then they shoved the dead baby under the bed, where it stays until the staff get around to removing the corpse. On weekends that can take two or three days. That's normal here. On the holiday, on "Children's Day," the children played undertaker...

Block Three, the terrible death house for handicapped infants and small children, normally remains forbidden to visitors. It lies hidden behind shrubs. "When

---

[109] Excerpted from Jürgen Kremb, "Der Kinder-Gulag von Harbin," *Der Spiegel* (No.37), September 11, 1995, pp.174-178. The full text of this article appears in Appendix P.

I set foot in here for the first time," says the Canadian teacher Peter Costello, "I thought to myself, 'I've entered hell.'"

The lecturer came to China with his wife Melanie in the fall of 1993. He heard about the establishment from a social worker he had befriended. He visited it and then came back almost every weekend. "I soon came to terms with the dirt and the filth, the almost medieval hygiene in which the children vegetate," the lanky young man reports. But then he discovered: again and again, babies disappeared from Block Three. He began to take notes for himself.

At the beginning of this year, the younger residents, separated between boys and girls, received a number—followed by the date on which they were first delivered. Under "status," Costello noted "died," or only "gone" when he couldn't confirm the exact cause of the departure. Under "details," he listed the reconstructed cause of death. As the most common single cause there stood: "starved, died of thirst."

The list grew into a gruesome accounting, comprehensive proof of the existence, denied by the Chinese government, of dying rooms in the country's orphanages. "We've seen about one hundred babies die here in the last two years," says the Canadian. Of the fifty children he has put down on his list since the beginning of January, thirty-six are certainly dead, possibly forty...

Guangxi Zhuang Autonomous Region

Civil affairs records for the southwestern province of Guangxi (technically a "minority autonomous region" for the Zhuang nationality) offer a striking contrast to the Harbin municipal annals. Guangxi is considered a relatively "leftist" province, and the radical political campaigns of the Communist period were often carried to especially destructive extremes there. Perhaps because of the provincial leadership's continuing hardline stance, the published history of civil affairs work in Guangxi is relatively forthcoming on the events of these periods and reveals their shattering impact on the institutionalized population in great detail.

Guangxi possessed a number of small orphanages and foundling homes in the late 1940s, several of which were established at the county and municipal levels during the war. By the end of 1948, there were fourteen child welfare institutes throughout the province, mainly operated by local governments but including as well three units established by foreign missions: a foundling home and an orphanage run by French Catholics in Beihai, and an American Protestant institution in Wuzhou, the

Wuguang Orphanage. These fourteen institutions held a total of 1,542 children in 1948.[110]

The Communists inherited only a handful of these orphanages, however. In 1949, in one of the last acts of the province's Nationalist-controlled civil affairs authorities, most of these institutions were reportedly "wound up" (*banli jieshu*). Only five children's institutions remained in Guangxi after the closures: the Nanning Foundling Home, the Guilin Municipal Relief Institute and Foundling Home, and the three Christian institutions.

Local governments in Guangxi also maintained urban old-age homes before the revolution, some dating as far back as the eighteenth century. By the late 1940s, however, the number of these institutions had dropped dramatically, as a result of the economic disruptions caused by the Anti-Japanese War and by a serious drought in 1945. By the time of the Communist takeover, only five old-age homes remained, one in each of the province's major cities of Guilin, Liuzhou, Wuzhou, Nanning, and Beihai.

Communist authority in southwestern China was established relatively late, and Guangxi was "liberated" only in 1950. By this time, the two state-run orphanages remaining in Nanning and Guilin reportedly held a total of just eighteen children, who were then "already breathing their last" (*yijing yanyan yixi*).[111] Rather than refurbishing these institutions, however, the new municipal authorities followed nationwide Party policy and shut them down altogether. The Nanning Foundling Home was immediately "wound up," and the Guilin Municipal Relief Institute and Foundling Home was amalgamated into the newly established Guilin Municipal Production-and-Rehabilitation Institute for the Disabled and Elderly (*Guilinshi Canlao Shengchan Jiaoyangyuan*).

Official policy towards the three remaining private children's homes was even more perverse. After a brief period during which these continued operating under their original Christian management, the Wuzhou People's Government took over the American-sponsored Wuguang Orphanage in 1951 and immediately closed it. The majority of its inmates were then settled in private families.[112] The measures taken in

---

[110] *Ins and Outs of Civil Affairs*, pp.66-67. The United Nations also operated an orphanage in Guangxi between 1946 and 1949, but it is unclear whether its inmates are included in the 1948 population totals.

[111] *Ibid.*, p.68.

[112] Along with the closure of most state-run orphanages by Guangxi's Nationalist government two years earlier, this suggests that the end of the Anti-Japanese war had sharply reduced the need for foster care. Most of the fifty children at the Wuguang Orphanage

Beihai were apparently much harsher: the city assumed control of the city's Catholic-run orphanage and foundling home in 1952, and the foundling home was then "wound up"–but the fate of its inmates is not recorded. The Beihai orphanage was closed at the same time, and its inmates transferred to the city's new Production-and-Rehabilitation Institute.[113]

The destruction of these institutions formed part of a policy of wholesale amalgamation of Guangxi's custodial welfare homes in the early Communist period: the official records add that "during the period 1950-1955, the task of fostering infants and children in cities such as Nanning, Guilin, Liuzhou, Wuzhou, and Beihai was assumed by foster care units attached to the production-and-rehabilitation institutes for the disabled and elderly in these cities."[114]

As elsewhere in China, this policy was suddenly reversed in 1956, and institutionalized minors were moved to newly established orphanages, but with no effort to separate orphans from delinquent children. On the principle of "establishing separate institutes as soon as possible for street children to be held together with orphans in areas where they are numerous," children held in the "production-and-rehabilitation institutes" of the five major cities were transferred to six new "child rehabilitation institutes" and "children's work-study schools."

It is difficult to determine what principles guided the "rehabilitation" of orphans during this period, but the history of Guangxi's urban old-age homes provides a disturbing indication of the province's general policies on institutional care in the late 1950s. The nationwide practice of screening the elderly by "class background" was implemented in a particularly drastic form in much of Guangxi, as later records reveal:

> In 1957, the social relief institutes in the five cities combined the whole people's rectification of workstyles (*zhengfeng*) and struggle against Rightists with undertaking socialist education for the inmates. In the four cities of Nanning, Guilin, Liuzhou, and Wuzhou, political investigations of the inmates were undertaken.

---

reportedly "had homes to return to" (*you jia ke gui*) in their native villages, possibly among other Protestant families.

[113] *Ins and Outs of Civil Affairs Work*, pp.68-69. As elsewhere in China, the Catholic charities in Beihai were singled out for special criticism: the official records claim, for example, that death rates at the Beihai Foundling Home had exceeded 95 percent since its foundation in 1921.

[114] *Ibid.*, pp.68-69.

According to statistics for the three institutions in Nanning, Guilin, and Liuzhou, after the political investigations, measures were taken against thirty-six persons, constituting 7.1 percent of the total institutional population. Two of these were sent to be dealt with by law-enforcement agencies, three were sent to be rehabilitated through labor reform (*laogai*), sixteen were sent to labor on vagrant farms (*youmin nongchang*), and fifteen were recalled to their former units for supervised labor.[115]

Guangxi thus extended its purge of "Rightists," which included the detention of those whose "crimes" were considered particularly serious, into the most vulnerable segment of the population, the institutionalized elderly without close relatives.

Punitive sanctions were not limited to those forcibly removed from the old-age homes, however. Although overtly coercive measures were only imposed on the basis of real or imagined individual offenses uncovered through "political investigation," a broader policy of class-based segregation was also introduced at the same time. The official history describes the shift in deceptively innocuous terms:

At the same time [as the detention of the "Rightist" elderly], segregated management and separate treatment were implemented for the rest of the inmates according to their class backgrounds. Disabled and elderly inmates with backgrounds from among the laboring people were grouped into "Retirement Departments" (*yanglaobu*), while those from the exploiting classes or with individual historical problems were grouped into "Rehabilitation Departments" (*jiaoyangbu*). The Retirement Departments "made care the priority" (*yi yang wei zhu*), and the Rehabilitation Departments "made education the priority" (*yi jiao wei zhu*).[116]

The ominous significance of this local policy can only be understood by comparison with its nationally accepted counterpart, as described in the 1959 "Draft Report on Problems in Civil Affairs Work." Although this document endorsed the segregation of elderly people by class background, it also specified that old-age homes

---

[115] *Ibid.*, p.63. The careful computation of the number detained, as a proportion of the total inmate population, suggests that, as happened in work units throughout China at that time, the urban retirement homes were officially assigned quotas of "Rightist" elements to discover within their midst.

[116] *Ibid.*, p.163.

should "make care the priority" for all their charges, including those from the "exploiting classes." Policy towards such inmates in Guangxi, by contrast, was explicitly punitive: the management principles of the "Rehabilitation Departments" rejected the function of "care" for their inmates in favor of ideological "education." The records later note in passing that the inmates of these departments "were discriminated against and attacked on political grounds."[117]

For the elderly in rural areas, custodial care was unavailable in any case until the massive institutional expansion of the Great Leap Forward. The first of the province's rural "respecting-the-aged homes" was established in June 1958 to house eighteen elderly inmates. Between mid-1958 and 1960, no fewer than 1,776 such homes were established and took in over 20,000 destitute old people, with rations supplied by local people's communes. During the economic retrenchment of the famine years, however, these institutions largely melted away:

> Because there was no way to resolve the problem of supply, the village "respecting-the-aged homes" which had been set up in one fell swoop (*yihong erqi*) were merged or abolished. By 1965, they had decreased in number to eighteen, containing 235 old persons, and the remaining old persons were returned to their original production teams for dispersed support (*fensan gongyang*).[118]

Child welfare policy in Guangxi between 1959 and 1961 also followed the principle of "making dispersed settlement [i.e., fostering in private homes] the priority, with concentrated settlement as a supplement." Although the early 1960s saw the widespread foundation of new "children's welfare institutes," these scarcely corresponded to the scale of the crisis. Only a small fraction of Guangxi's famine orphans were thus placed in institutional care ("concentrated settlement"), with the remainder being returned to their villages of origin ("dispersed settlement"):

> By the end of 1962, some 38,256 orphans had been publicly settled, of whom 32,639, or 85.3 percent, received dispersed settlement, and 5,617, or 14.7 percent, received concentrated

---

[117] *Ibid.*, pp.256-257.

[118] *Ibid.*, p.65.

settlement in 135 [newly] established children's welfare institutes.[119]

The records show that all but thirty-three of these institutions had closed by early 1965, as most of their inmates had "gradually reached adulthood." This indicates that as in Yunnan's Red River Prefecture, most of the Guangxi orphans held in "concentrated settlement" were older children and teenagers. Such institutional care was probably reserved largely for delinquent or "incorrigible" famine orphans, in accordance with the national regulations issued by the Interior Ministry on the subject. Younger orphans were instead returned to an uncertain fate on the rural communes, a process described euphemistically as "dispersed settlement."[120]

As in the rest of China, the civil affairs bureaucracy in Guangxi was abolished shortly after the outbreak of the Cultural Revolution and reconstituted only after 1972. Rural homes for the elderly were shut down altogether during those years; but the fate of the residents of nineteen urban retirement homes which remained intact at the outbreak of the Cultural Revolution was scarcely more appealing:

> Some [elderly persons] relief institutes undertook major accusations, exposures, criticisms and purges, conducting a "cleansing of the class ranks" among the institutional population (*zaiyuanmin*).... "Making care the priority" was seen as engaging in "welfarism" and criticized as "walking the capitalist road." By 1975, the entire Guangxi region had only seven urban social-relief institutes left.[121]

The treatment of orphans in Guangxi during the Cultural Revolution is apparently too sensitive a topic for the published records to discuss. It is recorded only that during this period "the child welfare institutes suffered severe sabotage," with the result that of the thirty-three such orphanages in the province in 1965, only two were still operating by 1978.

---

[119] *Ibid.*, p.69.

[120] For other targets of "social welfare work," even flimsier pretexts were invoked to wind down the institutional projects of the Great Leap Forward. The records note that by 1960, the province had established twenty-four "social relief institutes for the blind," housing 866 people, but that in 1962, these institutions were dissolved and their inmates were returned to their native places "in order to prepare for war." (*Ibid.*, p.63.)

[121] *Ibid.*, pp.63-64.

The political liberalization of the late 1970s led to the reversal of the most extreme civil affairs policies adopted in Guangxi during the Maoist era. "Making care the priority" was reaffirmed as the guiding principle of institutional welfare work, the class-based segregation system in the urban relief institutes (then renamed "social welfare institutes") was abolished, and inmates who had been unjustly designated as "targets of education" were rehabilitated, no doubt posthumously in many cases. A number of new social welfare institutes were also established after 1978, although the institutional capacity of the mid-1960s was never fully restored.[122] Apart from these efforts to undo the damage inflicted in previous decades, the most significant reform undertaken during this period was an increased reliance on "social forces," both domestic and foreign, for the financing and support of welfare institutions. Although the shift towards "self-paying care" in Guangxi's social welfare institutes had made only limited progress by the end of the 1980s, it accelerated substantially after 1990. Especially in the province's child welfare work, however, a more significant source of funding in recent years has been donations from charities based overseas, particularly in Hong Kong. But there is little evidence that orphans in Guangxi have in any way benefited from these donations; indeed, overseas press reports on conditions in one institution supposedly benefiting from such funding, the Nanning Municipal Social Welfare Institute, provided some of the earliest evidence of the abysmal conditions that are nowadays to be found throughout China's child welfare system.

By way of concluding this historical survey of the Chinese government's post-1949 reforms of the country's orphanage and social welfare system, the following official statement provides a concise explanation of the underlying philosophy which guided those reforms:

> Of course, when we speak of "inheritance," it is a critical inheritance, and we absolutely cannot inherit in their entirety things in civil affairs which are of a totally different basic nature or are mutually opposed....With respect to these, not only must we not inherit them, we must thoroughly destroy them (*chedi ba ta cuihui*), leaving them on record only as negative historical materials.[123]

---

[122] By 1987, for example, Guangxi had established thirty-two urban social welfare institutes housing 660 elderly inmates. This compares with nineteen apparently much larger institutions operating in 1965, caring for 1,278 inmates.

[123] *Ins and Outs of Civil Affairs*, pp.232-233.

"Condemned to Die–For Being A Girl"

The scene in the shabby upstairs room of what is little better than a squalid hovel is utterly heartbreaking. Nineteen newborn infants, crammed four or five to each rusty cot, lie sleeping on filthy mattresses, their tiny heads peeping out over torn blankets.

Beneath wispy tufts of black hair, their scalps are covered in weeping sores. Their bodies bear the stigmata of bleeding cuts where their little fingernails have tried to scratch away the discomfort of dry, cracking skin–skin which is of every hue from livid red to sickly, jaundiced yellow...

This is the place they call the Dying Room. This room, ten feet by twelve feet, is in a two-storey building which dares to call itself a 'children's welfare hospital'....We first heard of this place, the state orphanage in Nanning, the capital of Guangxi Province in Southern China, three months ago when an Australian charity worker discovered babies were being allowed to die of deyhdration, malnourishment, and plain neglect...

Worse, the party authorities of Nanning appear to have callously exploited Western sensibilities to line their pockets. Almost £500,000 raised by Hongkong charities to refurbish the Nanning orphanage has gone missing...."We need every kind of equipment," said Lin Jijie, the director of the orphanage since 1974. But wasn't the money from Hongkong supposed to help solve that? Mr. Lin shrugged. The fact that our small donation went not into a cashbox in his office but straight into his pocket is perhaps pertinent....

Mr. Lin says the orphanage has its own doctor, but no one ever knew where to find him. So the babies die of problems which could easily be remedied. Mr. Lin shrugged again. "Ten percent a month die at least. That's quite normal," he said, matter-of-factly.

(From: *The Daily Mail*, London, December 20, 1993)

The policies of the immediate postrevolutionary period aimed to accomplish just this destruction, and to build a system of social welfare free of any bourgeois taint. Ever since 1949, the political legitimacy of China's social welfare work itself has been in doubt, as the civil affairs departments aim to deal with problems whose very continued existence is politically unacceptable. For this reason, the institutional capacity of the pre-1949 custodial welfare system has yet to be fully restored, almost fifty years later, let alone expanded to match the country's growing population. By the 1990s, the government's disdain for institutional welfare work had produced grotesquely inhumane conditions in nearly all of China's state-run orphanages and foundling homes. These conditions have been documented not only by the evidence of outside observers but also–and far more thoroughly–by the authorities' own published statistics. The following chapter analyzes this official record in detail.

III. CHINA'S ORPHANS: THE OFFICIAL RECORD

In addition to various historical texts which document socialist welfare policy in previous decades, the Chinese authorities have also published extensive statistics, recently obtained by Human Rights Watch/Asia, on present-day conditions in the country's custodial welfare homes. These figures demonstrate that China's urban orphanages and other institutions for children serve a largely symbolic function, representing the state's public commitment to the humane treatment of abandoned infants but in practice making almost no effort to keep them alive. According to the authorities' own published statistics, the nationwide ratio of deaths to new admissions among institutionalized children is well over 50 percent, and many individual institutions appear to serve, in effect, as death camps for orphans. Worse, there are indications that even some of these published statistics may underestimate actual death rates among institutionalized orphans in China.

Contrary to some recent reports in the Western media, the government's statistics also show that Chinese orphanages are, at least on the face of it, neither underfinanced nor understaffed. In fact, the budgets of most such institutions are clearly adequate to assure minimum standards of care and sustenance to the number of children in their care at any given time. In practice, however, only a small fraction of available funding is used to provide children with the necessities of life. By far the largest share of most institutions' budgets is spent instead on various staff benefits, including salaries, bonuses, and retirement pensions. Many institutions employ astonishingly large numbers of people–although it is not always clear whether all of these employees actually exist or are required to report to work.[124] The overwhelming majority of the thousands of unnatural deaths which occur each year in China's orphanages result from deliberate neglect and abuse, and not from a lack of needed resources.

Finally, the published statistics show that only a small percentage of abandoned infants in China are being placed in any form of institutional care. Although it is possible that some of those orphans who remain unaccounted for have been placed in private foster care, there is stong evidence that such care is employed only as a measure of last resort, when institutional space is unavailable. The whereabouts of all but a tiny fraction of China's abandoned children are thus completely unaccounted for in official records. A full accounting of conditions in the country's child welfare system awaits official clarification of their fate.

---

[124] See, for example, note 160 for details of the peculiar staffing situation at the Shanghai Children's Welfare Institute.

77

Children in Urban Institutional Care

Since 1990, the Ministry of Civil Affairs has published a detailed annual accounting of China's urban institutional population as one section of a broader abstract, the *China Civil Affairs Statistical Yearbook*. Human Rights Watch/Asia has obtained five consecutive editions of this unclassified but very narrowly circulated publication, dated 1990 through 1994 and covering the calendar years 1989 through 1993.[125] Evidence from the ministerial yearbooks, particularly the 1990 edition, provides the basis for much of this chapter, supplemented where necessary by other official statistical sources. The comprehensiveness of these figures often leaves something to be desired, but what China's bureaucrats omit is often as revealing as what they choose to include.

Urban welfare institutes run by the Ministry of Civil Affairs are divided into three categories for statistical purposes:

- social welfare institutes (*shehui fuliyuan*);
- child welfare institutes (*ertong fuliyuan*);
- psychiatric welfare institutes (*jingshenbingren fuliyuan*).[126]

As noted in Chapter 2, the general-purpose "social welfare institutes," which hold an indiscriminate assortment of elderly, orphaned, handicapped, and mentally ill inmates, now constitute the overwhelming majority of custodial institutions run by the Ministry of Civil Affairs. According to the 1993 *China Civil Affairs Statistical Yearbook*, the most recent edition which includes the relevant figures, there were 950 "social welfare institutes" throughout the country at the end of 1992, compared with 129 "psychiatric welfare institutes" and just sixty-seven specialized orphanages.

---

[125] *China Civil Affairs Statistical Yearbook* (*Zhongguo Minzheng Tongji Nianjian*), 1990 edition, compiled by Ministry of Civil Affairs General Planning Office (Beijing: Zhongguo Shehui Chubanshe, December 1990); 1991 edition, compiled by Ministry of Civil Affairs General Planning Office (Beijing: Zhongguo Shehui Chubanshe, October 1991); 1992 edition, compiled by Ministry of Civil Affairs General Planning Office (Beijing: Zhongguo Shehui Chubanshe, October 1992); 1993 edition, compiled by Ministry of Civil Affairs General Planning Office (Beijing: Zhongguo Shehui Chubanshe, May 1993); 1994 edition, compiled by Ministry of Civil Affairs Planning and Finance Office (Beijing: Zhongguo Shehui Chubanshe, April 1994).

[126] In addition to these three categories, there are a small number of specialized welfare institutions in China which serve other functions. The civil affairs authorities of Liaoning Province, for example, maintain a separate system of retirement homes for the urban elderly.

The ministerial yearbooks list inmate totals for all social welfare institutes under Ministry of Civil Affairs jurisdiction and include separate figures for the number of infants and children in each, making it possible to calculate the total number of minors in urban institutional care. According to the 1994 yearbook's figures, children in the ministry's care at the end of 1993 were distributed as follows:

Table 3.1 Minors in the Care of the Ministry Of Civil Affairs, Year-End 1993[127]

Type of Institute	Number of Minors
Social Welfare Institutes	10,161
Child Welfare Institutes	7,002
Psychiatric Welfare Institutes	327
Total	17,490

These figures approximately correspond to other official claims on the number of institutionalized orphans in China. For example, a recent editorial in the *People's Daily*, China's main national newspaper, stated that "there are now more than 1,200 government-funded orphanages and social welfare institutions in the country, taking care of nearly 20,000 orphans."[128]

The statistics in Table 3.1 show that, as of the end of 1993, only some two-fifths of minor children living in Ministry of Civil Affairs institutions were held in specialized "child welfare institutes." Apart from a handful of children confined to psychiatric hospitals, the rest live in all-purpose "social welfare institutes," which contain an broad assortment of inmates. In most provinces, the majority of those held in the "social welfare institutes" are elderly people, but many such institutions also care for orphans, mental patients, the severely retarded and the physically disabled.

China's reliance on such institutions to care for most urban orphans represents the culmination of several decades of rhetorical commitment to "segregated management" for the institutionalized. More than thirty years after the June 1959

---

[127] *China Civil Affairs Statistical Yearbook* (1994 edition), pp.108-113. These figures exlude a very small number of minors held in other types of custodial welfare institutes.

[128] "Devote More Love," *Renmin Ribao (People's Daily)*, Beijing, May 10, 1995. p.3.

"Draft Report on Problems in Civil Affairs Work," which called for the establishment of separate welfare institutions for minors, virtually no progress has been made on this front. Indeed, the urban child welfare system appears have deteriorated in recent years, with access to specialized orphanage care diminishing for most abandoned infants and children.

The sixty-seven "child welfare institutes" operating throughout China in late 1993 varied widely in size and function, and not all of them were custodial institutions providing round-the-clock care.[129] Moreover, the geographical distribution of China's orphanages is highly uneven: eight of China's twenty-nine provinces and autonomous regions (Hebei, Shanxi, Jiangxi, Inner Mongolia, Hainan, Ningxia, Qinghai, and Tibet) had no specialized orphanages at all at the end of 1993. Abandoned children in the cities of these regions were held exclusively in "social welfare institutes."[130]

Even in provinces which do operate separate institutions for children, the "social welfare institutes" often hold the majority of urban orphans. The following table shows the distribution of infants and children between orphanages and "social welfare institutes" in each province and autonomous region at the end of 1993:

---

[129] Shanghai Municipality, for example, contains two "children's welfare institutes" operated by the municipal Civil Affairs Bureau. One of these, however, is a small district-level institution which provides daytime care for disabled children living with their families.

[130] More recently, however, a dedicated orphanage has been established in at least one of these regions. A report in the newspaper *Shanxi Ribao (Shanxi Daily)* dated May 11, 1995, refers to the existence of a specialized child welfare institute in Taiyuan, the capital of Shanxi Province.

Table 3.2 Distribution of Minors in Ministry of Civil Affairs Institutions, Year-End 1993[131]

Region	Child Welfare Institutes		Social Welfare Institutes		Percentage of Minors in Child Welfare Institutes
	Number of Institutions	Number of Minors	Number of Institutions	Number of Minors	
National Total	67	7,002	950[132]	10,161	40.8
Beijing	1	630	5	5	99.2
Tianjin	2	289	8	1	99.7
Hebei	0	0	21	254	0.0
Shanxi	0	0	12	697	0.0
Inner Mongolia	0	0	31	346	0.0
Liaoning	2	178	20	217	45.1
Jilin	1	540	12	120	81.8
Heilongjiang	5	739	17	105	87.6
Shanghai	2	690	14	40	94.5
Jiangsu	5	747	49	770	49.2
Zhejiang	6	603	38	452	57.2
Anhui	2	137	54	1,280	9.7
Fujian	2	112	43	475	19.1
Jiangxi	0	0	90	941	0.0

---

[131] Figures from the *China Civil Affairs Statistical Yearbook* (1994 edition), pp.108-111, except as noted.

[132] Figures in this column are from the 1993 edition of the *China Civil Affairs Statistical Yearbook* (pp.88-89). For reasons that are not clear, the 1994 edition of the yearbook omits information on the number of "social welfare institutes" in the country.

Region	Child Welfare Institutes		Social Welfare Institutes		Percentage of Minors in Child Welfare Institutes
	Number of Institutions	Number of Minors	Number of Institutions	Number of Minors	
Shandong	1	17	21	259	6.2
Henan	1	32	60	363	8.1
Hubei	6	408	103	917	30.8
Hunan	6	267	56	567	32.0
Guangdong	4	86	56	965	8.2
Guangxi	2	29	32	488	5.6
Hainan	0	0	1	21	0.0
Sichuan	6	504	56	264	65.6
Guizhou	4	194	35	73	72.7
Yunnan	3	276	40	36	72.7
Tibet	0	0	1	13	0.0
Shaanxi	1	155	26	179	46.4
Gansu	2	182	19	97	65.2
Qinghai	0	0	5	45	0.0
Ningxia	0	0	10	99	0.0
Xinjiang	3	187	15	72	72.2

As the figures in Table 3.2 indicate, abandoned children in densely populated provinces such as Shandong and Henan, each of which contained a single small orphanage as of December 1993, have virtually no hope of receiving appropriate care. Nor is there evidence of any systematic effort in recent years to remedy the deficiencies in the orphanage system. Between 1990 and 1994, according to successive editions of the *China Civil Affairs Statistical Yearbook*, the total number of child welfare institutes in China increased from sixty-four to sixty-seven, while the number of available beds rose from 6,830 to 8,645.[133] However, none of the newly-opened institutions were located in the seven provinces and autonomous regions which contained no orphanages at the end of 1989. In addition, the only orphanage in Hebei Province was closed during this period.

The institutional placement of abandoned children in China has thus become increasingly haphazard, even as their numbers have increased. Figures from successive years of the *China Civil Affairs Statistical Yearbook* show that the percentage of Chinese orphans being brought up in specialized children's institutions has actually fallen in recent years, decreasing from 44.9 percent at the end of 1989 to 40.8 percent at the end of 1993.

Urban "Child Welfare Institutes": Death Camps For Orphans

In most countries, reports of such disorganized institutional child-care policies would lead to calls for an expansion of the main orphanage system. In China, unfortunately, there is no reason to believe that this would improve children's living conditions without much broader reforms. With isolated exceptions, China's orphanages are places of no return for the majority of abandoned infants who enter them. Incredibly, the *China Civil Affairs Statistical Yearbook*, an unclassified public document, included detailed statistics on mortality rates in all urban welfare institutes in its 1990 edition, the first to be published by the Ministry of Civil Affairs. These figures show that conditions in China's orphanages in 1989 were easily among the worst in the world, with death rates far exceeding those recorded in Nicolae Ceausescu's Romania during the same period.

The editions of the *China Civil Affairs Statistical Yearbook* dated 1991 through 1994 omit all information on inmate deaths, however, giving only the number of inmates in each province's custodial welfare system at the end of the previous year. There are several possible explanations for this shift: the ministry may have acted in response to a perceived change in the political climate after the suppression of the

---

[133] The column in the *China Civil Affairs Statistical Yearbook* headed "beds [number]" (*chuangweishu [zhang]*) implies, from the use of the counter *zhang*, that infants and children in Chinese orphanages sleep in individual beds. This is generally not the case, however, and these figures should be interpreted as the maximum number of *persons* each institution is capable of holding. Moreover, in many orphanages where capacity has reportedly been expanded, it is often substantially unused. The combined capacity of the two child welfare institutes in the city of Nanjing, for example, rose from 440 beds at the end of 1989 to 590 beds at the end of 1992, the latest year for which municipal figures are available. The actual population of these institutes, however, increased from 325 to only 346 during the same period. Standards of institutional child welfare in Nanjing are apparently among the worst in China, with too few orphans surviving infancy to fill the beds available (see below, Table 3.3).

popular protest movements of early 1989, or may simply have concluded that the 1990 yearbook was needlessly explicit.[134] Since much of the work of the Ministry of Civil Affairs is highly sensitive, it is not surprising that the frankness of the 1990 yearbook was not duplicated in following years. Indeed, a directive issued jointly in July 1989 by the Ministry of Civil Affairs and the State Secrets Bureau, entitled "Regulations on the Specific Range of State Secrets in Civil Affairs Work and their Classification Level," specifies that certain types of "national statistical data" in the ministry's possession must be kept classified.[135]

However, the available statistics speak for themselves. The 1990 edition of the ministerial yearbook specifies the disposition of inmates in the ministry's child welfare institutes during calendar year 1989, as follows:

---

[134] It is also possible that the decision to stop publishing mortality statistics was related to an official investigation launched in 1990 into conditions at one of the country's largest specialized orphanages, the Shanghai Children's Welfare Institute (see Chapters 4, 5, and 6).

[135] Human Rights Watch/Asia has been unable to obtain the text of this directive. However, an official gloss on the directive's implementation, circulated in August 1991, appears in Appendix L.

Table 3.3 Official Population Statistics on China's Child Welfare Institutes, 1989[136]

Region	Data on Changes in the Institutionalized Population				Population at Year End				Year-end Breakdown of Population in Care			
	Population at End of Previous Year	Admitted During Current Year	Departed During Current Year	Died During Current Year	Total	Preferential Care Targets	"Social Three Nones"	Self-Paying Inmates	Disabled Adults	Children Over Six Years Old	Infants and Children Under Six Years Old	Mental Patients
National Total	5,539	3,210	1,233	1,857	5,659	246	4,756	657	222	3,516	1,787	113
Beijing	345	155	39	83	378	—[137]	322	56	22	133	221	—
Tianjin	213	106	21	84	214	—	207	7	—	130	84	—
Hebei	22	—	—	1	21	—	21	—	—	20	1	—
Shanxi	—	—	—	—	—	—	—	—	—	—	—	—
Inner Mongolia	—	—	—	—	—	—	—	—	—	—	—	—
Liaoning	152	12	10	—	154	—	124	30	1	150	3	—
Jilin	517	71	60	1	527	—	387	140	—	527	—	—

[136] Figures from *China Civil Affairs Statistical Yearbook* (1990 edition), China Social Press, pp.100-103. NB: The statistics in this table refer only to China's specialized urban orphanages.

[137] Dashes mean that a blank space, signifying a value of zero, appeared in the original table.

Region	Data on Changes in the Institutionalized Population				Population at Year End				Year-end Breakdown of Population in Care			
	Population at End of Previous Year	Admitted During Current Year	Departed During Current Year	Died During Current Year	Total	Preferential Care Targets	"Social Three Nones"	Self-Paying Inmates	Disabled Adults	Children Over Six Years Old	Infants and Children Under Six Years Old	Mental Patients
Heilongjiang	589	42	30	6	595	31	517	47	–	491	99	–
Shanghai	458	276	112	141	481	–	393	88	–	292	189	–
Jiangsu (Nanjing)	851 335	473 316	118 63	349 263	857 325	–	776 281	81 44	137	315 195	299 130	104
Zhejiang (Ningbo)	451 75	528 65	206 41	284 14	489 85	–	458 68	31 17	12	270 55	204 30	3
Anhui	42	3	1	4	40	–	38	2	2	31	5	2
Fujian	81	109	6	109	75	–	75	–	–	44	25	–
Jiangxi	–	–	–	–	–	–	–	–	–	–	–	–
Shandong	16	4	1	–	19	–	19	–	2	17	–	–
Henan	23	72	4	66	25	–	23	2	–	12	13	–
Hubei (Wuhan)	314 165	466 415	269 264	184 156	327 160	–	273 113	54 47	11	175 60	140 100	–
Hunan	145	121	113	54	99	–	99	–	1	36	59	–
Guangdong	89	55	31	23	90	1	88	1	6	69	15	–

Data on Changes in the Institutionalized Population / Year-end Breakdown of Population in Care

Region	Population at End of Previous Year	Admitted During Current Year	Departed During Current Year	Died During Current Year	Population at Year End				Disabled Adults	Children Over Six Years Old	Infants and Children Under Six Years Old	Mental Patients
					Total	Preferential Care Targets	"Social Three Nones"	Self-Paying Inmates				
Guangxi	21	43	5	39	20	–	20	–	–	2	17	–
Hainan	–	–	–	–	–	–	–	–	–	–	–	–
Sichuan (Chengdu) (Chongqing)	382 120 112	247 92 124	86 50 29	140 55 68	403 107 139	85	283 86 134	35 21 5	6	238 110	158 106 29	–
Guizhou	130	31	28	8	125	–	96	29	9	86	30	–
Yunnan	222	70	28	22	242	–	222	20	3	204	33	1
Tibet	–	–	–	–	–	–	–	–	–	–	–	–
Shaanxi (Xi'an)	126 126	232 232	19 19	210 210	129 129	129 129	–	–	6 6	27 27	95 95	–
Gansu	108	44	14	26	112	–	91	21	3	70	38	–
Qinghai	–	–	–	–	–	–	–	–	–	–	–	–
Ningxia	–	–	–	–	–	–	–	–	–	–	–	–
Xinjiang	242	50	32	23	237	–	224	13	1	177	59	–

NOTES ON TABLE 3.3:

1) The Chinese terms used in the original document for certain of the column headings are as follows: "targets of preferential care": *youfu duixiang*; "social three-nones": *shehui san-wu*; "disabled adults": *canji qing-zhuang nian* (literally, "young and middle-aged disabled adults"); "children over six years old": *shaonian ertong*; and "infants and children under six years old": *ying-you ertong*.

2) In the case of several provinces and cities (Beijing, Heilongjiang, Jiangsu, Hubei, Guangxi, Sichuan, Yunnan, Shaanxi and Gansu), statistics shown under the heading "Year-End Breakdown of Population in Care" are inconsistent with other subtotals appearing in the relevant rows. Guangxi, for example, is listed as having a total year-end population of twenty, but the "year-end breakdown" figures account for only nineteen inmates.

3) For Liaoning, the original Chinese table includes subcategory rows for Shenyang and Dalian, two of the province's major cities. Similarly, additional rows are included in the table for Changchun (in Jilin Province), Harbin (in Heilongjiang Province), Xiamen (in Fujian Province), Qingdao (in Shandong Province) and Guangzhou and Shenzhen (both in Guangdong Province). All these rows are left empty, however, suggesting that none of these cities has any specialized orphanages. Several of these cities, such as Harbin, are known to have general-purpose "social welfare institutes" (see Chapter 2). The compilers' purpose in including the empty rows for these particular cities is unclear, and Human Rights Watch/Asia has omitted the empty rows in the present version. Apart from this change and the translation of headings into English, the table as shown above is identical to the original.

4) The only specialized orphanage in Shaanxi Province is the Xi'an Municipal Children's Welfare Institute.

Calculating Mortality Rates

Calculating mortality rates from the raw population statistics for a single year, as given in Table 3.3, poses a statistical problem. The most obvious method, namely dividing the number of orphan deaths in a given province during a year by the actual total inmate population over that year, is not possible because the latter figures are unavailable. Since the 1990 yearbook gives only population figures for year-end 1988 and year-end 1989, without indicating any fluctuations or turnover during the course of the year, the use of these figures as simple denominators is statistically unreliable.

Perhaps for this reason, the method customarily used to calculate death rates in China's orphanages (according to Dr. Zhang Shuyun, formerly a medical employee at the Shanghai Children's Welfare Institute) is to divide the number of deaths at each institution by the number of children admitted during the same calendar year.[138] This method generally produces higher annual mortality statistics than those obtained by means of the former calculation, since the extant population from the previous year is not taken into account.[139] While such figures should not be seen as representing the percentage of all children resident in a given province's orphanage system who have died in the course of a calendar year, the use of the deaths-to-admissions ratio provides, nonetheless, at least a rough basis for assessing patterns of mortality among residents.[140] This method of calculating mortality is hereafter referred to as "Method A."

An alternative method of calculation, one which produces a more conservative estimate of orphan mortality but is made feasible by the specific data provided in Table 3.3, is to divide the number of deaths during a given year by the overall sum of the new admissions to a province's welfare system during the year and the previous year-end population figure, less the number of live departures during the

---

[138] As Table 4.1 shows, this is certainly the method that has been employed during the past few decades at the Shanghai Children's Welfare Institute, an orphanage promoted by the Chinese government as being a model for the entire country.

[139] An orphanage with a starting population of 100 children, for example, which took in an additional twenty children during the year and recorded fifteen deaths, would be assigned a mortality rate of 75 percent according to this methodology.

[140] Detailed statistics obtained from the Shanghai Children's Welfare Institute show that the majority of infants and children who die at the orphanage do so within a few weeks or months of their admission (see Chapter 4, "Mortality Statistics, 1960–91.") Assuming this is true for China's child welfare system as a whole, most of the orphans recorded as dying in institutional care in each province during a given calendar year are from among the group admitted during the same year. The ratio of deaths to admissions, as calculated by Method A, thus provides probably the most relevant and meaningful indicator of the actual mortality situation. Survival beyond the first critical months of institutional care, in other words, greatly improves a child's prospects of emerging from the child welfare system alive.

year. This method of calculation, referred to below as "Method B," still does not provide definitive mortality rates, since the length of each child's stay during the year is unknown, but in many cases it gives a truer picture of annual mortality as spread throughout the broader resident population. It should be emphasized, however, that the annual death rates produced by this method tend to considerably overstate the actual survival prospects of a child entering institutional care. Repeated exposure, year after year, to even the lower of the annual probabilities of death listed in the second column below, leaves children in many provincial welfare systems with little hope of surviving to adulthood.

The following table shows parallel sets of 1989 mortality statistics for the child welfare systems of each Chinese province (excluding those provinces with no specialized orphanages), calculated on the basis of data shown in Table 3.3 and in accordance with the two methods described above:

Table 3.4 Death Rates in China's Child Welfare Institutes, 1989[141]

Region	Death Rate By Method A (%)	Death Rate By Method B (%)
National Total	57.9	24.7
Shandong[142]	0.0	0.0
Liaoning	0.0	0.0
Jilin	1.4	0.2
Heilongjiang	14.3	0.9
Guizhou	25.8	6.1
Yunnan	31.4	8.3
Hubei *(Wuhan)*	39.5 *37.6*	36.0 *49.4*
Guangdong	41.8	20.4

[141] Figures in this table are derived from values in Table 3.3, with regions ranked by ratio of deaths to new admissions in ascending order.

[142] The calculated death rates for the provinces of Shandong, Anhui, and Hebei, each of which contained only a single small orphanage in 1989, should not be considered statistically valid.

Region	Death Rate By Method A (%)	Death Rate By Method B (%)
Hunan	44.6	35.3
Xinjiang	46.0	8.8
Shanghai	51.1	22.7
Beijing	53.5	18.0
Zhejiang *(Ningbo)*	53.8 *21.5*	36.7 *14.1*
Sichuan *(Chengdu)* *(Chongqing)*	56.7 *59.8* *54.8*	25.8 *34.0* *32.9*
Gansu	59.1	18.8
Jiangsu *(Nanjing)*	73.8 *83.2*	28.9 *44.7*
Tianjin	79.2	28.2
Shaanxi	90.5	61.9
Guangxi	90.7	66.1
Henan	91.7	72.5
Fujian	100.0	59.2
Anhui	133.3[143]	9.1
Hebei	—[144]	4.5

As can be seen, the death rates in Chinese orphanges as calculated by either method are, in all but a minority of provinces, extraordinarily high by any conceivable

---

[143] The only children's welfare institute operating in Anhui Province in 1989 admitted three children during the year and recorded four deaths.

[144] The figure for Hebei Province, which tops the list with an infinite death rate, is a statistical fluke. The only children's welfare institute operating in the province in 1989 admitted no children during the year and recorded one death. (This institution was closed in 1990.)

standard of judgement. Several more specific conclusions can be drawn from the figures in Table 3.4. First, there appears to be no systematic relationship between the standard of living in a given province and the mortality in the provincial child welfare system. Orphanages in Guizhou Province, in China's impoverished southwest, recorded death rates well below the national average in 1989, while those in several affluent areas, such as Fujian and Jiangsu provinces and Tianjin Municipality, ranked among the worst in the country.

Towards the upper range of the mortality statistics, it is also possible to identify several orphanages as genuine "death camps" for abandoned children, with annual intake and death rates exceeding the fixed capacity of the institution. The single specialized "child welfare institute" in Henan Province is one such institution.[145] This small orphanage, which in 1989 had a stated capacity of thirty beds, began the year with a population of twenty-three infants and children. During the year, seventy-two orphans were admitted to the institution, four left the orphanage alive, and sixty-six died, leaving the year-end population at twenty-five.

The *China Civil Affairs Statistical Yearbook* also divides year-end orphanage population figures into four categories of inmates: "adults with disabilities (*canji qing-zhuangnian*)," "children (*shaonian ertong*)," "infants and toddlers (*ying-you ertong*)," and "mental patients (*jingshen bingren*)."[146] Since the distinction between "children" and "infants and toddlers" is drawn at a child's sixth birthday,[147] it is possible to use these figures to estimate the age distribution of inmates at the Henan Province orphanage. Of the twenty-five surviving inmates at the end of 1989, twelve were classified as "children" and thirteen as "infants and toddlers." This suggests that the institute's population on any given date can be divided into two categories: recently arrived infants, virtually none of whom live for more than a few

---

[145]The exact location of Henan Province's only orphanage is unclear, as Human Rights Watch/Asia has been unable to obtain a comprehensive list of the names and addresses of all custodial welfare institutions in China. However, a selective list of "major" institutions can be found in *Compilation of Statistical and Historical Reference Materials on Civil Affairs, 1949-1992 (Minzheng Tongji Lishi Ziliao Huibian, 1949-1992)*, ed. Ministry of Civil Affairs Planning and Finance Office (Beijing: Zhongguo Shehui Chubanshe), pp.641-649.

[146] The existence of the first and last categories indicates that some orphanages house groups of inmates for which they are not officially designated. According to figures in the 1994 *China Civil Affairs Statistical Yearbook*, the practice of holding disabled and mentally ill adults in "children's welfare institutes" occurs chiefly in Jiangsu Province.

[147] "Explanation of Major Statistical Standards in Civil Affairs Work," reprinted in *Selected Compilation of Documents on Civil Affairs Work (Minzheng Gongzuo Wenjian Xuanbian)*, 1986, p.494.

months, and a small group of older children who have somehow survived infancy and who constitute the orphanage's only long-term inmates.

The high death rate at the Henan Province institute is particularly significant because it appears to perform a stabilizing function, maintaining the orphanage's total population at just below its declared capacity of thirty beds.[148] Indeed, one pattern which emerges from the 1990 statistics is the remarkable stability of the inmate population at most child welfare institutes.

An equally striking example is the child welfare system in Nanjing, Jiangsu Province, which began the year with 335 orphans and admitted an additional 316 during 1989. After 263 children died and another sixty-three left alive during the year, the inmate population had actually decreased to 325 by the end of 1989. Similarly, the specialized orphanages in Fujian Province recorded a total of 109 admissions and 109 deaths during the year, producing a death rate of 100 percent as calculated by Method A. With only six children leaving the institutes alive in 1989, the system's total inmate population decreased from eighty-one to seventy-five during the year.[149]

Population figures for orphanages in several other provinces, such as Guangdong, Guangxi, Sichuan, Shaanxi, and Gansu, show a similar constancy. Although some of these provinces maintain much larger child welfare systems than others, and calculated mortality rates during 1989 also varied substantially, the combined total of deaths and live departures in each province was very close to the number of new admissions, suggesting a deliberate policy of adjusting death rates to maintain a constant population in each institution. Human Rights Watch/Asia has confirmed that such a policy did exist before 1993 in at least one orphanage, the Shanghai Children's Welfare Institute (see Chapter 4: "Unnatural Deaths At The Shanghai Orphanage").

Preferential Care

One peculiar feature of China's orphanages which deserves special mention is the existence of a *de facto* class system within most institutions, based on the background of each child and exerting a powerful influence over orphans' prospects for survival. The majority of institutionalized minors are children of dead or unknown

---

[148] The reporting of capacity figures is apparently rather arbitrary, however. The number of children at the Henan orphanage increased slightly over the four years from 1989 to 1993, and the 1994 *China Civil Affairs Statistical Yearbook* gives the institution's capacity as 32 beds, exactly equal to the resident population at the end of 1993.

[149] Fujian Province contains two specialized orphanages. One of these, probably the larger of the two, is the Fuzhou Municipal Children's Welfare Institute, located in the provincial capital.

parentage and are therefore classified as "social three-nones" (*shehui san-wu*). With the implementation of economic reforms since 1978, however, the Ministry of Civil Affairs has begun encouraging orphanages to supplement their budgets by taking in so-called "self-paying" inmates (*zifei renyuan*), generally retarded or disabled children whose parents cannot care for them during the day. Evidence from the Shanghai Children's Welfare Institute indicates that standards of care for these children are far higher than for the "social three-nones," and that deaths of "self-paying" children in institutional care are very uncommon.[150]

In addition to the "self-paying" patients and "social three-nones," however, some 246 of the 5,659 inmates in urban child welfare institutes at the end of 1989 fell into a third category described as "targets of preferential care" (*youfu duixiang*). The majority of these were living in a single institution, the Xi'an Children's Welfare Institute in Shaanxi Province, with the rest in orphanages in Guangdong, Sichuan, and Heilongjiang provinces. Statistical evidence from the Xi'an orphanage in 1989 reveals that such "preferential care" almost invariably meant the difference between life and death.

In many respects, the pattern of children's deaths in Xi'an resembles that observed in Henan Province. The Xi'an Children's Welfare Institute is the only dedicated orphanage in Shaanxi Province, and in 1989 it is recorded as having taken in 232 children. During the same year, 210 children died and nineteen left the orphanage, resulting in a net increase in the inmate population from 126 to only 129. If there had been a large number of short-stay inmates or frequent transfers out during the year, with new children being admitted as beds became available, this close correspondence between successive year-end population figures might possibly be considered normal. But this was clearly not the case: there were only nineteen live departures, and all of the rest resulted from death. As in many other Chinese orphanages, the high death rate in Xi'an almost seems designed to maintain the institute's population at just below its stated capacity of 150 beds.

In one respect, however, the Xi'an orphanage was unique in China during 1989: all of the 129 children surviving at the end of the year were classified as "targets of preferential care." Since no status classification is available for the group of children who entered the orphanage during 1989, it is not possible to calculate the proportion of these children who constituted "targets of preferential care," or the percentage of such children who died during the year. However, since there were no

---

[150] The best-known of the "self-paying" inmates at the Shanghai orphanage is Hu Fangfang, the severely retarded grandson of the late Communist Party leader Hu Qiaomu (see Chapter 6). According to Dr. Zhang Shuyun, the death rate even among less exalted "self-paying" patients at the Shanghai Children's Welfare Institute was typically no more than 1 to 2 percent annually.

surviving orphans at the end of 1989 in any other categories, it is clear that the "social three-none" orphans, who probably constituted the overwhelming majority of new admissions, suffered a mortality rate of 100 percent during the year. Assuming that the 232 newly-admitted children arrived at roughly the same rate throughout the year, this implies that most of the "social three-nones" survived no more than a few days at the institute, since even those admitted in late December do not appear in the year-end statistics. The high death rate among the "social three-nones" in 1989 thus served not only to stabilize the population of the orphanage, but to maintain its exclusive status as an institution for socially and politically privileged children.

At some time during 1990, however, there appears to have been a dramatic change in official policy towards institutionalized children classified as "targets of preferential care." According to the 1991 edition of the *China Civil Affairs Statistical Yearbook*, the number of such children in urban orphanages dropped to one, in Guangdong Province, while the remaining 245, including all those in Xi'an as well as those in Sichuan and Heilongjiang provinces, disappeared from the published statistics. Since then, the Xi'an Children's Welfare Institute has apparently reverted to the status of an ordinary state orphanage: figures for the end of 1990 show that the institute contained only 115 children, nearly all of whom were classified as "social three-nones." Since the statistics in the ministerial yearbook are not annotated, the exact nature of this policy shift is likely to remain unexplained.

Death Rates: Exclusion of Infants

Another conspicuous feature of the 1990 yearbook's statistics is the unusually low death rate recorded at orphanages in Northeast China, which comprises the provinces of Liaoning, Jilin, and Heilongjiang. During the whole of 1989, a total of only seven children are recorded as having died in all of the northeastern orphanages, including six deaths in Heilongjiang and one in Jilin. However, a closer examination of the statistics shows that these low mortality figures do not indicate a higher standard of care for orphans in these three provinces. Rather, it appears that children's welfare institutes in Northeast China do not admit infants and small children or admit them only in very small numbers. Since child mortality rates are normally much higher among the youngest age groups, the low recorded death rates provide no evidence that the overall quality of care for abandoned children is higher in the Northeast than elsewhere in the country.

The clearest example of this can be seen in Jilin Province, whose lone orphanage is apparently one of the largest in China. Of the 525 orphans living in the institution at the end of 1989, however, all were classified as *shaonian ertong*, children over the age of six. Likewise, the single specialized orphanage in Liaoning Province, which recorded no deaths at all during 1989, housed a total of 153 children at the end of the year, of whom 150 were over age six.[151] In the four orphanages of Heilongjiang Province, the age distribution was somewhat less skewed: these institutions held ninety-nine "infants and toddlers" as well as 491 children over age six.[152] Not surprisingly, Heilongjiang's recorded death rate is considerably higher than that of the other northeastern provinces.

The same practice of excluding the youngest children from care appears to apply at orphanages in Shandong and Yunnan provinces, whose recorded mortality rates were also among the lowest in the country during 1989. This suggests that all Chinese provinces and regions whose orphanages reported deaths-to-admissions ratios of less than one-third[153] were in fact benefiting from the effects of an atypical age distribution, as the civil affairs authorities in these regions admitted orphans to specialized child welfare institutes only after they had survived for several years after birth.

It is not known, however, where these children had spent their earliest years before being transferred to Ministry of Civil Affairs orphanages. Some of them may have come from urban "social welfare institutes" in the same province, while others may have been placed originally in private foster care.[154] The unexplained surfacing of these older children–after years of statistical invisibility during the period when their expected mortality rate was presumably highest–represents part of the much larger problem of "missing" orphans in contemporary China.

It should be reiterated that the figures analyzed above refer only to orphans held in dedicated "children's welfare institutes." Mortality rates for the larger group of urban children in China's general-purpose "social welfare institutes," which would

---

[151] The Liaoning Province orphanage also held one disabled adult at the end of 1989.

[152] The statistics for Heilongjiang Province in the 1990 *China Civil Affairs Statistical Yearbook* appear to be slightly inaccurate. Although these 590 children are the only inmates recorded as living in Heilongjiang's child welfare institutes at the end of 1989, the total population of the orphanage system is given as 595.

[153] With the possible exception of Guizhou–ironically, one of the poorest provinces in China.

[154] The northeastern provinces may also be following a policy observed in some other areas, such as the city of Wuhan, by transferring abandoned children to orphanages with attached schools only when they reach the age of compulsory education. In Wuhan, however, orphans below school age are also cared for in Ministry of Civil Affairs institutions, which is apparently not the case in Northeast China. See Kay Johnson, "Chinese Orphanages: Saving China's Abandoned Girls," *The Australian Journal of Chinese Affairs*, no. 30 (July 1993), p.79.

presumably offer an even lower standard of care, cannot be calculated from the published statistics of the Ministry of Civil Affairs. Although the 1990 edition of the *China Civil Affairs Statistical Yearbook* includes statistics on the number of inmate deaths reported from "social welfare institutes" in each Chinese province and region in 1989, these do not specify how many deaths were of minor children (rather than of elderly, disabled, or mentally ill adults). It is significant, however, that the nationwide ratio of deaths to new admissions for the "social welfare institutes" in 1989 was 53.3 percent.[155] Despite the fact that these units care for a largely elderly population, many of whom might reasonably be expected to end their lives in institutional care, this figure is actually lower than the corresponding figure of 57.9 percent reported from specialized orphanages.

As high as these official figures are, they may in fact underestimate the true death rate in China's orphanages. Evidence from the Shanghai Children's Welfare Institute suggests that the number of deaths in this institution was consistently underreported during the 1980s, and that the actual ratio of deaths to admissions may have been well over 90 percent throughout this period (see Chapter 4). If similar practices are widespread elsewhere in China, conditions for the country's orphans may be almost unimaginably grim.

Orphanage Staffing and Budget Levels

The official statistics cited above illustrate the staggering death rates in China's orphanages, but offer no indication of *why* the number of deaths is so high. The handful of Western journalists who have succeeded in gaining access to particular institutions have generally blamed the appalling conditions there on a lack of adequate funding and staff levels—an argument likely to be echoed by the Chinese government as this issue begins to attract greater attention internationally. However, detailed budget and employment statistics published in the *China Civil Affairs Statistical Yearbook* demonstrate that China's child welfare system appears to be adequately financed and staffed to support the number of children in its care. The same figures, moreover, demonstrate a consistent disregard for orphans' well being on the part of the civil affairs authorities. Expenditures on children's food, clothing, and other basic needs are extremely low, and in the three years between 1989 and 1992 were actually reduced in many Chinese provinces, despite rising currency inflation.[156] The wages and benefits of orphanage staff, however, have increased substantially over the same

---

[155] Calculated from data in the *China Civil Affairs Statistical Yearbook* (1990 edition), p.94.

[156] The annual rate of inflation in China averaged 9.6 percent over the period 1985–93. (*The Europa World Yearbook 1995*, Europa Publications Ltd., London, 1995.)

period in inflation-adjusted terms, reflecting the increasing priority given to employees' interests over those of the children in their care.

The unusually high staffing expenses in most Chinese orphanages are in part a reflection of very low child-to-staff ratios–in principle, an ideal condition for the healthy development of children in an institutional setting. The following table, calculated from figures in the 1990 ministerial yearbook, shows inmate-to-staff ratios in children's welfare institutes in each Chinese province and region in 1989.

Table 3.5 Staffing Ratios in China's Child Welfare Institutes, Year-End 1989[157]

Region	Number of Staff	Number of Inmates	Inmates Per Staff Member
National Total	2,722	5,659	2.08
Beijing	214	378	1.77
Tianjin	123	214	1.74
Hebei	9	21	2.33
Liaoning	104	154	1.48
Jilin	137	527	3.85
Heilongjiang	182	595	3.27
Shanghai	348	481	1.38
Jiangsu	510	857	1.68
Zhejiang	193	489	2.53
Anhui	34	40	1.18
Fujian	58	75	1.29
Shandong	4	19	4.75
Henan	7	25	3.57

---

[157] Figures in columns 1 and 2 are from the *China Civil Affairs Statistical Yearbook*, 1990 edition, pp.98-99; ratios in column 3 were calculated by Human Rights Watch/Asia. Column 2 includes inmates other than children.

Region	Number of Staff	Number of Inmates	Inmates Per Staff Member
Hubei	160	327	2.04
Hunan	44	99	2.25
Guangdong	53	90	1.70
Guangxi	14	20	1.43
Sichuan	195	403	2.07
Guizhou	56	125	2.23
Yunnan	76	242	3.18
Shaanxi	57	129	2.26
Gansu	57	112	1.96
Xinjiang	87	237	2.72

Judging from the recorded death rates in 1989, however, these apparently excellent staffing levels have provided no significant benefits to China's institutionalized children.[158] Indeed, the lowest child-to-staff ratios are found in some of the worst provincial orphanage systems, including those of Fujian, Guangxi, and Jiangsu. By contrast, the child welfare institutes in Jilin and Shandong provinces, whose mortality rates in 1989 were among the lowest in China, reported two of the highest child-to-staff ratios in the country.[159] This paradox may be partly explained by anecdotal evidence from the Shanghai Children's Welfare Institute, where large

---

[158] The inmate-to-staff ratio in China's child welfare institutes has risen slightly since the end of 1989, due to an increase in the number of children in these institutions. According to figures in the 1994 *China Civil Affairs Statistical Yearbook*, the average number of inmates per employee had increased to 2.38 by the end of 1993.

[159] As noted above, however, the Jilin and Shandong orphanages do not hold children under six years of age.

numbers of people supposedly employed by the orphanage apparently do not exist or do not report to work.[160]

In any case, a more detailed analysis of the provincial civil affairs budgets suggests that the main function of children's welfare institutes in China is to provide employment and relatively attractive working conditions for orphanage staff. During the three years between 1989 and 1992, these conditions improved substantially. Not only did the number of orphanage employees rise slightly, from 2,722 to 3,054, but average staff salaries also kept well ahead of China's inflation rate during the same period, as the following table shows.

Table 3.6 Expenditure on Personnel in China's Child Welfare Institutes, 1989-92[161]

Region	1989		1992		Percentage Increase in Average Employee Earnings (1989-92)
	Personnel Expenditure (yuan/year)	Average Employee Earnings (yuan/month)	Personnel Expenditure (yuan/year)	Average Employee Earnings (yuan/month)	
National Total	6,253,000	167.7	12,123,000	283.2	68.9

---

[160] According to the confidential minutes of a meeting held on April 17, 1992, between Shanghai city officials and members of the local People's Congress, the Shanghai Children's Welfare Institute then had a total of 327 staff. This is broadly consistent with the figure of 336 given in the *Shanghai Statistical Yearbook* and with estimates given by orphanage director Han Weicheng (author's interview, March 1995). However, it is visually obvious that the orphanage, which consists mainly of several low-rise buildings scattered around a small walled compound, cannot possibly employ such a large number of people. According to sources within the orphanage, by mid-1993, many local child-care workers had been replaced by rural women from Anhui Province, who performed the same duties for much lower wages; the original staff members, however, continued to draw their original salaries without reporting for work.

[161] *China Civil Affairs Statistical Yearbook*, pp.504-507 (1990 edition) and pp.320-321 (1993 edition). The column headed "Personnel Expenditure (yuan/year)" includes employees' base wages, allowances (*buzhu gongzi*), "welfare fees" (*fulifei*), and benefits for retired employees, as well as a "price subsidy for major non-staple foods" *(zhongyao fushipin jiage butie)* paid during 1992. Figures in the column headed "Average Employee Earnings (yuan/month)" denote wage and benefit expenditures (excluding retirement benefits) divided by number of staff at year-end.

Region	1989		1992		Percentage Increase in Average Employee Earnings (1989-92)
	Personnel Expenditure (yuan/year)	Average Employee Earnings (yuan/month)	Personnel Expenditure (yuan/year)	Average Employee Earnings (yuan/month)	
Beijing	521,000	190.0	897,000	307.3	61.7
Tianjin	246,000	150.4	497,000	252.8	68.1
Hebei[162]	11,000	101.9	–	–	–
Liaoning[163]	–	–	527,000	343.5	–
Jilin	368,000	198.3	627,000	313.1	57.9
Heilong-jiang	395,000	161.6	737,000	226.1	40.0
Shanghai	978,000	196.1	1,831,000	355.5	81.3
Jiangsu	1,210,000	177.8	2,357,000	290.9	63.6
Zhejiang	487,000	181.3	884,000	284.6	57.0
Anhui	50,000	112.7	120,000	201.9	79.1
Fujian	133,000	179.6	256,000	274.4	52.8
Shandong	5,000	104.2	7,000	145.8	40.0
Henan	15,000	178.6	21,000	250.0	40.0
Hubei	332,000	149.5	589,000	231.5	54.8
Hunan	58,000	104.2	176,000	197.0	89.1
Guangdong	134,000	187.1	184,000	243.8	30.3
Guangxi	26,000	119.0	86,000	433.3	264.1

[162] The only children's welfare institute in Hebei Province was closed in 1990.

[163] The 1990 edition of the *China Civil Affairs Statistical Yearbook* lists the 1989 budget of Liaoning Province's orphanages as zero, perhaps indicating a failure of the provincial Civil Affairs Bureau to report budget data to central authorities on time.

Region	1989		1992		Percentage Increase in Average Employee Earnings (1989-92)
	Personnel Expenditure (yuan/year)	Average Employee Earnings (yuan/month)	Personnel Expenditure (yuan/year)	Average Employee Earnings (yuan/month)	
Sichuan	442,000	155.6	782,000	243.5	56.5
Guizhou	139,000	150.3	260,000	257.9	71.6
Yunnan	195,000	173.2	331,000	288.2	66.4
Shaanxi	97,000	137.4	191,000	237.4	72.8
Gansu	165,000	214.9	306,000	306.3	42.5
Xinjiang	244,000	205.0	457,000	318.3	55.3

Table 3.6 demonstrates again that there is little correlation between the financing of a given province's orphanage system and the quality of care provided. Staff salaries during 1989 were somewhat higher than the national average in Jiangsu and Fujian provinces, where death rates were extremely high, while wages and benefits at the Shandong Province orphanage, which recorded no deaths during the year, were among the lowest in China.

It should also be noted that average employee earnings in the state-financed orphanage system in 1992, although still fairly modest, were comparable to those in the foreign-financed "SOS Children's Villages" and in some provinces considerably higher. In early 1991, the highest combined wage and bonus payments authorized for the staff of the SOS Children's Villages were of 290 yuan per month, for the directors of each institution. Ordinary "mother's helpers" in the villages, presumably among the most numerous employees, received a combined wage and bonus of only 210 yuan per month.[164]

One particularly striking feature of Table 3.6 is the dramatic increase in employee earnings at the two specialized orphanages in the Guangxi Zhuang

---

[164] "Directive of the Office of the Ministry of Civil Affairs Regarding the Adjustment of Standards for Employees' Salaries and Orphans' Living Expenses at the SOS Children's Villages in Tianjin and Yantai" (promulgated February 6, 1991), in *Selected Compilation of Documents on Civil Affairs Work (Minzheng Gongzuo Wenjian Xuanbian)*, ed. Ministry of Civil Affairs Policy and Regulations Office (Beijing: Zhongguo Shehui Chubanshe, 1991), pp.238-239.

Autonomous Region. At the end of 1992, the Guangxi orphanages together cared for twenty-seven inmates, of whom twenty-one were children over age six, and employed fifteen staff.[165] Over the past three years, average monthly earnings for the Guangxi employees had nearly quadrupled, making them by far the best-paid orphanage staff in China.

The huge increase in staff compensation between 1989 and 1992 may reflect the substantial funds donated by Hong Kong charities to the Guangxi Civil Affairs Bureau during this period to improve conditions in the province's orphanages. Much of this money is apparently missing, and it is clear that the funds provided little benefit to Guangxi's institutionalized children. As Table 3.4 indicates, the province's specialized orphanages reported deaths-to-admissions ratios of over 90 percent in 1989. Mortality figures for later years are not available, but it appears that these two institutions had substantially changed their function by 1992: children under age six, who made up the large majority of inmates in 1989, had all but vanished three years later. These infants and young children may have been transferred to Guangxi's much larger network of "social welfare institutes" in an effort to make the specialized orphanages more presentable to foreigners–a phenomenon similar to that observed in Shanghai during the mid-1990s (see Chapter 7). Reports in late 1993 from one such general-purpose institution, in Guangxi's provincial capital of Nanning, suggest that infant mortality rates there were then still very high. (See Chapter 2, "Condemned to Die–For Being a Girl.".)

The relatively generous wages and benefits offered to employees of China's child welfare institutes are not matched by an equal concern for the financial needs of the orphans themselves. Most provincial child welfare systems spend only a small fraction of their total budgets on "inmates' living expenses" (*zhuyuan renyuan shenghuofei*), the budget category which covers food, clothing, and other incidental expenses for children's individual needs. As the following table shows, such expenditures, already at a very low level in 1989, increased far more slowly over the following three years than did expenditures for staff compensation:

---

[165] The two Guangxi orphanages also held one child under age six, four disabled adults, and one adult mental patient.

Table 3.7 Children's Living Expenses in China's Child Welfare Institutes, 1989-92[166]

Region	1989		1992		Percentage Increase in Expenditure Per Child, 1989-1992
	Children's Living Expenses (yuan/year)	Expenditure Per Child (yuan/month)	Children's Living Expenses (yuan/year)	Expenditure Per Child (yuan/month)	
National Total	3,192,000	47.0	5,394,000	64.9	38.1
Beijing	253,000	55.8	528,000	78.9	41.4
Tianjin	83,000	32.3	106,000	34.4	6.5
Hebei	13,000	51.6	–	–	–
Liaoning	–	–	167,000	80.0	–
Jilin	429,000	67.8	516,000	81.9	20.8
Heilong--jiang	521,000	73.0	741,000	85.2	16.7
Shanghai	248,000	43.0	543,000	69.5	61.6
Jiangsu	264,000	25.7	519,000	47.3	84.0
Zhejiang	216,000	36.8	488,000	65.7	78.5
Anhui	24,000	50.0	70,000	42.9	-14.2
Fujian	54,000	60.0	68,000	58.4	-2.6
Shandong	9,000	39.5	12,000	33.3	-15.7
Henan	11,000	36.7	23,000	59.9	63.2
Hubei	161,000	41.0	337,000	62.3	52.0
Hunan	37,000	31.1	130,000	53.6	72.3
Guangdong	61,000	56.5	51,000	47.2	-16.5

---

[166] Figures from *China Civil Affairs Statistical Yearbook*, pp.504-507 (1990 edition) and pp.320-321 (1993 edition). The column headed "Expenditure Per Child (yuan/month)" denotes monthly children's living expenditure divided by number of inmates at year-end.

Region	1989		1992		Percentage Increase in Expenditure Per Child, 1989-1992
	Children's Living Expenses (yuan/year)	Expenditure Per Child (yuan/month)	Children's Living Expenses (yuan/year)	Expenditure Per Child (yuan/month)	
Guangxi	9,000	37.5	12,000	37.0	-1.3
Sichuan	253,000	52.3	380,000	70.3	34.4
Guizhou	67,000	44.7	65,000	38.4	-14.1
Yunnan	150,000	51.7	187,000	59.0	14.1
Shaanxi	59,000	38.1	105,000	56.5	48.3
Gansu	68,000	50.6	115,000	47.2	-6.7
Xinjiang	202,000	71.0	231,000	84.1	18.5

The average increase in spending per child over this three-year period, of just over 38 percent, represents virtually no change in inflation-adjusted terms.[167] Several provinces, in fact, actually reduced spending per child even in nominal terms. Guangxi, for example, spent a total of 9,000 yuan to feed and clothe the twenty inmates in its orphanage system at the end of 1989, but budgeted only 12,000 yuan in 1992 to support a larger year-end population of twenty-seven inmates–most of whom were older children rather than infants. In per capita terms, this represented a reduction of just over one percent, even before allowing for inflation. (Expenditures on wages and salaries, by contrast, rose from 26,000 to 86,000 yuan over the same period, while the number of orphanage employees increased from fourteen to fifteen.)

Guangxi was not the only province to reduce expenditures on orphans' welfare during this period, despite China's rapid economic development. Indeed, the deepest cuts were made in the orphanage system of Guangdong Province, the wealthiest region of China and one of the fastest-growing. Civil affairs authorities in Guangdong cut spending on orphans' living expenses by nearly one-sixth between 1989 and 1992, reducing the province's expenditures per child to substantially less

---

[167] See note 156.

than the national average. Cuts of almost equal magnitude occurred in several other provinces, including Anhui, Shandong, and Guizhou.[168]

The shift in orphanage budget priorities during this period clearly demonstrates the unwillingness of China's provincial governments to finance improved standards of care in the country's child welfare institutes, depite the rapid growth of the Chinese economy during the early 1990s and the staggeringly high death rates recorded during 1989. It should be emphasized, however, that there is no clear correlation between spending levels and orphan death rates in the various Chinese provinces. The 1989 statistics show, for example, that relatively ample living expenses could be found not only in some of the better-managed provincial child welfare systems, such as those of Jilin and Heilongjiang, but also in Fujian, which recorded a deaths-to-admissions ratio of 100 percent during the year.[169]

Even in less generously funded regions, although levels of expenditure on children's basic needs may not have been sufficient to provide comfortable living conditions even in 1989, they clearly cannot explain the recorded orphanage death rates in and of themselves. Rather, it appears to be the other way around: only the very low survival rate for institutionalized minors allows the child welfare system to be maintained at its present miniscule size, with relatively modest budgets sufficing to feed and clothe the small number of orphans in institutional care at any given time. If the thousands of deaths occuring each year in China' orphanages are the result of inhumane conditions, these cannot be blamed on a lack of necessary funds–although the goal of saving public money may well be one reason such high death rates are tolerated.

Instead, the evidence available to Human Rights Watch/Asia strongly suggests that mortality rates in China's orphanages are maintained at their present level by a deliberate policy of starvation and medical neglect. Detailed records from the Shanghai Children's Welfare Institute, generally considered the best state-run orphanage in China, leave little doubt that most deaths at this institution in recent years have resulted from the intentional acts of child-care and medical staff (see Chapter 4).

---

[168] In some areas, these "cuts" reflected a failure of provincial spending to keep pace with an increase in the number of institutionalized orphans, rather than an actual budget reduction. Anhui Province, for example, was one of the few regions of China to increase its orphanage capacity between 1989 and 1993, by opening a second specialized orphanage in 1992.

[169] State-run orphanages in these provinces spent only slightly less per child in 1989 than the private SOS Children's Villages. Before an upward adjustment in early 1991, authorized living expenses per child were set at 75 yuan per month at the Tianjin village and 80 yuan per month in the Yantai village ("Directive of the Office of the Ministry of Civil Affairs..." p.239).

There is a basic economic policy-making dilemma that has been faced by the government in this area since the advent of the national population control policy. On the one hand, it costs only a negligible proportion of the country's economic resources to maintain the roughly 20,000 orphans now in state care in healthy condition until their legal majority. On the other hand, to assume such responsibility for the entire population of abandoned and orphaned children–a number that would increase exponentially if each year's cohort of infants survived–would indeed place a strain on the national budget.The humanitarian need is, in fact, so much greater than the government's policies have been designed to meet that, were the survival of children to become a policy priority, it would require much more than increasing subsistence allowances at existing welfare institutions. So far, however, the government appears to have avoided even addressing this reality, far less making the critically needed budgetary allocations.

Missing Orphans In the 1990s

An editorial in the *People's Daily* of May 10, 1995, gave China's orphan population as approximately 100,000.[170] Four years earlier, the Ministry of Civil Affairs had provided the considerably higher figure of 140,000 orphans nationwide.[171] Given the officially acknowledged surge in child abandonment in recent years, either figure seems implausibly low for a total population of 1.2 billion. Moreover, even if the lowest official figure of 100,000 orphans is accepted as valid, barely one-sixth of these children can be traced in the records of the Ministry of Civil Affairs. As noted earlier, only just over 17,000 Chinese orphans are accounted for in the ministry's published figures for 1994, as inmates of urban orphanages and "social welfare institutes."

Official Chinese sources have sometimes sought to imply that the more than 80,000 orphans missing from these statistics are cared for in rural areas by welfare homes for the elderly run by township and village governments, the so-called "respecting-the-aged homes." For example, the Chinese government has told the United Nations that "[in] the countryside, orphans and infants tend to be looked after in old folks' homes.[172] Similarly, a press release issued in June 1995 by the Chinese Embassy in London on the question of orphans' welfare claimed that "at present, there

---

[170] "Devote More Love," p.3.

[171] Cited in Sheryl WuDunn, "China's Castaway Babies: Cruel Practice Lives On," *New York Times*, February 26, 1991.

[172] *Addendum* to the *Report* submitted by the People's Republic of China to the United Nations Committee on the Rights of the Child (March 27, 1995), paragraph 93.

are 40,000 welfare institutions, including orphanages, in China's rural area, and one hundred orphanages in urban area [sic]."[173]

Although the latter claim overstates the number of specialized urban orphanages in China, the figure of 40,000 rural welfare homes corresponds roughly to the 41,096 "socially-run respecting-the-aged homes" *(shehuiban jinglaoyuan)* which existed throughout urban and rural China at the end of 1993.[174] These small institutions, which are administered by urban "street committees" or by rural local governments, are largely dedicated to the care of the destitute or infirm elderly, but some also shelter abandoned children, disabled adults, and other persons unable to care for themselves. Their role is thus analogous to that of the larger "social welfare institutes" in China's cities.

However, the Chinese government's implicit claim that these institutions hold large numbers of orphans is demonstrably false. Although the total capacity of the rural "respecting-the-aged homes" is far larger than that of China's urban welfare institutions, the overwhelming majority of the homes' inmates are, in fact, elderly, as figures from the 1994 *China Civil Affairs Statistical Yearbook* show:

Table 3.8 "Respecting-the-Aged Homes" in China, Year-End 1993[175]

Region	Number of Institutions	Total Inmate Population	Of Which:	
			Old Persons	**Other**
National Total	41,096	586,418	549,804	36,614
Beijing	301	4,707	4,508	199
Tianjin	259	3,005	2,986	19
Hebei	3,157	33,496	31,951	1,545
Shanxi	1,191	6,624	6,237	387
Inner Mongolia	987	12,019	10,835	1,184

---

[173] "Briefing by the Chinese Embassy on China's Orphanage [*sic*]" (June 1995), p.1. (See Appendix Q.)

[174] *China Civil Affairs Statistical Yearbook* (1994 edition), p.116.

[175] Figures in columns 1, 2, and 3 from the *China Civil Affairs Statistical Yearbook* (1994 edition), p.116; figures in column 4 calculated by Human Rights Watch/Asia.

Region	Number of Institutions	Total Inmate Population	Of Which:	
			Old Persons	Other
Liaoning	1,222	29,104	24,828	4,276
Jilin	900	26,722	24,022	2,700
Heilongjiang	1,102	25,549	21,832	3,717
Shanghai	331	6,365	5,934	431
Jiangsu	3,206	52,914	50,253	2,661
Zhejiang	1,282	15,017	14,865	152
Anhui	2,684	40,184	39,195	989
Fujian	642	6,757	6,290	467
Jiangxi	2,015	35,298	32,198	3,100
Shandong	4,589	82,237	81,316	921
Henan	2,350	34,744	34,084	660
Hubei	2,834	39,760	36,755	3,005
Hunan	1,927	20,394	19,055	1,339
Guangdong	1,598	25,542	24,789	753
Guangxi	282	2,687	2,596	91
Hainan	176	1,810	1,626	184
Sichuan	3,901	49,650	43,658	5,992
Guizhou	866	6,653	6,417	236
Yunnan	701	7,577	7,267	310
Tibet	107	743	654	89
Shaanxi	1,174	8,313	7,721	592
Gansu	559	2,837	2,752	85
Qinghai	110	746	695	51
Ningxia	246	1,446	1,347	99

Region	Number of Institutions	Total Inmate Population	Of Which:	
			Old Persons	Other
Xinjiang	397	3,518	3,138	380

Table 3.8 shows clearly that the "respecting-the-aged homes" hold, at most, only a fraction of China's "missing" orphans. Even assuming that all the inmates of these institutions are either elderly people or orphans (and not, for example, disabled or mentally ill adults), the entire non-elderly population of the "respecting-the-aged homes" nationwide is just over 36,000–less than half the gap between the acknowledged number of orphans in China and the number living in larger urban institutions.

Moreover, the population of the "respecting-the-aged homes" varies substantially from region to region, with a handful of provinces (Sichuan, Liaoning, Heilongjiang, Jiangxi, and Hubei) accounting for well over half of the non-elderly inmates in the entire system. In other provinces, such as Shanxi, Zhejiang, Guangxi, and Gansu, the elderly make up all but a minuscule fraction of the inmates in the homes, and the large majority of institutions have no non-elderly inmates at all. In these areas, contrary to the Chinese government's claims, it is clearly not official policy to care for orphans in the rural old-age homes–and in China as a whole, even given the most generous possible assumptions, these homes cannot account for the majority of the country's abandoned children.

Nor can the gap be adequately explained by including orphans who have been placed with adoptive families. The number of Chinese children adopted by foreigners, although rapidly increasing, is still very small in absolute terms and was insignificant before the early 1990s. The domestic adoption of abandoned children is also relatively uncommon (see below) and it is clearly impossible that children placed through adoption represent more than a small fraction of the country's "missing" orphans.

If the majority of China's orphans are not in any form of institutional care, then where are they? Some of them may have been placed in foster care with private families, a practice documented in Shanghai (see Chapter 7) and reportedly used in other parts of China as well. It appears, however, that the civil affairs authorities try to avoid such arrangements whenever possible, and resort to private foster care only when no institutional space is available. One official comment on the country's child welfare system states, for example, "Orphans and infants that cannot be institutionalized are educated and supported individually, as the law requires."[176] The Hong Kong representative of a major international children's charity confirms that the practice of Chinese authorities is to discourage private fostering, commenting that "they look upon it as the worst option" for abandoned children.[177]

Many developed countries once followed a similar policy of favoring institutional "warehousing" for orphans over decentralized foster care, which is generally more expensive. If conditions in China's orphanages today were comparable to those which prevailed in the West several decades ago, the government's refusal to abandon this discredited practice might be condemned as needlessly inhumane. However, given that many Chinese orphanages are not merely warehouses, but death camps, the policy of the Ministry of Civil Affairs appears in a far more sinister light. The ministry, which presumably continues to compile statistics on orphanage mortality rates even though it no longer chooses to publish them, is well aware of the fact that most abandoned children die shortly after being placed in institutional care. Its apparent refusal to consider alternatives which might offer a better chance of survival to these children suggests that the extraordinarily high death rates in China's orphanages are seen as desirable from the perspective of cost control–and perhaps for other reasons as well.

The civil affairs annals of Lianjiang County, in the southern province of Guangdong, provide circumstantial evidence for this view. One section of the annals describes the history of the Lianjiang County Children's Welfare Institute as follows:

> Since the establishment of New China, the civil affairs departments of Lianjiang County have always paid attention to the work of fostering orphans, abandoned infants, and disabled children. Before the Institute was established, these foster children were given to individual residents to care for, [and the foster parents received] forty yuan per month for each [child]. In 1979, the Welfare Institute was constructed with the permission of the provincial Civil Affairs Bureau, and it began operations in July 1980.[178]

---

[176] *Addendum* to the *Report* submitted by the People's Republic of China to the United Nations Committee on the Rights of the Child (March 27, 1995), paragraph 93.

[177] Author's interview, September 1995.

[178] *Lianjiang County Civil Affairs Annals (Lianjiangxian Minzhengzhi)*, ed. Lianjiang County Civil Affairs Bureau, Guangdong Keji Chubanshe, March 1991, p.139.

Between July 1980 and December 1987, according to the county annals, the new orphanage admitted a total of 645 children. Their subsequent fate is described as follows:

> ... many of those admitted were seriously ill, and a rather large number died *(siwang de jiao duo)*. One hundred twenty-nine were adopted through lawful procedures, and twenty-eight were sought out and retrieved by their birth parents. At the end of 1987, there were just fourteen persons in the institute.[179]

These figures imply that the remaining 474 children died in the care of the orphanage, representing over 73 percent of the total number admitted and more than *97 percent* of those not removed from the orphanage by their natural or adoptive parents. Although it is quite possible that some of these orphans were, in fact, seriously ill upon arrival, this can hardly explain fatalities on such a collossal scale .[180]

Since the orphans privately fostered in the county before 1980 provided what was then a relatively generous income to their foster parents, it is very unlikely that the death rate among such children was even a fraction of that recorded in later years. It is therefore difficult to avoid suspecting that the speedy death of nearly all infants abandoned in Lianjiang County after 1980 was, in fact, the purpose for which the county orphanage was established.

Chinese Adoption Policy

The apparent determination of the Ministry of Civil Affairs to place as many abandoned children as possible in institutional care, despite its predictably lethal results, is only one element of China's child welfare policy which raises questions about the authorities' underlying motives. Another is the state's policy of discouraging the legal adoption of such children by Chinese families, even as it aggressively promotes cross-border adoptions by childless couples from the United States and elsewhere. These apparently contradictory aims are embodied in China's 1991 Adoption Law, which was enacted to formalize what had previously been a somewhat haphazard process. Human Rights Watch/Asia believes that certain provisions of the

---

[179] *Ibid.*, p.140.

[180] It is apparently a standard policy for officials of the Ministry of Civil Affairs to claim (particularly when asked by foreigners) that the high death rate in Chinese orphanages is the result of diseases contracted by abandoned infants before their arrival (see, e.g., Johnson, p.75). However, an analysis of medical records from the Shanghai Children's Welfare Institute shows that this is rarely the case (see Chapter 4).

Adoption Law, and of later implementing regulations issued by the Ministry of Civil Affairs, suggest an unstated link between the management of Chinese orphanages and efforts to control the country's population.

Section 4 of the 1991 Adoption Law[181] identifies three categories of minors who may be lawfully adopted: "orphans who have lost their parents [*i.e.*, through death]"; "abandoned infants and children whose parents cannot be found after investigation"; and children whose natural parents cannot support them. Although children in all three categories are eligible for adoption, some are clearly more eligible than others.

Section 6 of the Adoption Law stipulates that adults seeking to adopt children must be over thirty-five years of age and may not have children of their own.[182] Section 8 of the law further specifies that adoptive parents may adopt no more than one child. The last two requirements suggest that the law's intent is to treat the adoption of a child as legally equivalent, for family-planning purposes, to a natural birth, and hence subject to the constraints of China's population policies.

China's practice of limiting adoption to childless adults predates the compulsory family-planning policies in place since the late 1970s, and was originally imposed to prevent foster children from being adopted for ulterior motives, as servants or prospective daughters-in-law.[183] However, the text of the 1991 Adoption Law strongly suggests that this provision now has a basis in China's population policy. Despite the fact that concerns about the possible exploitation of foster children would seem to apply equally to all categories of adoptions, Section 8 of the Adoption Law goes on to relax some of these supposedly protective restrictions, stating: "Those who adopt orphans or disabled children need not be childless or have reached the age of thirty-five, nor need they observe the limit of adopting one [child]."

The new law thus creates a legal distinction between "orphans" (*gu 'er*) in the strict sense, children whose natural parents are both dead, and "abandoned infants and children" (*qiying he ertong*), whose natural parents are unknown but presumably still living. Children in the latter category, unless handicapped, have very limited prospects for domestic adoption. Moreover, the Ministry of Civil Affairs is apparently very concerned to ensure that this distinction is properly observed. A set of implementing regulations for the Adoption Law, promulgated by the ministry on August 11, 1992, emphasizes that the term *gu 'er* refers only to a child whose parents' deaths can be legally verified, either by the existence of death certificates or by judicial

---

[181] An excerpted translation of the Adoption Law appears in Appendix M.

[182] In addition, an unmarried man who seeks to adopt an orphan girl must be at least 40 years older than the child.

[183] Johnson, p.79.

declarations of death. Local adoption registrars are enjoined to "strictly investigate evidence of the deaths of orphans' parents" before allowing adoption procedures to go forward.[184]

Neither the Adoption Law nor these implementing regulations attempt to justify this apparently arbitrary distinction, which seems to bear no relationship to the well-being of foster children. The most plausible explanation for the policy, however, is that genuine orphans, like most Chinese children, will usually have been born in conformity with official family-planning regulations. Infants abandoned by their natural parents, on the other hand, are likely to be so-called "black registration" (*hei hukou*) births, the result of pregnancies not authorized by the state.[185] In effect, therefore, the provisions of the Adoption Law deny the very legitimacy of these children's existence, allowing them to be adopted only if their foster parents forego the right to bear a child of their own, thereby canceling the "offense" of the abandoned child's natural mother.

In addition, China's family-planning authorities often appear to treat adoptions as equivalent to natural births, however illogically. In Shanghai, for example, official policy states that "couples who have long suffered from infertility, and who become pregnant after adopting one child according to the relevant regulations, may give birth to the one [natural] child."[186] Although this provision is clearly meant to exempt such unexpected pregnancies from the compulsory abortion which would otherwise prevent the birth of a second child, it also reinforces the

---

[184] "Notice of the People's Republic of China Ministry of Civil Affairs On Strictly Distinguishing, In the Handling of Adoption Registrations, Between Orphans and Abandoned Infants Whose Birth Parents Cannot Be Found After Investigation," in *Selected Compilation of Documents on Civil Affairs Work (Minzheng Gongzuo Wenjian Xuanbian)*, 1992 edition ed. Ministry of Civil Affairs Policy and Regulations Office (Beijing: Zhongguo Shehui Chubanshe, October 1993), p.354. Excerpts from this document appear in Appendix M.

[185] Since conceiving a child in China requires a permit from local family-planning authorities, most parents would presumably find it very difficult to secretly abandon an infant resulting from an authorized pregnancy, even if female or disabled. On the origins of abandoned infants in Wuhan, see Johnson, pp.73-74.

[186] Article 11, "Shanghai Municipal Family Planning Regulations," in *Compendium of Laws and Regulations of the People's Republic of China (Zhonghua Renmin Gongheguo Falü Fagui Quanshu)*, ed. Legal Work Subcommittee, Standing Committee of the National People's Congress (Beijing: Zhongguo Minzhu Falü Chubanshe, April 1994), p.942.

principle, laid down in the Adoption Law, that only childless couples may adopt children.[187]

It is significant that although the standards of eligibility for prospective foster parents under the Adoption Law apply equally to all nationalities, their practical effect is to restrict domestic adoptions far more severely than adoptions by foreigners. Western couples seeking to adopt Chinese children are generally infertile, and are thus unaffected by the requirement that adoptive parents be childless. The minimum age requirement, likewise, is often no obstacle to couples who have spent years trying to conceive a child naturally. In addition, China's unusually liberal policy of permitting adoption by single adults as well as married couples has made the country a popular destination for would-be foster parents who would find it difficult to adopt children elsewhere.[188] For these reasons, the terms of the new law have not prevented China from rapidly becoming one of the world's main source countries for cross-border adoptions.[189]

As noted in Chapter 2, the foreign adoption program has become an increasingly important source of revenue for the Ministry of Civil Affairs since the early 1990s, as individual welfare institutions are authorized to collect fees of several thousand U.S. dollars for every child adopted out of their custody.[190] At the same time, the provisions of the Adoption Law banning adoption by young adults and by couples with children make it very difficult for most institutionalized children to be placed in private homes in China itself. This policy appears particularly irrational in light of China's rigorous population policy. Unlike most countries, the People's Republic

---

[187] For one citizen's protest against similar family-planning regulations in Shaanxi Province during the early 1980s, see Appendix N. A rare official criticism of the humanitarian consequences of China's adoption policies, published in April 1995 in the newspaper *Shanghai Legal News*, appears in Appendix Q.

[188] The United States Consulate in Guangzhou now employs a full-time staff member to process adoption applications, a large number of which are reportedly from homosexual couples who face discrimination under the adoption laws of many U.S. states.

[189] United States citizens make up the large majority of overseas foster parents adopting children from the People's Republic of China. Figures from U.S. immigration authorities indicate that the number of adopted Chinese children arriving in the United States rose from 28 in 1990 to 748 in 1994. (Cited in Benjamin Marrison, "Baby, Baby," *Cleveland Plain Dealer*, August 6, 1995.)

[190] Domestic adoptions, by contrast, cost no more than a few hundred Chinese yuan, thus producing virtually no financial benefit for the welfare institutions involved (Johnson, p.83).

possesses a large pool of potential adoptive parents who are not infertile for medical reasons. The existence of tens of millions of married couples who wish to have larger families than the authorities now permit should make it possible to place most abandoned infants out with adoptive parents almost as soon as they are discovered. However, the Adoption Law rules out this straightforward solution for most such infants–particularly healthy or mildly disabled baby girls, who make up the majority of child abandonment cases nationwide.

IV. UNNATURAL DEATHS AT THE SHANGHAI ORPHANAGE

The Shanghai Children's Welfare Institute

Despite the outwardly normal appearance of daily life at the Shanghai Children's Welfare Institute, the city's oldest and largest specialized state-run orphanage and one that has been widely promoted by the central government in recent years as a model for orphanages throughout the country, visitors there often observe a disturbing anomaly. Senior staff have consistently maintained that all children admitted to the orphanage, except for the small proportion adopted by Chinese or foreign foster parents, remain there until the age of fifteen or sixteen. Apparent to even the most casual observer, however, is that, despite the presence of up to one hundred infants in the only building dedicated to their care, there is in fact a marked absence of older children on the orphanage grounds. During the early 1990s, according to former staff members, only a few dozen children in the five- to ten-year age bracket ever lived at the orphanage at any one time, with teenagers amounting to little more than a handful. By 1995, while the composition of the orphan population had significantly changed, only a small fraction of the officially claimed 470 non-infant inmates were anywhere to be found.[191]

Since March 1995, thanks mainly to the efforts of a fifty-three-year-old physician and former employee of the Shanghai Children's Welfare Institute, Zhang Shuyun, who escaped from China that month carrying with her a substantial archive of secretly obtained orphanage documents, the answers to the disquieting mystery of the lack of older children at the orphanage have become all too clear. The documents, covering mainly the period 1988–92, paint a picture of day-to-day life at that time for the institutionalized orphans and abandoned children of Shanghai–one of China's most prosperous cities–that seems marked by such extremes of official callousness and brutality as to challenge normal belief. In this chapter, the evidence contained in those documents is presented in comprehensive detail, with particular attention given to the core question of extremely high mortality at the orphanage and to the pseudo-medical diagnostic and treatment practices that appear, in many cases, to have been its primary cause.

---

[191] For further details on the current situation at the Shanghai orphanage, see Chapter 7.

A Brief History of the Orphanage

The Shanghai Children's Welfare Institute, located at what is currently known as 105 Puyu West Road in the city's Nanshi District, was founded in 1911, the last year of the imperial era, by a Chinese Catholic named Lu Bohong, and was initially called the Shanghai Hall of New and Universal Succour *(Shanghaishi Xin Puyu Tang)*. Administration of the charitable center, which from the outset gave shelter to all types of destitute persons ranging from abandoned newborn infants to eighty- or ninety-year-old sick and homeless people, was later taken over by a group of French Catholic nuns. After 1949, like most other foreign-run orphanages and benevolent relief societies in China, the center soon found itself the target of a government-inspired campaign of public vilification and demonization. According to a confidential history of the Nanshi site written in October 1964 by Yang Jiezeng, the orphanage director at that time,[192]

> The institute was formerly managed by a French imperialist nun named Aodila, who fled China shortly after Liberation.[193] Thereafter, it was nominally run by the Chinese Catholics, but the real power and interests remained in the hands of the imperialists and their running-dogs....Before Liberation, the institute was financially corrupt beyond description, especially during Aodila's time. In effect, she turned the place into an execution ground for the abuse and murder of Chinese children. For her, death was but a game.
>
> When the children fell sick, for example, she never gave them any medical treatment, and if they caught chicken pox or ran a high fever they never got so much as a cup of boiled water to drink. She made them take cold showers every day, even in freezing cold weather. And all they ever got to eat and drink was rice congee and watery milk with the curds removed. As a result of this severe ill-

---

[192] The document is a handwritten manuscript titled "Materials for the Shanghai Children's Welfare Institute's 'Symposium on Urban Welfare Work'"; although undated, it is clear from numerous aspects of the forty-two-page draft that this symposium was scheduled to be held in October 1964 and that the document was drafted just prior to the meeting. It should be emphasized that Human Rights Watch/Asia has not communicated with Yang Jiezeng, who is now living in retirement in Shanghai, and we have therefore been unable to obtain her permission to use these and other citations from the manuscript.

[193] "Aodila" is a Chinese transliteration, probably of the name "Odile."

treatment, the children often used to die of illness. But all Aodila would say was, "We only save their souls; we don't save their bodies. They may die young, but they go to Heaven and find eternal happiness."

During Aodila's tenure at the institute, the death rate among newborn infants consequently rose to more than 98 percent. Sometimes, the number of deaths even exceeded the number of admissions.[194] On January 5, 1949, for example, there were five new arrivals and twelve deaths in a single day; on January 6 that year, there were seven new arrivals and eight deaths; and on January 8, there were three new arrivals and eleven deaths.

In 1952, according to the account, the government dispatched to the institute a work team from the Shanghai branch of the Chinese People's General Relief Association *(Zhongguo Renmin Jiuji Zonghui)*, a newly established body that had been charged with the task of gradually taking over the functions and responsibilities of all charitable and philanthropic organizations that had survived the 1949 transfer of state power in China. The following year, the institute's status was officially changed to that of a "privately run and publicly assisted entity," and a few months later, a second governmental team was sent to investigate its affairs, this time from the religious affairs department. In 1956, the Hall of New and Universal Succour was formally taken over by the government and renamed the Shanghai Municipal Home for Foundlings *(Shanghaishi Yu'er Tang)*. In July 1964, the center was further reorganized and renamed as the Shanghai Municipal Children's Welfare Institute *(Shanghaishi Ertong Fuliyuan)*, the name it bears today.

Almost no information has come to light concerning the precise nature of the various administrative reorganizations that took place at the orphanage during the 1950s: for example, whether or not, as happened in most parts of the country after the Communist takeover, older orphans were relocated to multi-purpose holding centers

---

[194]Concerning the pre-1949 situation at the main orphanage in Wuhan, one Western writer recently noted: "[I]n fact, such high death rates were common at other orphanages in China at the time, whether foreign or Chinese-run; extremely high rates of mortality, ranging from 70 to over 90 percent, were also characteristic of orphanages in Europe and America in the eighteenth and nineteenth centuries." (Kay Johnson, "Chinese Orphanages: Saving China's Abandoned Girls," *The Australian Journal of Chinese Affairs*, no. 30, July 1993.) Such factors as the relative lack of effective antibiotics in the first part of this century and the scarcity of medical services generally are among the likely causes of the persistence of high deaths rates at Chinese orphanages before 1949.

and confined together with mentally ill adults and the unsupported elderly or dying; the extent to which the institute followed the national pattern of combining the custody of abandoned infants and younger orphans with that of juvenile delinquents ("incorrigible children"); and what happened to the destitute elderly who had previously accounted for a large proportion of the inmate population. It is known, however, that what is now probably the largest state-run welfare site in the Shanghai area, the Shanghai No.2 Social Welfare Institute, located on Chongming Island and currently run largely as a restricted-access adjunct of the Shanghai Children's Welfare Institute (see Chapter 7 for details), was in the early 1950s reorganized by the government as a "production-and-rehabilitation institute" *(shengchan jiaoyangsuo)*; so it is likely that some similar arrangements took place at the Nanshi site. But in general, it seems that the latter was unusual in that by the early 1960s at the latest, it had become a more or less genuine example of the "segregated management" orphan-care policy which the government has claimed to pursue since 1956 but has only rarely achieved in practice.[195] In addition to providing shelter to orphaned and abandoned children, the institute also served as a home for children whose two parents or sole surviving parent were prisoners serving sentences of "labor reform." According to official accounts, most of the prison population at this time consisted of sentenced "counterrevolutionaries," or political prisoners.

Director Yang's account provides, uniquely, a detailed statistical insight into the impact on China's orphanages of the terrible famine that swept the country in the aftermath of the Great Leap Forward.[196] Without anywhere referring to the causes of the dramatic increase, she listed the following figures for new admissions to the Shanghai orphanage:

> According to incomplete annual statistics, in 1956 there were 591 new admissions; in 1957, there were 896; in 1958, there were 1,901; in 1959, there were 3,616; in 1960 there were 8,853; in 1961, there were 2,197; in 1962, there were 960; in 1963, there were 555; and in 1964, as of October, there were 262. According to complete statistical records, altogether 18,344 children were admitted [to the orphanage] between 1959 and October 1964, and a total of 18,362 were discharged during the same period....The

---

[195] As Table 3.2 indicates, China's three directly administered municipalities (Beijing, Shanghai and Tianjin) are among the few areas of the country where relatively few children were held in "social welfare institutes" during the early 1990s.

[196] For a comprehensive history of the period, see *The Great Leap Forward Famine*, by Jasper Becker, to be published by John Murray (London) during 1996.

peak period was February 1960, when altogether 2,361 children arrived in a single month; and the heaviest single day was December 28 of that year, when 109 children were admitted.

Those familiar with the layout of the medium-sized orphanage compound at 105 Puyu West Road will probably find it hard to imagine how such large numbers of abandoned and destitute children could ever have been accommodated at the site, particularly during 1960, the worst year of the famine. In fact, it appears that the orphanage served as little more than a brief transit center for the children at that time, as the authorities strove to implement a two-pronged, emergency mass-adoption program known respectively as "collective outward transferral" *(jiti waisong)* and "doorstep fostering" *(menkou lingyang)*. The former practice, which accounted for the great majority of the more than 18,000 children discharged from the orphanage during those years, appears to have consisted of little more than organized mass transferrals of children back to the famine-stricken countryside whence most of them had just recently fled. The implication in the account is that temporary foster parents were first found for the children, although this seems highly implausible given the appalling conditions of famine, not to mention administrative collapse, then prevailing in most rural areas of the country.

Where "doorstep fostering" was concerned, attempts were reportedly again made from the outset to find foster parents from the countryside rather than the city, with the main official policy emphasis being on maintaining a tight restriction over the urban population. Thus by October 1964, the orphanage authorities were able to report, with evident satisfaction, "The number of fosterings by families within Shanghai Municipality dropped from 38.8 percent in 1961 to only 4.3 percent in 1964, while the number of collective outward transferrals to the countryside rose annually, reaching 84 percent by 1964...thereby according with the Party's policy."

While it may be inappropriate to tax the authorities too severely for responding weakly in this case to what was a crisis of staggering proportions, an emerging new policy orientation can nonetheless be discerned in the official response to the post-Great Leap famine which seems, in retrospect, to have exerted a decisive influence over the fate of China's orphans for the subsequent three decades and more. The first element of the policy was, as noted above, an official determination to restrict the urban population and prevent any further influx of the rural destitute. The second, however, lay in the leadership's apparent wish that the population of individual orphanages be maintained, henceforth, at a basically stable level. This trend could already be discerned in the practice of "collective outward transferral" in Shanghai, whereby the city's main orphanage, rather than seeking ways–however difficult of access–to expand its resources and facilities in order more properly to fulfill its ostensible purpose, instead engaged in a kind of zero-sum population transfer exercise whose effect was mainly to re-export the orphans crisis and return it to its place of origin. A foretaste of the new policy could also be found in the October 1964 Shanghai orphanage manuscript, where it was estimated "that from now on, barring any further changes in the situation, the number of new admissions will probably remain steady at around 200 to 300 per year."

For an institution the size of the Shanghai orphanage, annual admissions on this scale would imply either a rapidly increasing population or else a large number of annual departures, whether through adoption, children reaching adulthood, or death. Given the huge surge in intakes during the post-Great Leap famine, it is understandable that the orphanage would have wished to see a reduction toward more stable annual intake levels. The point is, however, that with the exception of the Cultural Revolution decade, when even the absolute population level probably fell, annual admissions to the Shanghai orphanage appear to have remained more or less at the level called for in the passage cited above. If large numbers of orphans were leaving the institute through adoption or by reaching adulthood in the early 1960s, they are apparently not doing so now. As can be seen from Table 3.3, the majority of annual departures from Chinese orphanages nowadays are through death.

As revealed in the nationwide orphanage population statistics for 1989 shown in Table 3.3, orphanages throughout the country were reporting end-of-year inmate population figures that were more or less identical to those reported at the preceding year's end—notwithstanding the huge variations in the numbers of new admissions, and similar variations in the ratios of deaths to admissions, that occurred between one orphanage and another in the course of 1989.[197] Since that time, leading officials of the Shanghai Children's Welfare Institute have consistently maintained to visitors that the orphanage population remains stable at a level of between 600 and 650 inmates. While the stated population range is greatly inflated,[198] the claim of long term numerical stability is essentially true. The only problem with this seemingly tranquil statistical tableau is this: the death rates at the orphanage have been so

---

[197] This striking regularity can be seen by comparing, in Table 3.3, the figures for each province in the "Population at End of Previous Year" with those in the "Total" subcolumn under the heading "Population at [current] Year End." The figures remained virtually the same from one year to the next in the majority of provinces, seemingly irrespective of the numbers of new admissions and deaths that took place. The same regularity could, theoretically, be the result of the orphanage taking in new admissions as and when the existing inmates depart, but the death rates are far too high to make this explanation plausible.

[198] See Chapter 7, under "Eyewitness Accounts from 1995", under "Potemkin Orphanage: The Children's Welfare Institute Since 1993."

consistently high that, since at least the mid-1980s, very little stable population has survived over any extended period.

A third and final element of the official policy which seems to have emerged during the early 1960s was that orphanage populations, henceforth, should consist mainly of disabled children. For another "quota-like" set of statistics cited approvingly in the orphanage's 1964 draft report were ones relating to the recent annual ratios between normal or healthy orphan inmates and those suffering from disabilities of various kinds. From a level of only 6.03 percent of all new admissions in 1961, the proportion of disabled children living in the orphanage had reportedly risen, as of October 1964, to 75 percent. After discounting the seventy-four members of the current total inmate population of 452 who were either proper orphans (in the legal sense) or the sons or daughters of sentenced prisoners, moreover, the proportion of disabled children among the remainder–the abandoned infant and child population–had risen to over 90 percent. As will be further explained, this focus on "disablement" levels or quotas, although no doubt originally reflective of the positive attempts made by orphanage staff at that time to place healthy abandoned infants in foster care, appears to have become, in the post-1978 period, a key and sinister factor in the emergence of worsening mortality.

The last figures available for the orphan population at the Shanghai Children's Welfare Institute prior to the onset of the Cultural Revolution are for October 1964, and read as follows: "Three hundred and seventy-three abandoned infants (of whom, thirty-four healthy and 339 sick or disabled); five strays and waifs; ten orphans from families of the working people; and sixty-four sons and daughters of prisoners undergoing reform-through-labor. Total: 452."[199] At that point, the statistical record goes blank. Sometime in 1966 or 1967, Yang Jiezeng was summarily deposed as orphanage director by a rebel faction led by her chief protégée at the orphanage, Qian Pei'e, a woman of only primary-school educational level; in the process, Director Yang was thrown from a window at the orphanage and left crippled in one leg.[200] Qian then assumed power at the orphanage and in 1982 was formally appointed as director, a post she held until her retirement in 1988, the year of Dr. Zhang Shuyun's transferral to the orphanage from her previous post at the Shanghai Municipal Research Institute for the Prevention and Cure of Occupational Diseases.[201] Sources report that the

---

[199] From Yang Jiezeng's October 1964 account, see note 192 above.

[200] In the mid-1980s, Yang Jiezeng was permitted to travel to the United States, where she underwent remedial surgery that restored her ability to walk again.

[201] While many of the professionally unqualified people who rose to positions of prominence in China during the Cultural Revolution were removed from power after 1978, Qian Pei'e was able to keep her *de facto* power at the Shanghai orphanage because (according

orphanage continued to function in a limited way during the Cultural Revolution decade, but no information is available on what became of most of the orphan population during that tumultuous period.

The case information trail resumes in May 1972, when an abandoned newborn boy suffering from infantile poliomyelitis, a good-looking child whom the staff named Ai Ming, was admitted to the compound at 105 Puyu West Road. Ai Ming, who escaped from China in the summer of 1995 at the age of twenty-two, naturally has no memory of his earliest years. He knows, however, that he is the only survivor among all the children who were admitted to the orphanage in May 1972. Like most other orphanages in China, the Shanghai Children's Welfare Institute always assigned the same surname to each new admission within a given month, and, as far back as Ai can remember, there were no other children at the orphanage sharing his surname. He recalls seeing corpses being carried out of the orphanage's Disabled Section at an average rate of nearly one a day, and that the orphanage gates were kept locked and under constant guard, with the children never being allowed to leave the compound except on once- or twice-yearly escorted trips to local parks or other public amenities.

His most vivid memory of orphanage life, however, is of how, at the age of twelve, he was made to carry the corpse of a recently deceased child to the orphanage's morgue. So complete was the isolation of children at the orphanage from the wider world that most of them regarded daily life there as probably being the normal condition of childhood. While removing the corpse, however, Ai Ming felt genuine fear for the first time, for he realized that the same fate could as easily befall him. Years later, he stood in the orphanage's morgue and took a series of photographs, several of which are reproduced in this report, of the emaciated corpses of infants and children who had died at the orphanage from malnutrition and neglect.

In retrospect, it seems possible that the nature of the trauma inflicted by the post-Great Leap famine on China's political leadership—both in respect of its own perceived ability to run the country effectively or at least safely, and, still more, with regard to the new state's self-legitimizing belief in the fundamental "superiority of socialism" over other social systems—was simply so great that it drove the leadership to take refuge in wilfully false and self-deluding perceptions of the society it was ruling over. The legions of orphaned and abandoned children, emerging in numbers apparently unprecedented in twentieth-century China's history,were not only the most visible and shocking of the many dire products of Mao's Great Leap Forward: they

---

to Zhang Shuyun) her husband sat on the Shanghai Economic Committee.

were also, for the political leadership, the most deeply intolerable.[202] Above all, they were an affront to socialism. At this point, a process of official denial appears to have set in. Henceforth, China would have only the number of orphans that it deserved–no more and no less. Just the right quantity, perhaps, to be commensurate with the political system's allegedly intrinsic, though as yet incompletely manifested, superiority.

Mortality Statistics, 1960–92

Soon after commencing employment at the Shanghai Children's Welfare Institute in September 1988 as a senior physician whose main duty was to carry out analysis of medical samples from the sick orphans, Zhang Shuyun began to discover the disturbing realities of everyday life there.[203] Over the next five years, she and numerous other dissident staff members waged an unremitting campaign to bring the facts to the attention of officials at the highest levels of the Shanghai government, in the hope that action would be taken to halt the severe abuses against the city's orphan population. In December 1991, the Shanghai Bureau of Supervision, a government body responsible for investigating cases of alleged administrative malfeasance, sent an investigative team comprising three senior officials to the Shanghai Children's Welfare Institute to monitor all aspects of the situation there and to prepare a comprehensive report on its findings. The three-person team remained at the orphanage on a daily basis for the following eight months. During the same period, moreover, a total of sixteen directly elected members of the Shanghai People's Congress–the local legislature–conducted an independent, diligent, and at times necessarily clandestine investigation into the orphanage's high levels of child mortality and associated abuses. Both teams of investigators confirmed and substantiated, in all major respects, the serious allegations of deliberate child abuse and neglect that Zhang Shuyun and her colleagues had been persistently raising since 1989.

---

[202] The estimated total number of deaths that resulted from the post-Great Leap famine is around twenty-seven million. For further details, see note 29, above.

[203] During the first year of her employment at the Shanghai Children's Welfare Institute, Dr. Zhang worked primarily on administrative duties relating to the orphanage's construction of a new therapy and rehabilitation block; in addition, she worked two or three shifts each month performing routine medical checkups on the children. After June 1989, when the Rehabilitation Center opened, she began working in the orphanage's laboratory, where she was mainly responsible for carrying out analyses of medical samples. She continued to perform medical examinations of sick children in all parts of the orphanage, however, until 1991, when she was prevented by the orphanage leadership from continuing to do so as punishment for her efforts to expose abuses against the children.

The eventual outcome of the dissident staff members' campaign, however, was that by 1993 all had been dismissed or driven from their jobs, and all but one of the People's Congress delegates who supported them had been prevented from standing for second terms in office. Meanwhile, all those directly responsible for the abuses at the orphanage had consistently been shielded and protected by the senior Shanghai authorities and sometimes even promoted. The city government imposed a complete news blackout on the controversy, and to this day not a single orphanage staff member or responsible official from the municipal Civil Affairs Bureau has ever been punished or seriously disciplined for their actions. The story of this extraordinary episode, including details of the Supervision Bureau's subsequent attempt to downplay the evidence of abuses and the final official cover-up campaign by the government, is related more fully in Chapter 6, below; while an account of the cosmetic changes and reforms that have been carried out at the Shanghai Children's Welfare Institute by the city authorities since 1993, when Zhang Shuyun was finally forced to tender her resignation, appears in Chapter 7.

Human Rights Watch/Asia's nine-month-long investigative collaboration with Dr. Zhang Shuyun began a matter of days after her escape from China. We were already aware of the severe situation at the Shanghai Children's Welfare Institute, thanks to a brief but highly disturbing report on the topic that had been published in 1992 by the U.S.-based monitoring group Human Rights in China.[204] But two items among the hundreds of pages of official and unofficial documentation on the Shanghai orphanage that Zhang Shuyun had brought with her from China compelled immediate attention.[205] These were, firstly, a set of thirty-four color photographs showing the severely malnourished bodies of ten infants and young children who died at the orphanage during June-July 1992, and depicting an eleven-year-old boy in an extreme state of emaciation who had been tied by his wrists and ankles to a bed, and who died just over a week later. Several of these photographs, which were taken secretly by Ai Ming over a several-week period in the orphanage's "waiting for death room" *(dengsijian)* and the morgue *(taipingjian)*, are reproduced below. (See "Scenes from the Morgue".)

---

[204] *Shanghai Ertong Fuliyuan Cuican Ertong (Devastation of Children At The Shanghai Children's Welfare Institute)*, Human Rights In China, November 1992 (New York). The seven-page, Chinese-language report comprised two documents: an internal report by the Shanghai Municipal General Labor Union on child abuse and high death rates at the orphanage (see Appendix F, below, for a complete translation of the document); and an introductory article written by the pseudonymous author Wen Shangtian.

[205] Since then, the volume of primary documentation on the Shanghai Children's Welfare Institute obtained by Human Rights Watch/Asia has increased several-fold.

The second main item of evidence in Zhang Shuyun's possession was a documentary archive containing the medical records of numerous children who had died at the orphanage since 1988; official registers of deaths for the years 1988 through 1992; and a set of officially compiled annual statistics of new admissions and deaths at the orphanage, together with annual fatality rates, dating back in part to 1960 and extending up to as recently as 1991. These mortality statistics are presented in tabular form below.

Table 4.1   Deaths at the Shanghai Children's Welfare Institute, 1960–64 and 1978–91[206]

Year	Deaths	NewAdmissions	Ratio of Deaths to Admissions (%)
1960	_[207]	–	6.19
1961	–	–	2.8
1962	–	–	2.08
1963	–	–	2.34
1964[208]	–	–	2.32
1965–77	–	–	–
1978	79	231	34.2
1979	66	232	28.4

---

[206] Death rates for the period 1960-64 are taken from the October 1964 manuscript by former orphanage director Yang Jiezeng. Figures for the period 1978-1991 have been gleaned from a variety of official records of the Shanghai Children's Welfare Institute and also from the internal minutes of six separate meetings that were convened by members of the Shanghai People's Congress in 1992 to investigate the abusive conditions at the orphanage. In 1993, Zhang Jinnuan, the orphanage administrator responsible for compiling the mortality figures since at least the late 1970s, was promoted to become director of the institute's Business Department *(Yewuke)*.

[207] Dashes indicate that the relevant information is unavailable.

[208] January through October only.

Year	Deaths	NewAdmissions	Ratio of Deaths to Admissions (%)
1980	69	209	33
1981	70	189	37
1982	80	191	41.9
1983	73	153	47.7
1984	72	102	70.6
1985	49	99	49.5
1986	89	161	55.3
1987	95	162	58.6
1988	101	188	53.7
1989	146	235	62.1
1990	126	224	56.3
1991[209]	211	272	77.6

Following the customary practice in China's orphanages, the mortality percentages shown in Table 4.1, representing the ratio of deaths to admissions, have been calculated according to Method A, which is described above in Chapter 3. The limitation of this method, namely that it omits from the calculation the extant population from the previous year, was also mentioned in Chapter 3. It is important to note, however, that these ratios are the ones referred to by Chinese orphanage staff and officials themselves as representing the "death rate" *(siwang lü)*. Since previous-year-end population statistics for the Shanghai orphanage are not available, with the exception of the three-year period 1989–91, for the range of years listed above, Method B can only be used to estimate annual death rates for those three years. This method is also described above in Chapter 3. The relevant figures are as follows: for

---

[209] January through October only.

1989, 22.2 percent; for 1990, 19.5 percent; and for 1991, 31.0 percent.[210] As shown in Table 4.1, the corresponding death rates as calculated by Method A were, by contrast, 62.1 percent, 56.3 percent and 77.6 percent.

The wide divergence between these two sets of figures can largely be explained by reference to another set of statistics. According to a detailed breakdown of the extensive mortality data that appears below in Tables 4.4 to 4.6, no fewer than 78.4 percent of all the children officially recorded as having died at the Shanghai orphanage between December 1988 and December 1989 had been resident there for one year or less. Similarly, for the period November 1991–October 1992, altogether 80.7 percent of the deaths that occurred during that period occurred among children who had been resident for one year or less. In other words, the new intakes accounted for the overwhelming majority of all the mortality that occurred, and thus represented an inordinately high-risk group; by comparison, the risk of mortality faced by the "stable" population was low.[211]

The conclusion that can be drawn from these data is that while Method B may provide a more reliable indicator of annual mortality throughout the orphanage population as a whole, nonetheless Method A–showing the ratio of deaths to admissions–offers a more meaningful picture of the actual mortality situation. The annual mortality figures derived by Method B appear to disguise heavily the fact that the brunt of mortality that occurs is being borne by subgroups within the orphanage population. China's orphanage leaderships' customary focus on mortality among new admissions may therefore actually generate more significant and relevant insights than

---

[210] It should be noted that the full formula for Method B was not applied in these calculations, since the annual figures for live departures were not available; deduction of the latter from the denominator of the calculation would have had the effect of raising the Method B death rates by at least several percentage points for each of the three years. The basic statistical data from which the above calculations were made were provided by Yu Ming, a deputy head of the Shanghai Supervision Bureau, at a closed meeting of the bureau's officials and delegates to the Shanghai Municipal People's Congress held on April 17, 1992. The raw figures–given in the sequence: extant population, new admissions, and deaths– were as follows: for 1989: 400, 235, and 141. For 1990: 422, 224, and 126. And for 1991: 407, 272, and 211. Surprisingly, the death rates for these years that Yu himself presented at the meeting–namely, 35.25 percent for 1989; 29.8 percent for 1990; and 51.8 percent for 1991–were calculated simply as the ratio of deaths to extant population, omitting the new admissions from the denominator of the calculation, and were thus actually higher than those obtained via Method B and shown above. (Details taken from internal minutes of the April 17, 1992 meeting.)

[211] In real terms, however, the mortality risk faced by even the "stable" population is still remarkably high; see note 224, below. For further details on the statistical breakdown of deaths, see below: "Demographic Trends."

the alternative method. For while Method B is more broadly representative, Method A may be more programmatically useful.

The available case data makes it possible, moreover, to calculate with precision the death rate among a specific cohort of new admissions in one recent year at the orphanage, namely a group of fifty-five infants and children who arrived during January–February 1992. (See Table 4.5.) Of the forty children whose disposition was known as of October that year, no fewer than twenty-four had already died, giving an authentic mortality rate of 60 percent over an eight- to nine-month period alone. Extended over the full year, the rate would almost certainly have been higher still. Furthermore, it should be remembered that all the above ratios only represent annual rates of death. If such severe mortality as these various figures indicate is, as the data suggest, sustained at the orphanage each year, then simply put, once a child enters the orphanage, his or her chances of eventually leaving the orphanage alive become close to nil.

In April 1992, after being confronted with the Shanghai orphanage's annual mortality figures by Zhang Shuyun and other dissident staff members, the investigative team from the Shanghai Supervision Bureau produced a novel alternative to either of these methods of statistical calculation. Orphanage mortality rates, they declared, should comprise only the ratio of deaths from among new admissions in a given year to the total number of new admissions in that year. While this method of calculation certainly lowered the mortality rates, it also meant, as the critics were swift to point out, that all children who died during any year other than the one in which they were admitted to the orphanage would henceforth vanish from the statistical record.[212] Around the same time, in its annually published statistical yearbooks, the Ministry of Civil Affairs began to deploy, in place of the former category "population at end of previous [or current] year," the new concept of "total annual person-days,"[213] presumably in an effort to quantify and record more adequately than before the demographic complexities of orphanage life. While this approach should theoretically have allowed more definitive mortality rates to be calculated, such promise was not

---

[212] This exchange appears in the Minutes of the fourth meeting, held on April 17, 1992, between members of the Shanghai People's Congress and officials from the Supervision Bureau. The "alternative" death rates were unveiled at the meeting by Yu Ming, deputy head of the Shanghai Supervision Bureau; even using this statistical sleight of hand, however, they were still extremely high: 42.5 percent for 1989, 37.5 percent for 1990, and 49 percent for 1991.

[213] The Chinese term is *"bennian zaiyuan zong-rentianshu"* (China Civil Affairs Statistical Yearbook: 1991, p.92).

to be fulfilled–for the authorities had by that time begun scrupulously excising all mention of orphanage fatalities from the public record.

Turning to the statistics themselves, the first noteworthy feature of Table 4.1 is that recorded mortality rates for the early 1960s seem extremely low in comparison with those of the post-Cultural Revolution period. Since virtually all the 18,000 or so abandoned and orphaned children who were admitted to the orphanage during the famine years, however, were dealt with under the policies of "collective outward transferral" and "doorstep fostering," and thus mostly remained at the orphanage only for very brief periods, the officially reported figures for 1960-64 probably only refer to deaths that occurred among the relatively small "stable" population.[214] Fatalities among all the others, although almost certainly high, are unlikely to have been recorded or even known about by the orphanage's staff. Even so, the relatively low mortality figures for those years suggest that those children who comprised the stable population may have enjoyed better conditions of treatment than those experienced by the majority of their counterparts since 1978.

Secondly, for the period 1964–78, encompassing mainly the decade of the Cultural Revolution, the fragmentary information given in Table 4.1 would seem to indicate that a fifteen-fold aggregate increase in mortality rates took place. Since the entire period itself is a statistical blank, however, one can only speculate as to what the actual death rates were during those years. Archival material from other provinces (of the kind presented in Chapter 2), shows that many orphanages around the country were simply closed down during the Cultural Revolution. Actual mortality among Shanghai's orphans during this period may have been considerably higher than the 34.2 percent figure recorded for 1978.

By far the most startling aspect of Table 4.1, however, is the dramatic increase in mortality that is recorded as having occurred at the Shanghai orphanage between 1978, the year of Deng Xiaoping's political ascendancy in China, and 1991, the last year for which official death-rate figures are available. An unusually high deaths-to-admissions ratio of 70.6 percent was reached, for reasons unknown, in 1984, but the highest mortality level on record since the orphanage began compiling such statistics in 1960 occurred in 1991, when the deaths-to-admissions ratio spiralled to

---

[214] Alternatively, all the children may have been included in the denominator of the mortality calculation, despite the lack of information on what became of those "outwardly transferred." Non-inclusion of deaths among the latter group in the numerator of the calculation would then have produced fallaciously low death rate figures, concealing much higher mortality among the children who remained.

77.6 percent.[215] While only the Chinese authorities are in any proper position to explain this appalling mortality trend, the underlying causes for the phenomenon may well derive from two major policy changes that were introduced by the government between the late 1970s and early 1980s.

The first was the introduction of the one-child-per-family population control policy, which produced a rapid rise in the number of abandonments of newborn baby girls by couples seeking to ensure, in line with the traditional Chinese stress on the importance of securing male heirs, that their only legally permitted child would be a boy.[216] This trend has apparently continued unabated over the past decade, to the point where abandoned baby girls are now widely reported to account for over 90 percent of the inmate populations of many orphanages in China.[217] (The great majority of these

---

[215] The mortality calculations obtained from the Shanghai Children's Welfare Institute are, as was indicated above, technically suspect, and the method of reporting deaths may have changed from time to time. For this reason, caution should be observed in assessing mortality trends over the longer term. What is clear, however, is that mortality has been astonishingly high for a long period, and it appears to be getting worse. One conceivable explanation would be that the orphanage has been accepting an increasingly high proportion of medically high-risk children over the past ten to fifteen years. For an evaluation of the medical aspects of the orphanage's affairs, see below, "The Medical Context."

[216] Human Rights Watch takes no position on the Chinese government's stated policies to achieve control over the phenomenon of population growth; such a matter is outside our mandate as a human rights organization. We condemn unreservedly, however, the severe human rights abuses, notably forced abortions and forced sterilizations, that often arise in the course of the government's coercive implementation of its one-child-per-family policy. The latter are fundamentally in violation of a right to privacy that is inherent in the major international human rights standards, and, since in essence committed with violence, they also violate the right to physical integrity of the person.

[217] Kay Johnson, for example, lists (on p. 72) the percentage of girls resident at the main Wuhan orphanage during the period from 1988 to 1992 as being "90+ percent." See also "Discarding of Baby Girls 'Serious' in Fujian," China News Service (Zhongguo Tongxun She), Beijing, March 22, 1989; in Foreign Broadcast Information Service (FBIS-CHI 89-056), March 24, 1989, p. 61. While the gender distribution of the orphan population as a whole at the Shanghai Children's Welfare Institute is not known, the mortality data presented in Tables 4.4 and 4.6 for the years 1989 and 1992 indicate that there was no major gender imbalance among the fatalities, suggesting that a roughly equal number of boys and girls has been admitted to the orphanage in recent years. It is unclear why the Shanghai orphanage apparently departs from the national trend in this respect. Interestingly, however, in the only period for which complete information on the gender ratio of new admissions is available, namely January–February 1992, a marked gender imbalance is evident: out of fifty-five new admissions over the two months, forty-four were female. (See below, "Demographic Trends" for further information.)

female infants, moreover, are by all accounts quite normal, whereas most of the relatively small number of abandoned boys in orphanage care appear to be either physically or mentally disabled.) The other, closely related policy change that occurred around the same time was the introduction of the seemingly perverse government rule whereby couples who already had one child were no longer permitted to adopt an abandoned child, although they could still adopt a "legal orphan."[218] As was explained in Chapter 3, in what appears to reflect an official perception of abandoned children as somehow being only potentially additional members of the population, they may now only be adopted by childless couples.[219]

In the early 1960s, staff at the Shanghai Children's Welfare Institute made strenuous efforts to find suitable foster homes for as many abandoned child victims of the post-Great Leap famine as possible. As Yang Jiezeng recalled in October 1964, "We gave the children away for fostering to anyone who would take them." Many of the "collective outward transferrals" and "doorstep fosterings" carried out at that time were probably an unmitigated disaster for the orphans concerned. But in principle, the policy of attempting to find new homes in Chinese society for children who had been abandoned was surely irreproachable. And the fact remains that at least the children who were transferred *en masse* to the countryside from Shanghai in the early 1960s were given a chance of survival, which would probably not have been the case had they remained at the orphanage, given the huge numbers arriving there daily at that time and in view of the leadership's evident unwillingness, even under those desperate conditions, to allow the orphanage to function significantly beyond normal "stable population" levels.

The following extracts from a letter that was published in June 1982 in a confidential newsletter compiled by the official newspaper *China Youth Daily* illustrate how drastically the adoption prospects of abandoned children in China had been curtailed by this time. In June of the previous year, the author of the letter, a woman named Liu Yu who was then on a business trip to the city of Hanzhong,

---

[218] It is unclear when this policy was first introduced in China. The first formal codification appears to have been in the 1991 Adoption Law, but anecdotal evidence suggests that it had by then already been in application for at least a decade. (See, for example, the letter by Liu Yu cited below.)

[219] The drawing of a legal distinction between abandoned children and orphaned children, and the requirement that certification of death in the case of both parents is necessary to establish the latter status, serves a potentially valid and important purpose, which is to discourage trafficking in abandoned children, a phenomenon which has reemerged in many parts of China in recent years. Once *bona fide* abandonment status has been determined, however, the distinction should clearly be seen as irrelevant to the question of the children's need to secure foster homes.

Shaanxi Province, learned that an abandoned baby girl had recently been brought in to the local police station. After explaining that she "felt sympathy for this abandoned infant and hatred for the immoral action of her natural parents," Liu, who already had a child, recounted her story as follows:

> I was determined to adopt this abandoned baby, with the aim of fulfilling my duty to society. After we had made the decision and had brought her home, we were then censured by the family planning office at the factory, which stubbornly insisted that this constituted having a second child in defiance [of the rules], and wanted us to send the baby back where she came from. Otherwise, we would be dealt with according to the family planning regulations of Shaanxi Province. We said that since the police station had agreed to give us the baby, and had issued us a certificate, we had therefore acted responsibly towards the [government] organization and the baby, and it would be wrong for us to send her back. Although we explained this many times, it was no use. Since then, the factory's family planning office has not only withdrawn our single-child certificate and canceled only-child treatment for my son,[220] but at the same time has fined us both 20 percent of our wages every month, greatly affecting the livelihood of our entire family....I really can't understand it.[221]

In November 1995, commenting on the current situation, a senior representative of one of the main Hong Kong-based charitable organizations involved in assisting Chinese orphanages stated to Human Rights Watch/Asia: "It's impossible for anyone who already has a child to adopt an abandoned infant."[222] This official closing off of the main potential path to fostering for most of the country's orphanage population—a development which has occurred, moreover, both within the context of a more or less static nationwide orphan-care network whose main institutional priority seems to be maintaining its inmate populations at basically stable levels, and, simultaneously, with the generation by other government policies of steadily growing numbers of abandoned baby girls—provides perhaps the single best explanation as to

---

[220] Single-child families in urban China are entitled to preferential treatment in areas such as housing and school assignment.

[221] For the complete text of this letter, see Appendix N, below.

[222] For professional reasons, the source wishes to remain anonymous.

why such pernicious mortality trends as those indicated in Tables 3.3 and 3.4 are currently being experienced by orphanage populations around the country.[223]

A further point of importance is that Table 4.1, which is based on the Shanghai orphanage's own internal records, records a higher death rate for 1989 (62.1 percent), than that derived by the same method of calculation from the openly published government figures presented in Table 3.3, namely 51.1 percent. If typical for the table as a whole, this official underreporting in the case of Shanghai would mean that even the extraordinarily high mortality levels reported for other provinces in 1989 actually understated the true situation. It should be remembered, moreover, that the figures in question are only annual death rates; when such high incidences of death as these are sustained even for a limited number of years, overall mortality rises to attritional levels. There is compelling evidence, in fact, that the Shanghai orphanage's own mortality figures for the period 1978-91 are severe underestimates. Assuming the orphanage's total population remained approximately constant during this period, the official statistics would imply that scores of children were leaving the orphanage alive each year, either by adoption or by "graduation" into society at the age of sixteen. According to Zhang Shuyun, however, during her five years of employment at the orphanage, adoptions were relatively infrequent, only a handful of teenagers were living at the institute, and the number of children reaching the age of sixteen and being discharged each year was in single digits. Ai Ming confirms that during the late 1980s, there were fewer than two dozen children at the orphanage of roughly his own age. Since it is clear that the total number of children at the institute has not increased substantially in recent years–and is in fact much smaller than the orphanage's management is willing to admit–the inescapable conclusion is that actual mortality rates at the orphanage have probably hovered somewhere in the region of 90 percent for the past decade and more.[224]

Finally, the table contains the only known official indication on record, for any part of China, of orphanage mortality trends subsequent to 1989. According to the authorities, the deaths-to-admissions ratio at the Shanghai Children's Welfare

---

[223] See, for example, the account recently published in the German magazine *Der Spiegel* concerning conditions at the Harbin Municipal Social Welfare Institute, a translation of which appears below as Appendix P.

[224] The decisive factor in determining a child's chance's of mortality, as noted above, is not the annual mortality rate, but rather the likelihood of encountering death at some point during his or her overall stay at the orphanage. The speculated mortality of around 90 percent at the Shanghai orphanage would even be consistent, seen in this context, with the very conservative nationwide annual death rate estimate of 24.7 percent shown in Table 3.3 that was calculated on the basis of Method B.

Institute, which is officially said to be the finest and best-run orphanage in China, continued its rapid ascent, increasing between the years 1989 and 1991 (after a slight dip during 1990) by an officially reported margin of almost 25 percent. Incomplete statistics for 1992, moreover, suggest that the ratio of deaths in that year may well have exceeded the 77.6 percent recorded in 1991. This state of affairs left almost no grounds for optimism as to the probable direction of post-1989 mortality trends at orphanages elsewhere around the country.

An Outline of the Attritional Process

The parallels, and also the contrasts, between what is happening nowadays in Chinese orphanages and the crisis in child welfare produced by the famine of the early 1960s seem eerily clear. Once again, huge numbers of abandoned infants are being generated across China, and again, the proximate cause of the crisis is the nationwide imposition by Beijing of an inflexible and punitive set of policies–this time, the one-child policy and the population control program. As happened more than thirty years ago, moreover, the unsettling evidence of the damage and suffering caused by its doctrinal rigidity is apparently being denied by the country's leadership and the blame cast elsewhere (even today, official Communist Party histories continue to claim that the early-1960s famine was caused by "bad weather"). Today's orphans and abandoned children, like their counterparts at that time, form a stark and perhaps intolerable reminder of the failures of official policy, and their existence must therefore, it seems, be largely denied. Just as before, there has been no commensurate expansion of the orphanage system to accommodate them, and orphanage populations have thus remained, to all outward appearances, reassuringly stable.

Unlike in the early 1960s, however, abandoned children in the 1990s have been unable to expect any "outward transferral," "doorstep adoptions" or other emergency responses to be forthcoming from the government. Such measures are officially deemed to be somehow inadvisable, since they might further imperil the core goal of restricting national population. Instead, the abandoned children are in practice accorded second-class orphan status and thereby condemned, in most cases, to spend the remainder of their lives in institutional care. And finally, since the orphanages are not expanding significantly in size or number, while the nationwide crisis of infant abandonment continues unchecked, curtailment of individual life expectancy would appear to represent, for orphanage staff, the only viable solution.

The sinister practical mechanics of the process whereby many of the children who formed the actual subjects of the mortality statistics listed above reportedly met their deaths are discussed in a subsequent section of this chapter. In outline, however, the process appears to have consisted of two main stages. The first stage took the form of a collective institutional decision—one made either explicitly or implicitly by the staff members, but apparently always in tacit pursuit of a single goal, that of maintaining a pre-ordained level of stasis within the orphanage population—that a certain orphan or group of orphans was medically "unviable" and was therefore destined to die. The subsequent stage involved the application by orphanage staff of a broad range of quasi-medical and pseudo-medical concepts, techniques and treatments whose practical effect was generally to ensure that these individual judgments of non-viability would in due course become a self-fulfilling prophecy. Orphanage staff, acting as judge and jury in the matter, could then rest in collective good conscience, apparently firm in the belief that "due process" had been observed.

On other occasions, however, no such pretense was made, and the elimination of the unwanted child would take place in a manner more reminiscent of a street lynching than a courtroom trial. In a single episode spanning the last four days of December 1991, only three months after the passage of a "Law of the People's Republic of China on the Protection of Minors," no fewer than fifteen children died at the orphanage in quick succession. The primary cause of death officially recorded in twelve of the cases was second- or third-degree malnutrition, and the secondary cause recorded in five instances was pneumonia. What is not found in the official record, however, is the fact that, as reported by Zhang Shuyun, at least nine of these fifteen deaths resulted from hypothermia and associated medical complications caused by the fact that the children had been left tied by orphanage staff to "potty chairs," in freezing weather conditions and wearing only a single layer of thin cotton clothing each, for more than twenty-four hours. When summoned to the scene of this atrocity-in-progress by a dissident staff member, the Supervision Bureau investigators personally witnessed the ugly, blue-black swellings that had emerged on the children's tightly bound arms and legs. Moreover, they saw with their own eyes that several of the children had already lapsed into unconsciousness. Upon hurriedly arriving at the scene, however, the orphanage's Party Secretary, Zhu Meijun, flatly refused the government investigators' timidly-put request that the children be untied and given emergency medical treatment. The deaths followed in due and inevitable course.[225] Neither Zhu Meijun nor any other staff member at the Shanghai Children's Welfare Institute was ever subsequently punished for this act—an act which at a minimum, under Chinese law, should have constituted the crime of multiple manslaughter.

---

[225] The name, gender and age at time of death of each of the fifteen children who died at the orphanage between December 28 and December 31, 1991, are as follows: Hu Ping, female, seven years; Yuan Jie, female, seven months; Yu Xin, female, three and a half months; Xie Cheng, female, one month; Jia Jun, male, two years and nine months; Zeng Xin, female, three months; Lou Mao, female, five and a half years; Hua Yi, female, one year and eight months; Peng Jun, male, three and a half years; Xing Mao, male, one year and four months; Zeng Yuan, female, two months; Xing Lan, female, four months; Xi Liang, male, eight months; Zeng Jun, male, three years; and Chen Jun, male, two years and seven months. (Further information on these cases can be found in the relevant section of Table 4.6, below.)

Even this, however, did not represent the high point in fatalities during the orphanage that year. On October 20, 1991, Ma Mimi, Gao Junzhu and Xu Xinyuan, three elected members of the Shanghai People's Congress, made a covert visit to the compound at 105 Puyu West Road, in an attempt to ascertain for themselves the truth or otherwise of the dissident employees' allegations. Gao later summarized, for the benefit of assembled senior leaders of the Shanghai Supervision Bureau and the municipal People's Congress's Legal Affairs Committee, what they found:

> The gates to the orphanage were all tightly locked....The weather was already very cold, but inside the children were going around in bare feet and single layers of clothing, looking like little piglets. In the canteen, the menus seemed fine, but when we asked the children whether they'd eaten or not, it turned out [the menus] were all phony. The children also told us that whenever foreign visitors came, they were given new clothes to wear and allowed to play ping-pong, but before the guests had even departed, [the clothes, bats and balls] were all taken away from them again.

And on a subsequent visit,

> We looked into the morgue *(tingshifang)*. There were seven bodies piled up there! Over a twelve-hour period between December 19 and December 20, 1991, no fewer than seven children had died. We went inside to look closer, and I wept at what I saw. The children's corpses hadn't even been properly shrouded, and they were no more than bags of skin and bone. It was unspeakable. How could this possibly be an orphanage of the New China? I came out of the place realizing that the allegations made by the critics were neither false accusation nor slander, and I went straight to the People's Congress's Legal Affairs Committee, absolutely furious.[226]

According to other witnesses, children's bodies would often be left lying in the orphanage morgue for several days before arrangements were made to dispose of them. As a result, the corpses had sometimes deteriorated so badly by the time the staff from the local crematorium arrived, especially in summer, that they would simply

---

[226] Passages taken from confidential minutes of the fourth meeting, held on the afternoon of April 17, 1992, between representatives of the Shanghai People's Congress and senior officials of the municipal government to discuss the situation at the Shanghai orphanage.

refuse to take them away. As an inducement to the crematorium workers, orphanage staff reportedly began leaving small cartons of fruit juice standing just outside the door to the orphanage morgue—one carton for each of the small bodies to be removed.

As was noted above in Chapter 2, China's civil affairs authorities not only run the country's network of orphanages and all other "social welfare" institutions, together with much of the country's custodial psychiatric care system; they also administer all of the crematoria. This fact alone serves to explain, to a large extent, the puzzling question of how the darkest secret of China's post-1949 orphan-care policy could until just recently have been kept so securely, in the bureaucratic sense, "within the family." Copies of over 200 crematorium slips that have been obtained by Human Rights Watch/Asia for infants and children who died at the Shanghai orphanage during 1991–92 show that staff often failed to enter on the forms even the most basic legally required information, such as the deceased child's date of birth, date and time of death, and cause of death.[227] According to Zhang Shuyun, the Public Security Bureau kept the Shanghai orphanage regularly supplied with blank death certificates, and those required for the children who had died in the course of a particular month would typically be filled out all at once at the end of that month, often weeks after the children concerned had actually died and already been cremated, and by one of the junior nursing staff rather than by a physician. In other words, the bodies were often illegally cremated. So sloppily and inaccurately was this task often carried out, moreover, that in several of the crematorium slips examined by Human Rights Watch/Asia, the recorded dates of cremation actually precede the children's respective dates of death as found in their individual medical records.

Strict municipal regulations on the disposal of corpses, issued by the Shanghai Bureaus of Public Security and Civil Affairs in 1987, clearly specify that in any case where there is a suspicion that death may have resulted from abnormal or unnatural causes, an additional certificate of death, to be issued by the Public Security Bureau after its completion of a detailed investigation of the circumstances, is legally required before the corpse can be cremated.[228] Among the well over 1,000 deaths that

---

[227] In China, a crematorium slip *(huohuachang cungen)* forms the final section of an official three-part document constituting the deceased's certificate of death; the bulk of the form is to be completed by the physician who certifies death, but the third section must be completed by crematorium officials prior to the cremation and then detached and retained in their files as a legal record of the corpse's final disposal.

[228] "Notification Concerning Methods of Implementation In the Handling of Corpses of Persons Who Die From Abnormal Causes" (*Guanyu Chuli Feizhengchang Siwang Shiti de Shixing Banfa de Tongzhi*), issued by the Shanghai Municipal Bureaus of Public Security and Civil Affairs, March 13, 1987; in *Shanghai Public Security Yearbook, 1988 (Shanghai*

are officially admitted to have occurred at the Shanghai orphanage since the early 1980s, not a single case, so far as is known, has ever been referred to the Public Security Bureau for investigation on suspicion of foul play. Nor has the Shanghai Municipal Bureau of Public Health, the government body responsible for monitoring, documenting and compiling detailed year-end statistics on all fatalities in the Shanghai area, ever, apparently, seen fit to take the initiative of independently investigating the possible causes and reasons for the massive, long-term incidence of shockingly high mortality at the Shanghai orphanage. Finally, there are indications that orphanage fatalities are not included in any of the publicly released statistics for child mortality in the Shanghai municipal area; the inclusion of such figures would probably result, especially for the various post-infancy age brackets, in significantly higher mortality rates than those officially reported by the Shanghai city authorities.

Ai Ming's Memories of Orphanage Life

When we were small, four or five years old, they kept us tied to chairs for part of the day. The child-care workers didn't want us running around freely. We were tied down between lunch and dinner, from 2:00 to 4:30 in the afternoon. Some of the child-care workers would tie us up before bedtime as well, from around 6:30 to 9:00 at night. In the Children's Section they didn't tie us to our beds, though, only in the Disabled Section. We never knew any of the kids in there.

They had a lot of ways to punish you. Sometimes they would make a kid stand with the top of his head against a wall for a whole morning or evening. Or they would scald your butt with hot water—really hot! Or not give you anything to eat. I can't remember how many times I got the "choking on water" (qiang shui) treatment.[229] When we were little, there was a tub full of dirty water, and they'd use it on you if you didn't mind. Once the child-care workers asked me and a friend to carry a pail of water, and I tripped and spilled it on the floor, because of my legs. They made us clean it up, and then we had to "ride the motorcycle" (zuo

---

Gongan Nianjian, 1988), Shanghai Social Sciences Academy Press, December 1988, pp.240-241 (volume marked "for internal distribution only").

[229] In this punishment, staff would hang children upside down with their heads submerged in water, until nosebleeds and near-suffocation ensued.

motuoche).[230] Even if your legs are good, you can't do it for very long. At two o'clock that day, they also gave us the "choking on water."

In the Children's Section, we started working at seven or eight years old, helping the child-care workers. The kids in the Disabled Section didn't do much of that, but I know they worked, unravelling yarn ends, because we did that too, and sometimes the work got sent from our section over to theirs.

We had classes from 8:00 to 10:30 every morning: language, math, natural sciences, geography. Some of the teachers were okay, but some just left us alone to read. In my age group, the teachers were better. But in some of the other classes, if the kids didn't pay attention they hit them with erasers until their heads were bleeding. I can read characters, but I can't write them very well. They never taught writing, only asked us to read. But the teachers in my time were a little more responsible. Nowadays they don't teach very much at all.

When I was around thirteen, I got hepatitis. I was in the infirmary for almost a year, from the summer of 1985 onward. Lots of kids got it, but none of them were sick for as long as I was. That was how I got to know Lu Yi.[231] I don't think he was really retarded, and I don't know why he was put in the Disabled Section. Maybe his head was a little small, so they sent him there. They brought in another boy with hepatitis, just as I was getting better. I never knew what his name was. Maybe he didn't know his own name; I don't think he could talk. They simply stopped feeding him, and he got thinner and thinner. Once I brought a popsicle and fed it to him, but he threw it up. After he died, the child-care workers made me help them carry his body to the morgue. That was the first time I realized I might die as well. It had a very deep effect on me.

I had just finished sixth grade in 1988, when they forced me into the mental hospital.[232] In August 1989, after I got back, I started working full days. The kids mostly started working full-time at twelve or thirteen. They gave us a little more than ten yuan (about US $2) per month in those days. When we were smaller and only worked in the afternoons, they gave us just one or two yuan each month.

---

[230] This involved making the child sit unsupported at half-squat with arms stretched forward horizontally for long periods of time.

[231] For details of the severe abuse suffered by fourteen-year-old Lu Yi, see Chapter 5.

[232] For details of this arbitrary and unjustified action, see Chapter 5.

> *We all understood what our situation was, why we were there. Some of the kids discussed it once in a while, a few times when other children were adopted or their parents came to take them back. But we didn't like to talk about it much.*

(Conversation with Human Rights Watch/Asia, October 1995)

The Medical Context

Primary Mortality Data: A Summary of Evidence

Who were all these children, the seemingly countless numbers of abandoned infants and orphans who have died or disappeared while being held in what passes for state-run institutional care in China over the past four and a half decades? What were their names; were they mainly boys or girls; what age did they generally survive to? Above all, what caused their deaths? The answers in most cases will probably never be known. As a result of the painstaking efforts of former staff members of the Shanghai Children's Welfare Institute and their numerous supporters, however, at least one small portion of this hitherto undifferentiated toll in young human life has now been quantified, identified, and thus partially redeemed from historical oblivion.

On the basis of this extensive primary monitoring work, Human Rights Watch/Asia has compiled and translated a substantial body of case documentation and mortality data, which collectively appear below as the final section of this chapter.[233] The first item of evidence it contains is a complete list of 153 infants and children who died at the Shanghai orphanage between December 1, 1988, and December 22, 1989. (See Table 4.4.) The list, consisting of a full translation of a handwritten document compiled by orphanage medical staff at the time, which was temporarily removed from the wall of the nurses' duty room in the orphanage's Medical Ward and secretly photocopied by Zhang Shuyun in late December 1989, contains the deceased children's names, genders, dates of birth, dates of admission to the orphanage and

---

[233] Throughout this report, English renderings of all medical terms contained in the original Chinese documents have been taken from a standard mainland-Chinese reference work: the *Han-Ying Yixue Da Cidian (Chinese-English Medical Dictionary)*, compiled by the Chinese University of Medical Science, Beijing, and published by *Renmin Weisheng Chubanshe* (People's Health Publishing House) in association with *Shangwu Yinshuguan* (The Commercial Press), January 1988; and the *Ying-Han Yixue Da Cidian (English-Chinese Medical Dictionary)*, same compiler and publishers, February 1988. The two-volume set comprises more than 3,500 pages of bilingual medical-terminological definitions and is, to Human Rights Watch/Asia's knowledge, the most comprehensive such reference work ever compiled by Chinese medical authorities.

dates of death, together with the officially recorded causes of death.[234] In no fewer than 119 of the cases, the officially stated cause of death was "congenital maldevelopment of the brain";[235] the second most common ostensible cause of death, recorded in twenty-two of the cases, was, implausibly enough, "mental deficiency."[236] Below in this chapter, we discuss the apparently spurious and invalid nature of many of these diagnoses, together with the extensive resort which they betray, on the part of the Shanghai orphanage management, to the use of quasi-eugenic medical concepts and what appears to have constituted a form of unjustified euthanasia.

The second item of documentary evidence, Table 4.5, is a complete list of the fifty-five infants and children admitted to the orphanage during January and February 1992; the list provides similar information to that found in the 1989 register of deaths, but also includes important details of the children's original state of health and nutrition at the time of their arrival. Out of the fifty-five new admissions, the status of only forty children was known as of October 1992 (the date of last information), with fifteen others remaining unaccounted for. As noted, however, these data allowed a calculation of the real death rate to be made. Of the forty "status known" cases, twenty-four children had already died, representing an authentic mortality rate of 60 percent; eight were reportedly still in orphanage care; seven had been adopted; and one recently arrived ten-year-old child (the only one among the group, incidentally, who was old enough to do so) had reportedly run away. It should be stressed that information appearing in the final column of Table 4.5 was current as of October 1992 at the latest; it is not known what eventually became of the children who were still

---

[234] Since most of the children were abandoned by their parents, it may be wondered how orphanage staff could have known their dates of birth. In a certain proportion of such cases, the parent abandoning the child leaves a note indicating the child's name and date of birth. In most cases, however, orphanage staff simply have to estimate the child's age. In the various cases compiled and reproduced in list form below, Shanghai orphanage staff often recorded the "birth date" as being the estimated number of months or years exactly prior to the day when the child was admitted to the orphanage, thereby giving rise to the wistful but erroneous impression that large numbers of the children arrived on their birthdays.

[235] "Congenital maldevelopment of the brain" was recorded as being the principal cause of death in 111 of the cases and as a secondary cause in a further eight cases.

[236] "Mental deficiency" was recorded as being the principal cause of death in ten of the cases and as a secondary cause in a further twelve cases. The apparently more respectable, but in practice equally suspect, diagnosis of "cerebral palsy" shared second place on the list in terms of overall frequency; it was recorded as being the principal cause of death in four of the cases and as a secondary cause in a further eighteen cases. For a complete listing of the various recorded causes of death, see Table 4.2, "Breakdown of 1989 and 1992 Cases of Infant and Child Deaths by Recorded Cause."

alive and in orphanage care at that time. Even if one assumes, however, that all fifteen of the children whose cases were of unknown disposition remained alive (the most conservative scenario), the authentic mortality rate would have been 44 percent, still an extraordinarily high figure.

Table 4.5 is especially valuable for the information it provides concerning the general state of health of the new admissions. While details of the children's weight, height, state of nutrition and intelligence level at time of arrival are fragmentary or missing in many cases, the details recorded for most new admissions upon arrival flatly contradict the official claim, namely that the high death rates at the Shanghai Children's Welfare Institute and at orphanages throughout China are mainly attributable to the "terminal condition" in which most abandoned infants are allegedly found. Of fourteen children admitted during January-February 1992 who were later recorded as having died mainly from malnutrition, for example, only two were actually diagnosed as being in "poor" or "rather poor" nutritional condition when they first arrived at the orphanage. Even more damningly, the nutritional status of no fewer than eight of the fourteen children was explicitly recorded as being either "satisfactory" or "moderate" upon first arrival. The speed of the nutritional decline undergone by these and a high proportion of other children who arrived at the orphanage is astonishing, and points at best to grossly inadequate clinical and nutritional practices. In three of the cases documented below, moreover, death was secondarily attributed to "mental deficiency," while in another case, the latter was even recorded as the sole cause of death. A similar pattern of medically suspect, improbable or quite unexplained fatality can be discerned throughout the case data appended below. The diagnosis of "terminal condition" (lin zhong) is certainly to be found in the orphanage's medical lexicon; but among the hundreds of individual case records examined by Human Rights Watch/Asia, it was actually stated as being the cause of death in only three cases.

The third item of evidence appearing below, Table 4.6, is a list of 207 infants and children who died at the orphanage between the months of November 1991 and October 1992.[237] Despite the unprecedented level of official scrutiny to which the orphanage's affairs were subjected by both legislative and executive branches of the government during 1992, the mortality trend still—and by any normal standards of bureaucratic behavior, inexplicably—continued undiminished.[238] The list provides details of the deceased children's names, genders, medical condition and ages upon

---

[237] Human Rights Watch/Asia has also obtained extensive name lists and other data on deaths that occurred at the Shanghai orphanage during 1990 and in the first ten months of 1991; these lists are incomplete, however, and have been omitted below for reasons of space.

[238] Since the total number of new admissions for 1992 remains unknown, the death rate for that year cannot be calculated; it certainly rivaled the historic peak of the previous year, however, and may even have exceeded it.

admission, dates of "consultation" (see below for an explanation of this important term), and dates and recorded causes of death. Case information for the three-month period December 1991–February 1992 is probably the most comprehensive of any thus far obtained by Human Rights Watch/Asia for the Shanghai Children's Welfare Institute, and includes important supplementary information on many of the cases listed in Table 4.5. Available case documentation for the months of November 1991 and March–October 1992 is relatively fragmentary, but nonetheless suffices to confirm the pernicious diagnostic trends and treatment patterns that emerge so clearly in the December 1988–December 1989 official register of deaths.

Even a cursory comparison of the various case materials presented in Tables 4.4 and 4.6 makes one factor stand out with extraordinary clarity, namely, the startling transformation that ostensibly occurred between 1989 and 1992 in the medical composition of fatalities at the orphanage. Over a mere three-year period, the percentage of those who were reported to have died primarily from "congenital maldevelopment of the brain" dropped from over 74 percent to less than 9 percent, while the percentage of those reported to have died mainly from malnutrition ("second-degree," "third-degree" or "severe") rose from a mere 1.3 percent to 50 percent.[239] Apparently, this brisk revolution in the sphere of terminal diagnostics was prompted by dissident staff members' queries as to the plausibility of such a high proportion of the children, most of whom were in any case too young to have made such a diagnosis possible, having died from congenitally malformed brains.[240] For some bizarre reason, one no doubt linked to the elusive realities of bureaucratic accountability and non-accountability in China, orphanage doctors evidently felt, by 1992, that in recording the cause of death more honestly–and in a list that was peppered, moreover, with a grotesque admixture of supposedly more mainstream and organic causes of death, notably "albinism," "harelip and cleft palate," "small, malformed cranium," "missing left forearm," "squint neck," "congenital idiocy" and "blind in both eyes"–they would somehow succeed in erecting a cast-iron medical alibi for their activities, thus disarming the critics. Table 4.6 provides, in short, a detailed profile of the monstrous mortality trend that dominated life at the Shanghai Children's

---

[239] For further information on the distribution of causes of death, see Table 4.2, below. ("Breakdown of 1989 and 1992 Cases of Infant and Child Death by Recorded Cause.")

[240] It is theoretically possible that the diagnosis of "congenital maldevelopment of brain" served as a convenient and routinized catch-all term for all severe neurologic conditions that could, in certain cases, be associated with a terminal course–especially in the absence of adequate nutritional or medical care. As the discussion of individual cases presented below indicates, however, the available evidence points clearly in the contrary direction: that the diagnosis was in fact a convenient, medicalized pretense for active or neglectful practices leading to unnecessary deaths.

Welfare Institute during the early years of this decade, and which almost certainly, despite the cosmetic changes recently carried out at the orphanage, continues to prevail throughout Shanghai Municipality's child welfare system as a whole.

The fourth item of evidence, which appears below under the heading "Individual Case Histories," has been drawn from the hundreds of pages of Shanghai orphanage medical records that were smuggled out of China in 1995, and consists of detailed, illustrative case histories of just twelve of the numerous infants and young children who appear to have died needlessly at the orphanage since 1989. The first five of these case histories are of the children depicted in the photographs shown below; four were already dead when the photographs were taken, and one died ten days afterwards. The next two comprise translations of the complete medical records of an infant girl and a two-year-old boy who died at the Shanghai Children's Welfare Institute in August 1989; in both cases, the sole officially recorded diagnosis of death was "congenital maldevelopment of brain." Since the latter condition was recorded as being the ostensible main cause of death in most of the orphanage fatalities during 1989, these two cases serve to illustrate and exemplify the deplorable medical diagnostic and treatment practices that prevailed more generally at the orphanage at that time.

The remaining five case histories, of infants who died at the orphanage between December 1991 and February 1992, consist of tabulated summaries compiled by Human Rights Watch/Asia of all key entries that were found in those children's medical records. The principal diagnosis of death recorded in four of these cases was "malnutrition" (second- to third-degree or severe), while the remaining death was attributed to "congenital maldevelopment of brain function"; secondary stated causes of death included "severe dehydration," and, once again, "mental deficiency."

"Summary Resolution" and "Consultation"

The Shanghai Children's Welfare Institute, during Zhang Shuyun's period of employment (1988-1993), was administratively divided into a number of sections or divisions. These included the Reception Unit (Shouyingshi), where new admissions of all ages usually remained for the first thirty to forty days after arrival; the Infants' Section (Ying'erbu), where relatively healthy infants under the age of five years were placed; the Disabled Section (Shangcanbu), to which children with obviously severe handicaps were sent directly from the Reception Unit upon arrival, and where most others either genuinely or falsely diagnosed as mentally or physically "defective" were eventually placed, regardless of age; the Children's Section's Young Children's Group (You'erzu), where children of between the ages of six and ten lived; and the Children's Section (Ertongbu) proper, where children who survived to the age of ten or older were placed. As the mortality data in Tables 4.4–4.6 indicate, deaths occurred relatively rarely in the Young Children's Group, and were extremely rare in the

Children's Section proper. In addition, there was the General Medical Ward *(Zonghe Yiwushi)*, which until approximately 1990 was known as the "critical ward" *(bingweijian)* and served as the orphanage's "dying room";[241] thereafter, a separate "waiting for death room," located adjacent to the part of the orphanage where healthy children spent their days, was instituted.[242] Until mid-1993, however, many children were simply left to die on wards in the Reception Unit and the Disabled Section, without first being transferred to this special room. Finally, there was the orphanage morgue, which was located well away from the dormitory buildings.

According to Zhang Shuyun, the great majority of the deaths that occurred during her several-year period of employment at the orphanage were the deliberate result of a policy known as "summary resolution" *(jiudi jiejue)*.[243] The purpose of the policy was apparently to limit artificially the number of children on a given ward in order to maintain the workload at a more or less constant level. The procedure was reportedly as follows. Upon the arrival of a new orphan or group of orphans on the ward, child-care workers *(baoyuyuan)* from each of the three working shifts would agree among themselves to eliminate an equal number of the children already living on the ward, thereby holding the population constant.[244] Usually, some pretext would be found to provide a semblance of legitimation for the decision, for example that the child concerned was terminally sick or weak; or that he or she had some serious congenital abnormality rendering him or her unviable in some unspecified way. Senior medical staff at the orphanage were reportedly fully aware that child-care staff were pursuing such measures, and accorded them their tacit endorsement.

---

[241] The critical ward was known colloquially among orphanage staff as the *"tingseegay,"* which is the Shanghai dialect version of the Mandarin term *"dengsijian"*: "waiting for death room."

[242] It appears that the orphanage itself no longer contains a "waiting for death room," although this cannot be confirmed.

[243] All of the information concerning the practice of "summary resolution" has come from Zhang Shuyun, and Human Rights Watch/Asia has been unable to obtain independent corroboration of her account. The lack of documentary evidence in itself, however, is scarcely surprising, given that this stage of the process was reportedly an informal one made by ordinary child-care workers at the orphanage, and since it is most unlikely that any of the staff members concerned would have been incautious enough to have left any written trace or record of their activities.

[244] Each ward *(xiaozu,* or "group") at the Shanghai Children's Welfare Institute at that time normally housed between twenty and thirty children and was staffed by five child-care workers, two each during the morning and afternoon shifts and one at night.

According to Zhang Shuyun, the process was often quite arbitrary, and it was clear that many of the children who were targeted for "summary resolution" were those whom child-care workers on the wards found it excessively time-consuming or troublesome to care for (because of incontinence, for example, in the case of older children) or simply those whom they found to be physically unattractive. Once selected, the children would reportedly be denied virtually all food and medical care, and would sometimes even be given no water. As the children's health rapidly deteriorated, staff would sometimes find it necessary to administer sedative drugs in order to keep them quiet and docile; but more often than not, even the older children would simply lapse into a state of terminal listlessness and begin to fade away. When Zhang Shuyun expressed concern about the children's condition, she would be told: "They just won't absorb the food."[245] Those within one or two days of death would then be transferred to the orphanage's "waiting for death room," from where the corpses would in due course be sent to the orphanage morgue. The process as a whole accomplished a further vital aim: it ensured shared and collective responsibility for such actions on the part of the staff members concerned, while at the same time creating an overall diffusion of individual guilt.

Zhang Shuyun first learned about the practice of "summary resolution" on June 23, 1991, during the Supervision Bureau's investigations at the orphanage and more than two years after she had started working there, in the course of a conversation with a child-care worker on Ward 18 of the Disabled Section. Around the same time, the Supervision Bureau investigators were also informed about this practice, but they reportedly chose to ignore the information. According to the staff member, use of the measure was decided upon unilaterally in her ward by a woman named Liu Zhanying, the chief child-care worker on the ward. (Liu was subsequently promoted to become head of the Disabled Section.) The ward's capacity was twenty-five children, and "summary resolution" was used to hold it constant at this level. Acccording to the staff member, during the two-year period since June 1989, there had been twenty-five children's deaths on Ward 18, of which two had resulted from illness and the remaining twenty-three from "summary resolution." She also said that at least two other wards, namely Wards 11 and 13, which had capacities of twenty-one children each, followed the same methods, although "summary resolution" was decided upon collectively by staff on those wards.

Dr. Zhang knew of one ward, headed by a more conscientious child-care worker, in which "summary resolution" was definitely not used, and there may well

---

[245] Another comment that Zhang Shuyun heard frequently from the child-care staff while doing her monthly round of medical examinations on the wards was: *"Duo he, duo niao, duo chi, duo la"* ("The more they eat and drink, the more they shit and piss.")

have been others. Significantly, given the official claim that most deaths at the orphanage result from serious illness, child deaths were very rare on that particular ward. Orphanage records suggest that fatalities were considerably higher on certain wards (for example, Ward 7) than on others, and it seems likely that these wards were the main focus of the process of attrition tacitly encouraged by more senior staff. It is clear, however, that staff on the wards concerned tried to maintain strict secrecy about the practice.

Although the "summary resolution" measure reportedly was applied mainly against the newly admitted infants, there are several known cases of much older children having been intentionally starved to death. One such was Di Qiang, a twelve-year-old boy from Ward 9 of the orphanage's Disabled Section. In February 1992, shortly after being targeted for "summary resolution," Di attempted to steal food from other children, and was then drugged with chlorpromazine by the staff and tied down to his bed. During a visit to the orphanage by a group of foreigners later that month, Di was briefly untied from his bed and managed to escape to a bathroom on the ward, where he drank urine from a toilet. This incident occurred in the midst of the investigation by the city's Supervision Bureau into conditions at the orphanage, and a child-care worker on the ward informed Xu Jianrong, a member of the investigating team, about what had happened. Xu duly brought the matter to the attention of Zhu Meijun, the orphanage's Party Secretary, who reportedly then arranged for Di's medical records to be falsified and for a nurse and a child care-worker to testify to the investigating team that the boy had been given plenty to eat and drink. Di Qiang died from third-degree malnutrition on February 23, 1992.

While no documentary evidence exists to show that the policy of "summary resolution" was practiced at the Shanghai Children's Welfare Institute, the same cannot be said of what is reported to have formed the subsequent stage of the process described above–that of the final "doctoring to death" of the infants and children concerned. For if "summary resolution" involved no written records and was concluded only through discussions among non-professional child-care staff, the final stage of a child's deliberate starvation required, apparently, a signed endorsement from the orphanage's most senior medical officials. These documents of endorsement, which, together with the orphanage's medical records more generally, provide the principal "smoking gun" in this issue, took the form of a single-page entry in a child's medical records known as the "Consultation Record Form" *(huizhen jiludan)*. The completion of this document by one or more senior leaders of the Medical Department, usually the deputy head, Luo Xiaoling (a nursing-college graduate) or one of her colleagues, appears to have formed, at least prior to March 1992, the institutional prerequisite for transferring a child who was near to death from one of the ordinary wards to the orphanage's "waiting for death room." This authorizing document would typically identify the child as suffering from (as in 1989) "congenital maldevelopment of brain," or (as in late 1991 and 1992) "third-degree malnutrition"; the documentary evidence clearly suggests, moreover, that ordinary child-care workers at the orphanage then interpreted this as constituting official approval for the final withholding of food and medical attention from the child concerned.

Out of fifty-seven cases of death recorded in Table 4.6 as having occurred at the orphanage during the three-month period December 1991–February 1992, for example, "consultation" *(huizhen)*, a quasi-medical ritual that was generally undertaken upon formal request by a child's individual physician, was performed in at least thirty-six cases. According to the relevant medical records, the child's death normally followed within one to seven days after completion of the Consultation Record Form–a standard, two-part orphanage document–by the relevant authorities.[246] The first part of the form comprised a brief summary of the child's medical history; a summary of the most recent medical examination; and a preliminary diagnosis of the ostensible medical problem, and it had to be completed by the child's regular physician at the orphanage. The second part recorded the results of the actual "consultation" examination; a brief statement of diagnosis regarding the patient's condition; and finally, instructions as to his or her subsequent treatment. This part of the document had to completed, dated and signed by Luo and/or her chief deputies.

Two distinguishing features of the Consultation Record Form can be discerned from among the numerous specific examples of the document examined by Human Rights Watch/Asia. First, the so-called diagnoses entered in the second part of the form appear, from a detailed scrutiny of the wider relevant case records, for the most part to be medically misleading, specious or downright fraudulent. Second, the so-called treatment instructions which followed on the form–and which purported, crucially, to be a last-minute, emergency medical intervention by the orphanage's most senior and experienced physicians–consisted in most cases of no more than a single, solitary line of almost macabrely formulaic prose: "treat the illness in accordance with the symptoms" *(duizheng zhiliao)*. Most tellingly, from the date of "consultation" onwards and until more or less the time of actual death, the medical record of the child concerned, in the majority of cases, either goes completely blank or else contains, at best, little more than a few, sporadic entries indicating the adoption of merely token or perfunctory efforts toward the saving of life.

The case of Chen Zhong, a two-year-old boy who died at the orphanage in August 1989, provides a stark illustration of this general pattern. The first entry on the infant boy's medical record, dated May 5, 1989, reads as follows:

---

[246] In several of the cases recorded in Table 4.6, however, a period of as long as several weeks elapsed between "consultation" session and death of the child; and in the clearly exceptional case of Nan Shi (see Case #43), fully eighteen months elapsed.

Chen Zhong: male. Child was admitted to the orphanage yesterday afternoon. Nutritional state and development average. Heart rate: 90/min. Lungs: (–) [normal]. Abdomen soft. Good movement in all limbs. Absence of vocalization, but crying loudly. No icteric sclera or xanthochromia [yellowish discoloration of eye membrane or skin].

So far, so good. Chen appears to have been a child in average health, albeit one of somewhat delayed speech development. He had survived the first two years of life in generally acceptable condition. By July 31, 1989, however, less than three months after his admission to the orphanage, Chen's health had undergone a dramatic deterioration. According to the Consultation Record Form signed by Luo Xiaoling and others that day:

> *Examination:*   Afflicted child is listless. Complexion ashen. Nutritional development poor. No response to external stimuli. Heart sound satisfactory. Respiratory harshness. Abdomen concave. Subcutaneous fat all gone. High flexion and tension in all limbs.
>
> *Diagnosis:*   Cerebral palsy (all limbs). Mentally defective (severe). Third-degree malnutrition.

> *Treatment Instructions:*
> Treat illness in accordance with the symptoms.

No further entries appear on Chen Zhong's medical record until August 12, 1989, the day of his death. The sole recorded cause of death was "congenital maldevelopment of brain," and Chen evidently received no medication or other medical treatment during the twelve days prior to death. On July 30, it had been dutifully noted, "After two months at the orphanage, afflicted child's general condition is poor. Appetite poor; frequent trismus [lockjaw]; feeding extremely difficult." The same day's diagnosis reads: "Cerebral palsy. Mentally defective. Malnutrition." But if this reference to feeding difficulties were indeed true, which in the context seems improbable, staff evidently failed to adopt even the most basic of measures to alleviate that condition.

There is strong evidence to suggest, moreover, that the diagnosis of "cerebral palsy," a condition which in any case should not have proven fatal, was probably false and fraudulent, since the first mention of this alleged condition appears on Chen's medical record in a clearly different handwriting and pen line than any of the other entries for the period concerned. According to Zhang Shuyun, soon after the arrival of the three-man Supervision Bureau investigation team on the Shanghai orphanage's grounds in December 1991, Han Weicheng and other members of the leadership, in a blatant attempt to tamper with and conceal the documentary evidence of widespread deaths at the orphanage, had mobilized their supporters among the staff to carry out a systematic and around-the-clock rewriting of many of the medical records of children who died there during the previous few years. (For a particularly egregious and obvious example of this several-week-long campaign of forgery, see the case of Yu Lei in "Seven Medical Histories," below; a complete translation of Chen Zhong's medical records appear in the same section.)

The close collaboration between certain child-care workers and senior members of the orphanage's Medical Department in achieving the goals of "summary resolution" and "consultation" can be seen in the case of Sun Zhu, a baby girl who was admitted to the orphanage in June 1989 at the age of one month, and who died two months later. In several of the medical records examined by Human Rights Watch/Asia, including those of Sun Zhu, the words "frequent food refusal" (*shichang jushi*) or "refused food for no reason" (*wugu jushi*) were entered by orphanage doctors. According to Zhang Shuyun, what actually occurred in such cases is that child-care staff would wait until a child who had been marked down for "summary resolution" was completely listless from hunger, then spoon a little food into his or her mouth; by this time, of course, the child was usually unable to swallow the food. The child-care staff would then summon one of the chief doctors, generally either Sheng Xiaowei, the head doctor in the Infants' Section, or Jiang Huifang, the head doctor in the Disabled Section, to see the food on the child's lips, and the doctor would duly make a record of the child's "refusal to eat." All parties to the charade, however, were reportedly fully aware of what was going on.

Zhang Shuyun, who performed medical checkups on the children in the wards only once a month, saw Sun Zhu three separate times. On the first occasion, soon after the baby's arrival at the orphanage, she appeared to be in reasonable condition, apart from somewhat sunken eyes apparently caused by a bout of diarrhea. Dr. Zhang instructed that the child be given saline solution to rehydate her, but this was not done, since it was night time and the pharmacy was closed. The next time Dr. Zhang saw Sun, a month later, she had become little more than skin and bones. On the third and final occasion, August 12, the baby was so hungry that she trying to chew flesh off her hand. She died later the same day. The cause of death that appears in the medical record, however, is "congenital malformation of brain." (A complete translation of Sun's medical records appears in "Seven Medical Histories," below.)

The pernicious character of the "consultation" protocol emerges in numerous other recorded cases of children, including ones much older than Sun, who arrived at the orphanage in apparently good health, but who were then branded by orphanage staff with one or another "disability" diagnosis and who mysteriously passed away sometime thereafter. At best, the relevant medical documentation reveals a degeneration of medical ethics on the part of orphanage doctors to the point where they appear to have played little role other than passively to record the children's gradual decline. It appears, moreover, that none of the children who were dealt with under "consultation" procedures, despite being by definition the medically most critical cases, were ever transferred from the orphanage to proper local hospitals to receive emergency life-saving treatment. The following cases provide a few brief examples:

- Chen Ping, a five-month-old boy born with a harelip and cleft palate, who was admitted to the orphanage on May 31, 1989. "Consultation" was performed two and a half years later, on December 3, 1991, and he died the following day. Recorded causes of death: "third-degree malnutrition; harelip and cleft palate; mentally defective (severe)."

- Lou Mao, a four-year-old girl who was admitted to the orphanage on September 28, 1990, and was diagnosed by staff as having a "small, malformed cranium." "Consultation" was performed fifteen months later, on December 18, 1991, and she died eleven days after that. Recorded causes of death: "third-degree malnutrition; small, malformed cranium."

- Jia Jun, a six-month-old boy, blind in both eyes but weighing 5.5 kilograms and apparently otherwise quite normal, who was admitted to the orphanage on September 11, 1989. "Consultation" was performed on July 10, 1991, and he died five months later, on December 29. Recorded causes of death: "third-degree malnutrition; mentally defective (severe)."

- Xie Yong, a five-year-old girl who was admitted to the orphanage on December 18, 1991, and was diagnosed by staff as having a "small, malformed cranium" and being "mentally defective." "Consultation" was performed on December 25, 1991, and she died the following day. Recorded causes of death: "second-degree malnutrition; small, malformed cranium; mentally defective."

- Jiang Lin, a seven-year-old girl who was admitted to the orphanage on May 19, 1991, and was diagnosed by staff as being of "poor intelligence." "Consultation" was performed on December 14, 1991, and she died four days later. Recorded causes of death: "third-degree malnutrition; mentally defective."

It is unlikely that the policy of "summary resolution" was continued by the Shanghai orphanage's child-care staff after mid-1993, when the orphanage first began to be opened up to the local and overseas public. All mention of "consultation," moreover, appears to have disappeared from the medical-documentary record sometime around March 1992, just as serious pressure began building on the orphanage's management from the separate investigations by the People's Congress and the Supervision Bureau.[247] The practice of starving infants to the point of death on the regular wards has obviously now been discontinued, since foreigners visit these wards almost every day and observe no such blatant abuses. It is possible that a small number of infants or children selected for death are being transferred to more remote wings of the orphanage before any clearly visible signs of malnutrition appear. As will be explained in Chapter 7, however, the most recent evidence suggests that a new policy which came into force in early 1993, under which large numbers of infants and young children have been secretly transferred from 105 Puyu West Road to the Shanghai No.2 Social Welfare Institute on Chongming Island, now serves as the Shanghai orphanage's principal means of disposing of surplus inmates.

Medical Staff and Standards of Treatment

In view of the foregoing, the question inevitably arises whether the Shanghai Children's Welfare Institute is in fact, as officially claimed, an orphanage. From the evidence presented thus far, it would appear that the institute is, by contrast, a hospice for terminally ill infants and young persons, and one specializing, moreover, in the very specific fields of congenital brain abnormality and third-degree malnutrition. It might be reasonable to assume, therefore, that the orphanage would at least be minimally equipped with the kinds of pediatric medical expertise and facilities needed to provide appropriate care for children suffering from such severe disorders, especially those in the terminal phases of their condition.

The mundane reality, however, is that the majority of medical staff at the Shanghai orphanage, although dignified with the titles of either "doctor" *(yishi)* or "physician" *(yisheng)*, are not actually proper graduates, in the currently accepted sense of the word, of university or college medical departments. As was noted earlier, Luo Xiaoling, who at the time of her retirement in 1994 was head of the entire Medical

---

[247] This point cannot be confirmed, but it is striking that none of the medical records for the period subsequent to February 1992 that have been examined by Human Rights Watch/Asia contain Consultation Record Forms; it is possible, although unlikely, that this certification practice was continued thereafter and the relevant documents stored separately.

Department *(Yiwuke)*, is a nursing school graduate; she reportedly rose to that position, in what Chinese refer to as a "helicopter-style" professional ascent *(zhisheng feiji)*, because of her good relations with Han Weicheng, the former orphanage director. Ding Yi, who heads the orphanage's General Medical Ward *(Zonghe Yiwushi)*, graduated in medicine sometime before 1978, but as a "worker-peasant-soldier" student, that is, someone admitted to college or university under the profoundly anti-intellectual enrollment policies initiated by Mao Zedong in 1970, when China's universities and colleges were reopened after the havoc of the early Cultural Revolution years.[248]

One of the very few university-trained doctors at the orphanage was Lu Hongyan, a senior physician on the Medical Ward. The extent of Lu's professional diligence, however, may be gauged from two clinical observations which he recorded on January 17, 1992 in the medical record of Yu Lei, a fifteen-month-old boy who died three days later of third-degree malnutrition and severe dehydration, namely: "not exactly in high spirits" and "nutritional state not ideal." (A detailed summary of Yu's medical records appears below, under the heading "Seven Medical Histories.") Another was Zhang Shuyun, a graduate of the Beijing University of Medical Science, but as punishment for her efforts to expose the continuing abuses at the orphanage, she was reassigned in July 1990 to perform Chinese massage therapy, and in 1991 was barred from carrying out any further medical examinations of the children.

The foregoing should not be taken to mean that all "worker-peasant-soldier" or "special-middle school" graduates are necessarily incompetent as doctors. The methods by which the Chinese authorities choose to train the country's medical staff is something which falls outside Human Rights Watch's mandate; and we recognize that the scarce resource of highly-trained specialist doctors is something which would not, in the normal course of events, be found in an orphanage. Our point in detailing

---

[248] Ostensibly a means by which "politically correct" members of China's laboring classes could, upon "recommendation by the masses," gain access to tertiary-level education, the policy of "worker-peasant-soldier" enrollment *(gong-nong-bing xueyuan)* is now almost universally recognized in China as having resulted in the wholesale admission through "backdoor channels" *(zou houmen)* of politically activist young people whose chief characteristic was that they excelled in currying favor with local Communist Party cadres. Other "worker-peasant-soldier" graduates who served on the orphanage's medical staff during Zhang Shuyun's period of tenure were Wu Junfeng, deputy head of the Medical Department, and Jiang Huifang, until 1991 a doctor in the Infants Section and thereafter head of the Disabled Section. In several other cases, medical staff had benefited from an even lower level of professional training than this. Sheng Xiaowei, the head of the Infants Section, and Lu Yin, a doctor in the same section, for example, both received their medical education at "special-middle school" *(zhong-zhuan xuexiao)*, a type of secondary-level vocational training institution attended by many young people in China in lieu of senior high school.

the professional training of the Shanghai orphanage's medical staff is to highlight the striking disparity between the evidently low level of that training and the specialist nature of the prevalent diagnoses (in particular, "mental deficiency" and "congenital malformation of brain") which were made in the cases of most of the infants and children who ostensibly fell sick at the orphanage. This disparity is particularly critical given that the children in question actually died of the alleged conditions.

The administratively most senior member of the orphanage's medical staff, Han Weicheng, who served as director of the orphanage from 1988 until 1994, claims to be one of China's leading experts in the treatment of childhood cerebral palsy. The validity of this claim, and even of his status as a genuine doctor, is highly suspect. (According to a member of the Shanghai Municipal People's Congress: "In fact, he has never treated even a single case of cerebral palsy."[249])

Han Weicheng began working at the Shanghai Children's Welfare Institute in 1985, as part of an official "propaganda work team" charged by the city government with the task of "sweeping away filth" *(sao huang),* that is, rooting out alleged "pornography" and moral dissolution among the staff. His main activity during this initial period at the orphanage reportedly consisted of campaigning against staff members who enjoyed listening to Voice of America, the BBC World Service and overseas Chinese pop music. Qian Pei'e, the woman who had overthrown Yang Jiezeng during the Cultural Revolution and then taken over her job, apparently took a liking to Han, and in 1986 she appointed him as the orphanage's deputy director of logistics. Upon Qian's retirement in 1988, Han succeeded her as acting director, becoming full director the following year. In 1994, one year after Zhang Shuyun and all the other dissident staff members had finally been sacked or driven out of the orphanage, Han was promoted to the position of vice-director of the Shanghai Civil Affairs Bureau's Department of Social Welfare Work *(Shanghaishi Minzhengju*

---

[249] See note 251, below. The principal basis for Han's claim to be an expert in the treatment of child cerebral palsy is a slim volume on the subject that was published in Shanghai in 1989 and which bears his name as author. (*Naoxing Tanhuan Ertong Jiating Yundong Kangfu Xunlian Wen-Da [Questions and Answers on Family-Based Motor Rehabilitation Therapy for Children With Cerebral Palsy],* by Han Weicheng, Shanghai Scientific Popularization Press, March 1989.) Han entered college as a medical student sometime in late 1965 or early 1966, but his professional studies were halted after only a few months by the onset of the Cultural Revolution. From 1970 until 1981, he worked in a remote rural area of Xinjiang Uygur Autonomous Region, situated in the far northwest of China, in the health clinic of a large oil-processing installation. He returned to Shanghai in 1981, where he found employment at a workshop for the disabled run by the municipal Civil Affairs Bureau, which made artificial limbs and was staffed mainly by blind people.

Shehui Fuli Shiyechu) and he has since assumed the concurrent post of acting department director, following the retirement of his former superior.[250] He is, in other words, an administrator more expert in politics than in medicine.

As regards the actual medical facilities and equipment available for the benefit of orphans or abandoned infants who fall ill at the Shanghai orphanage, the overall picture is similarly bleak. Despite the phenomenally high death rates at the orphanage, which (as was noted above) the victims' medical records consistently attribute to a wide range of "terminal conditions" whose medical legitimacy is at best highly suspect, members of the orphanage management will, when pressed, insist that they never take in seriously ill children, claiming instead that all such cases are sent to local hospitals for the kinds of specialized treatment which the orphanage itself is ill-equipped to provide. At other times, however, orphanage officials will assert that the institute is in fact a highly advanced center for the treatment of seriously disabled orphans. In other words, they try to have it both ways, depending upon which particular types of questions are asked, and in which particular direction–toward the city leadership, the general public, or foreign visitors–they happen to be facing at the time.

One fact stands out: with extremely few exceptions, neither the reportedly small number of genuinely "terminal cases" who arrived at the orphanage during Zhang Shuyun's time there, nor the large number of infants and children who were rendered critically ill by deliberate abuse and neglect at the hands of the staff, were sent to local hospitals to receive emergency treatment or any other kind of proper medical attention. And even if were true that all of the ostensibly terminal medical diagnoses recorded in the cases of children who died at the orphanage were in fact genuine, and that the institute therefore functioned, in effect, as a child hospice, the shocking fact remains that almost nowhere in the medical records can any indication or evidence be found of those children–even the ones suffering from "third-degree malnutrition," who in addition were seemingly not put on any supplementary nutritional regime–having been granted analgesic medication or any other forms of pain-relieving care during the final days of life.

In June 1989, the construction of a new, seven-story medical treatment block, named the Shanghai Municipal Rehabilitation Center for Disabled Children, was completed on the orphanage's grounds, using funds provided by the city goverment. During Zhang Shuyun's time at the orphanage, the rehabilitation center was used more

---

[250] The offices of the Department of Social Welfare Work are located at 105 Puyu West Road, adjacent to the Children's Welfare Institute and contained within the same walled compound. The department is responsible for supervising the management of the Shanghai orphanage and all other custodial welfare institutions under the jurisdiction of the Shanghai Civil Affairs Bureau.

or less exclusively for the out-patient therapeutic treatment of disabled children from Shanghai or other parts of China whose parents were able to pay for the services provided, and the sick inmates of the orphanage itself were very rarely transferred or admitted there for treatment of any kind.

The Public Image of the Rehabilitation Center

Brief Introduction

The Rehabilitation Centre for Disabled Children of the Municipality of Shanghai is a social welfare institute engaged in the health and rehabilitation work for the children. The Centre's main rehabilitation treatment is physical exercises and it provides multi rehabilitation services for the disabled children in the society, including physiotherapy, speech therapy, occupational therapy, special education, etc. The Centre now has only eighty rehabilitation beds for in-patients in its wards....[It] is financed by the Bureau of Civil Affairs of Shanghai Municipal Government with a budget of approximately 5.6 million yuan...

The Rehabilitation Center for Disabled Children has modernized advanced rehabilitation equipments donated by UNICEF. The workers participating in the career of children's rehabilitation mostly have received professional technical training, at home or abroad....The Rehabilitation Centre for Disabled Children will try its best to catch up with and overtake the advanced standard for the benefits of disabled children.

(From a pamphlet issued by the Shanghai Children's Welfare Institute
on International Children's Day, June 1, 1989.)

The consequences of this discriminatory medical treatment emerge in a comparison of the orphanage's fatality records and an academic article on the treatment of cerebral palsy which was published by Han Weicheng during this period.[251] Cerebral palsy was listed as being a cause of death in approximately 10 percent of the 360 or so deaths officially recorded as having occurred at the orphanage during the two years 1989 and 1992, a figure apparently accounting for a large proportion of all the inmates so diagnosed. In his published article, however, Han

---

[251] *"124 Li Naoxing Tanhuan Ertong Yundong Gongneng Kangfu"* ("Rehabilitation of Motor Function in 124 Cases of Cerebral Palsy"), published in *Zhongguo Kangfu* (China Rehabilitation), Vol.4, No.2, pp.58-60 (date of issue unavailable.) According to one member of the Shanghai Municipal People's Congress: "As for [Han's] speech to the Ministry of Civil Affairs about [the success rate of] 97.85 percent out of the 124 cases, in fact he's never treated even a single case of cerebral palsy. When the families of sufferers used to come to him, he'd say: 'I haven't got time right now'." (Passage taken from internal minutes of the sixth meeting between SMPC delegates and Shanghai government officials, June 8, 1992.)

claimed to have achieved, using the standard Bobath method of physical therapy, a success rate (comprising all "conspicuously effective" or "effective" cases) of as high as 97.58 percent among 124 target cases treated at the Shanghai Child Welfare Institute. In only six of the cases was the treatment said to have had "no effect," and there is no mention in the article of any deaths having occurred, even among the latter small group. It is clear from references found in the article to supplementary "home therapy" by the children's parents that the sample group consisted of out-patient cases of cerebral palsy, rather than afflicted orphans from among the inmate population–a fact which is anyway evident from the contrasting death rates. Thus, either Han was grossly misrepresenting the standards and effectiveness of treatment services available at the orphanage's rehabilitation center, or the children suffering from cerebral palsy who were actually resident at the orphanage were systematically denied access to a remarkably effective set of therapeutic resources, ones that were available on their very doorstep.[252] According to physicians consulted by Human Rights Watch/Asia, moreover, cerebral palsy is rarely a fatal condition, unless accompanied by severe neglect and lack of medical care.

The orphanage's main gate also carries a plaque announcing it to contain, in addition to the rehabilitation block, the "Shanghai Municipal Hospital for Disabled Children," thus further bolstering the impression usually received by outsiders that the institute is a specialized center for the treatment of sick and disabled orphans. This hospital appears, however, to exist only in name. At least prior to mid-1993, in fact, it would probably have been a gross exaggeration to describe even as rudimentary the facilities that were actually available to the orphan inmates. When medical staff recorded "harelip and cleft palate" as being the cause of numerous infant deaths, for example, they were doing no more than stating the facts. Many infants who were admitted to the orphanage suffering from these minor and easily correctable birth defects died because orphanage medical staff had failed to carry out the most basic remedial surgery; unable to feed properly because of their disability, the children simply starved to death. In addition, although many of the infants and small children were officially recorded as having had "feeding difficulties," the orphanage apparently did not even possess suction machines (simple devices used for clearing blockages of the oesophagus which can otherwise lead to suffocation). The orphanage does own radiography equipment, but it was apparently almost never used, despite the reported

---

[252] Increased morbidity factors of the kind found in most institutional medical settings mean that mortality could be expected to have been somewhat, or even considerably, higher among the in-patient population than among the out-patient population; but clearly not to this extent. The key point, moreover, is that apparently no attempt was made to grant the orphans with cerebral palsy any access to immediately available therapies and treatments.

prevalence of, for example, bronchial and respiratory ailments among the newly admitted infants.

Standard drugs and pharmaceuticals were available throughout Zhang Shuyun's time at the orphanage, but they were generally administered in a highly parsimonious manner, if at all. An exception was made in the case of orphans held in the Disabled Section, many of whom, besides being regularly tied to their beds all night, were kept almost permanently sedated with powerful psychotropic and muscle-relaxant drugs such as chlorpromazine, phenobarbital and dilantin; while these drugs can have a distinct therapeutic purpose in certain severe types of psychoneural disorder (schizophrenia, for example, or advanced cases of cerebral palsy), the actual purpose of such medication was reportedly to keep the children docile and compliant for the convenience of

the child-care staff. In certain other cases, drugs for medically legitimate use were prescribed with reckless abandon. In the case of a one-month-old baby girl named Ba Jun, who was admitted to the orphanage in good health on January 2, 1992, but then swiftly developed a pulmonary infection, for example, orphanage doctors prescribed no fewer than five different types of antibiotic medication within the short space of three weeks. This prescriptive abundance, however, made no difference at all, since on February 7, her doctor recorded in the medical record: "To date, staff have neglected to carry out my instructions to administer antibiotics." Ba Jun died the following day; the officially recorded cause of death was "severe malnutrition and pneumonia"; and no staff member was ever reported, let alone disciplined or legally prosecuted, for causing a death through gross medical negligence. (For full details of this case, see "Seven Medical Histories.")

Epidemiologic Aspects

In analyzing and evaluating medical case data, especially in cases where the patients have died, experts in infant and child epidemiology generally seek answers to two broad types of questions. First, was there any pronounced mismatch between the medical risk involved in the patient's illness, and thus the degree of medical need, and the quality of the medical services provided? And second, can any clear irregularities in the broader epidemiology be discerned, that is, were the outcomes of the illnesses or diseases, especially as regards the death rate, markedly different from those usually found elsewhere? The latter point can also be expressed as the question of possible mismatch between medical risk and course of illness. In situations where, judged by these two general criteria, a consistent pattern of improbable fatalities occurs, the evidence points toward fatal medical neglect or death from abnormal or unnatural causes. In this section of the report, the medical data recorded by doctors and nursing staff at the Shanghai Children's Wefare Institute in the cases of numerous infant and child fatalities that occurred there during the period 1988–92 will be more closely examined to see how they rate on this general scale of assessment.

In evaluating the data presented below, it is useful to be aware of the standards of medical ethics adopted by the international community, both governments and the medical profession. For example, the International Code of Medical Ethics, adopted by the World Medical Association in 1949 and amended in 1968 and 1983, states:

> A physician shall always maintain the highest standards of professional conduct....A physician shall act only in the patient's interests when providing medical care which might have the effect of weakening the physical and medical condition of the patient...A physician shall always bear in mind the obligation of preserving human life...A physician shall owe his patient complete loyalty and all the resources of his science.

The United Nations' Convention on the Rights of the Child, which came into force in September 1990 and was ratified by China in December 1991, contains wide-ranging protections for the physical and medical well-being of all children, especially those placed in state institutional care. Its Article 20 states: "A child temporarily or permanently deprived of his or her family environment, or in whose own best interests cannot be allowed to remain in that environment, shall be entitled to special protection and assistance provided by the State." States ratifying the convention undertake the obligation, under Article 24, "[t]o diminish infant and child mortality" and, under Article 23, to "recognize that a mentally or physically disabled child should enjoy a full and decent life, in conditions which ensure dignity, promote self-reliance and facilitate the child's active participation in the community."

The case material which follows provides sufficient comment on whether the Shanghai orphanage met these standards in the 1980s and early 1990s. (A further selection of relevant international standards appears below in Appendix R.)

DEMOGRAPHIC TRENDS

A brief summary of the demographic distribution of fatalities at the Shanghai orphanage should first be provided. According to a detailed statistical analysis of the case data contained in Tables 4.4 and 4.6 for the two periods December 1988–December 1989 and November 1991–October 1992, the gender and age distribution of the mortality that occurred was as follows.[253]

December 1988–December 1989. Of the total of 153 children who died, 49.7 percent were female and 50.3 percent were male. Among the "newborn" group, 54.7 percent were female. Fifty-three children were less than two months old at the time of admission, and their deaths accounted for 34.6 percent of the statistical cohort; the deaths of thirty-three children aged between two months and one year at the time of admission accounted for 21.6 percent of all deaths; the deaths of twenty-five children aged between one and three years at time of admission acounted for 16.2 percent; and the deaths of thirty-three children aged three years or older at time of admission accounted for 21.6 percent. Ages at time of admission were unavailable for the remaining nine members, or 5.9 percent, of the group.

Of the children who died, 20.3 percent survived for ten days or less after admission; 15.7 percent survived for between eleven and twenty-eight days; 16.3 percent survived for between twenty-eight days and two months; 26.1 percent survived for between two months and one year; and 13.7 percent survived for one year or more. Survival-from-admission data were unavailable in 7.9 percent of the cases. There appeared to be little statistically meaningful gender variation in the relative numbers of deaths that occurred within the various age-at-admission cohort brackets.

Altogether 78.4 percent of the deaths occurred within one year of the children's admissions to the orphanage. Among females, fatalities in the first year after admission were 76 percent.

November 1991–October 1992. Of the total of 207 children who died, 57 percent were female and 43 percent were male.[254] Among the "newborn group," 67.7 percent of the fatalities were female. Sixty-two children were less than two months old at the time of admission, and their deaths accounted for 30 percent of the statistical cohort; the deaths of thirty-five children aged between two months and one year at the time of admission accounted for 16.9 percent of all deaths; the deaths of seventeen

---

[253] Human Rights Watch/Asia acknowledges with gratitude the assistance of David Chappell, who carried out the arduous task of calculating this statistical data.

[254] The gender of sixty-six of the children was not recorded in the data available. The above figures were arrived at by assuming that the gender ratio was the same among those of unrecorded sex as among those whose gender was known.

children aged between one year and three years accounted for 8.2 percent; and the deaths of twenty-nine children aged three years or older at the time of admission accounted for 14.1 percent. Ages at time of admission were unavailable for the remaining sixty-four members, 30.9 percent, of the group.

Of the children who died, 11.6 percent survived for ten days or less after admission; 21.7 percent survived between eleven and twenty-eight days; 15.5 percent survived for between twenty-eight days and two months; 31.9 percent survived for between two months and one year; and 18.3 percent survived for one year or more. Survival-from-admission data were unavailable in only 1 percent of the cases. Of the children who were admitted at age two months or less, 91.9 percent survived no more than one year and just under half survived for only two months or less. Again, there appeared to be little statistically significant gender imbalance among the fatalities. It is worth noting, however, that the gender ratio among new admissions during the only period for which complete data of this kind are available, namely January–February 1992, was highly imbalanced: out of fifty-five new admissions, forty-four were girls.

Altogether 80.7 percent of the deaths occurred within one year of the children's admissions to the orphanage. Among females, the figure was 85.6 percent.

RECORDED CAUSES OF DEATH

In addition, the general diagnostic trends shown in the Shanghai orphanage's documentation of infant and child deaths should be briefly considered. Table 4.2 shows the relative incidence of the various causes of death that were most commonly recorded in the orphanage's medical records and other mortality data during two twelve-month periods:

Table 4.2   Breakdown of 1989 and 1992 Cases of Infant and Child Death by Recorded Cause[255]

---

[255] The original sample groups, as listed in Tables 4.4 and 4.6, below, contained details of 153 and 207 infant and child deaths, respectively, which occurred at the Shanghai Children's Welfare Institute during the two separate periods specified in this table. In two of the 153 cases from the former period, and in eighty-four of the 207 cases from the latter period, the causes of death were either not recorded or have not been obtained by Human Rights Watch/Asia; those cases have been omitted from the present table, and the percentage breakdowns of listed causes of death have been calculated on the basis of the reduced totals for the two periods, namely 151 and 123. In most of the cases, several causes of death were recorded in the individual medical records; the term "secondary causes" denotes, in this table, all causes of death which did not appear to be listed as the primary one. As will be noticed, the first set of figures, for December 1988 to December 1989, covers a thirteen-month period rather than one year; this derives from the nature of the documentary evidence obtained and is largely irrelevant for the present purpose. For further information on the actual case populations from

Recorded Cause of Death (cases where known)	December 1988–December 1989			November 1991–October 1992		
	Primary Cause	Secondary Causes	Primary Cause as % of Cases	Primary Cause	Secondary Causes	Primary Cause as % of Causes
congenital maldevelopment of brain	112	10	74.2%	11	2	8.9%
malnutrition	2	10	1.3%	62	20	50%
mental deficiency	11	12	7.3%	4	25	3.3%
cerebral palsy	4	18	2.6%	8	14	6.5%
pneumonia	0	1	0%	4	15	3.3%
congenital heart disease	3	3	2%	8	2	6.5%
small, malformed cranium	5	3	3.3%	2	4	1.6%
harelip and/or cleft palate	1	3	0.7%	2	4	1.6%
premature birth	1	1	0.7%	5	1	4%
low-weight infant	1	0	0.7%	1	5	0.8%
congenital absence of anus	1	2	0.7%	2	0	1.6%
spina bifida	0	2	0%	1	0	0.8%
hydrocephalus	0	0	0%	3	0	2.4%

which the above data were derived, see Tables 4.4–4.6, below.

Recorded Cause of Death (cases where known)	December 1988–December 1989			November 1991–October 1992		
	Primary Cause	Secondary Causes	Primary Cause as % of Cases	Primary Cause	Secondary Causes	Primary Cause as % of Causes
miscellaneous low-incidence diagnoses[256]	10	15	6.6%	10	17	8.1%
Total Number of Cases	151	·	100%	123		100%

As can be seen, during the two periods as a whole, four diagnoses were used to account for the great majority of infant and child deaths at the Shanghai orphanage, namely: "congenital malformation of brain," "mental deficiency," "cerebral palsy" and "malnutrition." Some preliminary observations on each of these diagnoses should be made at this point.

1) "Congenital maldevelopment of the brain." This category of medical condition is listed in the World Health Organization's *International Classification of Diseases* (ICD-NA) under the general heading of "Congenital Anomalies." It is considered to be distinct from other severe cranial conditions such as anencephalus (absence of brain) and hydrocephalus (water-filled cranium), and also from certain

---

[256] "Miscellaneous low-incidence diagnoses" are ones which were recorded by orphanage officials in a total of only two or less cases of death during the periods December 1988–December 1989 and November 1991–October 1992 combined. The specific details of this incidence range were as follows (figures given as "total of primary + secondary causes for former period/total of primary + secondary causes for latter period"): "neonatal infection": 2/0; "necrosis": 0/2; "angioma": 2/0; "blind in both eyes": 2/0; "epilepsy": 1/1; "megacolon": 0/2; "heart failure": 1/1; "meningocele"(cerebral): 1/0; "respiratory failure": 0/1: "poor digestion": 1/0; "congenital obstruction of nephelium": 1/0; "deaf mute": 0/1; "choked on milk and suffocated": 0/1; "burn wounds": 0/1; "swollen liver and spleen"; "hepatitis": 1/0; "urinary tract fissure": 1/0; "viral meningitis sequelae": 1/0; bilateral retinal cytoma": 1/0; "congenital malformation of bone": 1/0; "skull defect with infection": 0/1; "hemorrhage": 0/1; "missing left forearm": 0/1; "lymphoma": 0/1; "tongue cancer": 0/1; "phlegmona": 0/1; "asthenia universalis": 0/1; megalodactyly (enlarged feet): 0/1; "sight impairment": 0/1; "torticollis" (squint neck): 0/1; and "albinism": 0/1. In addition, the "miscellaneous low-incidence" category includes five causes of death where the total case incidence was higher than two, but where they all occurred as secondary rather than primary causes, and hence their value in the "primary cause as percentage of cases" column was zero; these were: "septicemia": 0/7; "congenital idiocy" (Down's syndrome): 5/1; "severe dehydration": 0/5; "total circulatory failure": 0/4; and "terminal condition": 3/0.

other congenital anomalies such as spina bifida, a major disorder of the neural tube. Under Category No. 742.2, the ICD-NA lists several different types of congenital diseases known collectively as "reduction deformities of brain"; these include "agenesis of part of brain" and "hypoplasia of part of brain." According to the English-Chinese bilingual edition of the manual, both of these closely related medical conditions are expressed in Chinese by a single term: *"bufen nao de fayu bu quan."* In the medical records kept by the Shanghai Children's Welfare Institute, the term used is almost invariably *"xiantianxing nao fayu bu quan"*, which translates literally as "congenital incomplete development of brain"; the standard English-Chinese medical dictionary compiled and published in Beijing, however, gives the translation as "congenital maldevelopment of brain."

The term is a generic one and apparently covers a wide spectrum of brain disorders ranging from severe non-development of certain parts of the cerebellum, which is sometimes detectable by physicians at the time of birth, all the way through to minor maldevelopments which become manifest only in certain cognitive disorders, such as delayed or absent capacity for speech, much later on in infancy or childhood. All but the most overt forms of the disorder require specialist medical knowledge in order to be diagnosable, and identifying the lesser forms requires, at a minimum, some systematic testing of the child's cognitive abilities. In the medical records of the Shanghai orphanage that have been examined by Human Rights Watch/Asia, there is no reference to or record of any such testing having been carried out on any infants or children, including those diagnosed as suffering from "congenital malformation of brain," since the late 1970s.[257]

The ascription of "congenital maldevelopment of brain" as cause of death appears clearly fallacious in numerous cases to be found in the orphanages medical records, such as the case of Lü Lei, a boy who was admitted to the Shanghai Children's Welfare Institute in July 1983 at the age of six and a half years. Upon his arrival, Lü was self-reliant and capable in all major respects. According to the new admissions' medical record: "He is able to go to the toilet by himself; to eat on his own; to wash his face and hands, dry himself, and change his own clothes." By September 1984, moreover, according to orphanage records, "He is working [in the orphanage's workshop] at unravelling old garments to make [cleaning] rags." In other

---

[257] In several individual medical records dating from the mid- to late 1970s, there are entries indicating that an elementary form of cognitive or intelligence testing was sometimes carried out on children once they had reached the age of approximately three years old. These involved having the child make simple drawings of objects found in its day-today environment. There is no indication that cognitive tests were ever carried out on younger children, much less on newborn infants. All trace of such testing disappears from the medical records after about 1979.

words, Lü's brain was considered by the orphanage staff to be sufficiently well developed by the time he was seven years old as to allow him not merely to look after himself, but also to perform child labor. The details of Lü's eventual decline and death are noted in the records as follows: "December 6, 1991: general condition poor, complexion ashen, thin and drawn, poor digestion"; and "January 15: ashen complexion, disturbance of intestinal function". No further entries appear on Lü's medical record–that is, no medication or treatment seems to have been given–from January 16 until February 6, 1992, the day of his death.

2) "Mental deficiency." According to the ICD-NA (Category Nos. 317–318), there are four types of mental retardation: "mild," signified by an intelligence quotient (IQ) of between fifty and seventy; "moderate," where the IQ is thirty-five to forty-nine; "severe," where the IQ is twenty to thirty-four; and "profound," where the IQ is less than twenty. The correct Chinese equivalent of the term "mental retardation" is *"jingshen fayu chizhi"*; in the Shanghai orphanage's medical records, however, the term almost invariably appears as *"zhili buzu"*, a colloquial and rather pejorative phrase meaning "insufficient intelligence," and rendered in the standard bilingual medical dictionary as, variously, "mental deficiency" and "mentally defective." In international and standard Chinese diagnostic practice, the four types of mental retardation are designated in reverse order by the letters I-IV, with "mental retardation (I)" signifying the most severe level.

Beyond the absence of any cognitive or intelligence testing having been carried out at the Shanghai orphanage, at least prior to mid-1993, it is also worth noting that in the few instances where any specific category of mental retardation was noted in the medical records obtained by Human Rights Watch/Asia, it was almost invariably given as either "severe" or "(V)", that is, an even milder form of the condition than any thus far recognized by the World Health Organization.[258] In all other cases, a blunt and non-specific "mentally defective" was all that was recorded. And this was despite the fact that in October 1986, China's State Council had issued a detailed set of classifications for mental and physical disability, including precise definitions of the four internationally recognized levels of mental retardation;and that, moreover, in April 1989, the Chinese Association of Neurology and Psychiatry issued nationwide a document titled "Chinese Classification and Diagnostic Criteria of Mental Disorders" (CCMD-2), which again defined and stipulated the use of the four

---

[258] The one exception was in the case of Jian Xun, who was diagnosed as suffering from "mental deficiency (IV)"; see below for details of this case.

separate designations for mental retardation.[259] The results of this clear disregard for medical precision can be seen in the case of Ba Cheng, a two-year-old boy who died at the Shanghai orphanage on January 18, 1992, and whose death was attributed by orphanage medical staff to a combination of "third-degree malnutrition" and, ludicrously enough, "mental deficiency (v)."

The orphanage is quite capable, nonetheless, of maintaining reasonably high standards of care for the mentally disabled when it has a financial incentive to do so. Mortality rates among handicapped children whose families board them at the orphanage are reportedly no more than 1 or 2 percent annually.[260] One such child, Hu Fangfang, the profoundly retarded grandson of the late Hu Qiaomu, a senior Party leader who played a key role in launching China's economic reforms after 1978, is housed in a separate room in the orphanage's Rehabilitation Center, provided with round-the-clock nursing care, and reportedly thrives.[261]

There is strong evidence that, in practice, orphanage medical staff simply assumed that most newly admitted orphans and abandoned infants were mentally retarded. Time and time again, the words "monitor intelligence" appear in the medical records on the first day of a child's arrival at the orphanage. The Chinese term used throughout the medical records is *zhi-guan* (an abbreviation for *zhili guancha*), meaning "intelligence level to be determined through observation." Orphanage staff recorded this abbreviated term (which for convenience has been rendered in this report as "monitor intelligence") in the cases of almost all newly admitted children who showed no signs of mental retardation or deficiency. The underlying sense of the term was thus "provisionally normal."

It is worth noting that neither the term *zhi-guan* nor its expanded form, *zhili guancha*, can be found in the massive two-volume standard medical dictionary referred to above; both appear to be unauthorized medical terms that have little or no currency or usage in contemporary Chinese medicine beyond the confines of the

---

[259] The former document is titled "Five Categories of Disabled Persons in the Nationwide Survey Investigation (Criteria of Disablement)" *(Quanguo Canjiren Chouyang Diaocha [Canji Biaozhun])*, issued by the State Council on October 30, 1986. The latter document, of which only an English translation has been obtained, was passed by the Association for Chinese Neurology and Psychiatry at a national conference held in the city of Xi'an in April 1989.

[260] Information provided by Lu Ming, deputy head of the Shanghai Municipal People's Congress's (SMPC) Legal Affairs Committee, in the third meeting, held on April 8, 1992, between SMPC delegates and city government officials to discuss the orphanage's affairs; details taken from internal minutes of the meeting.

[261] Hu Qiaomu also served as Chairman Mao's personal secretary.

country's institutional care network. On a more anecdotal note, according to Zhang Shuyun, older orphans at the Shanghai Children's Welfare Institute used to complain to her that Han Weicheng, the orphanage director, would often describe them to foreign visitors as being "cured mental defectives," when in fact they were quite normal. The pseudo-medical labelling process thus began, in many cases, from the moment of a child's arrival at the orphanage. And whatever the truth of individual diagnoses of "congenital brain maldevelopment" may have been, the absurdity of recording "mental deficiency" as a cause of death is self-evident.

3) "Cerebral palsy." This broad and diverse category of illness is classified in the ICD-NA under the heading "Other Disorders of the Central Nervous System," and is seen as medically distinct from "congenital maldevelopment of brain." Category No. 343, "Infantile Cerebral Palsy", lists among other conditions: "spastic infantile paralysis," "congenital spastic paralysis (cerebral)," "spastic [or atonic] diplegia," "hemiplegia," "quadriplegia," "monoplegia" and "ataxic cerebral palsy." Excluded from the category are certain hereditary forms of the condition, such as "hereditary cerebral paralysis" and "athetoid cerebral palsy" (Vogt's disease). Mainly a disease of the neuromuscular system, cerebral palsy has no necessary connection with mental retardation. Afflicted persons do, however, require special care and attention at mealtimes, particularly in the case of infants or the severely affected elderly, in order to ensure proper nutrition. Details of the grossly neglectful infant feeding practices at the Shanghai orphanage are presented in Chapter 5. According to Zhang Shuyun, starvation-induced "listlessness" was sometimes recorded by orphanage doctors as being a sign of cerebral palsy during the "consultation" sessions.

4) "Malnutrition." This is in some ways a fairly obvious and self-explanatory medical condition, but certain important observations can nonetheless be made. In infants, especially those with congenital disabilities such as cleft palates, improper or negligent feeding practices will swiftly result in severe malnutrition and even death. Infant malnutrition can also be the result of feeding difficulties caused, for example, by severe muscular spasms or slackness of the types found in cases of cerebral palsy. But under conditions of proper medical care, it usually proves tractable and only rarely results in death. In particular, serial and massive infant death from malnutrition is something which is normally only ever associated with severely famine-struck regions of the world, and certainly not with state orphanages located in thriving metropolitan centers.

In the case of the Shanghai orphanage, moreover, there may be more than a passing connection between the prevalence of third-degree malnutrition among the orphan population until mid-1993 and the frequency with which inmates were diagnosed as being "mentally defective." According to the World Health Organization, lack of proper nutrition forms a major cause of mental retardation worldwide. (ICD-NA Category No. 263.2, "arrested development following protein-calorie malnutrition" is listed as including both "physical retardation due to malnutrition" and "psychomotor retardation due to malnutrition." Excessive administration of psychotropic and muscle-relaxant drugs can also induce psychomotor retardation in children.) It is evident that in many of the cases listed in this report, Shanghai orphanage doctors observed "listlessness" (*shen-wei*) caused by malnutrition, recorded this as being evidence of "mental deficiency" and then perversely adduced the latter as being a secondary (and on occasions even the primary) "cause of death."

As Table 4.2 shows, from the early 1990s onward orphanage medical staff began ascribing far more deaths to "third-degree malnutrition" and far fewer to "congenital malformation of brain." This diagnostic shift appears mainly to have been prompted by dissident staff members having raised their suspicions about the latter diagnosis with the Supervision Bureau investigating team. It is also conceivable that orphanage doctors simply altered their system of recording deaths on some more legitimate medical procedural grounds, although all the available documentary evidence and witness testimony suggests otherwise. In either event, malnutrition is, as noted above, a treatable condition. A detailed regimen of treatment for infants and young children suffering from malnutrition is set forth in the *Standard Rules of Nursing*, a volume distributed by the Ministry of Public Health for use by all qualified nurses in China. The book prescribes a wide range of therapies and remedial measures that should be adopted in the case of any child suffering from first-, second- or third-degree malnutrition, ranging from high-protein and high-vitamin diets and measures to avoid throat or intestinal infections, to the intensive use of intravenous drips and blood transfusions.[262] Judging from the Shanghai orphanage's medical records and the eyewitness testimony of Zhang Shuyun, however, most medical staff there appear not to be familiar with this volume.

INDEPENDENT EVALUATION OF DATA

In an attempt to ascertain whether, given a particular risk status upon admission, any inconsistency could be found between a child's documented risk on admission and the subsequent illness course and recorded cause of death, a group of U.S. physicians affiliated with the Boston–based organization Physicians For Human Rights recently analyzed, on Human Rights Watch/Asia's behalf, the case data shown in Table 4.6 documenting the infant and child deaths that occurred at the Shanghai

---

[262] See *Standard Rules of Nursing (Huli Changgui)*, Volume 1, People's Health Press (Beijing), June 1991, pp.308-310 and pp.441-442. An even more explicit set of nursing instructions for the treatment of infant malnutrition sufferers is set forth in the People's Liberation Army nursing manual, *Standard Technical Operating Rules for Medical Nurses (Yiliao Huli Jishu Caozuo Changgui)*, published by People's Army Medical Press (Beijing), 1987, pp.C430-C432.

orphanage from November 1991 through October 1992. The major issue they addressed was whether the high recorded mortality could be attributed to the fact that the orphanage admits an unusually high-risk population of children who, despite appropriate care, tend to succumb at high rates; or alternatively, to the fact that clinical and other needed care for the admitted children appeared to have been inadequate, inappropriate or denied altogether. They specifically examined the data on children who died from malnutrition, and noted their apparent nutritional status upon admission, based upon the children's recorded admission diagnoses and/or recorded weights upon admission.

According to the physicians' findings, 47 percent of the children died from malnutrition and had an admission weight recorded. Of these children, eighteen, or 38 percent of the total, had weights that placed them at less than the fifth percentile for their age, as reckoned by a comparison with U.S. National Center for Health Statistics growth charts for American children. (It should be noted in passing that Chinese children are typically somewhat smaller in size and weight than children in Western countries.) However, the remaining twenty-nine children, or 62 percent of the total, had recorded weights greater than the fifth percentile. The physicians' conclusion was that the majority of children dying of malnutrition at the Shanghai orphanage for whom admission data were available had been admitted without a diagnosis of significant malnutrition. Almost three-quarters of these children died, moreover, within six months of entering the orphanage.[263]

Individual Case Studies

In this section of the report, twelve individual cases of infant and child death at the Shanghai Children's Welfare Institute are described and examined in as much detail as the medical documentation available in each case permits.

Table 4.3 Summary of Cases

---

[263] One caution is useful in interpreting these findings. Many of the children with a dramatic downhill course were young infants, and a finding of adequate nutrition may in some cases have failed to reflect serious underlying disorders that could possibly have led to rapid nutritional deterioration. This is because certain such children may have been adequately nourished in the womb, but were unable to sustain proper nutritional growth after birth. The physicians' analysis indicates clearly, however, that the great majority of infants who died at the orphanage during the year examined did not, in fact, arrive at the orphanage critically malnourished. Rather, they found that the deterioration leading to death appeared, according to the official records, to have occurred during the children's stay at the orphanage.

#	Name	Sex	Died	Age	Recorded Cause of Death
1	Ke Yue	F	6/10/92	2 ½ years	severe malnutrition; congenital maldevelopment of brain
2	Huo Qiu	F	6/23/92	4 years	severe malnutrition; cerebral palsy; mental deficiency
3	Xie Ying	F	6/24/92	3 years	malnutrition; mental deficiency
4	Ba Zhong	F	6/30/92	6 months	malnutrition; severe dehydration; phlegmona
5	Jian Xun	M	7/17/92	11 years	recorded cause of death unknown
6	Chen Zhong	M	8/12/89	2 years	congenital maldevelopment of brain
7	Sun Zhu	F	8/12/89	3 months	congenital maldevelopment of brain
8	Guo Qing	F	12/24/91	2 ½ years	third-degree malnutrition; mentally defective
9	Zeng Yuan	F	12/29/91	2 months	congenital maldevelopment of brain function; collapse of body functions
10	Xing Qian	F	1/2/92	5 months	second or third-degree malnutrition; mentally defective (severe)
11	Yu Lei	M	1/20/92	15 months	third-degree malnutrition; severe dehydration; mentally defective
12	Ba Jun	F	2/8/92	2 months	severe malnutrition; pneumonia

Scenes From The Morgue

The photographs of dead children reproduced below are among approximately seventy such photographs that were taken by Ai Ming during June–July 1992 in the Shanghai orphanage's morgue and "waiting for death room." Of the two rolls of film shot by Ai, one was confiscated shortly afterwards by orphanage officials, who had been keeping dissident staff members and orphans under surveillance, at the privately owned photographic studio in Shanghai where it was being developed. Ai was then interrogated at length by the officials, who suspected but could not prove his involvement, but he denied all knowledge of the film or of how it had been taken. The second roll of film, which contained photographs of eleven different children, was kept hidden for the next three years at various locations around China, however, and was successfully smuggled out of the country in late 1995. The distressing physical appearance of the five children shown in the photographs below speaks eloquently for itself: all five clearly died from starvation. The case histories behind these photographs are briefly as follows:

- **Ke Yue**, a girl, was admitted to the orphanage in November 1989, the month of her birth. Two and a half years later, on June 9, 1992, orphanage doctors recorded that she had developed "third-degree malnutrition," was "breathing in shallow gasps" and had a "weak heartbeat, 88/minute." In addition, she was said to be displaying "poor response to external stimuli." On June 10, she was admitted to the Medical Ward, where she died later the same day. Two separate causes of death were diagnosed by her physician, Wu Junfeng: "severe malnutrition" and "congenital maldevelopment of brain." (Date of photographs: June 11, 1992.)

- **Huo Qiu**, a girl born in approximately February 1988, arrived at the orphanage on January 3, 1991, at the age of three. One and a half years later, on June 16, 1992, she was diagnosed as suffering from "severe malnutrition" and "cerebral palsy." By a week later, at 7:55 a.m. on June 23, she was dead. According to her medical records, she died of the two illnesses just mentioned, together with, for good measure, "mental deficiency." In a striking example of diagnostic inconsistency, however, Huo's crematorium slip, completed and signed by a person named Zhou Bing, records that she died of "congenital maldevelopment of brain"—and that, moreover, she was "male."[264] (Date of photographs: June 23, 1992.)

---

[264] Two similar cases should be mentioned in passing, if only as an illustration of the disregard for orphans' individuality and well-being which apparently prevails throughout China. The first is that of Di Qiang, a boy noted in his own medical records at the Shanghai orphanage as being "female," who died of starvation there in February 1992. (Di's case is discussed above under the heading "Summary Resolution" and "Consultation.") The second is that of "Mei Ming" ("No Name"), an infant girl found lying under a pile of blankets in an appalling state of medical neglect at the Zhaoqing Social Welfare Institute, Guangdong Province, in early 1995 by undercover filmmakers for U.K.'s Channel 4 documentary film, "The Dying Rooms," and who died three days later. After the film was screened on television in June 1995, the Chinese government issued a statement claiming that "Mei Ming" was actually a boy—despite the fact the the Channel 4 crew had photographic evidence of the girl's gender. The line drawing which appears on the front cover of this report was done on the basis of one of the photographs of "Mei Ming" taken shortly before her death

- **Xie Ying**, a girl born on April 22, 1989, was admitted to the orphanage on December 12, 1991 at the age of two and a half years. Little is known about her medical history, except that she died six months later, at 4:20 a.m. on June 24, 1992, and that the sole causes of death recorded by her physician, Lu Hongyan, were "malnutrition" and "mental deficiency." The space on Xie's crematorium slip for recording cause of death was simply left blank. (Date of photographs: June 24, 1992.)

- **Ba Zhong**, a baby girl, was admitted to the orphanage on January 3, 1992, the day after her birth, weighing a respectable 2.8 kilograms. That same day, the words "monitor intelligence" were noted down on her medical record. On the night of April 27, in Group No.7 of the Infants Section, she developed a slight fever. By May 1, her temperature had risen to 39.5°C and she was given an injection of compound amidopyrine (a drug for reducing fever). On June 17, she was admitted to the Medical Ward and diagnosed as suffering from "severe malnutrition" and "severe dehydration." Three days later, she developed a head infection caused by a bedsore, and was recorded as being "listless." She died at 7:10 a.m. on June 30, at the age of six months. Death was noted in the medical records as having resulted from "malnutrition," "severe dehydration" and "phlegmona" (an uncontrolled form of subcutaneous necrotic infection). Again, however, the crematorium slip tells a different story. According to Wu Junfeng, who filled out the form, Ba died of "congenital maldevelopment of brain." (Date of photographs: June 30, 1992.)

- **Jian Xun**, a boy born in February 1981, was admitted to the orphanage on February 24, 1988, at the age of seven. The photographs of this child were taken ten days before his death. On the day of Jian's admission, all of the indicators entered on his medical record at the time of the initial checkup show that he was in satisfactory health in all but two respects: he was deaf-mute, and apparently he had minor motor-coordination difficulties. The entries for February 24, 1988 read: "Nutritional condition satisfactory; weight twenty-nine kilograms; subcutaneous fat normal; ear, nose and throat normal; heart and lungs normal; motor development slightly imperfect; deaf-mute." Although there is no record of any intelligence tests having been carried out (something which given Jian's age would, for once, have been entirely feasible for orphanage doctors to do), he was also marked down as being "mentally deficient." He was accordingly assigned to the Disabled Section, Group No.9.

After about one year at the orphanage, Jian began showing signs of having a minor digestive problem, and in June 1989 he developed an infection of the upper respiratory tract, for which antibiotics were prescribed. His medical record then goes blank, apart from a series of brief entries showing the results of six-monthly general checkups, for a period of almost three years. These entries, however, are revealing. By June 1988, after only four months at the orphanage, his body weight had dropped from twenty-nine to twenty-two kilograms; a year later it was under twenty-four kilograms; and by June 1990 it was still only 24.5 kilograms. By November 1991, Jian's body weight had fallen to twenty-three kilograms–six less than he had weighed upon his admission to the orphanage more than three and a half years earlier. One of the nursing staff informed Zhang Shuyun that during this three-year period, Jian had begun bleeding from the stomach.

On March 9, 1992, the medical records resume again with the observations: "Frequent vomiting after eating; general condition poor; abdomen concave; subcutaneous fat sparse." A course of metoclopramide (a digestive medication for stomach upsets) and vitamin B1 was prescribed by Jian's physician on the Disabled Section, Jiang Huifang. On April 22, Jiang noted as follows: "Nutritional condition poor. Transfer [patient] to the Medical Ward. Gastritis?"

It was at this point that Jian Xun's problems began in earnest. Over the next three months, he was shunted back and forth between the Disabled Section and the Medical Ward at least four times, but the medical records show that no serious effort was made to diagnose or treat his illness during this period, despite the fact that it appears he was suffering from nothing more serious than a deteriorating gastric condition. More crucially, Jian's real problem–that he was in an advanced state of malnutrition which had been progressing steadily and without treatment since at least mid-1988–was almost entirely overlooked.[265] In April 1992, it was instructed that he receive "two [260cc] bottles of milk daily" (approximately one pint per day) for the limited period of five days, and that he be put on a further course of metoclopramide, supplemented by cephalosporin (another antibiotic.) By this time, however, he was so badly malnourished that his appearance had become severely skeletal and he could barely walk.

---

[265] Starvation itself can produce ulceration and vomiting of blood, as the peptic acids attack the stomach wall.

Above all, the medical records suggest that the main concern of both Jiang Huifang and Lu Hongyan, a senior physician on the Medical Ward, during the last three months of Jian's life was that he should not die on their respective watches and in their particular parts of the orphanage. For Jian posed a problem not usually encountered by the staff: unlike most of the orphans and abandoned children who passed through the orphanage's attritional process, he was neither an infant nor an older child classified as a "no-hoper" or "terminal" case on arrival; he was eleven years old and had been admitted in quite satisfactory health. The principal culprit in this sinister medical conspiracy appears to have been Lu Hongyan, Jian's doctor on the Medical Ward. The contrasting entries on the medical record tell the story, and in the process betray a degeneration of medical ethics to the point where the physician's role has apparently been reduced to one of merely recording the patient's slow decline, in passive but meticulous fashion, and with no meaningful effort being made to save life:

> *April 22* [1992]: General condition poor; nutritional development poor; abdomen concave; response to external stimuli just perceptible. Send to Medical Ward. (Jiang Huifang)

> *April 28, 8:00 a.m.*: After bleeding from stomach, the afflicted child was transferred to Medical Ward. After treatment, his condition has much improved...appetite is good, and no vomiting or diarrhea. Upon discharge [today], to receive two bottles of milk daily and supplementary nutritional gruel. Diagnosis: bleeding from upper digestive tract. (Lu Hongyan)

> *April 28, 9:00 a.m.*: After period of transfer to the Medical Ward, afflicted child's condition poor; thin and drawn; complexion ashen; lungs normal; heart rate and sound normal; abdomen concave; subcutaneous fat reduced; skin elasticity poor; response to external stimuli still perceptible. Diagnosis: gastritis. Treatment: two bottles of milk per day for five days. (Jiang Huifang)

On April 30, Jian Xun was prescribed a joint course of phenobarbital, metoclopramide and gentamicin (an antibiotic).[266] On May 4, Jiang again

---

[266] It is unclear why antibiotic medication was given, since there is no indication in the medical record of any infection having been suspected.

transferred him to the Medical Ward. Nine days later, Lu discharged him and recorded the following:

> *May 13, 8:00 a.m.:* After several days of treatment, the afflicted child's condition has improved. Appetite good; no vomiting or diarrhea; no positive [morbidity] indicators upon examination.
>
> Treatment: After returning to the [Disabled] Section, should get out of bed during the day. In the evenings before sleeping, tie him to bed by the hands to prevent him clutching at his throat. *(Wanshang shui shi, jiang shou zhazhu, bimian zhua hou.)* (Lu Hongyan)
>
> *May 13, 10:00 a.m.:* Upon return after ten days in the Medical Ward...afflicted child's general condition is poor; thin and drawn; complexion ashen; nutritional condition extremely poor; lungs normal; heart rate regular; abdomen soft but concave; subcutaneous fat reduced; skin elasticity poor; knee-joints chafed, red and swollen.
>
> Diagnosis: gastritis; malnutrition; mentally defective.
> Treatment: Reinforce nursing. (Jiang Huifang)

According to an orphan who later spoke with Zhang Shuyun, Jian Xun was from this time onward placed in nappies and kept tied to his bed by the hands and feet almost continuously for twenty-four hours a day. Moreover, according to Dr. Zhang, the "chafed, red and swollen" knee-joints were the result of staff having beaten them with a wooden stick to prevent Jian from struggling while he was tied down. Again, these measures were applied in the midst of the Supervision Bureau's investigations into allegations of child abuse at the orphanage. On June 2, noting that Jian's condition had become "extremely poor," Jiang Huifang again transferred him to the Medical Ward. Sixteen days later, however, Lu discharged him yet again and recorded the following:

> *June 18, 8:00 a.m.:* After treatment on the Medical Ward...afflicted child's appetite is good, with no vomiting or diarrhea. Was given gentamicin $80,000^u$ twice daily (M); vitamin B_6, 5mg (M) twice daily; vitamin B complex. Can now walk by himself, and physical strength has improved. (Lu Hongyan)

June 18, 9:00 a.m.: Afflicted child's general condition poor; malnourished; complexion ashen; lungs and heart normal; subcutaneous fat reduced; skin elasticity poor. Check for improvement in vomiting. Treatment: reinforce nursing. (Jiang Huifang)

No pain-relieving medication was prescribed at this or any other stage of Jian's protracted and probably agonizing physical decline. His medical records were temporarily removed from the orphanage's files on July 7, the day of his final admission to the Medical Ward and ten days prior to his death, by an orphan who was helping dissident staff members to document the needlessly continuing deaths at the institute. On the same day, Ai Ming went into the Medical Ward and took the photographs of Jian that appear below. The final entries in the copy of the medical record obtained by Human Rights Watch/Asia are for the same day and read, in part, as follows:

July 7, 8:00 a.m.: Afflicted child is breathing in sharp gasps; appetite poor for the past ten days; frequent vomiting. Complexion ashen; poor response to external stimuli; respiration rate 21/minute; heart rate 108/minute; nutritional state of entire body extremely poor; abdomen concave.

Diagnosis: Severe malnutrition (with metabolic acidosis?)[267]
Treatment: Standard pediatric nursing regime; regular nutrition; take temperature twice daily; vitamin B complex, two tablets twice/day orally; metoclopramide, one tablet twice/day orally. (Lu Hongyan)

It is not known on which of the two doctors' watches Jian Xun finally died. On his crematorium slip, no cause of death was recorded, and no signature was appended. (Date of photograph: July 7, 1992.)

Seven Medical Histories
In the following seven cases, the medical records of the children concerned are presented in extended format. The first two medical histories take the form of a

---

[267] Metabolic acidosis is a pH imbalance caused by severe dehydration or protein deficiency. It can also sometimes result from diabetes. Although it can be treated with bicarbonate of soda or other alkalis, the root cause–in this case, malnutrition–must be cured above all else.

complete translation of the deceased children's records, including the Consultation Record Forms. In the remaining five cases, all key entries from the children's medical records have been compiled in tabular form; in creating the tables, only substantively irrelevant items and instances of non-significant textual repetition were excluded, and particular care was taken to include any entries from the original records which might reflect creditably upon the orphanage's standards of medical care and its treatment of individual children.

- **Chen Zhong**, a boy born in May 1987 whose case was briefly mentioned above, was admitted to the orphanage in May 1989 at the age of two. He arrived in reasonable health apart from the fact that he appeared to be a deaf-mute. Despite the fact that the check-box for "Mental Development" on Chen's admissions examination form was left blank, indicating that no intelligence testing was performed, his doctor instructed staff to "monitor intelligence" in his case. Less than three months after arriving at the orphanage, Chen's health had severely deteriorated. On July 31, the "consultation" ceremony was duly carried out: Chen was diagnosed as having cerebral palsy, malnutrition and being mentally retarded. (For evidence of apparent fraudulence by staff in making the diagnosis of "cerebral palsy," see above under the heading "'Summary Resolution' and 'Consultation'.") As the medical records show, no medication or pain-relieving care was administered to Chen over the subsequent twelve days prior to his death.

[Document 1:]

SHANGHAI MUNICIPAL CHILD WELFARE INSTITUTE
SHANGHAI MUNICIPAL REHABILITATION CENTER FOR DISABLED CHILDREN [268]

INFANT AND CHILD HEALTH EXAMINATION RECORD

Name:	Chen Zhong	*Sex:*	Male	*Age:*	2 years
Born:	May 5, 1987	*Admitted:* May 5, 1989			

Date of Examination: May 6, 1989

---

[268] The Shanghai orphanage made rather indiscriminate use of the various headed notepapers at its disposal. Thus, the fact that the name "Shanghai Municipal Rehabilitation Center for Disabled Children" appears at the top of this form does not mean that the children in question were actually examined at the Rehabilitation Center; in fact, they were almost always examined in the orphanage's Reception Unit.

Exact Age:	2 years	*Heart:*	(–)
Weight:	9.25 kg	*Lungs:*	(–)
Height:	81 cm	*Liver and Spleen:*	(–)
Sitting Height:	–	*Genital Organs:*	–
Head Circumference:	46 cm	*Deformity:*	–
Chest Circumference:	48 cm	*Skeleton:*	–
Anterior Fontanelle:	Closed	*Motor Development:*	–
Subcutaneous Fat:	(–)[269]	*Mental Development:*	–
Hair:	Fine	*Evaluation of Physique:*	–
Lymph Nodes:	(–)	*Diagnosis:*	Monitor intelligence
Eyes, Ears, Nose & Throat:	(–)		Deaf-mute?
Mouth Cavity:	(–)		Cerebral palsy[270]
Teeth: Number:	10/10	*Other:*	–
Caries:	0	*Examined by:*	Jiang Huifang

[Document 2:]

SHANGHAI MUNICIPAL REHABILITATION CENTER FOR DISABLED CHILDREN

MEDICAL RECORD

Name: Chen Zhong

Admission Record

5/5/89, 3 PM:

Chen Zhong: male. Child was admitted to the orphanage yesterday afternoon. Nutritional state and development average. Heart rate: 90/min. Heartbeat regular. Lungs: (–). Abdomen soft. Good movement in all limbs. Absence of vocalization, but crying loudly. No icteric sclera or xanthochromia [yellowish discoloration of eye membrane or skin.]

△   monitor intelligence

Jiang Huifang

7/30/89, 10 AM:

After two months at the orphanage, afflicted child's general condition is poor. Appetite poor; frequent trismus [lockjaw]; feeding extremely difficult.

---

[269] The frequently occurring entry "(–)" on the medical records signifies "negative" and means that the examination showed the infant or child to be normal on the health indicator in question. By contrast, the entry "–" (i.e. with no brackets) denotes that orphanage staff recorded no details and simply left the column or check-box empty.

[270] The characters for "cerebral palsy" appear on Chen Zhong's medical record in a different handwriting and pen line than all the other entries, and appear to have been added at a later date.

PE: Listless (*shen-wei*). Thin and drawn. Nutritional development
poor. Heart: (–). Respiratory harshness. Abdomen concave.
High tension in all limbs. Light edema in lower limbs.

△   Cerebral palsy. Mentally defective. Malnutrition.

Rx: Treat illness in accordance with the symptoms.
Request Medical Department to perform Consultation.

Sheng Xiaowei

[July 31:]

Consultation performed by Luo Xiaoling, Zhao Wanhua and Jiang
Huifang of the Medical Department.

PE: Afflicted child is listless. Ashen complexion. Nutritional
development poor. No response to external stimuli. Heart sound
satisfactory. Respiratory harshness. Abdomen concave.
Subcutaneous fat all gone. High flexion and tension in limbs.

△   Cerebral palsy (all limbs); mentally defective; third-degree
malnutrition.

Rx: Treat illness in accordance with the symptoms.

Jiang Huifang

8/12/89, 2PM:

Child's pupils dilated [platycoria]; absence of response to light shone in
pupils. Respiration and heart beat ceased. Dead.

Death diagnosis: Congenital maldevelopment of brain.

Jiang Huifang

[Document 3:]

SHANGHAI MUNICIPAL CHILD WELFARE INSTITUTE
CONSULTATION RECORD FORM

Patient's Name:	Chen Zhong	*Sex:*	Male
Age:	2 years+	*Group:*	Infants' Group No.3

Summary of Medical History: After two months in the orphanage,
afflicted child's general condition is poor.
Appetite poor; has difficulty feeding;
frequent trismus; food refusal.

Summary of Examination: Thin and drawn. Listless. Nutritional
development poor. Heart (–). Respiratory
harshness. Abdomen concave. High
tension in all limbs. Light edema of lower
limbs.

Preliminary Diagnosis: 1) Cerebral palsy
2) Mentally defective

3) Malnutrition

Infants Section, Physician:
[signed:]   Sheng Xiaowei
July 31, 1989

- -

CONSULTATION RECORD
Date of Consultation: July 31, 1989

Examination: Afflicted child is listless. Complexion ashen.
Nutritional development poor. No response to
external stimuli. Heart sound satisfactory. Respiratory
harshness. Abdomen concave. Subcutaneous fat all
gone. High flexion and tension in all limbs.

Diagnosis: Cerebral palsy (all limbs).
Mentally defective (severe).
Third-degree malnutrition

Treatment Instructions: Treat illness in accordance with the symptoms

Consultation Performed By Physician: [signed:]
Luo Xiaoling, Zhao Wanhua, Jiang Huifang

- **Sun Zhu**, a baby girl born in May 1989, was admitted to the orphanage at the age of one month. Medical staff recorded her general condition on arrival as "poor," although her weight was normal and, according to Zhang Shuyun, she was merely suffering from the effects of diarrhea. No entry was made in the "Mental Development" check-box, but Sun was nonetheless branded as being "mentally defective." In late July, after a seven-week gap in the medical records, Sun was suddenly said to be suffering from third-degree malnutrition, for which condition nothing more substantial than vitamin supplements was prescribed. "Consultation" was performed ten days later, the girl was again diagnosed as being "mentally defective"; a query was raised that she might also have cerebral palsy, although the only indications were that she was "listless" and had "high muscular tension in all limbs," probably because she was starving. In any event, no medication or treatment was prescribed, and three days later Sun died, ostensibly of "congenital maldevelopment of brain."

[Document 1:]

SHANGHAI MUNICIPAL CHILD WELFARE INSTITUTE
SHANGHAI MUNICIPAL REHABILITATION CENTER FOR DISABLED CHILDREN
INFANT AND CHILD HEALTH EXAMINATION RECORD

| *Name:* | Sun Zhu | *Sex:* | Female | *Age:* | 1 month |
| *Born:* | May 6, 1989 | *Admitted:* | June 6, 1989 | | |

Date of Examination: June 7, 1989

Exact Age:	1 month	*Heart:*	(–)
Weight:	3.5 kg	*Lungs:*	(–)
Height:	46 cm	*Liver and Spleen:*	(–)
Sitting Height:	–	*Genital Organs:*	–
Head Circumference: 34 cm		*Deformity:*	–
Chest Circumference: 32 cm		*Skeleton:*	–
Anterior Fontanelle: 2 x 2 cm		*Motor Development:* –	
Subcutaneous Fat: little		*Mental Development:* –	
Hair:	none	*Evaluation of Physique:* –	
Lymph Nodes:	(–)	*Diagnosis:*	Mentally defective
Eyes, Ears, Nose & Throat: (–)			
Mouth Cavity:	0		
Teeth: *Number:* 0		*Other:*	–
Caries: 0		*Examined by:*	Jiang Huifang

[Document 2:]

SHANGHAI MUNICIPAL REHABILITATION CENTER FOR DISABLED CHILDREN
MEDICAL RECORD

Name: Sun Zhu

Admission Record

6/7/89, 10AM:

Child was admitted to orphanage yesterday; female infant of around one year old. General condition poor. Slight respiratory harshness. Heart rate 140/min; heartbeat regular. Abdomen soft. Liver and spleen not palpable [i.e., both normal]. No icteric sclera or xanthochromia. Poor response to external stimuli.

Δ　　　Mentally defective.

Jiang Huifang

7/29/89, 10AM

Nurse reports child is listless, appetite poor.

PE:　　General condition poor. Thin and drawn. Ashen complexion.
　　　　Lungs (–). Heart rate 98/min. Heartbeat regular. Abdomen soft.
　　　　Liver and spleen not palpable.

Δ　　　Third-degree malnutrition.

Rx:　　Reinforce nutrition.
　　　　Vit. C + Vit. B complex x 20 packets
　　　　　　　1 tablet, 3 times/day (general supplies)

Jiang Huifang

8/9/89, 3PM

Nurse reports child's general condition has been poor since admission to orphanage. Frequent food refusal.

PE:　　General condition poor. Thin and drawn. Ashen complexion.
　　　　Lungs (–). Heartbeat regular. Abdomen soft. High muscular
　　　　tension in all limbs. Poor response to external stimuli.

Δ　　　Mentally defective.
　　　　Malnutrition.

Rx:　　Request Medical Department to perform consultation.

Jiang Huifang

[8/9/89:]

Consultation performed by Luo Xiaoling, Zhao Wanhua and Jiang Huifang of the Medical Department.

PE:　　Afflicted child is listless. Nutritional development poor. Thin
　　　　and drawn. Ashen complexion. Poor response to external
　　　　stimuli. Heart sound satisfactory. Heartbeat regular. Both lungs
　　　　(–). Abdomen soft. High muscular flexion and tension in all
　　　　limbs.

Δ　　　1) Mentally defective. 2) Cerebral palsy?

Rx:　　Treat illness in accordance with the symptoms.

8/12/89, 6AM
Child's pupils dilated; absence of response to light shone in pupils.
Respiration and heartbeat ceased. Dead.
Death diagnosis: Congenital maldevelopment of brain.

Jiang Huifang

[Document 3:]

SHANGHAI MUNICIPAL CHILD WELFARE INSTITUTE
CONSULTATION RECORD FORM

Patient's Name:	Sun Zhu	*Sex:*	Female
Age:	3 months	*Group:*	Infants' Reception Unit

Summary of Medical History: Since admission to orphanage, child's general condition rather poor. Frequent food refusal.

Summary of Examination: General condition poor. Thin and drawn. Ashen complexion. Lungs: (–). Heartbeat regular. Abdomen soft. High tension in all limbs. Poor response to external stimuli.

Preliminary Diagnosis: Mentally defective.
Malnutrition.

Infants Section, Physician:
[signed:] Jiang Huifang
August 9, 1989

CONSULTATION RECORD
Date of Consultation: August 9, 1989

Examination: Afflicted child is listless. Nutritional develoment poor. Thin and drawn. Ashen complexion. Poor response to external stimuli. Heart sound satisfactory; heartbeat regular. Lungs: (–). Abdomen soft. High flexion and tension in all limbs.

Diagnosis: Mentally defective.
Cerebral palsy?

Treatment Instructions: Treat illness in accordance with the symptoms.

Consultation Performed By Physician: [signed:]
Luo Xiaoling, Zhao Wanhua, Jiang Huifang

• **Guo Qing**, a baby girl born on April 2, 1989, with a harelip and cleft palate, was admitted to the orphanage on April 19 at the age of two weeks. Her vital signs were all recorded as "normal" on admission; she developed bronchitis eight months later, but this was treated with antibiotics and she apparently recovered well. In January 1990, she was fortunate enough to be transferred to the Rehabilitation Center for a harelip repair operation, which was carried out without major incident. A month later, she contracted an upper respiratory infection and in May 1990 had a bout of enteritis, but again recovered well from both. On September 10, the upper respiratory infection returned, and she received preliminary medication. The medical record then goes blank for a period of fifteen months, apart from brief entries indicating that her weight dropped from 6.05 kilograms at age fourteen months to a perilous 5.25 kilograms in November 1991, by which time she was more than two and a half years old. On December 14, 1991, "consultation" was performed and Guo was diagnosed as suffering from third-degree malnutrition and being "mentally defective." There then follows a ten-day period in which no entries appear on the medical record. On December 24, 1991, Guo died. The causes of death were recorded as "third-degree malnutrition" and "mental deficiency."

GUO QING (♀)		
Date	**Examination and Symptoms**	**Diagnosis and Treatment**
April 19, 1989	*Admitted to orphanage and placed in Infants Section's Reception Unit. Examined by Jiang Huifang (JH), a doctor in the Infants Section:* * Two-week-old infant with harelip and cleft palate * Nutritional development quite OK * Complexion ruddy * Movement in all limbs normal * Weight: 3.25 kg * Lungs (–) [All other indicators recorded as "normal"]	*Recorded by JH:* * Harelip and cleft palate * Monitor intelligence *(zhi-guan)*
April 20 –May 18	*Reception Unit. No entries on medical record for one month.*	
May 19	*Recorded by JH:* *Reception unit now full, so infant has been temporarily transferred to care of the sick ward	

GUO QING (♀)		
Date	**Examination and Symptoms**	**Diagnosis and Treatment**
May 20 –Dec.12	*No entries on medical record for almost seven months. Guo Qing's location during this period is not recorded.*	
Dec.13	*Location still unknown. Recorded by JH at 10:00 a.m.:* * Severe coughing * No temperature [sic], diarrhea or vomiting * General health OK * Conscious * Respiratory harshness in both lungs, no dry or moist rales [gurgling sounds from lungs]	*JH's diagnosis:* * Cough *JH's treatment instructions:* * Cephalosporin, 125 mg tabs. x 3, 1/6 tab. three times/day * Cough mixture 15^{cc} mixed with Phenergan 15^{cc}, administer 1^{cc} [sic] three times/day
Dec.14	[Same symptoms as previous day]	*JH's treatment instructions:* * Fosfomycin in syrup 10 gm, 1/6 three times/day
Dec. 15	*No entries on medical record.*	
Dec. 16	*Recorded by JH at 10:00 a.m.:* * Severe coughing [Other symptoms same as on Dec. 13] * Presence of phlegm audible in lungs	*JH's diagnosis:* * Bronchitis *JH's treatment instructions:* * Penicillin K, 400,000^{u} bottles x 6, 400,000^{u} twice/day IM [intramuscular]
Dec. 17–18	*No entries on medical record*	
Dec. 19	*Recorded by JH at 10:00 a.m.:* * Coughing improved * No temperature, vomiting or diarrhea * General health acceptable * Respiratory harshness in both lungs, no dry or moist rales	*JH's diagnosis:* * Bronchitis *JH's treatment instructions:* * Penicillin K, 400,000^{u} bottles x 6, 400,000^{u} twice/day IM
Dec 20– Jan. 5, 1990	*No entries on medical record. Guo Qing's location still not recorded.*	

GUO QING (♀)		
Date	**Examination and Symptoms**	**Diagnosis and Treatment**
Jan. 6	*Recorded by JH at 11:00 a.m.:* * General health acceptable * Conscious * Temperature steady * Appetite good, takes milk five times/day and powdered-rice paste [*naigao*] twice/day * Transfer infant to Rehabilitation Center's (RC) Medical Ward to carry out repair of harelip *4:00 p.m.: Examined by Xu Weihe (XW), head doctor in RC Medical Ward:* * Heart rate 120/min., steady, no pathologic murmur * Respiration rate 40/min. * Second-degree harelip on left side, with cleft palate	*XW's treatment instructions:* * Prepare to conduct harelip repair operation
Jan. 7–19	*RC's sick ward. No entries on medical record for 12 days.*	
Jan. 20	*Recorded by XW:* * Weight: 5.2 kg * Tested for allergy to Procaine and Penicillin	
Jan. 21	*No entries on medical record*	
Jan. 22	*RC Medical Ward. Recorded by XW at 12:50 p.m.:* * Harelip repair operation carried out at 9:30 AM * Operation successful, little blood loss	*XW's treatment instructions:* * Penicillin G procaine, 10 x 400,000^u bottles, 400,000^u twice/day IM
Jan. 23	*No entries on medical record*	
Jan. 24	*Recorded by XW at 8:00 a.m.:* * General health good * Temperature (at anus) 38.3°C * Appetite good * Basically recovered from operation	
Jan. 25	*RC's sick ward. No entries on medical record*	
Jan. 26	*Recorded by XW:* * Avoid any stretching of lip wound	*XW's treatment instructions:* * Penicillin G procaine, 10 x 400,000^u bottles, 400,000^u twice/day IM

Guo Qing (♀)		
Date	**Examination and Symptoms**	**Diagnosis and Treatment**
Jan. 27–30	*No entries to medical record for three days.*	
Jan. 31	*RC Medical Ward. Recorded by XW:* * Physical condition excellent * Appetite good, temperature normal * Stitches removed today * Wounds not healed well at base of nose and on lips, but no bleeding or infection	
Feb. 1–21	*RC Medical Ward. No entries on medical record for 11 days.*	
Feb. 22	*Recorded by XW:* * Condition good: child to be returned to its group *(xiao zu)* at the Infants Section today	
Feb. 23–25	*Infants Section. No entries on medical record.*	
Feb. 26	*8:40 a.m.: Recorded by Lu Jingdi (LJ), a paramedic responsible for orphanage's X-ray work:* * Coughing for two days, no fever * General condition fair * Respiratory harshness in both lungs	*LJ's diagnosis:* * Upper respiratory infection *LJ's treatment instructions:* * Erythromycin estolate 0.125 x three days, one tab. three times/day * Cough mixture 50ᶜᶜ
Feb. 27– May 25	*No entries on medical record for two months.*	
May 26	*Infants Section, 10:00 a.m.. Examined by Jiang Huifang (JH):* * Complexion rather ashen * Runny diarrhea twice * No vomiting or fever * General condition fair * Conscious * Lungs normal	*JH's diagnosis:* * Enteritis *JH's treatment instructions:* * Furazolidone 0.1 x two tabs. and Vitamin B_6 x two tabs., each 1/6 three times/day
May 27–29	*No entries on medical record.*	
May 30	*Recorded by JH at 10:00 a.m.:* [Symptoms same as on May 26]	*JH's diagnosis and treatment instructions:* [Same as listed on May 26]

GUO QING (♀)		
Date	**Examination and Symptoms**	**Diagnosis and Treatment**
May 31 –Sep. 9	*Infants Section. No entries on medical record for three months, apart from following:* * June 19: [age 14 months:] weight 6.05 kg	
Sep. 10	*Infants Section, 10:00 a.m.. Examined by Lu Yin[271] (LY), paramedic in the section:* * Temperature 39°C * No coughing, diarrhea or vomiting * General condition still fair * Repiratory harshness in both lungs, no dry or moist rales	*LY's diagnosis:* * Upper respiratory infection *LY's treatment instructions:* * Compound amidopyrine ampoule 2^{cc} x 1, 1/3^{cc} ST [immediately],IM * S.M.Z. co 0.2 x 6 tabs., ½ tab. twice/day
Sep. 11, 1990– Dec. 13, 1991	*No entries to medical record for fifteen months, apart from following:* * Nov. 1990: age 1½ years; weight 5.5kg * Nov. 1991: age 2½ years; weight 5.25 kg [NB: weight at age 14 months was 6.05 kg]	
Dec. 14	*Infants Section, 10:00 a.m.. Sheng Xiaowei (SX), a paramedic and head of the Infants Section, requests Luo Xiaoling (LX), head of the Medical Department, to perform Consultation.* *Recorded on Consultation Record Form (huizhen jiludan), signed by LX:* * Listless * Complexion ashen * Nutritional development extremely poor * Thin and drawn, hair falling out * Poor response to external stimuli * Abdomen concave; subcutaneous fat all gone; skin elasticity poor * Limb flexion and tension low * Skin temperature cold * Respiratory harshness in both lungs * Cleft palate, repaired harelip	*SX's diagnosis:* * Mentally defective * Third-degree malnutrition * Cleft palate, repaired harelip *Recorded on Consultation Record Form, signed by LX:* *Diagnosis:* * Mentally defective * Third-degree malnutrition * Cleft palate *Treatment:* * Treat illness in accordance with the symptoms
Dec. 15–23	*Still in Infants Section. No entries on medical record for eight-day period.*	

---

[271] Lu Yin was reportedly one of the more conscientious members of the orphanage's medical staff; she frequently criticized the low level of medical ethics that prevailed and sought to raise the overall standard of treatment of the children.

GUO QING (♀)		
Date	**Examination and Symptoms**	**Diagnosis and Treatment**

Dec. 24	*Infants Section. Lu Yin notes in medical record that Guo Qing died at 3:00 p.m.:*
	 * Respiration and heartbeat ceased
	 * Both pupils dilated
	 * No response to light shone in pupils
		LY's diagnosis:
		 * Death from:
		   1) Mental deficiency
		   2) Third-degree malnutrition

- **Zeng Yuan**, a baby girl born on October 25, 1991, was admitted to the orphanage on November 30, 1991 weighing a bouncing 4.5 kilograms and reportedly well in all other important respects. However, she was marked down as a "monitor intelligence" case. Three days later, implausibly enough, her physician recorded that she was suffering from "second-degree malnutrition." By December 12, she was "listless," showed "poor response to external stimuli," and her subcutaneous fat layer had vanished and the shape of her intestines had become visible. The next day, "consultation" was carried out and she was diagnosed as suffering from "congenital maldevelopment of brain." The doctor ordered the nursing staff to "take measures in accordance with the symptoms," followed as usual by a complete blank on the medical records. Two weeks later, Zeng died, ostensibly of "congenital maldevelopment of brain function" and "total circulatory failure."

ZENG YUAN (♀)		
Date	**Examination and Symptoms**	**Diagnosis and Treatment**
Nov.30, 1991	*Admitted to orphanage and placed in Infants Section's Reception Unit. Examined by Lu Yin (LY), a paramedic in the Infants Section:* * General health acceptable * No fever, coughing, vomiting or diarrhea * Conscious *(shen qing)* * Appetite fair * Limb movement normal * Weight: 4.5 kg * Heart and lungs (–) [All other indicators recorded as "normal"]	*Recorded by LY:* * Monitor intelligence
Dec. 1	*Reception Unit. No entries on medical record.*	

ZENG YUAN (♀)		
Date	**Examination and Symptoms**	**Diagnosis and Treatment**
Dec.2	* Listless *(shen wei)* * Appetite rather poor * No fever, coughing, vomiting or diarrhea * Conscious * Heart and lungs normal	*LY's diagnosis:* * Second-degree malnutrition *LY's treatment instructions:* * Keep under observation *(ji guan)*
Dec.3-5	*Reception Unit. No entries on medical record.*	
Dec.6	* Listless * Appetite poor * Heart and lungs normal	*LY's diagnosis:* * Second-degree malnutrition *LY's treatment instructions:* * Keep warm, pay attention to nutrition
Dec. 7-11	*Reception Unit. No entries on medical record.*	
Dec.12	* Listless * Appetite poor * No fever, coughing, vomiting or diarrhea * Heartbeat low and shallow * Respiration normal, no unusual sounds * Shape of intestines visible through abdomen * Subcutaneous fat layer thin and sparse * Poor response to external stimuli	*LY's diagnosis:* * Second to third-degree malnutrition *LY's treatment instructions:* * Request head of Medical Department to perform Consultation
Dec.13	*Reception Unit. Consultation performed by Wu Junfeng (WJ), a doctor and deputy-head of Medical Department, with LY also present.* *Recorded on Consultation Record Form, signed by WJ:* * Expression blank and withdrawn * Anterior fontanelle sunken * Heartbeat shallow and weak, 84/min. * Lungs normal * Subcutaneous fat all gone * Outline of intestines visible	*Recorded on Consultation Record Form, signed by WJ:* *Diagnosis:* * Congenital maldevelopment of brain * General collapse of body functions *Treatment:* * Take measures in accordance with the symptoms
Dec. 14-28	*Reception Unit. No entries on medical record for two weeks.*	

ZENG YUAN (♀)		
Date	**Examination and Symptoms**	**Diagnosis and Treatment**
Dec.29	*Reception Unit. LY notes in medical record that Zeng Yuan died at 9:00 a.m.:* * Heart beat and respiration ceased * Both pupils dilated * No response to light shone in pupils	*LY's diagnosis:* * Death from congenital maldevelopment of brain-function; general collapse of body functions; total circulatory failure

● **Xing Qian**, a girl born on August 9, 1991, was admitted to the orphanage one month later on September 9. Her weight on arrival was 3.6 kilograms, her heart and lungs were normal, and she had no deformities, but again, nurses were instructed to "monitor intelligence." From late October until mid-December, she is said to have suffered from various respiratory tract infections, which were treated with antibiotics. During the second half of December, she developed a lymph node infection, but this responded to penicillin, and by December 22, Xing was recorded as having fully recovered. There then follows an eight-day period in which no entries appear on the medical record. On December 31, "consultation" was performed: the recorded symptoms included "extremely poor response to external stimuli," "hoarse and barely audible moanings", and "subcutaneous fat layer thin and sparse." She was duly diagnosed as suffering from "second- or third-degree malnutrition"–and as being "mentally defective (severe)." The nurses were told to "treat the illness in accordance with the symptoms," and two days later Xing was dead. The causes of death were recorded as "second- to third-degree malnutrition" and "mental deficiency (severe)."[272]

---

[272] The medical record was subsequently tampered with by orphanage officials in an attempt to show that Xing Qian was mentally retarded. On the new admissions' medical examination form (*Ying-You Er Jiankang Jiancha Jilubiao*) the characters *zhi-guan* ("monitor intelligence") were clearly entered on the day of admission. But in the entry for the same day (September 9) on the main medical record (*Bing Shi Jilu*), the character *guan* was later partially deleted and clumsily altered to read *li* (it actually ended up resembling the similar character *jiu*, "a long time"), and the new characters *bu zu* added. The revised entry on the main medical record thus reads *zhili bu zu:* "mentally defective." The forgers evidently forgot, however, to alter the entry on the new admissions' medical form, thus leaving clear trace of their activities.

XING QIAN (♀)		
Date	**Examination and Symptoms**	**Diagnosis and Treatment**
Sep. 9, 1991	*Admitted to orphanage and placed in Infants Section's Reception Unit. Examined by Lu Yin (LY) a paramedic in the Infants Section:* * Conscious * Weight: 3.6 kg * Lymph nodes (–) * Heart and lungs (–) * No deformities [All other indicators recorded as "normal"]	*Recorded by LY:* * Monitor intelligence
Sep. 10–Oct. 29	*No entries on medical record for seven weeks.*	
Oct. 30	*Xing Qian's location in orphanage not recorded. Examined by Wang Jihong (WJ), a paramedic in the Infants Section:* * Running high fever: 39.1°C * Coughing, no sputum or diarrhea * Appetite fair * Heart and lungs normal	*WJ's diagnosis:* * Infection of upper respiratory tract *WJ's treatment instructions:* * Penicillin 400,000^u twice/day IM, eight bottles [i.e. a four-day course]
Oct.31–Nov. 20	*Location unrecorded. No entries on medical record for three weeks.*	
Nov. 21	*Examined by Lu Yin (LY), a paramedic in the Infants Section:* * Coughing and vomiting milk for two days * Listless * Appetite poor * Breathing in gasps * Heart rate: 100/min. * Respiratory harshness; rales audible in lungs	*LY's diagnosis:* * Bronchitis *LY's treatment instructions:* * Penicillin K, 3 x 400,000^u bottles, 200,000^u twice/day IM [i.e. three-day course] * Cough syrup: 30^{cc} bottle (x 1), 0.5^{cc} three times/day orally
Nov. 22 –Dec. 3	*Location unrecorded. No entries on medical record for eleven days.*	
Dec. 4	*Examined by LY:* * Coughing for two days * Severe vomiting of milk * Conscious * Appetite fair * Respiratory harshness and rales in both lungs	*LY's diagnosis:* * Bronchitis *LY's treatment instructions:* * Penicillin K, 3 x 400,000^u bottle, 200,000^u twice/day IM
Dec. 5-15	*Location unrecorded. No entries on medical record for ten days.*	

XING QIAN (♀)		
Date	**Examination and Symptoms**	**Diagnosis and Treatment**
Dec. 16	*Examined by LY:* * Swelling below left jaw for two days, with coughing * No fever, vomiting or diarrhea * Listless * Appetite rather poor * Respiratory harshness in both lungs; no rales	*LY's diagnosis:* * Acute suppurating infection of lymph node *LY's treatment instructions:* * Penicillin K, 6 x 400,000ᵁ bottles, 200,000ᵁ twice/day IM * Cough mixture: 30ᶜᶜ bottle (x 2), 5ᶜᶜ three times/day orally
Dec. 17	*LY requests Luo Xiaoling (LX) to examine patient:* * Acute suppurating infection of lymph node * Conscious * Appetite fair * Heart and lungs normal * Abdomen and skin normal	*LX's treatment instructions:* * Add Kanamycin, 1 x 1gm bottle, 0.1gm twice/day IM
Dec. 18-21	*No entries on medical record*	
Dec.22	*Examined by LY:* * Appetite poor, vomiting milk * No fever, coughing, vomiting [sic] or diarrhea * Recovered from lymph node infection * Listless * Heart rate 130/min. * Respiratory harshness in both lungs, no rales	*LY's diagnosis:* * Second-degree malnutrition * Poor digestion *LY's treatment instructions:* * Lactasin complex, five tablets, ½ tablet three times/day * Vitamin C, five 0.1 tablets, one tablet three times/day
Dec. 23-30	*No entries on medical record* for one week.	

XING QIAN (♀)		
Date	**Examination and Symptoms**	**Diagnosis and Treatment**
Dec. 31	*In Medical Ward (date of transfer not recorded). Examined by LY:* * Listless * Appetite poor for past week, refused last two meals * All four limbs cold * Poor response to external stimuli * Heartbeat: low and shallow * Respiratory harshness in both lungs; no rales *Consultation performed by Luo Xiaoling (LX). Recorded on Consultation Record Form, signed by LX:* * Listless * Extremely poor response to external stimuli * Hoarse and barely audible moanings * Poor state of nutrition and growth * Heartbeat low and weak * Respiratory harshness in both lungs * Subcutaneous fat layer thin and sparse * All limbs very cold	*LY's diagnosis:* * Second or third-degree malnutrition * Mentally defective (severe) *LY's treatment instructions:* * Request head of medical department to perform Consultation. *Recorded on Consultation Record Form. signed by LX:* *Diagnosis:* * Third-degree malnutrition * Mentally defective *Treatment:* * Treat illness in accordance with the symptoms * Reinforce nursing and observation
Jan 1, 1992	*No entries on medical record*	
Jan. 2	*3:10 p.m.: LY notes in medical record:* * Respiration and heartbeat ceased * Both pupils dilated * No response to light shone in pupils	*LY's diagnosis:* * Death from: 1) Second to third-degree malnutrition 2) mental deficiency (severe)

- **Yu Lei**, a boy born on October 5, 1990, was admitted to the orphanage on October 14, 1991 at one year of age. On arrival, his vital body signs were all recorded as "normal," but he was diagnosed as being "mentally defective." In addition, his weight appears on the medical record for the day of admission as "6 kg." Upon close examination, however, it is clear that the numeral "6" has been superimposed over the original entry, since it appears in considerably larger handwriting and a thicker pen line than any other entries on the record; as far as can be ascertained, the original entry reads

"10 kg."[273] Contrary to what the record shows, therefore, it would seem that Yu Lei was in fact rather well-fed at the time of his arrival at the orphanage.

After a two-month period during which no entries were made on the medical record, on December 14, Yu was diagnosed by Wu Junfeng, his physician, as being "listless" and having "third-degree malnutrition." Luo Xiaoling performed "consultation" later that day and entered on the record: "complexion ashen," "subcutaneous fat all gone" and (strangely enough) "forehead small." In addition to confirming Wu's diagnoses of third-degree malnutrition and mental deficiency, she added that Yu had bronchitis, but prescribed no medication. Five days later, on December 19, the record states that Wu prescribed a course of antibiotics, although this may also represent a later falsification.[274] In any event, there is the clearest possible evidence–namely, the existence of two entirely different versions–to show that from December 20, 1991, until January 20, 1992, the day of Yu's death, his medical record was entirely rewritten by orphanage staff at a later date. Both versions of the record are included below for purposes of comparison.

According to the first and apparently authentic version, no entries were made to the record for an entire month between December 19, 1991 and January 18, 1992, on which day Yu was transferred to the Medical Ward and observed by Lu Hongyan, a doctor there, to be in an utterly deplorable condition. Lu failed, however, to leave any record indicating that Yu was suffering from anything other than sheer starvation and dehydration. No remedial measures were apparently adopted, and two days later, Yu died. The diagnoses of death recorded by Lu were: "third-degree malnutrition," severe dehydration" and "mentally defective."

---

[273] The same forgery appears on both the new admissions' medical examination form and the main medical record.

[274] The entry for December 19 seems to have been either altered–the date appears to have been superimposed over an original "Dec. 17"–or fabricated in its entirety. The latter is suggested by the fact that Sheng Xiaowei reentered verbatim here the symptoms and diagnosis written by Luo Xiaoling on the Consultation Record Form five days earlier, but this time prescribed a course of medication–something that was conspicuously absent from the Consultation Record Form. Since there remains a modicum of doubt as to the inauthenticity of the "December 19" entry, however, we have included it here as part of the pre-altered portion of the medical record. In most other such cases from the Shanghai orphanage, the alteration and/or fabrication of the medical records was performed so clumsily as to be immediately apparent.

The main features of the second version of the medical record are that it attempts to indicate that Yu suffered a bout of middle-ear infection, that he was suspected of having cerebral palsy, and that he received a limited amount of medication. However, the eventual causes of death recorded are identical to those appearing on the first version of the document. Moreover, the fabrication was apparently done in such haste that a "clerical error" of considerable importance occurred: in the final entry, dated "January 20, 1992, 8:00 a.m.," it is recorded that Yu Lei "died on the evening of January 20."

YU LEI (♂)		
Date	**Examination and Symptoms**	**Diagnosis and Treatment**
Oct. 14, 1991	*Admitted to orphanage and placed in Infants Section's Reception Unit. Examined by Lu Yin (LY), a paramedic in the Infants Section:* * Conscious (*shen-qing*) * Weight 6 kg [falsified entry: see above] * Heart and lungs (–) * Mental retardation *(jingshen fayu chi)* [All other indicators recorded as "normal"]	*LY's diagnosis:* * Mentally defective *LY's treatment instructions:* * Keep under observation
Oct.15– Dec. 13	*Infants Section. No entries on medical record for two months.*	

Yu Lei (♂)		
Date	**Examination and Symptoms**	**Diagnosis and Treatment**
Dec. 14	*Infants Section, Group #3. Recorded at 2:00 p.m. by Sheng Xiaowei (SX), a paramedic and head of the Infants Section:* * After over a month in the orphanage, general health poor, no response to external stimuli * Appetite poor, has difficulty feeding * No clear improvement after feeding and drinking adjustments * Listless * Abdomen concave	*SX's diagnosis:* * Mentally defective (severe) * Third-degree malnutrition
	SX requests Luo Xiaoling (LX), head of the medical department, to perform Consultation. Recorded on Consultation Record Form, signed by LX: * Listless * Poor nutritional state; thin and drawn * Forehead small *(qian'e zhaixiao)* * Hair thin and sparse * Complexion ashen * No response to external stimuli * Moist rales in both lungs * Abdomen concave * Subcutaneous fat all gone * All limbs cold	*Recorded on Consultation Record Form, signed by LX:* *Diagnosis:* * Third-degree malnutrition * Mentally defective * Bronchitis *Treatment:* * Treat illness in accordance with the symptoms
Dec. 15–18	*Still in Infants Section [i.e., not transferred to Medical Ward]. No entries on medical record for four-day period.*	
Dec. 19	*Infants Section. Recorded by SX at 2:00 p.m.:* * Consultation performed by Luo Xiaoling, Wu Junfeng (WJ) and others * Symptoms as above [i.e., Dec. 14]	*[Repeat of (LX's and WJ's) Dec. 14] Diagnosis:* * Third-degree malnutrition * Mentally defective * Bronchitis *[Repeat of Dec. 14] Treatment instructions:* * Treat illness in accordance with the symptoms *SX's treatment instructions:* * Erythromycin estolate 0.125 x 7 tabs, one tablet three times/day * Phenergan 1^{cc} + cough mixture 2^{cc}, three times/day

YU LEI (♂)		
Date	**Examination and Symptoms**	**Diagnosis and Treatment**
VERSION I: DEC.20, 1991–JAN. 20, 1992		
Dec. 20– Jan. 17, 1992	*Infants Section. No entries on medical record for period of four weeks.*	
Jan. 18	*Yu Lei moved to Medical Ward. Examined by Lu Hongyan (LH), a doctor on the ward:* * Third-degree malnutrition * Severely dehydrated * General condition poor * Appetite poor * Low response to external stimuli * Listless * Face thin and drawn, yellowish hue * Respiration weak, heartbeat audible * No dry or moist rales in lungs * Abdomen soft * Other indicators: normal	*LH's diagnosis:* * Third-degree malnutrition * Severe dehydration * Mentally defective *LH's treatment instructions:* * Adjust eating and drinking * Take measures in accordance with the symptoms *(duizheng chuli)*
Jan. 19–20	*Medical Ward. No entries on medical record.*	
Jan. 21	*Medical Ward, 8:00 a.m.: Recorded by LH:* * Respiration and heartbeat ceased at 20:15 hrs on Jan. 20 * Absence of response to light shone in pupils * No pulse detectable in main arteries * All limbs rigid * No body temperature	*LH's diagnosis:* * Third-degree malnutrition * Severe dehydration * Mentally defective *LH's instructions:* * Remove [the corpse] *(yichu)*
VERSION II: DECEMBER 20, 1991–JANUARY 20, 1992		
Dec. 20–30, 1991	*Infants Section. No entries on medical record for ten days.*	
Dec. 31	*Infants Section. Recorded by SX at 3:00 p.m.:* * Otitis media [middle-ear infection] on both sides; pus emerging; giving off bad smell * General condition poor * Conscious * Nutritional development extremely poor * No response [to external stimuli] * Heart and lungs (−)	*SX's diagnosis:* * Otitis media *SX's treatment instructions:* * Cephalosporin 0.125 x 7 tabs, one tablet three times/day

YU LEI (♂)		
Date	**Examination and Symptoms**	**Diagnosis and Treatment**
Jan. 1–13, 1992	*Infants Section. No entries on medical record for twelve days.*	
Jan. 14	*Infants Section. Recorded by SX at 10:00 a.m.:* * No apparent results after treating illness in accordance with the symptoms and adjusting eating and drinking in recent period * Currently has considerable difficulty eating * Listless; thin and drawn; general condition poor * Eyes set in fixed stare *(shuangyan ningshi)* * Heartbeat low and weak * Both lungs (–) * Abdomen concave * Subcutaneous fat all gone * All four limbs highly tense * No response to external stimuli	*SX's diagnosis:* * Third-degree malnutrition * Mentally defective (severe) *SX's treatment instructions:* * Treat illness in accordance with the symptoms * When necessary, transfer [patient] to the Medical Ward
Jan. 15–16	*Still in Infants Section. No entries on medical record.*	
Jan. 17	*Moved to Medical Ward. Examined by Lu Hongyan (LH), a doctor on the ward:* * Not exactly in high spirits *(jingshen qianjia)* * Fair response to external stimuli * Appetite poor * No fever, coughing, vomiting or diarrhea * Conscious * Nutritional state not ideal *(yingyang qianjia)* * Thin and drawn * All four limbs stiff and rigid, as in cerebral palsy syndrome *(cheng nao-tan zhuang)* * Severe eczema on both sides of lower body * Heart rate: 88/min. * Respiration in both lungs (–); no dry or moist rales * Abdomen soft, no pain on pressure	*LH's diagnosis:* * Severe malnutrition * Mentally disabled *(zhi-can)* *LH's treatment instructions:* * Administer *Ying'er Su* [a Chinese digestive medication for children], one packet three times/day * Feed with cows' milk: six measures, three times/day [i.e. a total of 180^{cc}/day] * GS [glucose solution] 10^{cc} + Vitamin C 0.3 gm, twice/day, orally
Jan. 18–19	*Medical Ward. No entries on medical record.*	

Yu Lei (♂)		
Date	**Examination and Symptoms**	**Diagnosis and Treatment**
Jan. 20	*Medical Ward. LH records at 8:00 a.m.:* * Failed to respond to treatment over recent period * Died on the evening of January 20 [sic] from severe imbalance/maladjustment *(yanzhong shitiao)* and severe dehydration * Respiration and heartbeat ceased * No pulse detectable in main arteries * No response to light shone in pupils * No body temperature	*LH's diagnosis:* * Third-degree malnutrition * Severe dehydration * Mentally defective *LH's instructions:* * Remove [the corpse] *(yichu)*

•   **Ba Jun**, a girl born on December 2, 1991, was admitted to the orphanage on January 2, 1992 at the age of one month. On the day of arrival, her medical record states: "general health quite satisfactory," limb movement normal" and "weight: 3.8 kg." Although the "Mental Development" check-box was left blank, nurses were nonetheless instructed to "monitor intelligence." For the next ten days, no entries appear on the medical record. By January 13, Ba's condition had drastically and inexplicably deteriorated, and Luo Xiaoling was summoned to perform "consultation." Noting that the infant was "listless" and of "ashen complexion," she diagnosed poor digestion and second-degree malnutrition. Later that day, Ba's physician, Lu Hongyan, recorded that she was suffering from pulmonary infection–something which Luo had apparently overlooked–and prescribed a course of medication.

A strange shadow play then ensued, in which, over the subsequent three weeks, Ba's condition continued to decline despite her doctors having prescribed no fewer than five different types of antibiotic. By January 18, she had developed third-degree malnutrition, and bronchial pneumonia was diagnosed. The following day she was admitted to the Medical Ward. On January 28, Lu declared her "recovered from bronchial pneumonia" and to be of "rosy complexion." Three days later, she was diagnosed with bronchitis and medication was ostensibly resumed. But on February 4, Ding Yi, head of the Medical Ward, examined her and noted on the record: "all limbs cold," "triple concave syndrome"[275] and "has lost capacity to suckle."

---

[275] *I.e.*, sunken eyes, deep hollows on the sides of the neck and concave abdomen.

Although stating explicitly that her illness was "now critical," Ding casually wrote: "Had intended to administer oxygen therapy, but valve of oxygen cylinder blocked, so did not proceed with treatment." On February 7, he further recorded: "To date, staff have neglected to carry out my instructions to administer antibiotics." Ba Jun died the following morning, and the final entry on her medical record reads: "death from severe malnutrition and pneumonia."

BA JUN (♀)		
Date	**Examination and Symptoms**	**Diagnosis and Treatment**
Jan. 2, 1992	*Admitted to orphanage and placed in Infants Section's Reception Unit. Examined by Lu Yin (LY), a paramedic in the Infants Section:* * General health quite satisfactory. * No fever, coughing, vomiting or diarrhea * Conscious * Limb movement normal * Weight: 3.8 kg * Heart and lungs (–) [All other indicators recorded as "normal"]	*Recorded by LY:* * Monitor intelligence
Jan. 3–12	*Reception Unit. No entries on medical record for ten days.*	

BA JUN (♀)		
Date	**Examination and Symptoms**	**Diagnosis and Treatment**
Jan. 13	*Reception Unit. Lu Yin requests head of Medical Department to perform Consultation (huizhen). 11:00 a.m.: Consultation performed by Luo Xiaoling (LX), a nursing paramedic and head of orphanage's Medical Department.* *Recorded on Consultation Record Form, signed by LX:* * Ashen complexion * Listless * Poor response to external stimuli * Poor state of nutritional development * Heartbeat fair, 120/min. * Respiratory harshness in both lungs * Skin and limb temperature low * Diaper rash *2:30 p.m.: Examined by Lu Hongyan (LH), a doctor on General Medical Ward:* * Respiratory harshness in both lungs; no rales detectable	*Recorded on Consultation Record Form, signed by LX:* *Diagnosis:* * Poor digestion * Second-degree malnutrition *Treatment:* * Adjust eating and drinking * Treat illness in accordance with the symptoms * Reinforce nursing and observation *LH's diagnosis:* * Pulmonary infection *LH's treatment instructions:* * 25% GS [glucose solution] 20^{cc} with Vitamin C 250mg P.O., once/day * Lincomycin 0.6gm twice/day, IM
Jan. 14	*Reception Unit. Recorded by LY:* * Improvement in spirits * Conscious * Appetite better * Respiratory harshness in both lungs; no rales audible	*LY's diagnosis:* * Digestion poor * Malnutrition * Lung infection *LY's treatment instructions:* [Same as LH's of previous day]
Jan. 15	*Reception Unit. (LY):* * Ashen complexion * Appetite poor * Respiration: [no change from previous day]	*LY's diagnosis and treatment instructions:* [Same as on previous day]
Jan. 16	*Reception Unit. (LY):* * Listless * Appetite poor * Respiration: [no change] *LY requests examination by Lu Hongyan*	*LH orders change of medication:* * [Discontinue Lincomycin,] commence Penicillin K 400,000^{u} twice/day, IM
Jan. 17	*Reception Unit. (LY):* [Same entries as previous day]	*LY's treatment instructions:* [Same as on previous day]

BA JUN (♀)		
Date	**Examination and Symptoms**	**Diagnosis and Treatment**
Jan.18	*2:00 PM: Admitted to General Medical Ward:* * Listless * Weak response to external environment * Yellowish complexion; thin and drawn * Poor nutritional state * Severe coughing with sputum; gasping for breath * Sporadic dry and moist rales in both lungs	*LH's diagnosis:* * Third-degree malnutrition * Bronchial pneumonia *LH's treatment instructions:* * Feed with cow's milk: four measures, six times daily.[276] * [Discontinue Penicillin,] commence 5% GS 500cc with Erythromycin 400,000u once/day, GTT [intravenously]
Jan.19	*Medical Ward. No entries on medical record.*	
Jan.20	*Medical Ward (LH):* * Listless * Appetite better * Face thin and drawn * Respiration rapid and gasping: rate 60/min. * Lung condition: [same entry as on Jan.18]	*LH's diagnosis:* * Bronchial pneumonia *LH's treatment instructions:* * Commence Ampicillin 0.125gm twice/daily, IM
Jan. 21-27	*Medical ward. No entries on medical record for one week.*	
Jan.28	*Medical Ward (LH):* * Coughing and sputum production now stopped * Complexion rosy; conscious * Appetite returned; no sputum or diarrhea * Respiratory harshness in both lungs * No dry or moist rales	*LH's diagnosis:* * Recovered from bronchial pneumonia * Stop all medication tomorrow
Jan. 29-30	*Medical ward. No entries on medical record.*	*No medication given from Jan.29 until Jan.31*
Jan.31	*Medical Ward:* * Coughing with sputum resumed yesterday * Respiratory harshness in both lungs * Sounds indicating sputum in larynx	*LH's diagnosis:* * Bronchitis *LH's treatment instructions:* * Commence Kanamycin 0.075gm twice daily, IM
Feb. 1-2	*Medical Ward. No entries on medical record.*	

---

[276] One "measure" = 10cc, making a total prescribed daily milk intake of 240cc.

BA JUN (♀)		
Date	**Examination and Symptoms**	**Diagnosis and Treatment**
Feb. 3	*Medical Ward. Examined by Ding Yi (DY), a paramedic and head of General Medical Ward:* * Ashen complexion * Inadequate response to stimuli * Poor blood circulation in extremities * Respiratory harshness in both lungs * Moist rales in part of lower-right lung	*DY's Diagnosis:* * Severe malnutrition * Pneumonia *DY's treatment instructions:* * Continue use of Kanamycin * Place under close observation; pay attention to feeding
Feb.4	*Medical Ward (DY):* * All limbs cold; body temperature 35°C * "Triple concave" *(san aoxian)* respiratory syndrome * Lung condition: as above * No longer has strength or capacity to suckle	*DY's diagnosis:* * Illness now critical *DY's treatment instructions:* * Keep under close observation * Had intended to administer oxygen therapy, but valve of oxygen cylinder blocked, so did not proceed with treatment *(Yuan ni xi yang, yin yangqitong fa guzhang, wei zhixing)*
Feb. 5–6	*Medical Ward. No entries on medical record.*	
Feb. 7	*Medical Ward (DY):* * Complexion ashen * Poor response to stimuli * Body temperature: 36°C * Heart rate: 128/min. * Has lost capacity to suckle * Moist rales audible in lower-right lung	*DY notes on the medical record:* * To date, [staff have] neglected to carry out my instructions to administer antibiotics *(Qian yi jieduan, kangjunsu yizhu lou zhixing)* * New instructions: begin Kanamycin, IM
Feb.8	*Medical Ward. 8:00 a.m.: Nurse reports that Ba Jun died at 5:00 a.m.. Corpse examined by DY:* * Absence of response to light shone in pupil * Heart beat and respiration ceased	*DY's diagnosis:* * Death from severe malnutrition and pneumonia

Concepts Of "Disability"

A perplexing question emerges from the case data presented above. Why is such a large proportion of China's institutionalized orphan population, according to the official record, either physically or mentally disabled? The condition of legal orphanhood arises from parental loss, not from disability. While infant abandonment can certainly lead to physical or mental disablement (as a result of excessive exposure to heat or cold, for example, or from prolonged deprivation of food and water) and may easily prove fatal, the majority of abandoned babies in China, according to most authoritative accounts, are intentionally left by their mothers in public places such as bus and railway stations or outside government offices, and are quickly found by members of the public and handed over to the police or other authorities. Infants found in an obviously serious medical condition should be sent to hospitals rather than to orphanages, and if for any reason officials err in this regard, then it should be the orphanage's urgent responsibility to transfer the gravely ill babies to hospital.

Many babies in China are abandoned by their parents merely because they were born with conspicuous physical defects such as harelips or cleft palates; but as noted above, these are hardly fatal conditions. And as for such frequently alleged mental disabilities as "congenital maldevelopment of the brain": even in the few cases (if there are any) where this eventual diagnosis may actually have been genuine, the condition is scarcely one which the average Chinese peasant would be capable of diagnosing, and thus could seldom have provided the reason for abandonment. (One of the few types of congenital brain abnormality, in the case of a newborn infant, which would actually be visible to or otherwise detectable by the parent is anencephalus, an extremely rare condition.) The truth of the matter is that most babies who suffer abandonment in China today are mentally and physically normal–apart, that is, from one specific and instantly diagnosable "birth defect," that they are female.[277]

Why are China's orphanages, therefore, so disproportionately full of ostensibly disabled children, many of whom eventually die, and why are there so few physically and mentally normal orphans? Or rather: what has happened to most of them? The nationwide orphanage mortality rates provide the crude and straightforward answer. In Shanghai alone, during 1991, the ratio of deaths to new admissions was over 77 percent. Of those that remained alive at the end of any recent year, the majority were also said to be suffering from a number of serious disabilities, either

---

[277] As the statistical breakdown of the mortality data in Tables 4.4 and 4.6 which appears below under the heading "Demographic Trends" shows, the Shanghai orphanage is apparently unusual in that there was no major gender variation among the children who died there in 1989 and 1992. It is unclear why Shanghai differs from many other Chinese orphanages in this respect.

mental or physical; and since the population replacement rate was so high, most of these would also have succumbed to their alleged medical conditions before very long. In an internal policy document issued by the Shanghai Children's Welfare Institute in October 1992, the orphanage's leadership stated that out of an inmate population of 550 children, "98 percent are disabled."[278] The absurd implication of this situation would thus seem to be that it is somehow the genuinely disabled orphans who are surviving to constitute the orphanage's so-called stable or long-term population, while the healthier ones tend to fall by the wayside. Most likely, of course, this is simply an illusion generated by the orphanage's seemingly widespread practice of false medical labelling. But what role does the concept of "disability" actually play in the baffling demographic structure of China's orphanages?

In order to address this issue properly, we must consider China's contemporary theory and practice in the realm of "superior births science"–a literal English rendering of the Chinese term *youshengxue,* which is the original translation (and still the only term found) in Chinese for the word "eugenics." A set of quasi-medical concepts and theories deriving largely from Social Darwinian notions of competitive national evolution, eugenicism held that certain types of people, particularly the mentally disabled or those with various congenital physical defects represented a blemish upon human society which could be gradually removed by the adoption of various new and unorthodox medical interventions. By common consensus, eugenics remains a highly dangerous field of human endeavor, and one especially susceptible to political manipulation.[279]

Since approximately the mid-1980s, the Chinese government has been actively promoting the study and practice of eugenics as part of a long-term, systematic effort to "raise the quality of the population." This campaign is closely tied in with the government's continuing national birth-control program, in two distinct senses. One concerns the encouragement by the authorities of generally positive and medically enlightened methods aimed at improving the health of the single child which most Chinese couples may legally produce; this is the less controversial sense conveyed by

---

[278] "Report on Deputy Mayor Xie's Instructions Concerning 'A Request By Disabled Orphans to Be Given Access to the Nine-Year System of Compulsory Schooling," issued by the Shanghai Children's Welfare Institute on October 8, 1991.

[279] During much of the first half of this century, the practice of eugenics was much in vogue within certain medical circles, and also some governments, in Europe and North America. In practice, this now almost universally discredited set of ideas reached its nadir in the 1930s and 1940s in Germany, with the systematic and largely successful extermination campaigns waged by the Third Reich against European Jews, gypsies, homosexuals and the like. Some Western medical experts today see a legitimate place for certain purged and revised aspects of eugenics theory, for example in the field of genetic engineering.

the English rendering "superior births science." The other, however, concerns the government's increasingly overt intervention in the sphere of reproductive freedom by means of a growing body of legislation and policy aimed at preventing, often by coercive means, what it refers to as "inferior births" *(liesheng)*. Collectively, these embody some of the crudest pseudo-scientific tenets of unreconstructed eugenicism.

In November 1988, for example, the Gansu provincial government passed an item of legislation titled "Regulations Prohibiting Idiots, Imbeciles and Morons From Having Children."[280] The three types of mentally retarded persons so unengagingly referred to in this way (and hereafter referred to as "feeble-minded persons") are defined in Article 2 of the regulations as being all those: "1) whose disability is congenitally produced by family heredity, inbreeding or environmental factors affecting their parents;[281] 2) who have an intelligence quotient of forty-nine or below and are severely depressed in intelligence; 3) who are challenged in such functionsas language, memory, orientation and thought." ·

According to Article 3, upon medical discovery: "Feeble-minded persons are prohibited from having children. Feeble-minded persons must undergo surgical sterilization as a prerequisite of receiving permission to marry..."[282] And according to Article 5, "Female feeble-minded persons who are already pregnant must undergo termination of pregnancy and surgical sterilization." No upper time-limit is placed on the stage of gestation at which the forbidden pregnancies must be terminated.

In January 1990 the government of the northeasterly province of Liaoning passed a set of mandatory eugenics provisions which exceeded in scope and severity even the Gansu Province regulations. This law, the existence of which has never previously been reported outside of China, revealed by its title–"The Liaoning

---

[280] These regulations were passed on November 23, 1988 by the Standing Committee of the Fifth Session of the Gansu Provincial People's Congress and came into force on January 1, 1989. The designation "idiots, imbeciles and morons" *(chi-dai-sha*, an abbreviation for *baichi, daizi, shagua)* is used throughout the regulations.

[281] The reference to "environmental factors" would include, for example, cases of cretinism or other forms of brain damage caused by iodine deficiency during gestation, an epidémiological factor commonly found in remote inland rural parts of China and reportedly the cause of a large proportion of all cases of mental retardation nationwide.

[282] Article 4 adds: "Feeble-minded persons who have married before the proclamation of these regulations and who are able to bear children should undergo surgical sterilization in accordance with the provisions of Article 3."

Provincial Regulations on the Prevention of Inferior Births[283]–the real underlying agenda of China's "superior births" legislation. According to Article 7 of the regulations, for example, persons suffering from schizophrenia, manic-depressive psychosis, paranoia or epileptic psychonosema will only be allowed to marry if their illness has been in clinical remission for a period of not less than two years. Article 8 of the Liaoning regulations further stipulates that any fertile couples found to be suffering from one of the following conditions are prohibited from bearing children, and that all those "whose illnesses are serious," including prospective marriage partners, must undergo surgical sterilization:

> 1. A history of serious mental illness on both sides;
> 2. Moderate feeble-mindedness *(chi-dai-sha)* on both sides, or severe feeble-mindedness on one side;
> 3. Serious achondroplasty, osteogenesis imperfecta, Marfan's syndrome, pigmentary degeneration of the retina, progressive muscular degeneration (facioscapulohumeral type), or autosomal recessive inherited disease on one side.
> 4. Serious endemic cretinism on both sides.

In addition, in the case of pregnant women who have a family history of hemophilia or of severe hemophilia on the husband's side, or who have already given birth to a "severely defective child" or are found "to have too much or too little amniotic fluid," Article 10 stipulates: "If in the course of a checkup the birth is confirmed as being inadvisable, the pregnancy shall be terminated." Again, no time limit is placed on the stage of gestation at which the mandatory abortion is to occur. Article 4 of the Liaoning regulations ordered, moreover, the creation of a whole new tier of policy-enforcement officialdom, comprising "eugenics health-care supervisors" *(yousheng baojian jianduyuan)* placed at all levels of the administration and charged with "supervising and inspecting the work of preventing inferior births." An appeals process is laid out in Article 11, but the ultimate punishment for non-compliance with orders for termination of pregnancy and sterilization is nothing less than the payment,

---

[283] These regulations were passed on January 13, 1990, by the Standing Committee of the Seventh Session of the Liaoning Provincial People's Congress and came into force on July 1, 1990.

in one lump sum, of 140 percent of the couple's combined income for a full year. Moreover, this is the minimum fine specified.[284]

In October 1994, China's National People's Congress approved a major item of national legislation titled, innocuously enough, "Law of the People's Republic of China on Maternal and Infant Health Care."[285] When the penultimate draft of the law was first publicized by the government ten months earlier, it bore the somewhat different title of "Draft Law on Eugenics and Health Protection." The name change was apparently prompted by the wave of international protests that swiftly ensued. In a joint statement, for example, the European Society of Human Genetics and the European Alliance of Genetic Support Groups denounced the Chinese authorities for ordering the sterilization of people with genetic disorders, and pointed out that such measures contravened Article 16 of the Universal Declaration of Human Rights, according to which "men and women of full age, without limitation due to race, nationality or religion, have the right to marry to found a family."[286] Although the draft law was never made public, a glimpse of the content was provided by a press release issued by the official New China News Agency in December 1993. Among other things, the statement noted, the draft law would include "measures [on] deferring the date of marriage, terminating pregnancies, and sterilization" and specified that "those having such ailments as hepatitis, venereal disease or mental illness, which can be passed on through birth, will be banned from marrying while carrying the disease."

Moreover, it added: "The draft does not state whether China will adopt euthanasia to eliminate congenitally abnormal children, saying that the international community has not come to a conclusion on that issue..."[287] While there is currently some international controversy over the very specific question of whether or not

---

[284] Article 17, paragraph 1. By contrast, the punishment for child abandonment in China is as follows: "Those who abandon infants and children shall be fined not more than 1,000 yuan (approximately US $125) by the public security authorities." (1991 Adoption Law, Article 30.) Only when "the circumstances are especially grave" does child abandonment become an actual crime, punishable by up to five years' imprisonment. (Criminal Law, Article 183.)

[285] The law was passed by the Standing Committee of the Tenth Session of the Eighth National People's Congress on October 27, 1994, and came into force on June 1, 1995.

[286] See for example, Victoria MacDonald, "Geneticists Accuse Peking of Violating Family Rights," *The Sunday Telegraph*, September 3, 1995; the joint statement was timed to coincide with the holding in Beijing of the United Nations Fourth World Congress of Women.

[287] "State Plans Laws To Prevent 'Inferior' Births," Xinhua News Agency, December 20, 1993; English translation in Foreign Broadcast Information Service (FBIS-CHI-93-242), same day; for full text, see Appendix O, below.

newborn infants suffering from anencephalus (total absence of brain) should be subjected to euthanasia, there exists, to Human Rights Watch/Asia's knowledge, no significant body of respectable medical opinion anywhere in the world which would support the viewpoint that congenitally abnormal children more generally ought to be euthanized.[288] It would appear from the press statement, however, that at least some influential medical circles in China are already firmly behind the idea that congenitally abnormal children should be dealt with in this way: for merely by noting that the "draft does not state whether" China will adopt such legislation, it clearly implies that the issue is somehow already, if only provisionally, on the agenda.[289]

Which returns us to the question of China's orphanage population. First, the country's civil affairs bureaus, which run the orphanages, have been accorded a central role in the national eugenics program. As the government bodies responsible for approving and registering all marriages, they must check and authenticate the various certificates of eugenic acceptability that prospective couples need to provide in order to get married. But they also perform a planning and enforcement role in the process. As Article 4 of the Liaoning regulations forthrightly states: "The civil affairs,

---

[288] It is important to note that the passage of national-level legislation in China is usually preceded by a period of trial implementation of the legislative ideas concerned, and often occurs several years or more after the actual passage at provincial level of "trial regulations" in the same area. The example of the Gansu and Liaoning eugenics regulations, both of which preceded and laid the legislative and judicial groundwork for the eventual passage of the Law on Maternal and Infant Health Care, is a good case in point. It should also be stressed that the latter law, although containing none of the more overt and coercive provisions on such matters as sterilization and termination of pregnancy as are to be found in the former, conspicuously failed, in contrast to normal legislative practice in China, to state in its final "supplementary" provisions that the law either superseded or rendered invalid previous laws and provisions with which it might be in conflict. Hence, although the law states, "Any termination of pregnancy or application of ligation operation [surgical sterilization] shall be agreed and signed by the person concerned," this did not preclude the authorities in provinces such as Gansu and Liaoning from continuing to apply their existing mandatory, non-consensual regulations on the prohibition of "inferior births."

[289] See also, for example, "China: Delegates Propose 'Conditional Euthanasia' For Those Who Are A Burden," China News Service (Zhongguo Xinwenshe), March 20, 1994; English version in the British Broadcasting Corporation's Monitoring Service: Far East, March 23, 1994. According to the official news report, "At present, some old people have lost the ability to take care of themselves. They are confined to their beds, are incontinent and unable to control their bowels. Their minds are no longer clear and they must be looked after by their children. The aged are very painful. Not only do their children find this difficult to bear–both spiritually and financially–but they also are a burden on the state. Under this situtation, the implementation of euthanasia is very essential."

family planning and other authorities at provincial, municipal and county levels shall, together with the public security organs, assist [public health bodies] in diligently carrying out the task of preventing inferior births."[290]

Second, while there is no evidence that Shanghai orphanage authorities consciously or systematically applied a policy of eugenics-based euthanasia against the inmate population, it is clear that the pervasive nationwide influence of the kinds of ideas and legislation outlined above served to engender an intellectual and social atmosphere that in practice would have been highly conducive to abuses of this nature. At worst, government policies may have provided a ready-made alibi for such abuses. For if persons such as schizophrenics, the "feeble-minded" and even the incipiently blind are all officially deemed to lead such valueless lives, and to be such an intolerable burden on society, that they must be comprehensively eliminated in the next generation through mandatory sterilizations and termination of pregnancies, it probably requires less of a mental leap than might be imagined to begin viewing children already born with authentic congenital abnormalities like cerebral palsy, or those born moderately or profoundly mentally retarded, or even those "listless" due to medical neglect, as somehow leading such utterly empty and meaningless lives that it would be doing them a favor to euthanize them.

There is an inescapable problem, however, about all this. As the individual medical records repeatedly suggest, the deceased children appear not to have died, in most cases, from the various medical reasons recorded. They did not die, apparently, from "congenital maldevelopment of brain"; nor from having "small, malformed craniums"; nor even, in any medically meaningful sense, from being afflicted with "harelip and cleft palate." And they certainly did not die from being "mentally defective." Instead, the overwhelming weight of the evidence, both direct and circumstantial, points to the single conclusion that the great majority of them died from severe and protracted malnutrition. So why all the fuss? Why did the orphanage authorities seek, apparently, to establish such "eugenically correct" patterns of mortality for their young wards, and do so, moreover, in such exhaustive and laborious detail? Eugenics itself being largely pseudo-science, one hesitates to speak of any such thing as "pseudo-eugenics." But this, essentially, appears to have been what was applied: a fraudulent ascription of certain causes of death which happened neatly to conform with a set of national policies whose aim was to eliminate congenital disablement of all types from society as a whole.

---

[290] Article 3 adds: "In implementing measures for premarital health checkups, the municipal-level bureaus of public health and civil affairs shall put forward plans in accordance with local conditions and submit them for approval by the people's government at the same level."

Are the staff of the Shanghai Children's Welfare Institute, and the thousands of other orphanage staff members all over the country, simply evil people? Probably not, in most cases, although there is clearly an immanent evil to be found in the system, and members of the leadership, both collectively and individually, share a profound culpability. The missing part of the solution to this seemingly labyrinthine mystery may lie in the third of the elements, as briefly described early in this chapter, of the official policy line on orphanage affairs which began subtly to take form in the immediate aftermath of the post-Great Leap famine.[291] This was the apparent focus on "disablement quotas," the desire on the part of individual orphanage leaderships to establish an increasingly high ratio of sick and disabled orphanage inmates to the fit and healthy ones, with the former category comprising mainly the abandoned infants and accounting for the great majority, and the latter comprising the so-called legal or natural orphans. While in the early to mid-1960s efforts were made to find foster homes for both types of orphan, and the policy thus represented a largely benign, though often ineffectual, attempt to discharge as many healthy and adoptable children as possible out of state institutional care and back into society, by the late 1970s and the advent of the one-child-per-family policy, coupled to an extent with the growing market economy, the policy began to assume, it seems, a more malignant character.

By the 1980s, there was the growing epidemic of child abandonment to contend with, a phenomenon which, moreover, was taking place within the context of more or less static levels of institutional capacity. On top of this, there came the new rule forbidding the adoption of abandoned children by couples who already had one child. All these factors must have driven China's orphanages toward a situation of demographic crisis unparalleled even in comparison with the penny-pinching contexts of the 1950s and early 1960s. Above all, therefore, it was the ruthless arithmetic of the situation, the impossible disparity emerging between orphan supply and institutional capacity, which conspired to exacerbate further China's already staggering orphanage mortality rates during the prosperous 1980s and 1990s.

Once the low cost, more or less zero-population-growth solution had been decided upon by the government, the problem of what to do with the surplus-to-requirement population became an essentially technical one, namely, how to allocate survival ratios in such a way as to ensure the desired level of "stable population." By the 1980s, the appropriate medical diagnoses had been made available by the government: abandoned children were at first seen merely as social mistakes who should never have arisen, and then, apparently, for increasing reasons of staff convenience, as being medical or even political errors which should, by rights, have been prevented before birth. While there undoubtedly are many genuinely disabled

---

[291] See above, "A Brief History of the Orphanage."

children in China's orphanages today, the concept of "disability" thus appears to have been pressed into the service of medically quite illegitimate goals.

The bottom line, however, was that simply by restricting its annual budgetary allocations to a level commensurate with a notionally stable inmate population, the government could achieve its otherwise complex orphanage management goals with a stroke of the fiscal pen. And this, precisely, is what it appears to have done. By default, therefore, the brutal task of "readjusting" the inmate population has historically been left up to each individual orphanage to accomplish, by its own diverse means and in a more or less ad hoc way. The government, for the most part, has remained aloof, remote and detached from the process, although it is government policy that set it in motion and cynical government acquiescence that allows it to continue–even in the face of sustained exposure and demands for change, like those raised in the case of the Shanghai orphanage.

Until the Chinese government acknowledges, therefore, the true scale and proportions of the country's child abandonment crisis in the 1990s, and moreover undertakes a comprehensive expansion of the country's institutional care system, China's unwanted children seem doomed to continue spending their mostly brief lives in an environment that is blighted by such arbitrary competition for resources, and such random processes of attrition, that only the luckiest rather than the fittest can have any significant hope of survival.

Documentation of Deaths

The following tables contain a distillation of much of the primary data on infant and child deaths at the Shanghai Children's Welfare Institute that were compiled over the four-year period 1989–93 by dissident staff members of the orphanage. They comprise three sets of materials:

- An official list of 153 infants and children who died at the orphanage between December 1, 1988 and December 22, 1989 (Table 4.4).

- Details of the nutritional and medical condition of all fifty-five infants and children who were admitted to the orphanage during January–February 1992, together with information (where known) on their status as of October that year (Table 4.5).

- A list of 207 infants and children who died at the orphanage between November 5, 1991 and October 28, 1992 (Table 4.6).

(For Human Rights Watch/Asia's analysis and evaluation of the data contained in these tables, see the preceding sections of this chapter.)

Table 4.4   Official List of 153 Infant and Child Deaths at the Shanghai Children's Welfare Institute, December 1988–December 1989[292]

No.	Group	Name	Sex	Born	Died	Cause of Death	Admitted
					December 1988		
88	MW	Deng You	F	11/20/78	12/1/88	congenital maldevelopment of brain	5/14/82
89	MW	Jian Fa	F	5/15/87	12/2/88	congenital maldevelopment of brain	2/18/88
90	MW	Bi Shen	F	11/19/88	12/3/88	neonatal infection	11/23/88
91	MW	Dou Yan	F	11/25/88	12/5/88	congenital maldevelopment of brain	12/4/88
92	Grp.13	Qu Fan	F	9/12/83	12/7/88	congenital maldevelopment of brain	9/14/88
93	MW	Bi Shu	F	1/7/88	12/9/88	congenital maldevelopment of brain	11/14/88
94	MW	Shan Jiao	M	12/10/82	12/10/88	congenital maldevelopment of brain	5/7/88
95	MW	Qu Li	F	8/28/88	12/12/88	congenital maldevelopment of brain	9/18/88
96	MW	Dou Lan	F	12/1/88	12/13/88	congenital obstruction of nephelium; premature birth	12/7/88

[292] This document is a full translation of an official list, compiled by orphanage medical staff, of all infants and children who died at the Shanghai Child Welfare Institute during the thirteen-month period December 1988–December 1989. The handwritten document was temporarily removed from the wall of the nurses' duty room in the orphanage's Medical Ward and secretly photocopied by Dr. Zhang Shuyun in late December, 1989. Abbreviations used in the "Group" column are as follows: "MW": Medical Ward; "DS": Disabled Section; "RU": Infants Section's Reception Unit; "Grp.#": subgroup within Infants Section, Disabled Section, etc. Items appearing in *italics* in the "Cause of Death" column are ones that appear to have been entered on the list at a later date, presumably as part of the authorities attempts during 1992 to tamper with and conceal the documentary evidence concerning deaths at the orphanage. NB: In 1989, the section of the orphanage referred to in this list as the "Medical Ward" was more generally known as the "critical ward" (*bingweijian*)—or even (in common staff parlance) as the "waiting for death room" (*dengsi jian*). As can be seen from the overwhelming preponderance of cases on this list who died in the Medical Ward, it effectively represented, for most of the children transferred there, the penultimate stop on a preordained journey to the orphanage's morgue (*taipingjian*).

216

No.	Group	Name	Sex	Born	Died	Cause of Death	Admitted
97	MW	Bei Gang	F	3/12/87	12/17/88	congenital maldevelopment of brain	6/7/88
98	MW	Qiu Xian	F	12/20/86	12/23/88	cerebral palsy; mentally defective	12/15/88
99	MW	Qu Xia	M	12/7/80	12/23/88	cerebral palsy; mentally defective	9/17/88
100	MW	Chao Zhong	F	11/25/79	12/27/88	congenital maldevelopment of brain	11/25/87
101	MW	Su Ying	M	7/23/85	12/31/88	congenital maldevelopment of brain	8/9/86
102	MW	Bei Xiu	M	1/10/85	12/28/88	small, malformed cranium; mentally defective	6/20/88
					January 1989		
1	MW	Dou Kang	M	4/29/86	1/2/89	congenital maldevelopment of brain + cerebral palsy	12/8/88
2	MW	Dou Hu	F	12/15/86	1/3/89	congenital maldevelopment of brain + small, malformed cranium	12/1/88
3	MW	Ruan Ding	F	10/1/88	1/6/89	congenital maldevelopment of brain + harelip	10/11/88
4	MW	Shan Chun	M	5/8/88	1/8/89	congenital maldevelopment of brain + spina bifida	5/18/88
5	MW	Hang Yuan	M	3/14/81	1/14/89	congenital maldevelopment of brain + cerebral palsy	3/14/88
6	MW	Dou Jun	F	10/30/88	1/15/89	congenital maldevelopment of brain + congenital idiocy (xiantian yuxing); congenital heart disease	12/5/88
7	MW	Rong Ai	M	3/9/85	1/23/89	congenital maldevelopment of brain + cerebral palsy	9/7/86
8	MW	Pu Ying	M	10/30/85	1/26/89	congenital maldevelopment of brain + cerebral palsy	7/16/86
9	DS	Bei Hong	M	5/15/84	1/28/89	congenital maldevelopment of brain + cerebral palsy	6/15/88
10	MW	Yu Liao	M	12/2/88	1/30/89	congenital maldevelopment of brain + congenital idiocy; congenital heart disease	1/7/89

No.	Group	Name	Sex	Born	Died	Cause of Death	Admitted
					February 1989		
11	MW	Dou Yuan	F	10/15/88	2/1/89	congenital maldevelopment of brain + *angioma*	12/1/88
12	MW	Zong Zhou	M	9/2/87	2/5/89	congenital maldevelopment of brain + *congenital idiocy; malnutrition*	1/13/88
13	MW	Bi Wei	M	11/18/88	2/10/89	congenital maldevelopment of brain + *blind in both eyes; malnutrition*	11/23/88
14	MW	Hua Mao	M	6/5/83	2/11/89	congenital maldevelopment of brain + *cerebral palsy*	5/6/84
15	MW	Ruan Zhong	M	10/17/78	2/12/89	congenital maldevelopment of brain	10/17/88
16	Grp.17	Guang Rong	M	4/10/82	2/14/89	congenital maldevelopment of brain	1/2/87
17	RU	Li Yi	F	2/23/89	2/25/89	congenital maldevelopment of brain [NB: this was later scored out and replaced with:] *terminal condition*	2/25/89
					March 1989		
18	MW	Li Xuan	F	Nov. 88	3/5/89	congenital maldevelopment of brain + *malnutrition (severe)*	Nov. 88
19	MW	Li Feng	M	2/25/81	3/8/89	congenital maldevelopment of brain + *cerebral palsy*	2/21/89
20	Grp.18	Zhu Gang	F	6/8/78	3/8/89	congenital maldevelopment of brain	4/25/80
21	MW	Sha Chen	F	3/17/84	3/11/89	congenital maldevelopment of brain	3/21/84
22	MW	Li Wei	M	2/1/88	3/12/89	congenital maldevelopment of brain + *cerebral palsy*	2/21/89
23	MW	Ruan Qing	M	10/18/78	3/12/89	congenital maldevelopment of brain	10/18/88
24	MW	Hu Ze	M	2/12/85	3/17/89	congenital maldevelopment of brain + *cerebral palsy*	3/14/89

No.	Group	Name	Sex	Born	Died	Cause of Death	Admitted
25	MW	LI MING	M	1/28/89	3/17/89	low-weight infant; malnutrition + *congenital maldevelopment of brain*	2/28/89
26	MW	HU BIAO	F	3/8/89	3/25/89	neonatal infection; incomplete eyeball development + *congenital maldevelopment of brain*	3/18/89
27	MW	CEN PU	F	4/10/75	3/29/89	congenital maldevelopment of brain + *cerebral palsy*	9/26/78
28	MW	YING BAO	M	2/20/83	3/29/89	malnutrition + *congenital maldevelopment of brain*	2/18/86
					April 1989		
29	MW	YU KE	F	1/18/89	4/4/89	congenital maldevelopment of brain + *third-degree malnutrition*	1/10/89 [sic]
30	MW	HU JIAO	M	3/7/82	4/4/89	congenital maldevelopment of brain + *cerebral palsy, epilepsy*	3/7/89
31	MW	HU YU	M	3/5/89	4/6/89	congenital maldevelopment of brain + *congenital heart disease*	3/12/89
32	MW	DOU FEN	M	12/26/83	4/8/89	congenital maldevelopment of brain	12/26/83
33	Grp.13	DOU LI	M	12/5/83	4/14/89	congenital maldevelopment of brain + *third-degree malnutrition*	12/6/88
34	MW	GUO XIA	M	5/24/88	4/26/89	swollen liver and spleen (cause unclear); terminal condition; congenital maldevelopment of brain	4/24/89
35	MW	YU FA	M	12/1/84	4/30/89	hepatitis [NB: this was later scored out and replaced with:] *congenital maldevelopment of brain; mentally defective*	1/12/89
					May 1989		

219

No.	Group	Name	Sex	Born	Died	Cause of Death	Admitted
36	MW	Hu Sha	F	1/5/89	5/2/89	small, malformed cranium; third-degree malnutrition + *congenital maldevelopment of brain*	3/19/89
37	MW	Hu Shao	M	1/22/89	5/3/89	fissure in urinary tract; third-degree malnutrition + *congenital maldevelopment of brain*	3/15/89
38	MW	Chen Hao	M	2/19/89	5/18/89	congenital heart disease; pneumonia; heart failure	5/10/89
39	MW	Chen Jing	F	4/9/89	5/14/89	small, malformed cranium; mentally defective	4/9/89
40	MW	Hu Gui	M	3/2/83	5/15/89	incomplete brain development; cerebral palsy + *mentally defective; malnutrition*	3/18/89
41	MW	Chen Xing	M	2/13/88	5/18/89	mentally defective; small, malformed cranium	5/18/89
42	MW	Bi Yu	F	11/12/88	5/18/89	third-degree malnutrition; congenital absence of anus	11/10/89
43	MW	Guo Yuan	F	Dec. 88	5/23/89	congenital heart disease; incomplete brain development	—
44	MW	Hong Dao	M	9/11/82	5/25/89	mentally defective; blind in both eyes	12/10/89 [sic]
45	MW	Chen Lie	F	3/26/89	5/26/89	mentally defective	5/1/89
46	MW	Chen Jiang	F	5/22/87	5/27/89	mentally defective	5/29/89
47	MW	Hu Hong	F	3/21/85	5/27/89	mentally defective	3/21/89
48	MW	Xi Shi	F	10/28/82	5/29/89	congenital maldevelopment of brain; cerebral palsy	10/21/87
49	MW	Hu Chun	F	9/9/88	5/30/89	mentally defective; small, malformed cranium	3/23/89
					June 1989		
50	MW	Chen Bing	M	12/18/88	6/2/89	mentally defective; cerebral palsy	5/18/89

No.	Group	Name	Sex	Born	Died	Cause of Death	Admitted
51	MW	Sun Tao	M	6/18/87	6/10/89	mentally defective; terminal condition	6/9/89
52	MW	Chen Lu	M	5/13/81	6/12/89	congenital maldevelopment of brain; cerebral palsy	5/13/89
53	MW	Guo Xing	M	4/15/89	6/13/89	congenital maldevelopment of brain; harelip	4/20/89
54	DS	Bi Shi	M	11/25/88	6/23/89	congenital maldevelopment of brain; mentally defective	11/26/88
55	MW	Hu Ju	F	3/13/86	6/24/89	congenital maldevelopment of brain; mentally defective; cerebral palsy	3/13/89
_293	MW	Luo Qi	M	12/8/81	6/27/89	congenital maldevelopment of brain	_294
56	MW	Sun Pi	M	6/1/89	6/1/89	congenital maldevelopment of brain	6/12/89 [sic]
57	MW	Sun Po	M	6/25/88	6/30/89	congenital maldevelopment of brain	6/28/89
					July 1989		
58	MW	Sun Jiang	M	4/1/88	7/2/89	congenital maldevelopment of brain	6/30/89
59	MW	Qi Yan	M	6/30/89	7/10/89	congenital maldevelopment of brain	7/2/89
60	MW	Chen Guang	F	4/20/88	7/11/89	congenital maldevelopment of brain	5/20/88

---

[293] Entries for five deaths that occurred during 1989, starting with that of Luo Qi, were added to the list at a later date; these were not assigned case numbers by the list compilers. A total of 138 officially recorded deaths, i.e. five more than the 133 numbered cases on the list, thus took place at the orphanage between January 1 and December 22, 1989. The year-end death toll of 141 that was later admitted to by the authorities included deaths that occurred during the final week of 1989.

[294] Date of admission not entered on this list. Luo Qi's medical record, however, gives the date of admission as 12/8/84; it also states that he was placed in the orphanage's Disabled Section, rather than (as recorded above) the Medical Ward

No.	Group	Name	Sex	Born	Died	Cause of Death	Admitted
61	MW	CHEN NING	M	7/24/88	7/12/89	congenital maldevelopment of brain	5/24/89
62	MW	GUO SONG	F	12/1/88	7/12/89	congenital maldevelopment of brain	4/29/89
63	MW	HONG JIAN	M	early Aug. 81	7/15/89	congenital maldevelopment of brain	12/9/89
64	MW	QI GUAN	M	7/4/89	7/19/89	premature birth; congenital incomplete development [sic]	7/4/89
65	MW	QI HONG	F	5/16/88	7/26/89	cerebral palsy	7/16/89
66	MW	QIGUANG	M	7/22/89	7/26/89	congenital absence of anus	7/24/89
67	MW	QI QI	M	7/12/89	7/30/89	congenital maldevelopment of brain ; meningocele [swollen brain membrane]	7/20/89
68	MW	LIANG [?]	M	4/15/84	7/31/89	congenital maldevelopment of brain	4/16/88
69	MW	QI YING	M	7/12/89	7/31/89	congenital maldevelopment of brain	7/19/89
					August 1989		
70	MW	SUN LI	F	5/26/89	8/2/89	congenital maldevelopment of brain	5/26/89
71	Grp.11	SUN JING	M	6/15/85	8/7/89	congenital maldevelopment of brain	6/18/89
72	MW	CHEN LING	M	5/31/82	8/9/89	congenital maldevelopment of brain	5/3/89
73	MW	QI SHAN	F	7/22/89	8/8/89	congenital maldevelopment of brain	7/27/89
74	MW	SUN ZHU	F	5/6/89	8/12/89	mentally defective	6/7/89
75	MW	CHEN ZHONG	M	5/5/87	8/14/89	cerebral palsy; mentally defective; malnutrition	5/6/89
76	MW	QI XING	F	5/26/89	8/13/89	congenital heart disease; congenital idiocy	7/26/89

No.	Group	Name	Sex	Born	Died	Cause of Death	Admitted
77	MW	QI MING	M	9/22/88	8/17/89	small, malformed cranium; congenital maldevelopment of brain	7/22/89
78	MW	MING HUI	M	12/25/86	8/18/89	congenital maldevelopment of brain	2/10/87
79	MW	CHEN LI	F	1/26/82	8/20/89	congenital maldevelopment of brain	5/9/89
80	MW	QI LING	F	2/26/89	8/20/89	congenital maldevelopment of brain	7/26/89
81	MW	XIA JIE	F	7/30/89	8/21/89	congenital maldevelopment of brain; generalized angioma (quanshenxing xueguanliu)	8/15/89
82	MW	HU WEN	F	4/8/86	8/23/89	congenital maldevelopment of brain	3/22/89
83	MW	SUN JI	F	6/16/88	8/27/88	congenital maldevelopment of brain	6/10/89
84	MW	XIA REN	F	8/19/89	8/25/89	congenital maldevelopment of brain	8/19/89
					September 1989		
85	MW	QI JIAN	F	6/23/86	9/1/89	congenital maldevelopment of brain	7/28/89
86	MW	XIA SHU	M	9/2/88	9/1/89	congenital maldevelopment of brain	8/2/89
87	MW	SUN ZHI	F	6/24/89	9/2/89	congenital maldevelopment of brain	6/25/89
88	MW	XIA FEI	F	8/29/86	9/2/89	congenital maldevelopment of brain; cerebral palsy	8/29/89
89	MW	XI YI	M	10/26/82	9/5/89	congenital maldevelopment of brain	10/26/87
90	MW	XIA LING	F	3/29/89	9/5/89	congenital maldevelopment of brain	8/29/89
91	MW	GUO QI	F	1/1/89	9/5/89	congenital maldevelopment of brain	4/18/89
92	MW	XIA GANG	F	4/9/89	9/7/89	congenital maldevelopment of brain	8/19/89
93	MW	CHEN MIN	F	5/19/89	9/9/89	congenital maldevelopment of brain; harelip	5/24/89

No.	Group	Name	Sex	Born	Died	Cause of Death	Admitted
94	Grp. 7	Hu Ying	M	12/20/88	9/10/89	cleft palate; congenital maldevelopment of brain	3/6/89
95	MW	Bei Li	F	2/29/87	9/11/89	viral meningitis sequelae	6/15/88
96	MW	Sun Wu	M	5/29/89	9/11/89	congenital maldevelopment of brain	6/1/89
97	DS	Shi Ying	F	9/16/84	9/12/89	poor digestion; mentally defective	3/19/86
98	MW	Rong Jian	M	3/29/86	9/14/89	congenital maldevelopment of brain	9/18/86
99	MW	Yu Xu	F	7/6/84	9/14/89	congenital maldevelopment of brain	7/9/88
100	MW	Xia Mei	M	2/17/88	9/16/89	congenital maldevelopment of brain	8/17/89
101	MW	Jia Hong	M	9/11/87	9/19/89	congenital maldevelopment of brain	9/11/89
102	MW	Qi Chao	F	4/12/89	9/20/89	small, malformed cranium; cerebral palsy; mentally defective	7/12/89
103	MW	Guo Feng	M	3/16/88	9/22/89	congenital maldevelopment of brain; mentally defective	4/16/89
104	MW	Guo Yun	F	7/12/85	9/22/89	congenital maldevelopment of brain	4/10/89
105	MW	Zhang Wu	F	9/17/83	9/29/89	congenital maldevelopment of brain	9/20/83[295]
106	RU	Jia Wei	M	9/26/89	9/30/89	congenital maldevelopment of brain + congenital absence of anus	9/28/89
					October 1989		
107	RU	Jia Wen	F	9/17/89	10/4/89	congenital maldevelopment of brain	9/24/89
108	MW	Jia Ming	F	6/22/89	10/5/89	congenital maldevelopment of brain	9/22/89

[295] The year "83" appears to have been superimposed at a later date over the original entry for date of admission: "89"

No.	Group	Name	Sex	Born	Died	Cause of Death	Admitted
109	MW	Jia Lie	F	9/1/89	10/6/89	congenital maldevelopment of brain	9/15/89
110	MW	Ruan Qiao	F	5/18/86	10/7/89	congenital maldevelopment of brain	10/25/88
111	MW	Ruan Ying	F	8/21/88	10/8/89	mentally defective; congenital idiocy	8/21/88
112	MW	Xia Bao	M	8/2/89	10/10/89	mentally defective	8/12/89
—	MW	Xia [?]	F	8/29/86	10/12/89	—	—
113	MW	Dou Po	F	10/16/89	10/15/89 [sic]	congenital maldevelopment of brain	12/5/88 [sic]
114	MW	Jia Ying	F	8/29/89	10/28/89[296]	congenital maldevelopment of brain; spina bifida	10/28/89
115	MW	Die Yan	F	10/25/88	10/25/89	congenital maldevelopment of brain	10/28/89
116	MW	Die Qiang	F	3/27/89	10/29/89	bilateral retinal cytoma (shuangce yanqiu shimu xibaoliu)[297]	10/21/89
117	MW	Die Min	F	12/13/88	10/30/89	congenital maldevelopment of brain	10/13/89
—	—	Xia Jing	F	6/14/89	10/31/89	congenital incomplete bone development; mentally defective	10/31/89
—	—	Di Chun	M	10/20/88	10/31/89	—	—
November 1989							
118	MW	Jia Chong	F	2/22/87	11/2/89	congenital maldevelopment of brain	9/22/89

[296] The date of death given for Jia Ying, 10/28/89, represents a later alteration; the original entry on the record is impossible to make out.

[297] Chinese term not found in medical dictionary; literal English translation rendered.

No.	Group	Name	Sex	Born	Died	Cause of Death	Admitted
119	MW	Jia Zheng	M	9/7/88	11/5/89	congenital maldevelopment of brain	9/7/89
120	MW	Xia Sen	F	8/24/82	11/7/89	congenital maldevelopment of brain	8/24/89
—	—	Die Zhan	M	5/25/89	11/9/89	congenital maldevelopment of brain	—
121	MW	Ke Shan	M	10/21/89	11/9/89	congenital maldevelopment of brain	11/2/89
122	MW	Ke Hui	M	11/1/89	11/17/89	congenital maldevelopment of brain	11/2/89
123	MW	Jia Xin	M	11/4/88	11/18/89	congenital maldevelopment of brain	9/4/89
124	RU	Di Mei	M	10/8/86	11/18/89	congenital maldevelopment of brain	10/23/89
125	MW	Ke Li	M	11/5/89	11/20/89	congenital maldevelopment of brain	11/14/89
126	MW	Xia Guang	M	6/31/89	11/21/89	congenital maldevelopment of brain	8/31/89
127	MW	Qu Mou	M	6/11/86	11/24/89	congenital maldevelopment of brain	9/2/88
128	MW	Die Jia	F	2/16/85	11/25/89	congenital maldevelopment of brain	10/16/89
129	MW	Bi Jia	F	2/1/88	11/30/89	congenital maldevelopment of brain	—
December 1989 (Partial List)							
130	MW	Xia Yuan	F	6/27/89	12/1/89	congenital maldevelopment of brain	—
131	MW	Shou Hong	F	9/7/87	12/2/89	congenital maldevelopment of brain	7/7/88
132	MW	Xin Jian	M	11/3/89	12/15/89	congenital maldevelopment of brain	12/1/89
133	RU	Xin Bing	M	12/10/85	12/22/89	congenital maldevelopment of brain	12/10/89

Table 4.5   Medical Condition of All New Admissions to the Shanghai Children's Welfare Institute, January–February 1992[298]

No.	Name	Sex	Born	Admitted Age	Weight/ Height	State Of Nutrition	Intelligence Level	Type of Disability	STATUS AS OF OCTOBER 1992 (WHERE KNOWN) Recorded Cause of Death
				NEW ADMISSIONS, JANUARY 1992					
1	BA JUN	F	12/2/91	1/2/92 1 month	3.8 kg 50 cm	moderate	monitor intelligence[299]	–[300]	Died (2/8/92): third-degree malnutrition; pneumonia
2	BA ZHONG	F	1/1/92	1/3/92 2 days	2.8 kg 49 cm	satisfactory	monitor intelligence	–	Died (6/30/92): third-degree malnutrition, severe dehydration
3	BA WEI	M	–	1/3/92	–	–	–	–	Died (1/7/92): third-degree malnutrition, mentally defective

[298] This table is based on a handcopied version of the January–February 1992 section of the official Admissions Register maintained by the Infants Section's Reception Unit at the Shanghai Child Welfare Institute; all new arrivals were initially admitted to this unit, regardless of their age. The causes of death, where applicable, were recorded on a register of deaths (a handcopied version of which has also been obtained by Human Rights Watch/Asia) maintained by the Medical Ward. Five columns appearing in the original Admissions Register—headed respectively, "Anterior Fontanelle", "Liver Function", "Umbilical Cord", "Chest Circumference" and "Head Circumference"—have been omitted in the present version, with a few minor exceptions, all data entered in the first of those four columns appeared to indicate generally normal health on the part of the children concerned. (The exceptions were: Case #2, February 1992, where liver function was recorded as "GPT>4"; and Case #19, February 1992, where size of anterior fontanelle was recorded as "6 x 6cm." In addition, for Cases #10, 16, 24 and 28 from February 1992, "head circumference" was listed as being, respectively, "40cm", "40cm", "45cm" and "38cm"; all but the last of these entries appeared to fall well within the "normal" range of head sizes as indicated by other such entries for children of similar age. In the column headed "State of Nutrition," the Chinese terms used in the original document were, in order of nutritional health: *ke*—"satisfactory"; *zhong*—"moderate"; *lüe cha*—"rather poor"; and *cha*—"poor".)

[299] *"Zhi-guan"*, an abbreviation for *"zhili guancha"*, which means: "intelligence level to be determined through observation." For a detailed discussion and evaluation of this term, see above, "Recorded Causes of Death" under "Epidemiologic Aspects.")

[300] Dashes in this and the following table indicate that the relevant information is unavailable.

227

New Admissions, January 1992

No.	Name	Sex	Born	Admitted Age	Weight/Height	State Of Nutrition	Intelligence Level	Type of Disability	Status As Of October 1992 (Where Known) Recorded Cause of Death
4	Ba Jin	F	12/5/91	1/3/92 *1 month*	4.0 kg 55 cm	moderate	monitor intelligence	–	Infants Section, Group #7
5	Ba Gong	F	1/8/91	1/6/92 *1 year*	4.0 kg –	–	–	–	Died (1/8/92): *malnutrition; mentally defective*
6	Ba Cheng	M	1/15/90 (lunar)	1/6/92 *2 years*	12.0 kg 88 cm	poor	mentally defective (√)	mentally defective	Died (1/18/92): *third-degree malnutrition; mentally defective*
7	Ba Zheng	F	1982	1/7/92 *10 years*	29.0 kg 128 cm	poor	normal	none	Ran away
8	Ba Min	F	10/28/91	1/8/92 *2 ½ mths.*	6.0 kg 57 cm	poor	mentally defective (√)	mentally defective; epilepsy	Died (2/29/92): *cerebral palsy; malnutrition; pneumonia*
9	Ba Xue	F	12/5/91	1/9/92 *1 month*	3.0 kg 55 cm	satisfactory	normal	none	Died (7/9/92): *severe malnutrition; congenital maldevelopment of brain*
10	Ba Yue	F	1/9/87	1/9/92 *5 years*	18.5 kg 93 cm	satisfactory	normal	none	Toddler's Group (*you-er zu*)
11	Ba Qing	F	11/21/91	1/12/92 *1 ½ mths.*	3.7 kg 47 cm	satisfactory	monitor intelligence	–	Adopted
12	Ba Li	F	1/11/92	1/16/92 *5 days*	3.8 kg 49 cm	satisfactory	monitor intelligence	–	Adopted
13	Ba Chao	F	12/5/91	1/16/92 *1 ½ mths.*	3.0 kg 47 cm	satisfactory	monitor intelligence	six fingers on both hands; six toes on left foot	Died (2/17/92): *low weight; malnutrition; severe dehydration*
14	Ba Hong	F	1/9/92	1/18/92 *9 days*	3.5 kg 47 cm	satisfactory	monitor intelligence	–	Infants Section, Group #10

228

New Admissions, January 1992

No.	Name	Sex	Born	Admitted Age	Weight/ Height	State Of Nutrition	Intelligence Level	Type of Disability	Status As Of October 1992 (Where Known) Recorded Cause of Death
15	Ba Nan	F	12/24/91	1/19/92 26 days	3.5 kg 49 cm	satisfactory	monitor intelligence	harelip	Died (2/11/92): harelip; severe malnutrition; choked on milk
16	Ba Dong	F	12/11/91	1/20/92 1½ mths.	3.0 kg 52 cm	satisfactory	monitor intelligence	—	Died (5/6/92): malnutrition; high fever, diarrhea; septicemia
17	Ba Qun	F	10/18/91	1/21/92 3 months	5.0 kg 53 cm	moderate	monitor intelligence	—	Infants Section, Group #7
18	Ba Yue	F	12/4/89	1/22/92 2 years	10.0 kg 69 cm	moderate	monitor intelligence	blisters on skin (cause unknown)	Sent to Medical Ward on 1/23/92 [outcome unknown]
19	Ba Zhou	F	10/20/91	1/22/92 3 months	5.5 kg 54 cm	moderate	monitor intelligence	angioma on right leg	Infants Section, Group #7
20	Ba Quan	F	1/2/92	1/24/92 22 days	2.5 kg 45 cm	rather poor	monitor intelligence	—	Died (8/24/92): congenital maldevelopment of brain
21	Ba Xiu	F	1/21/92	1/26/92 5 days	2.5 kg 45 cm	poor	monitor intelligence	neonatal jaundice	Unknown
22	Ba Jing	F	12/10/91	1/26/92 1½ mths.	5.0 kg 51 cm	satisfactory	monitor intelligence	—	Unknown
23	Ba Rong	F	12/31/91	1/27/92 27 days	5.0 kg 53 cm	satisfactory	monitor intelligence	—	Adopted
24	Ba Qian	F	9/16/91	1/28/92 4½ mths.	7.0 kg 61 cm	satisfactory	mentally defective(v)	hydrocephalus	Died (8/20/92): hydrocephalus; congenital maldevelopment of brain
25	Ba Fan	F	12/26/91	1/29/92 1 month	4.25 kg 50 cm	satisfactory	monitor intelligence	—	Unknown

New Admissions, January 1992

No.	Name	Sex	Born	Admitted Age	Weight/ Height	State Of Nutrition	Intelligence Level	Type of Disability	Status As of October 1992 (Where Known) Recorded Cause of Death
26	Ba Hua	F	1/9/92	1/31/92 22 days	3.0 kg 48 cm	satisfactory	monitor intelligence	—	Unknown

New Admissions, February 1992

No.	Name	Sex	Born	Admitted Age	Weight/ Height	State of Nutrition	Intelligence Level	Type of Disability	Status As of October 1992 (Where Known) Recorded Cause of Death
1	Jiao Dong	F	12/28/91	2/1/92 1 month	4.1 kg 50 cm	good	monitor intelligence	—	Infants Section, Group #7 (as of 4/25/92)
2	Jiao Ling	F	5/20/91	2/1/92 8 months	6.5 kg —	—	monitor intelligence	—	Unknown
3	Jiao Qi	F	12/6/91	2/1/92 2 months	4.1 kg —	—	—	congenital heart disease	Died (9/3/92): malnutrition
4	Jiao Fang	F	11/25/91	2/7/92 2 ½ mths.	— 57 cm	—	—	mentally defective	Died (6/15/92): severe malnutrition; dehydration
5	Jiao Bing	F	2/3/91	2/9/92 6 days	2.8 kg 47 cm	satisfactory	monitor intelligence	—	Died (4/9/92): malnutrition
6	Jiao Min	M	2/1/83	2/12/92 9 years	— 122 cm	—	—	mentally defective	Unknown
7	Jiao Zheng	F	—	2/12/92 —	— —	—	—	—	Adopted, 2/17/92
8	Jiao Juan	M	1/25/89	2/12/92 1 year	— 79 cm	—	—	bow-legged (lack of calcium)	Unknown

No.	Name	Sex	Born	Admitted Age	Weight/ Height	State of Nutrition	Intelligence Level	Type of Disability	STATUS AS OF OCTOBER 1992 (WHERE KNOWN) Recorded Cause of Death
9	JIAO HONG	M	3/1/83	2/12/92 9 years	120 cm	–	–	mentally defective	Died (4/15/92); *mentally defective* [sic]
10	JIAO FENG	M	8/24/90	2/12/92 1 ½ years	– 75 cm	–	–	small, malformed cranium	Unknown
11	JIAO LI	F	–	2/14/92 –	–	–	–	–	Adopted (2/15/92)
12	JIAO WEN	F	10/2/85	2/14/92 6 ½ years	– 94 cm	–	–	mentally defective	Died (2/27/92); [recorded cause of death unknown]
13	JIAO YUN	M	2/5/92	2/15/92 10 days	– 50 cm	–	–	mentally defective	Died (3/1/92): *megacolon*
14	JIAO JING	F	2/6/92	2/16/92 10 days	– 46 cm	–	monitor intelligence	–	Unknown
15	JIAO XIANG	M	–	2/11/92 –	–	–	–	–	Adopted (2/20/92)
16	JIAO DONG	M	2/1/80	2/17/92 12 years	– 128 cm	–	–	small, malformed cranium	Unknown
17	JIAO MAO	M	3/1/88	2/17/92 4 years	– 94 cm	–	–	mentally defective	Unknown
18	JIAO JUE	F	2/8/92	2/18/92 10 days	– 48 cm	–	monitor intelligence	–	Unknown
19	JIAO HAO	F	4/10/91	2/18/92 10 months	62 cm	–	–	hydrocephalus	Died (7/22/92): *bronchial pneumonia; hydrocephalus*

New Admissions, February 1992

No.	Name	Sex	Born	Admitted Age	Weight/ Height	State of Nutrition	Intelligence Level	Type of Disability	STATUS AS OF OCTOBER 1992 (WHERE KNOWN) Recorded Cause of Death
20	JIAO FA	F	–	2/19/92 –	–	–	–	–	Adopted, 2/26/92
21	JIAO QI	M	1/10/92	2/19/92 1 month	– 54 cm	–	–	–	Died (4/30/92): malnutrition
22	JIAO QIANG	F	–	2/20/92 –	–	–	–	–	Died (2/23/92): malnutrition; convulsive high fever
23	JIAO CHU	F	1/2/90	2/23/92 2 years	12.5 kg 76 cm	moderate	–	mentally defective	Died (5/11/92): cerebral palsy
24	JIAO GANG	F	2/21/85	2/24/92 7 years	18.0 kg 117 cm	moderate	–	small, malformed cranium	Unknown
25	JIAO CHENG	F	2/24/92	2/24/92 newborn	3.1 kg 49 cm	satisfactory	monitor intelligence	–	Unknown
26	JIAO JIN	F	2/18/92	2/24/92 6 days	3.0 kg 49 cm	satisfactory	monitor intelligence	–	Died (6/17/92): malnutrition; head infection
27	JIAO HUI	F	4/19/91	2/24/92 10 months	8.0 kg 72 cm	moderate	–	mentally defective	Sent to Medical Ward on 2/28/92 with fever [outcome unknown]
28	JIAO PING	F	6/5/89	2/25/92 3 years	13.0 kg 88 cm	satisfactory	–	small, malformed cranium	Died (4/29/92): [recorded cause of death unknown]
29	JIAO WEI	F	12/12/91	2/28/92 2 ½ mths.	5.0 kg 56 cm	satisfactory	monitor intelligence	–	Unknown

Table 4.6   **List of 207 Infant and Child Deaths at the Shanghai Children's Welfare Institute, November 1991–October 1992**[301]

No.	Name	Sex	Born	Admitted	Age	Condition On Arrival	Died	Age	Cause of Death	Where Died
						NOVEMBER 1991				
1	BEI PEI[302]	M	1986	June 88	2 yrs.	–	11/5/91	5 yrs.	–	Disabled Section
2	YU JI	F	1990	Oct. 91	19 mths.	–	11/5/91	20 mths	–	Infants Section
3	RONG YA	M	1984	Sep. 86	2 yrs.	–	11/6/91	7 yrs.	–	Infants Section, Group #14
4	NAN QING	F	1986	April 90	4 yrs.	–	11/7/91	5 yrs.	–	Medical Ward
5	KE CHENG	F	1988	June 89	1 yr.	–	11/9/91	3 yrs.	–	Medical Ward
6	JIANG LI	M	1988	Sep. 90	2 yrs.	–	11/9/91	3 yrs.	–	Infants Section, Group #3
7	QIAO YA	M	1979	Feb. 90	11 yrs.	–	11/11/91	12 yrs.	–	Disabled Section, Group #9

[301] This list was assembled by Human Rights Watch/Asia from details contained in a variety of official documents from the Shanghai Children's Welfare Institute, and contains details of all known infant and child deaths that occurred at the orphanage during the twelve-month period November 1991–October 1992. The source documents used in compiling the list include individual medical records; crematorium slips; mortality lists compiled by dissident staff at the orphanage; information compiled by SMPC delegates; and other miscellaneous documentary materials. Since the list is a composite one and not a translation of an original document, figures appearing in the "No." column are ones assigned for reference purposes by Human Rights Watch/Asia; for the most part, they do not correspond to any case numbers appearing on the original source documents.

[302] No medical records were obtained for cases of death that occurred during November 1991. Details for that month were compiled by Human Rights Watch/Asia on the basis of entries secretly copied from the orphanage's Staff Duty Register (*Jiaoban Bu*). The columns headed "Condition On Arrival" and "Cause of Death" are thus left vacant; moreover, no dates or other details regarding "consultation" sessions were obtained for any of the November 1991 cases.

No.	Name	Sex	Born	Admitted	Age	Condition On Arrival	Died	Age	Cause of Death	Where Died
8	Shan Zhou	M	1988	May 88	? days	–	11/11/91	3½ yrs.	–	Infants Section, Group #15
9	Yu Xi	F	May 91	Oct. 91	5 mths.	–	11/12/91	6 mths.	–	Infants Section
10	Bian Xue	F	April 91	June 91	2 mths.	–	11/13/91	7 mths.	–	–
11	Gan Dong	?	–	–	–	–	11/13/91	–	–	–
12	Zeng Ya	M	11/11/91	11/11/91	newborn	–	11/14/91	3 days	–	I.S. Reception Unit
13	Yu Hong	M	Sep. 91	Oct. 91	1 mth.	–	11/14/91	2 mths.	–	I.S. Reception Unit
14	Zeng Pei	M	1989	Nov. 91	2 yrs.	–	11/15/91	2 yrs.	–	Medical Ward
15	Yuan Zhong	F	June 91	Aug. 91	2 mths.	–	11/15/91	5 mths.	–	Infants Section
16	Yu Wen	F	Oct. 91	Oct. 91	newborn	–	11/15/91	1 mth.	–	I.S. Reception Unit
17	Peng Hai	M	Nov. 90	July 91	8 mths.	–	11/15/91	1 yr.	–	Infants Section
18	Qu Jiang	F	8/27/88	9/27/88	1 mth.	–	11/16/91	3 yrs.	–	Disabled Section, Grp. #14
19	Zeng He	M	5/8/91	11/12/91	6 mths.	–	11/16/91	6 mths.	–	Medical Ward
20	Yu Lie	F	10/12/91	10/12/91	newborn	–	11/21/91	1 mth.	–	Medical Ward
21	Yuan He	F	6/17/91	8/29/91	2½ mths.	–	11/23/91	5 mths.	–	I.S. Reception Unit
22	Xing Fa	F	8/20/91	9/1/91	12 days	neonatal jaundice	11/25/91	3 mths.	–	Medical Ward
23	Tai An	F	7/10/88	8/5/88	1 mth.	–	11/26/91	3 yrs.	–	Infants Section, Group #3

NOVEMBER 1991

No.	Name	Sex	Born	Admitted	Age	Condition On Arrival	Died	Age	Cause of Death	Where Died
24	Yu Xiao	M	10/23/91	10/23/91	newborn	—	11/26/91	1 mth.	—	Medical Ward
25	Zeng Mao	F	10/27/91	11/27/91	1 mth.	—	11/27/91	1 mth	—	I.S. Reception Unit
26	Xi Ping	F	5/20/91	6/11/91	22 days	—	11/27/91	6 mths.	—	Infants Section, Group #7
27	Yuan Ding	M	Nov. 89	Aug. 91	1¾ yrs.	—	11/28/91	2 yrs.	—	Infants Section, Group #5
28	Zeng Qi	F	10/5/91	11/27/91	1½ mths.	—	11/28/91	1½ mths.	—	Infants Section, Group #4
29	Zeng Wan	F	Mar. 91	Nov. 91	8 mths.	—	11/28/91	8 mths.	—	I.S. Reception Unit
30	Peng Hao	F	7/13/91	July 91	newborn	—	11/28/91	4 mths	—	Infants Section, Group #7
31	Tai Yi	M	8/29/84	8/29/88	4 yrs.	—	11/29/91	7 yrs.	—	Infants Section, Group #13
32	Mao Lin	F	11/7/76	10/20/80	4 yrs.	—	11/30/91	15 yrs.	—	Medical Ward

DECEMBER 1991

No.	Name	Sex	Born	Admitted Age	Recorded Medical Condition On Arrival	"Consultation"	Died Age	Cause of Death	Recorded Cause of Death Location
33	Zheng Jue	?	2/27/91	11/27/91 9 months	—	—	12/1/91 9 months	—	Medical Ward
34	Yu Zhen	F	10/22/80	Oct. 91 11 years	—	—	12/2/91 11 years	—	Disabled Section, Group #9

No.	Name	Sex	Born	Admitted Age	Recorded Medical Condition On Arrival	"Consultation"	Died Age	Recorded Cause of Death Location
35	XI SHI	F	5/5/91	6/8/91 *1 month*	missing left forearm; monitor intelligence[303]	–	12/2/91 *7 months*	choked on milk and suffocated; second-degree malnutrition *Infants Section, Group #7*
36	YUAN JIA	M	8/20/90	Aug. 91 *1 year*	–	–	12/3/91 *15 mths.*	– *Infants Section*
37	CHEN PING	M	12/21/88	5/31/89 *5 months*	harelip and cleft palate; monitor intelligence; weight 5 kg	12/2/91	12/3/91 *3 years*	third-degree malnutrition, harelip and cleft palate; mentally defective (severe) *Infants Section, Group #15*
38	YU ZHE	?	10/21/85	Oct. 91 *6 years*	–	–	12/4/91 *6 years*	*Disabled Section, Group #9*
39	ZENG HUI	?	–	Nov. 91	–	–	12/7/91	– *Infants Section*
40	YU YUN	?	10/27/87	Oct. 91 *4 years*	–	–	12/8/91 *4 years*	*Disabled Section*
41	ZENG HUAN	F	8/11/89	Nov. 91 *2 years*	–	–	12/10/91 *2 years*	– *Medical Ward*
42	GU XIN	F	10/2/86	11/27/90 *4 years*	small, malformed cranium; weight 15 kg	12/9/91	12/10/91 *5 years*	third-degree malnutrition; mentally defective *Disabled Section, Group #18*

303 *"Zhi-guan"*, an abbreviation for *"zhili guancha"*, which means: "intelligence level to be determined through observation." For a detailed discussion of this term, see above, "Recorded Causes of Death," under "Epidemiologic Aspects."

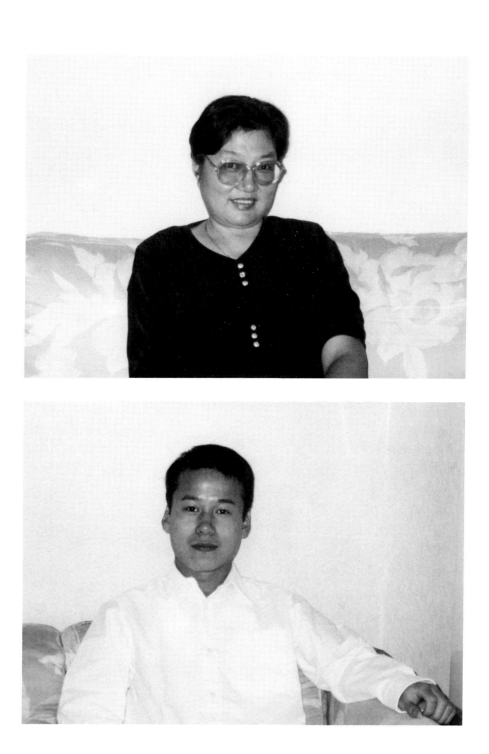

Above: Dr. **Zhang Shuyun**; born 1942; formerly a physician at the Shanghai orphanage; left China in March 1995. Below: **Ai Ming**, born 1972, spent twenty years at the Shanghai orphanage; left China in June 1995.

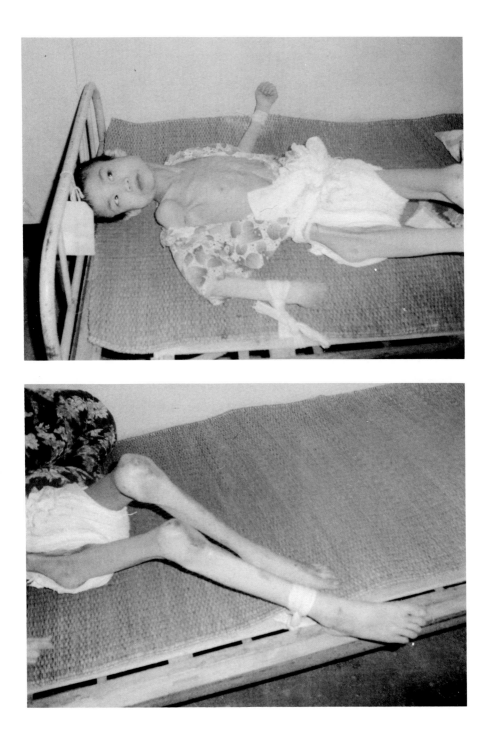

Jian Xun: Male; born February 1981; admitted to Shanghai orphanage February 24, 1988; died July 17, 1992. No causes of death entered on crematorium slip. Date of photographs: July 7, 1992.

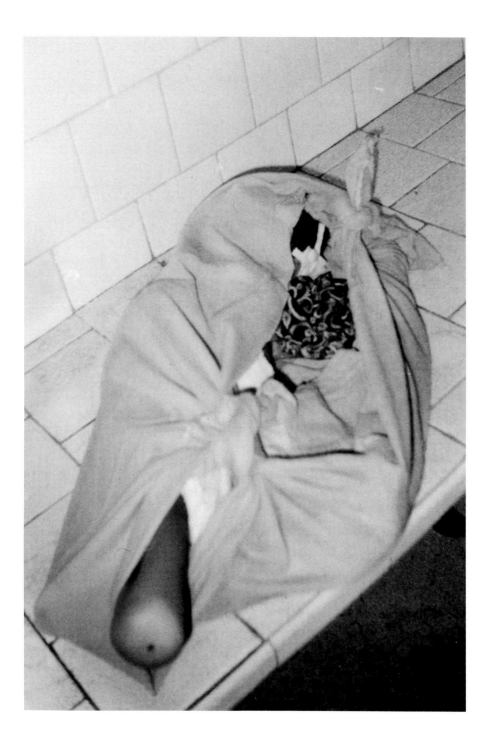

Shrouded body of **Huo Qiu**.

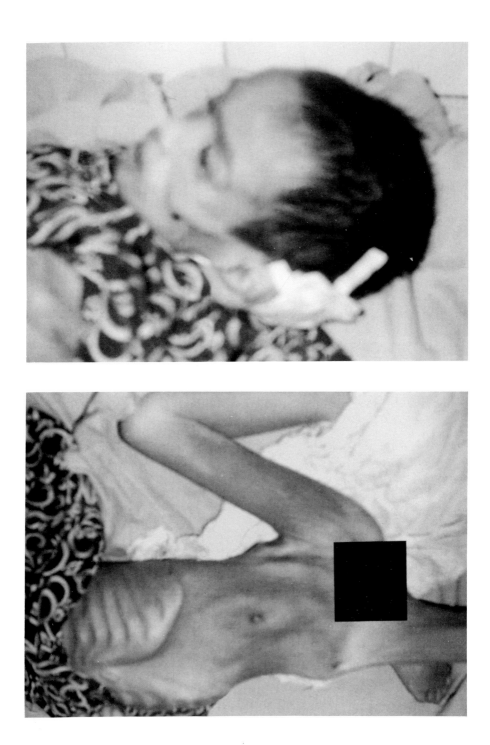

Huo Qiu: Female; born February 1988; admitted to Shanghai orphanage January 3, 1991; died June 23, 1992. Recorded causes of death: severe malnutrition, cerebral palsy and mental deficiency. Date of photographs: June 23, 1992.

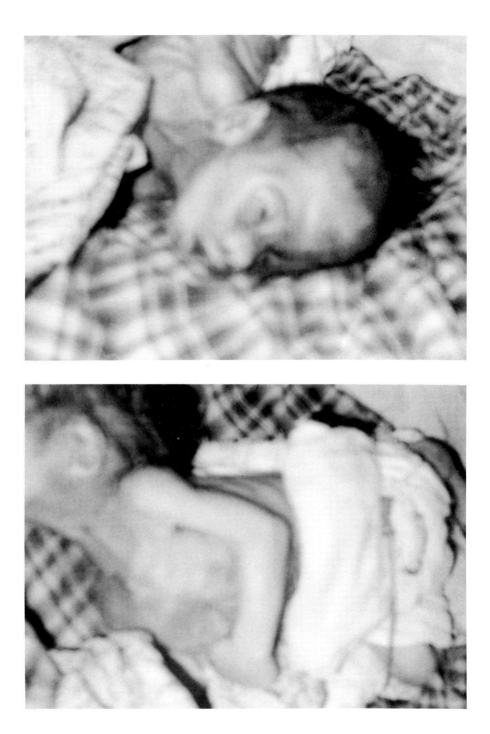

Ba Zhong: Female; Born January 2 1992; admitted to Shanghai orphanage January 3, 1992; died June 30, 1992. Recorded causes of death: malnutrition, severe dehydration and phlegmona. Date of photographs: June 30, 1992.

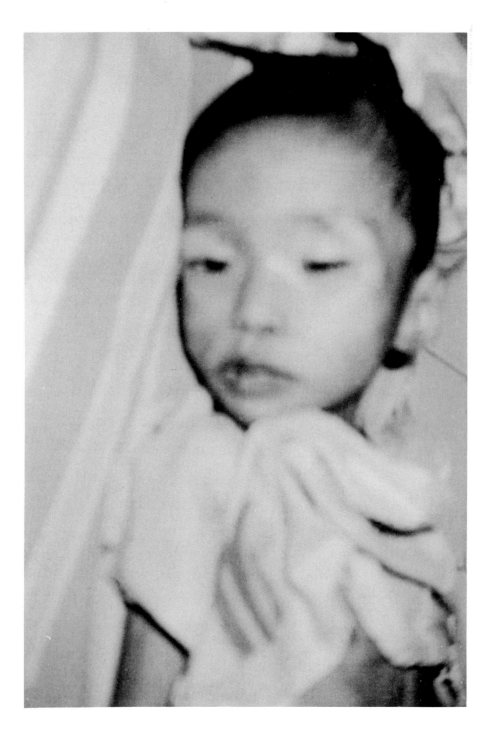

Ke Yue: Female; born November 1989; admitted to Shanghai orphanage same month; died June 10, 1992. Recorded causes of death: severe malnutrition and congenital maldevelopment of brain. Date of photograph: June 11, 1992.

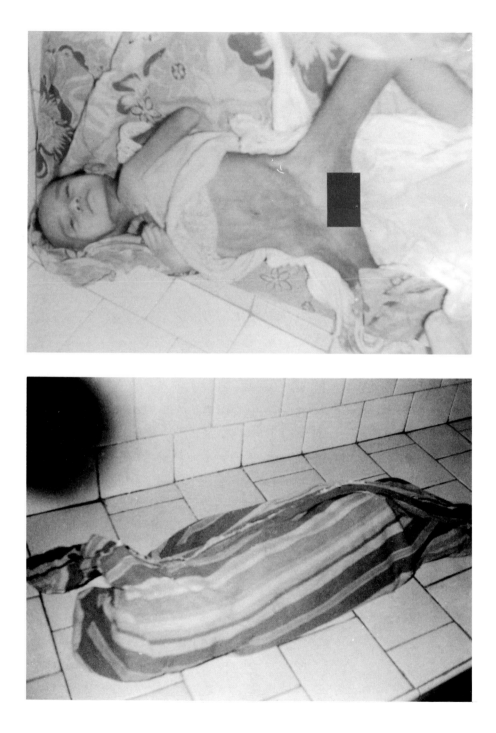

Above: **Xie Ying**.   Below: Shrouded body of **Ke Yue**.

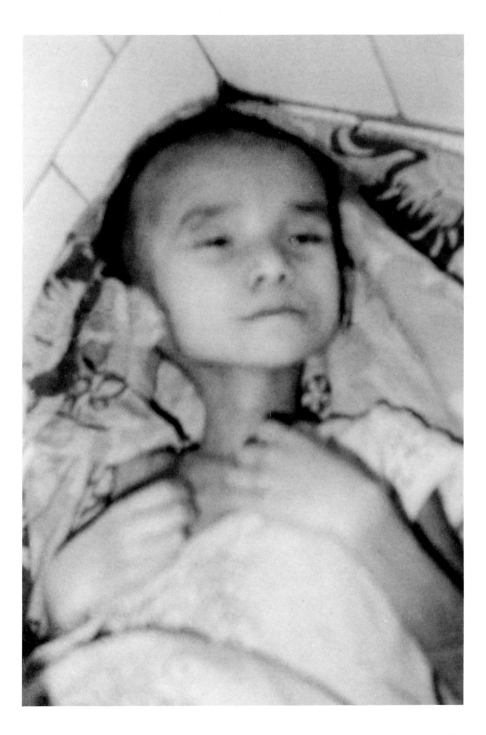

Xie Ying: Female; born April 22, 1989; admitted to Shanghai orphanage December 12, 1991; died June 24, 1992. Recorded causes of death: malnutrition and mental deficiency. Date of photographs: June 24, 1992.

No.	Name	Sex	Born	Admitted Age	Recorded Medical Condition On Arrival	"Consultation"	Died Age	Recorded Cause of Death Location
43	NAN SHI	M	12/1/89	5/21/90 6 months	blind in both eyes; monitor intelligence; weight 5 kg	6/19/90	12/11/91 2 years	malnutrition; mentally defective Medical Ward
44	YU CHENG	M	8/14/91	10/13/91 2 months	monitor intelligence; albino; weight 5.8 kg	12/12/91	12/13/91 4 months	third-degree malnutrition; albinism; mentally defective Infants Section, Group #7
45	QI FU	M	4/25/76	8/21/76 4 months	congenital heart disease; mentally defective	12/14/91	12/15/91 15 years	third-degree malnutrition; congenital heart disease; mentally defective Disabled Section, Group #18
46	JIANG LIN	F	3/2/84	5/19/91 7 years	poor intelligence (zhili cha)	12/14/91	12/18/91 7¾ yrs.	third-degree malnutrition; mentally defective Infants Section, Group #7
47	XI FAN	M	2/2/91	6/22/91 4½ mths.	small, malformed cranium; weight 5.5 kg	12/3/91	12/22/91 10½ mths.	third-degree malnutrition; small, malformed cranium Infants Section, Group #7
48	GUO QING	F	4/2/89	4/19/89 17 days	harelip and cleft palate; weight 3.25 kg	12/14/91	12/24/91 2½ yrs.	mentally defective; third-degree malnutrition Infants Section, Group #3
49	JIANG JUN	F	6/23/85	9/23/90 5 years	small, malformed cranium; cerebral palsy; weight 10.1 kg	12/24/91	12/25/91 6½ yrs.	third-degree malnutrition; mentally defective; cerebral palsy Disabled Section, Group #14

No.	Name	Sex	Born	Admitted / Age	Recorded Medical Condition On Arrival	"Consultation"	Died / Age	Recorded Cause of Death / Location
50	XIE YONG	F	10/1/86	12/18/91 / 5 years	small, malformed cranium; mentally defective; weight 13 kg	12/25/91	12/26/91 / 5 years	second-degree malnutrition; small, malformed cranium; mentally defective / Infants Section's Reception Unit
51	XIE LE	M	11/1/91	12/7/91 / 1 month	monitor intelligence; weight 2.25 kg	12/20/91	12/26/91 / 2 months	third-degree malnutrition; mentally defective; torticollis [squint neck] / Infants Section, Group #3
52	HU PING	F	1/20/85	3/26/89 / 4 years	paralysis of lower legs, withered calf-muscles; but able to speak, crawl and feed herself; weight 14.75 kg	—	12/28/91 / 7 years	congenital maldevelopment of brain / Disabled Section, Group #17
53	YUAN JIE	F	6/2/91	8/8/91 / 2 months	missing left forearm; weight 3.75 kg	12/19/91	12/28/91 / 7 months	third-degree malnutrition; mentally defective; missing left forearm; bronchial pneumonia / Infants Section, Group #7
54	YU XIN	F	9/8/91	10/8/91 / 1 month	monitor intelligence; weight 3.7 kg	12/27/91	12/28/91 / 3 ½ mths	third-degree malnutrition; bronchial pneumonia; total circulatory failure / Infants Section, Group #7
55	XIE CHENG	F	11/30/91	12/19/91 / 19 days	small, malformed cranium	12/20/91	12/28/91 / 1 month	third-degree malnutrition / Infants Section's Reception Unit
56	JIA JUN	M	3/5/89	9/11/89 / 6 months	blind in both eyes; weight 5.5 kg	7/10/91	12/29/91 / 2 ¾ yrs.	third-degree malnutrition; mentally defective (severe) / Infants Section, Group #3

No.	Name	Sex	Born	Admitted / Age	Recorded Medical Condition On Arrival	"Consultation"	Died / Age	Recorded Cause of Death / Location
57	ZENG XIN	F	9/22/91	11/19/91 / 2 months	mentally defective; congenital idiocy?; weight 3.5 kg	12/18/91	12/29/91 / 3 months	second to third-degree malnutrition; bronchial pneumonia; congenital idiocy? [sic] / Infants Section's Reception Unit
58	LOU MAO	F	6/20/86	9/28/90 / 4 years	small, malformed cranium	12/18/91	12/29/91 / 5 ½ yrs.	third-degree malnutrition, small, malformed cranium / Disabled Section, Group #18
59	HUA YI	F	4/6/90	7/16/90 / 3 months	monitor intelligence; weight 5.0 kg	12/28/91	12/29/91 / 1 ½ yrs.	third-degree malnutrition, mentally defective / Infants Section, Group #3
60	PENG JUN	M	7/1/88	7/22/91 / 3 years	mentally defective; weight 7.75 kg	12/26/91	12/29/91 / 3 ½ yrs.	third-degree malnutrition; cerebral palsy / Infants Section, Group #15
61	XING MAO	M	8/10/90	9/10/91 / 1 year	monitor intelligence; weight 14 kg	12/27/91	12/29/91 / 1 ⅓ yrs.	third-degree malnutrition; mentally defective; cerebral palsy[304] / Infants Section, Group #3
62	ZENG YUAN	F	10/25/91	11/30/91 / 1 month	monitor intelligence [record later altered to: "mentally defective"]; weight 4.5 kg	12/13/91	12/29/91 / 2 months	congenital maldevelopment of brain; total circulatory failure / Infants Section's Reception Unit

[304] The words "cerebral palsy" appear to have been added to the original record at a later date.

					DECEMBER 1991		
No.	**Name**	**Sex**	**Born**	**Admitted** *Age*	**Recorded Medical Condition On Arrival**	**"Consul- tation"**	**Died** *Age*	**Recorded Cause of Death** *Location*
63	XING LAN	F	8/26/91	9/17/91 *22 days*	monitor intelligence; weight 3.5 kg	12/29/91	12/30/91 *4 months*	third-degree malnutrition; severe pneumonia; asthenia universalis [collapse of body functions] *Infants Section, Group #7*
64	XI LIANG	M	4/26/91	6/28/91 *2 months*	monitor intelligence; weight 5.0 kg	12/30/91 10:30 AM	12/30/91 3:30 PM *8 months*	third-degree malnutrition; bronchial pneumonia and septicemia; total circulatory failure *Infants Section, Group #7*
65	ZENG JUN	M	2/8/89	11/17/91 *2 ¾ years*	cerebral palsy; weight 12 kg	12/30/91	12/31/91 *3 years*	severe malnutrition; mentally defective *Infants Section, Group #7*
66	CHEN JUN	M	5/12/89	5/24/89 *12 days*	monitor intelligence; weight 2.75 kg	12/30/91	12/31/91 *2 ½ yrs.*	third-degree malnutrition; mentally defective *Infants Section, Group #3*

240

JANUARY 1992

No.	Name	Sex	Born	Admitted Age	Recorded Medical Condition On Arrival	"Consultation"	Died Age	Recorded Cause of Death Location
67	BI FENG[305]	F	5/30/77	1985 8 years	–	–	1/1/92 14 ½ yrs.	no cause of death recorded
68	XING QIAN	F	8/9/91	9/9/91 1 month	monitor intelligence; weight 3.6 kg	12/31/91	1/2/92 5 months	second to third-degree malnutrition; mentally defective (severe) Medical Ward
69	ZENG XI	F	11/2/91	11/25/91 23 days	monitor intelligence; weight 2.8 kg	1/4/92 8:30 AM	1/4/92 10:00 AM 2 months	second-degree malnutrition; severe pneumonia; total circulatory failure Medical Ward
70	BA GONG	F	1/8/91	1/6/92 1 year	mentally defective; malnutrition; weight 4.0 kg	1/7/92	1/8/92 1 year	mentally defective; malnutrition Infants Section
71	BA WEI	M	12/2/91	1/3/92 1 month	mentally defective	1/6/92	1/7/92 1 month	third-degree malnutrition; mentally defective Infants Section
72	JI XING	M	11/10/89	2/27/90 3 ½ mths.	megalodactyly [oversized toes]; testicles swollen with fluid; lymphoma of right buttock and leg; weight 4.5kg	1/8/92	1/9/92 2 years	third-degree malnutrition; megalodactyly of right foot; lymphoma of right buttock and leg Infants Section, Group #15

---

[305] The case of Bi Feng was one of only three cases formally acknowledged by the Shanghai Bureau of Supervision, which in late 1991 began an eight-month-long investigation into the high death rates at the orphanage, as constituting "deaths from unnatural causes." Bi Feng had been entirely healthy until shortly before her sudden death in January 1992, and orphanage officials were unable to produce any explanation for her death. The other two such cases were those of Xi Liang (case #64) and Xing Fei (case #53). See Chapter 5 for further details on these cases.

241

JANUARY 1992

No.	Name	Sex	Born	Admitted / Age	Recorded Medical Condition On Arrival	"Consultation"	Died / Age	Recorded Cause of Death / Location
73	XIE SHAN	M	5/6/91	12/13/91 / *7 months*	post-operative hydro-cephalus; mentally defective; weight 8.5 kg	1/9/92	1/11/92 / *8 months*	post-operative hydrocephalus; mentally defective / *Infants Section's Reception Unit*
74	XIE JIAN	M	12/6/87	12/5/91 / *4 years*	mentally defective; cerebral palsy; weight 10 kg	–	1/15/92 / *4 years*	bronchial pneumonia; mentally defective; malnutrition / *Medical Ward*
75	BA CHENG	M	1/15/90 (lunar)	1/6/92 / *2 years*	mentally defective; weight 12 kg	–	1/18/92 / *2 years*	malnutrition / *Infants Section's Reception Unit*
76	YU LEI	M	10/5/90	10/14/91 / *1 year*	mentally defective; weight 6.0 kg	12/14/91	1/20/92 / *15 mths.*	third-degree malnutrition; severe dehydration; mentally defective / *Medical Ward*
77	ZENG XIANG	F	10/4/91	11/19/91 / *1 ½ mths.*	monitor intelligence; weight 3.8 kg	–	1/25/92 / *15 mths.*	malnutrition; heart failure; pneumonia; low-weight infant / *Medical Ward*
78	SHAO YI	F	2/7/76	12/5/81 / *5 ¾ years*	infantile poliomyelitis sequelae; deaf-mute? [sic]; weight 18 kg	–	1/26/92 / *16 years*	deaf-mute; third-degree malnutrition; *Disabled Section, Group #11*
79	XING YI	F	Aug. 91	Sep. 91 / *1 month*	–	–	1/27/92 / *1 ½ yrs.*	–

242

No.	Name	Sex	Born	Admitted / Age	Recorded Medical Condition On Arrival	"Consult-ation"	Died / Age	Recorded Cause of Death / Location
80	Lü Lei	M	12/1/76	7/19/83 / 6 ½ years'	deaf-mute?; mentally defective? [sic]; weight 37.5 kg	–	2/6/92 / 15 years	congenital maldevelopment of brain / Disabled Section.
81	Ba Jun	F	12/2/91	1/2/92 / 1 month	monitor intelligence; weight 3.8 kg	1/13/92	2/8/92 / 2 months	severe malnutrition; pneumonia / Medical Ward
82	Ba Nan	F	12/24/91	1/19/92 / 26 days	monitor intelligence; harelip; weight 3.5 kg	2/11/92	2/11/92 / 1 ½ mths	second-degree malnutrition; harelip / Medical Ward
83	Zeng Xian	F	11/16/91	11/24/91 / 8 days	monitor intelligence; weight 2.8 kg	2/13/92	2/15/92 / 3 months	third-degree malnutrition; pneumonia; low body weight / Infants Section's Reception Unit
84	Ba Chao	F	12/5/91	1/16/92 / 1 ½ mths.	Six fingers on hands, six toes on left foot, six intelligence; weight 3.0 kg	–	2/17/92 / 2 ½ mths	third-degree malnutrition; severe dehydration; low-weight infant / Medical Ward
85	Xing Fei	M	8/17/91	Sep. 91 / ? days	obstructed nephelium [thin layer of skin over eyeball]	–	2/19/92 / 6 months	bronchial pneumonia / Infants Section, Group #7
86	Jiao Qiang	F	12/4/89	2/20/92 / 2 years	cerebral palsy; weight 8.5 kg	–	2/23/92 / 2 years	– / Medical Ward
87	Di Qiang	M	1980	Oct. 1989	–	–	2/23/92 / 12 years	third-degree malnutrition / Disabled Section
88	Jiao Wen	F	10/2/85	2/14/92 / 6 ½ years	mentally defective	–	2/27/92 / 6½ years	third-degree malnutrition; mentally defective / Infants Section's Reception Unit

243

FEBRUARY 1992

No.	Name	Sex	Born	Admitted *Age*	Recorded Medical Condition On Arrival	"Consult- ation"	Died *Age*	Recorded Cause of Death *Location*
89	BA MIN	F	10/28/91	1/8/92 *2 months*	mentally defective; epilepsy; weight 6.0 kg	1/13/92	2/29/92 *4 months*	malnutrition; pneumonia; cerebral palsy? *Medical Ward*

MARCH 1992

No.	Name	Sex	Born	Admitted	Age	Condition On Arrival	Died	Age	Recorded Cause of Death	Where Died
90	JIAO YUN [306]	M	2/5/92	2/15/92	10 days	mentally defective	3/1/92	24 days	megacolon	MW[307]
91	MI ZHONG	M	–	March 92	–	–	3/14/92	–	respiratory failure	MW
92	MI JIA	?	–	March 92	–	–	3/15/92	–	–	–
93	JIANG BAO	?	–	Sep. 90	–	–	3/22/92	–	–	–

[306] Most of the subsequent case information is taken from death registers maintained by the orphanage's Medical Ward. NB: From March 1992 onwards, the medical records no longer contain specific mention of "consultation" being performed by Luo Xiaoling or other medical staff at the orphanage. It is unclear whether the practice was stopped at that point or continued covertly and without further documentary trace. It is important to remember that the Bureau of Supervision's eight-month-long investigation into the high death rate at the orphanage was moving into high gear by April 1992. Whatever the case, the fact is that the death rate continued unabated throughout the investigation and until October 1992, when the orphanage leadership finally succeeded in blocking all further access to the medical records and official death lists.

[307] Orphanage locations in the "Where Died" column are henceforth abbreviated as follows: "MW": Medical Ward; "IS": Infants Section; "DS": Disabled Section; "RU": Reception Unit; and "CS": Children's Section.

244

MARCH 1992									
No.	Name	Sex	Born	Admitted	Age	Condition On Arrival	Died	Age	Recorded Cause of Death	Where Died
94	XIE LONG	?	–	Dec. 91	–	–	3/24/92	–	malnutrition; cleft palate	MW
95	MI ZENG	M	–	March 92	–		3/28/92	–	cerebral palsy	MW
96	XIE LING	M	–	Dec. 91	–	–	3/28/92	–	severe malnutrition; bronchial pneumonia	MW

APRIL 1992									
No.	Name	Sex	Born	Admitted	Age	Condition On Arrival	Died	Age	Recorded Cause of Death	Where Died
97	DONG XI	M	–	April 92	–	–	4/4/92	–	premature; low weight	MW
98	MI XIA	?	–	March 92	–	–	4/4/92	–	–	–
99	JIAO BING	F	2/3/92	2/9/92	6 days	monitor intelligence; weight 2.8 kg	4/9/92	2 mths.	malnutrition; severe dehydration	MW
100	JIAO HONG	M	3/1/83	2/12/92	9 yrs.	mentally defective	4/15/92	9 yrs.	mentally defective	MW
101	MI FEN	F	–	March 92	–	–	4/16/92	–	malnutrition; cerebral palsy	MW
102	ZENG QUAN	F	–	Nov. 91	–	–	4/17/92	–	cerebral palsy, malnutrition	MW
103	DONG QI	F	–	April 92	–	–	4/17/92	–	hemorrhage of upper digestive tract	MW

245

APRIL 1992

No.	Name	Sex	Born	Admitted	Age	Condition On Arrival	Died	Age	Recorded Cause of Death	Where Died
104	DONG FAN	F	-	April 92	-	-	4/20/92	-	low weight, malnutrition	MW
105	MI QING	M	-	March 92	-	-	4/27/92	-	pneumonia	MW
106	JIAO PING	F	6/5/89	2/25/92	2 ¾ yrs.	small, malformed cranium	4/29/92	3 yrs.	malnutrition; pneumonia; small, malformed cranium	IS
107	JIAO QI	M	1/10/92	2/19/92	1 mth.	-	4/30/92	3½ mths.	malnutrition	MW

MAY 1992

No.	Name	Sex	Born	Admitted	Age	Condition On Arrival	Died	Age	Recorded Cause of Death	Where Died
108	XIE CHAO	F	-	Dec. 91	-	harelip	5/3/92	-	harelip; bronchial pneumonia; malnutrition	MW
109	LIANG ZU	M	4/3/84	4/9/88	4 yrs.	-	5/5/92	8 yrs.	malnutrition; mentally defective; cerebral palsy	MW
110	FA DONG	F	12/11/91	1/20/92	1 mth.	monitor intelligence; weight 3.0 kg	5/6/92	5 mths.	malnutrition; septicemia	MW
111	XING QIAN	M	12/3/90	-	-	-	5/7/92	1½ yrs.	cranial phlegmona	-
112	JIAO CHU	F	1/2/90	2/23/92	2 yrs.	weight 12.5 kg; mentally defective	5/9/92	1½ yrs.	malnutrition; cerebral palsy	DS, Grp. 18

May 1992

No.	Name	Sex	Born	Admitted	Age	Condition On Arrival	Died	Age	Recorded Cause of Death	Where Died
113	Xin Qian	F	-	May 92	-	-	5/20/92	-	congenital heart disease	MW
114	Xin Lu	F	1/5/92	5/7/92	4 mths.	-	5/23/92	4 ½ mths.	malnutrition, cerebral palsy	MW
115	Mi Sha	F	3/4/92	3/12/92	8 days	monitor intelligence; low weight (1.5 kg)	5/24/92	2 ½ mths.	premature birth; low-weight infant	MW
116	Xin Sheng	M	5/4/92	5/7/92	3 days	-	5/25/92	21 days	congenital absence of anus	MW
117	Xing Ju	-	-	Sep 91	-	-	5/30/92	-	congenital maldevelopment of brain	IS
118	Qiao Xiong	?	-	Feb 90	-	-	5/30/92	-	congenital heart disease	IS
119	Xin Shi	M	-	May 92	-	-	5/31/92	-	congenital heart disease	MW

June 1992

No.	Name	Sex	Born	Admitted	Age	Condition On Arrival	Died	Age	Recorded Cause of Death	Where Died
120	Xin Yuan	M	8/10/91	5/10/92	9 mths.	-	6/1/92	10 mths.	malnutrition; cerebral palsy	MW
121	Mi Gang	M	3/16/92	3/21/92	5 days	-	6/3/92	2½ mths.	congenital harelip and cleft palate; malnutrition; cerebral palsy	MW

No.	Name	Sex	Born	Admitted	Age	Condition On Arrival	Died	Age	Recorded Cause of Death	Where Died
						JUNE 1992				
122	MI ZHAN	F	3/18/90	3/17/92	2 yrs.	–	6/4/92	2 yrs. +	congenital maldevelopment of brain	MW
123	JIA SHUN	F	6/22/89	Sep. 89	3 mths.	–	6/5/92	3 yrs.	cerebral palsy	MW
124	KE SHEN	F	June 89	Nov. 89	5 mths.	–	6/6/92	3 yrs.	mentally defective; malnutrition	MW
125	KE YUE	F	–	Nov. 89	–	–	6/10/92	–	severe malnutrition; congenital maldevelopment of brain	MW
126	YUAN FENG	M	6/6/89	6/6/92	3 yrs.	–	6/12/92	3 yrs.	severe malnutrition; cerebral palsy	MW
127	JIAO FANG	F	11/25/91	2/7/92	2½ mths.	mentally defective	6/15/92	7 mths.	malnutrition; severe dehydration	MW
128	YAN HUA	F	5/28/92	6/3/92	6 days	–	6/17/92	20 days	malnutrition; infected swelling on side of head	MW
129	JIAO JIN	F	2/18/92	2/24/92	6 days	monitor intelligence; weight 3.0 kg	6/18/92	4 mths.	malnutrition; head infection	MW
130	HUO QIU	F	2/16/88	1/3/91	3 yrs.	–	6/23/92	4 yrs.	malnutrition; mentally defective; cerebral palsy	MW
131	XIE YING	F	4/22/89	12/12/91	2½ yrs.	–	6/24/92	3 yrs.	malnutrition; mentally defective	MW
132	YAN ZHAN	M	6/3/92	6/4/92	1 day	–	6/27/92	24 days	congenital spina bifida	MW

248

JUNE 1992

No.	Name	Sex	Born	Admitted	Age	Condition On Arrival	Died	Age	Recorded Cause of Death	Where Died
133	YAN LEI	M	10/8/91	6/23/92	8 ½ mths.	cerebral palsy; malnutrition; tongue cancer?; weight 5.5kg	6/29/92	9 mths.	malnutrition; tongue cancer? [sic]; cerebral palsy	MW
134	BA ZHONG	F	1/1/92	1/3/92	2 days	weight 2.8 kg; monitor intelligence	6/30/92	6 mths.	third-degree malnutrition; severe dehydration; phlegmona	MW

JULY 1992

No.	Name	Sex	Born	Admitted	Age	Condition On Arrival	Died	Age	Recorded Cause of Death	Where Died
135	XIN YING	M	5/15/92	5/23/92	8 days	–	7/3/92	1 ½ mths	skull defect, with infection; malnutrition	MW
136	DONG LIN	M	10/3/91	4/17/92	7 mths.	small, malformed cranium; congenital maldevelopment of brain; 1st-degree malnutrition; weight 7.0 kg	7/4/92	9 mths.	small, malformed cranium; infected right hand; malnutrition	MW
137	MENG YU	?	–	–	–		7/6/92		bronchial pneumonia	IS, Grp. 16
138	ZHAN GUI	M	7/1/92	7/4/92	–	congenital absence of anus; low weight	7/7/92	–	congenital absence of anus	MW

JULY 1992

No.	Name	Sex	Born	Admitted	Age	Condition On Arrival	Died	Age	Recorded Cause of Death	Where Died
139	Ba Xue	F	12/5/91	1/9/92	1 mth.	normal; weight 3.0 kg	7/9/92	7 mths.	congenital maldevelopment of brain; severe malnutrition	MW
140	Yan Jun	M	-	June 92	-	-	7/16/92	-	cerebral palsy	IS
141	Jian Xun	M	2/24/81	2/24/88	7 yrs.	mentally defective; deaf-mute; weight 29 kg	7/17/92	11 ½ yrs.	-	MW
142	Zhan Mao	?	-	July 92	-	-	7/18/92	-	-	IS
143	Zhan Bao	F	-	July 92	-	-	7/19/92	-	burn wounds on both legs; septicemia	MW
144	Fang Shen	M	-	April 91	-	-	7/21/92	-	malnutrition; mentally defective	MW
145	Xie Qi	M	-	Dec. 91	-	-	7/21/92	-	congenital maldevelopment of brain	MW
146	Jiao Hao	F	4/10/91	2/18/92	10 mths.	hydrocephalus	7/22/92	1⅓ mths	hydrocephalus; bronchial pneumonia	MW
147	Xin Hua	F	-	May 92	-	-	7/25/92	-	cerebral palsy; fatal necrosis of subcutaneous tissue; septicemia	MW
148	Dong Yang	M	10/6/90	4/20/92	1 ½ yrs.	congenital heart disease; pneumonia	7/26/92	2 yrs.	malnutrition; severe bronchial pneumonia; congenital heart disease	MW

JULY 1992

No.	Name	Sex	Born	Admitted	Age	Condition On Arrival	Died	Age	Recorded Cause of Death	Where Died
149	DONG HUAN	F	–	April 92	–	–	7/27/92	–	cerebral palsy; malnutrition	MW
150	XIN ZHAO	F	–	May 92	–	premature birth	7/28/92	–	premature birth	MW
151	HU FENG	M	–	March 89	–	–	7/30/92	–	–	MW

AUGUST 1992

No.	Name	Sex	Born	Admitted	Age	Condition On Arrival	Died	Age	Recorded Cause of Death	Where Died
152	ZHAN XU	F	–	July 92	–	–	8/1/92	–	congenital heart disease	MW
153	DONG FU	M	–	April 92	–	–	8/1/92	–	congenital megacolon	MW
154	DONG BEI	F	–	April 92	–	–	8/2/92	–	–	MW
155	XIN FANG	F	–	May 92	–	–	8/2/92	–	congenital heart disease	–
156	LUO HUAN	?	–	Aug. 92	–	–	8/5/92	–	–	–
157	XIN FEN	?	–	May 92	–	–	8/7/92	–	–	MW
158	DONG LAN	?	–	April 92	–	–	8/13/92	–	–	MW
159	YAN JIAN	?	–	June 92	–	–	8/13/92	–	–	MW
160	BA QIAN	F	9/16/91	1/28/92	4 mths.	weight 7.0 kg; mentally disabled (v); hydrocephaly	8/20/92	11 mths.	–	MW

August 1992

No.	Name	Sex	Born	Admitted	Age	Condition On Arrival	Died	Age	Recorded Cause of Death	Where Died
161	Luo Hao	F	8/11/92	Aug. 92	–		8/21/92	10 days	–	MW
162	Xin Yun	?	–	May 92	–		8/23/92	–	–	–
163	Xin Zhan	?	–	May 92	–		8/24/92	–	–	–
164	Ba Quan	F	1/2/92	1/24/92	22 days	monitor intelligence; weight 2.5 kg	8/24/92	7 ½ mths	congenital maldevelopment of brain	MW
165	Luo Jing	?	–	Aug. 92	? days		8/26/92	? days	–	–
166	Xin Wan	F	May 92	May 92	–		8/27/92	3 mths.	congenital maldevelopment of brain	MW
167	Luo Wei	M	April 92	Aug. 92	4 mths.		8/28/92	4 mths.	–	–
168	Luo Jun	M	Aug. 92	Aug. 92	–		8/28/92	1 mth.	–	MW
169	Luo Zhi	F	8/18/92	8/?/92	–		8/29/92	11 days	premature birth	MW

September 1992

No.	Name	Sex	Born	Admitted	Age	Condition On Arrival	Died	Age	Recorded Cause of Death	Where Died
170	Luo Wei	M	–	Aug. 92	–	–	9/1/92	–	third-degree malnutrition	MW

SEPTEMBER 1992

No.	Name	Sex	Born	Admitted	Age	Condition On Arrival	Died	Age	Recorded Cause of Death	Where Died
171	ZHAN LING	M	5/13/92	7/30/92	2 ½ mths.	small, malformed cranium; sight impairment	9/2/92	3 mths	congenitally small, malformed cranium; sight impairment	MW
172	LUO CHONG	M	Aug. 92	Aug. 92	–	–	9/2/92	1 mth.	–	RU
173	JIAO QI	F	12/6/91	2/1/92	2 mths.	congenital heart disease; weight 4 kg	9/3/92	9 mths	congenital heart disease; malnutrition	MW
174	LUO JING	F	–	Aug. 92	–	–	9/4/92	–	–	–
175	QIU LIE	M	7/3/88	9/4/92	4 yrs.	cerebral palsy; third-degree malnutrition; epilepsy; weight 8 kg	9/5/92	4 yrs	congenital maldevelopment of brain; epilepsy; malnutrition	RU
176	XING TING	?	–	Sep. 91	–	–	9/5/92	–	–	–
177	YAN GANG	?	–	June 92	–	–	9/7/92	–	–	IS
178	LUO YING	?	–	Aug. 92	–	–	9/10/92	–	–	RU?
179	LUO JIA	F	–	8/31/92	4 yrs.	–	9/13/92	4 yrs.	–	RU
180	XIN GUANG	?	–	May 92	–	–	9/13/92	–	–	CS?
181	LUO ZHUAN	M	8/14/92	8/24/92	10 days	malnutrition; limbs swollen; weight 2.9 kg	9/13/92	1 mth.	congenital maldevelopment of brain; third-degree malnutrition	MW

SEPTEMBER 1992

No.	Name	Sex	Born	Admitted	Age	Condition On Arrival	Died	Age	Recorded Cause of Death	Where Died
182	QIU LEI	F	–	Sep. 92	–	–	9/14/92	–	–	RU
183	LUO NING	M	7/27/92	8/3/92	7 days	harelip and cleft palate; weight 3.5 kg	9/16/92	1 ½ mths.	cranial subcutaneous necrosis; third-degree malnutrition; harelip and cleft palate	MW
184	QIU YONG	M	8/2/92	9/3/92	1 mth.	hydrocephalus; malnutrition; premature birth?	9/15/92	1 ½ mths.	hydrocephalus; premature birth; severe malnutrition	RU
185	XIE TONG	?	–	Dec. 91	–	–	9/17/92	–	–	–
186	ZHAN JU	M	June 92	July 92	–	–	9/18/92	3 mths	–	IS
187	LIANG SHAN	M	10/15/87	4/23/88	6 mths.	weight 6.0 kg; congenital heart disease; respiratory infection	9/18/92	5 yrs.	congenital heart disease; heart failure; third-degree malnutrition	MW
188	QIU YUAN	?	–	Sep. 92	–	–	9/25/92	–	–	RU
189	QIU E	?	–	Sep. 92	–	–	9/25/92	–	–	RU
190	QIU BING	M	–	Sep. 92	5 yrs.	–	9/27/92	5 yrs.	–	RU
191	QIU YI	?	–	Sep. 92	–	–	9/28/92	–	–	RU
192	QIU WU	M	Sep. 91	Sep. 92	1 yr.	–	9/29/92	1 yr.	–	MW
193	QIU LIANG	F	June 92	Sep. 92	3 mths.	–	9/30/92	3 mths	–	RU

OCTOBER 1992 (PARTIAL LIST)

No.	Name	Sex	Born	Admitted	Age	Condition On Arrival	Died	Age	Recorded Cause of Death	Where Died
194	ZHAN YING	F	May 92	July 92	2 mths.	congenital heart disease; high fever	10/3/92	5 mths.	recurrence of congenital heart disease	MW
195	SHOU RONG	F	–	Oct. 92	? days	–	10/6/92	? days	–	RU
196	QIU YAN	?	–	Sep. 92	–	–	10/6/92	–	–	RU?
197	LUO MIN	M	–	Aug. 92	5 yrs.	–	10/6/92	5 yrs.	cerebral palsy	MW
198	YAN HANG	F	Oct. 91	June 92	8 mths.	–	10/8/92	1 yr.	malnutrition	MW
199	QIU NING	F	Mar. 92	Sep. 92	6 mths.	–	10/9/92	7 mths.	–	MW
200	YAN ZHU	?	–	June 92	–	–	10/9/92	–	–	IS?
201	SHOU LONG	?	–	Oct. 92	–	–	10/9/92	–	–	RU
202	QIU ZHI	F	July 92	Sep. 92	2 mths.	premature birth	10/11/92	3 mths.	premature birth	RU
203	XIN JIE	M	Oct. 88	May 92	3½ yrs.	–	10/11/92	4 yrs.	cerebral palsy	MW
204	QIU DONG	F	Mar. 92	Sep. 92	6 mths.	–	10/13/92	7 mths.	–	MW
205	DONG YUE	?	–	April 92	–	–	10/14/92	–	–	–
206	QIU REN	F	Jan. 92	Sep. 92	9 mths.	–	10/23/92	10 mths.	congenital maldevelopment of brain	RU
207	SHOU JI	?	–	Oct. 92	–	–	10/28/92	–	–	–

V. ABUSE AND ILL-TREATMENT AT THE SHANGHAI ORPHANAGE: 1988-1993

Everyday existence for orphans at the Shanghai Children's Welfare Institute was accompanied not only by almost continual reminders of death, as the infant and child fatality lists so scupulously maintained by the medical staff continued to grow, but also by frequent acts of seemingly gratuitous brutality by many of the ordinary child-care workers and other staff. Eyewitnesses of numerous such events have provided detailed information to Human Rights Watch/Asia on a number of cases of abuse, neglect and ill-treatment of abandoned children which occurred at the orphanage between 1988 and 1993, many resulting in serious injury and sometimes death. On the basis of this evidence, Human Rights Watch/Asia has reached the following conclusions:

- Although a majority of the deaths recorded at the Children's Welfare Institute between 1989 and 1991, mainly of infants and very young children, appear to have been deliberately caused through the process of "consultation" described in Chapter 4, unnatural deaths from other causes were also fairly common at the orphanage during the same period. These usually resulted from lack of medical care or medical negligence, as well as from accidents such as choking. However, in addition to killings that resulted from "consultation," other acts of deliberate cruelty or indifference by staff members also led to a number of deaths.

- The policies and actions of Han Weicheng, acting director of the Children's Welfare Institute between 1988 and 1989 and the orphanage's full director from 1989 to 1994, led to a dramatic worsening of conditions for older children at the orphanage. Han Weicheng raped, beat, and physically abused orphans on a number of occasions, often with the knowledge of other staff members and children, and shielded orphanage employees responsible for deaths and injuries of children in their care. The resulting climate of impunity caused a substantial increase in the number of cases of cruelty and grave abuse by other staff members.

- Han Weicheng and his associates were given consistent support and protection by their superiors within the Shanghai Civil Affairs Bureau, one branch of which, the Department of Social Welfare (*Shehui Fulichu*), is responsible for overseeing the Children's Welfare Institute.

This support included active cooperation in the violent abuse and intimidation of orphans. In addition to the orphanage itself, the Shanghai Civil Affairs Bureau also administers several other custodial institutions in the city. These include the Shanghai No.2 Social Welfare Institute (*Shanghai Di'er Shehui Fuliyuan*); the Shanghai No.1 [Men's] Social Psychiatric Rehabilitation Institute (*Shanghai Diyi Shehui Jingshenbing Kangfuyuan*); the Shanghai No.3 [Women's] Social Psychiatric Rehabilitation Institute (*Shanghai Disan Shehui Jingshenbing Kangfuyuan*); and the Shanghai Municipal Civil Affairs Bureau Deportation Station (*Shanghaishi Minzhengju Qiansongzhan*). These four institutions were responsible for illegally detaining orphans removed from the Shanghai Children's Welfare Institute, at the request of Han Weicheng and other senior staff at the orphanage. Some of these children were beaten and tortured while in detention.

- Other branches of the Shanghai municipal government also colluded with senior staff at the orphanage to violate children's human rights. In particular, orphans were illegally arrested and held at official detention centers under the authority of the Shanghai Public Security Bureau. In one case, such a detention was carried out in a successful effort to protect Han Weicheng from prosecution for rape.

Categories of Abuse

Although Human Rights Watch/Asia has documented many individual cases in which children at the orphanage suffered severe or prolonged abuse and ill-treatment, certain policies at the institute which amount to cruel, inhuman, or degrading treatment appear to have been applied almost universally before 1993, and in some cases even more recently. These included the following:

Improper Feeding Practices, Leading to Severe Malnutrition or Death

Infants at the Children's Welfare Institute are normally bottle-fed on ordinary cow's milk. Once they are old enough to eat solid foods, this is supplemented by *naigao* (a sticky paste made from hot water and powdered white rice) and by rice porridge containing small quantities of meat and green vegetables. Although the orphanage diet itself is far from ideal, containing inadequate levels of protein and vitamins, the most critical shortcoming, in the period of Zhang Shuyun's employment, appeared to be in the feeding methods themselves. Former staff members and visitors to the institute reported that small infants were not normally bottle-fed by hand. Instead, child-care workers prepared bottles for feeding and then placed them in orphans' cribs, usually wrapped in a cloth diaper, for infants to nurse unattended.

The only apparent purpose of this practice was to save time and inconvenience for the child-care workers themselves, but its effects were frequently fatal. Up to the present time, a sizeable proportion of abandoned infants admitted to the orphanage suffer from cleft palates, which in most cases can be easily corrected through surgery. Zhang Shuyun has stated, however, that during her tenure at the institute, the scheduling of cleft palate operations at the orphanage was subject to delays which often lasted several months. Since infants with cleft palates cannot bottle-feed without assistance, however, this usually led to starvation and death long before surgery could be arranged.

Unattended bottle feeding is also extremely dangerous even for infants capable of nursing normally. Zhang Shuyun reports that before 1993, infants below one year of age frequently choked to death during feedings because they were normally tied to their beds almost continuously (see below). It was also not uncommon for infants to lose their grip on the nipple, and thus to consume only a portion of the allotted feed. Child-care workers routinely ignored these occurrences and provided no additional milk, resulting in chronic malnutrition among many infants. The resulting weakness appears to have been a contributing factor to the very high death rate from pneumonia and other contagious diseases among infants at the institute.[308]

Feeding practices for older children were often similarly haphazard. Child-care workers were normally responsible for feeding several toddlers simultaneously, and generally tried to complete the task as rapidly as possible by quickly spooning hot food into children's mouths. Zhang Shuyun reports that this practice frequently led to deaths by choking during her tenure at the institute. When signs of choking occurred, child-care workers often made no attempt to intervene or call in professional staff for assistance, instead waiting until after the group feeding was completed to report a child's death.

In at least one case, Han Weicheng acted personally to protect a negligent staff member who had allowed a child to choke to death. According to another former employee of the orphanage, who witnessed this incident in 1987, Han Weicheng ordered an orphanage medical employee, Ding Yi, to perform an unlawful autopsy on the child, despite his having no relevant training or authority to do so. After cutting open the child's throat, Ding used a cloth diaper to wipe out a lump of *naigao* blocking the windpipe. He then asserted that the child's death had resulted from natural causes.

---

[308] The practice has other hazards as well. Zhang Shuyun describes a case she witnessed in 1991 in which an apparently healthy infant developed a serious infection as a result of milk leaking from a bottle into the child's ear. The condition went untreated and the child died in less than a week, shortly before it was scheduled to be handed over for adoption to a married couple from the United States.

Tying of Children's Limbs

Numerous witnesses have reported that before 1993, infants and children at the Child Welfare Institute were routinely tied to cribs, beds, and chairs, chiefly as another means of reducing the staff workload. One early official acknowledgement of this appeared in the Shanghai newspaper *Labor News* in an article dated May 31, 1990. According to the reporter, who visited the orphanage as part of a delegation just before International Children's Day, "We saw close to 200 infants and young children lying in bed with their hands tied to the bed frames with gauze." (A full translation of the article appears in Appendix C.)

The policy of tying up children appears to have been a factor contributing to the deaths of a large number of orphans in the winter of late 1991, during a period of extremely cold weather in Shanghai. Shortly after the arrival of an investigation team from the Shanghai Bureau of Supervision in December 1991 (see Chapter 6 for details), members of the team reported that large numbers of children were being kept tied to their beds. The team also discovered several small children tied to chairs, often wearing only thin clothing with no shoes or socks, and able to relieve themselves only through holes in the chair seats into chamberpots placed underneath.[309] A number of these children had developed blue-black discolorations on their skin, apparently a symptom of advanced hypothermia aggravated by the immobilization of their limbs. However, the institute's then Communist Party secretary, Zhu Meijun, denied that the children were suffering from frostbite, instead telling the investigators that the marks were bruises caused by a "platelet disorder." Medical records obtained by Human Rights Watch/Asia indicate that at least fifteen children died at the orphanage over the four-day period December 28-31, 1991.[310]

Improper Medication

Prior to 1993, many orphans at the Children's Welfare Institute were routinely given powerful and medically inappropriate drugs solely for the convenience of their caretakers. Many of these drugs are habit-forming or have potentially serious side effects and have no recognized medical use in healthy subjects.

The main purpose of the drug regimen, which was applied only to older orphans in the Disabled Section (*Shangcanbu*), was apparently to keep severely handicapped children calm and sedated so that they could be kept in their beds almost continuously. The three medications most commonly used for this purpose were

---

[309] This is a common practice at other Chinese orphanages, reported by numerous foreign visitors to welfare institutions in other parts of the country.

[310] For further details of this case, see Chapter 4, "An Outline of the Attritional Process."

phenobarbital, chlorpromazine (a tranquilizer used in the treatment of schizophrenia), and dilantin (a muscle relaxant and anticonvulsant used to treat epileptic seizures).

The routine use of these drugs, combined with inadequate supervision of children, occasionally led to serious illness. In one case reported by Zhang Shuyun from late 1992, two blind girls, Bao Wei and Yu Feng, and a deaf-mute (name unknown) took massive overdoses of chlorpromazine after a staff member left several bottles of sugar-coated pills unattended. The three children lost consciousness but survived.

Zhang Shuyun also reports that girls at the orphanage were placed on a regimen of oral contraceptives after reaching puberty. The apparent purpose of this policy was not to prevent unwanted pregnancies but simply to suppress menstruation and avoid the associated inconvenience to orphanage staff.

Beatings, Torture, and Physical Abuse by Staff

Virtually all older orphans at the Children's Welfare Institute before 1993 suffered violent physical abuse at least occasionally at the hands of orphanage employees. Far from being normal disciplinary measures, these frequently involved elaborate punitive practices which in many cases amounted to torture. According to Zhang Shuyun, some of the most common methods employed included:

- forcing children to assume the "airplane" and "motorcycle" positions for long periods of time (respectively, bent forward horizontally at the waist with arms held vertically upward, and sitting unsupported at half-squat with arms stretched forward horizontally). In some cases, these techniques were supplemented by forcing children to balance bowls of hot water on their wrists, heads, or knees or to squat over bowls of boiling water, so that scalding occurred when the child fell;

- forcing children to kneel on ridged washboards for long periods of time;

- hanging children upside down with their heads submerged in water, until nosebleeds and near-suffocation ensued. This technique, known as *qiang shui* ("choking on water"), was reportedly the one most feared by children.

Ai Ming, a former inmate of the Children's Welfare Institute born in 1972 and now living overseas as a political refugee, has corroborated Zhang Shuyun's description of these techniques, and reports that they were often inflicted for relatively minor disciplinary infractions, or simply on the whim of the child-care workers themselves.

More common and less sophisticated methods used by some abusive child-care workers included blows to the head and face with wooden poles and heavy plastic slippers. The resulting cuts and bruises normally went without medical attention for fear of alerting professional staff to the abuse, and infections of these injuries sometimes resulted in deaths from untreated septicemia. Zhang Shuyun reports that such violent attacks were common enough before 1993 that many smaller children would instinctively duck and shield their heads when an adult approached.

In a number of individual cases, physical abuse by staff went far beyond even these brutal methods. The following five examples, selected from among cases documented by Human Rights Watch/Asia, illustrate the severity of the problem.[311]

Yue Yi (August 1988)

Yue Yi, a fifteen-year-old boy with one congenitally disabled leg, was physically assaulted and beaten by Han Weicheng in his office, shortly after Han assumed the position of acting orphanage director in 1988. Afterwards, Yue was locked in a disused building for several days, with only limited food. Although many orphans and staff members witnessed this incident, Han Weicheng later forced other administrators to deny publicly that the beating had taken place. One staff member who refused to do so was demoted as a result. Han Weicheng's conduct on this occasion sent a clear signal to his subordinates that children could be abused with impunity and paved the way for even more extreme cases of cruelty in future years (see below).

One morning in August 1988, Yue overslept and had to be woken by a teacher. Grabbing the teacher's leg, Yue Yi accidentally tripped her, causing her to fall and sprain her wrist. Although Yue Yi wrote a "self-criticism" as a result of this incident, he was ordered to report to Han Weicheng's office later the same day. Han had earlier warned Tang Youhua, then a staff teacher and director of the Children's Department (*Ertongbu*) at the orphanage, which cares for older orphans without severe disabilities, that "Yue Yi hurt a teacher, so I'm going to whop him (*zhou ta*)." Tang then warned Yue Yi to "be careful" when he went to see Han.

On his way to Han Weicheng's office, Yue Yi passed Zhen Weiming, then director of the orphanage's Personnel Department, who struck him on the side of the head before he entered.[312] When Yue Yi arrived at the office, Han began threatening him, telling him, "I'm returned from Xinjiang, and I've studied judo." He then

---

[311] Sources for the following case reports include testimony from Zhang Shuyun and Ai Ming, and also documentation compiled by members of the Shanghai People's Congress who investigated the allegations, often by taking direct testimony from the victims themselves.

[312] Zhen Weiming was later promoted to vice-director of the orphanage.

knocked Yue to the ground and began punching and kicking him. The beating continued intermittently for some ninety minutes and was witnessed by a number of other orphans, including Ai Ming, who watched through the window of Han's office. Both Tang Youhua and another teacher tried to intervene during the beating but were sent away. Tang Youhua later saw Han bring Yue out of the office; his shirt was torn and he was covered with sweat. "I whopped him," Han reportedly told her. Two other senior staff members, then vice-director Tao Xinzhong and then Communist Party secretary Zhu Qingfang, told Yue at the time that he deserved a beating.

Yue Yi was then locked in a disused shed on the orphanage grounds for four days and three nights. In spite of the hot summer weather, he was given only rice and soup to eat, with no meat, vegetables, or cold drinks, and provided with only a spittoon as a chamberpot. Orphanage staff members were warned not to bring Yue any other food or drink, although some secretly brought refreshments such as popsicles and sliced watermelon. Some teachers reportedly brought other children to the shed to show them Yue's punishment as an example.

The beating of Yue Yi resurfaced as an issue during an internal investigation launched by the Shanghai Civil Affairs Bureau in early 1990, based on a series of complaints made by Zhang Shuyun and other staff members critical of Han Weicheng's management. On June 2, 1990, at a mass meeting of the institute's employees, Han Weicheng forced other staff members to deny that this incident had taken place, asking them, "Did I beat Yue Yi or not?" Except for Tang Youhua, all those present agreed that he had not. Tang was then denounced by a number of senior staff members at the meeting, including Han Weicheng, Zhu Qingfang, and Zhen Weiming. She was later demoted to a minor administrative position managing the institute's supplies, and retired in late 1994.

Yue Yi has since been adopted by a married couple in Shanghai and lives at home. He is reported to manifest severe psychological problems as a result of the abuse he suffered at the orphanage, and has been unable to find a permanent job.

HONG NA (April 1991)

Hong Na, a six-year-old girl with a disfiguring birthmark on her face, suffered brutal and sadistic abuse from a senior staff member over a period of more than twenty-four hours. The employee responsible was penalized by a token fine, but only after intense pressure from critics of the orphanage management.

On the morning of April 30, 1991, Hong Na stole several pieces of candy from a pile which was to be distributed in advance of an official visit to the orphanage by Xie Lijuan, Shanghai's deputy mayor for health, education, and social welfare. The institute's head child-care worker, Feng Ya'an, discovered the stolen candy hidden in Hong Na's clothing. Feng then began beating the child with her plastic shoe and a wooden mop pole. Hong ran away and attempted to jump off the balcony of the two-story dormitory building, shouting, "I want to die!" Feng Ya'an held her back and tied Hong's wrists with a cloth diaper. She used this to hang the child from the metal frame of a high window in the building, so that Hong was forced to stand on tiptoe, and then began pummelling her with her fists.

This incident was witnessed by a number of other children, some of whom secretly visited Zhang Shuyun in her office to notify her.[313] Dr. Zhang responded by telephoning attorneys at the Shanghai No.2 Legal Affairs Agency, who had earlier provided legal support for critics of the orphanage management. The agency dispatched two female staff members to investigate, who succeeded in entering the orphanage compound but were detected and thrown out before they could locate Hong Na.

Hong Na was left hanging from the window frame until late that day and was allowed no lunch or mid-day nap. She was eventually found and given food by Chen Dongxian, the orphanage driver, whom Zhang Shuyun had sent to look for her. Hong was later taken down from the window frame but was not allowed to go to sleep; she was kept tied up in a standing position for the entire night.

The next morning (May 1), Feng Ya'an forced Hong Na to assume the "airplane" and "motorcycle" positions, and repeatedly beat the child's palms with her plastic shoe. Later the same day, Feng placed a dead rat in Hong Na's bed before the children's mid-day nap, causing hysteria among Hong and other orphans.

Both orphanage director Han Weicheng and Zhu Qingfang, then the institute's Communist Party secretary, publicly denied that this incident had occurred. Several months later, after repeated complaints by critics among the orphanage staff, Feng Ya'an was fined sixty yuan for her treatment of Hong Na. However, Han Weicheng and vice-director Huang Jiachun later gave Feng twenty yuan in cash as a partial reimbursement (officially described as a "merit bonus"), and apologized to her for having imposed the fine, explaining that they had been forced to do so by pressure from others.

Feng Ya'an allegedly threatened Hong Na after the incident took place, warning her not to discuss what had happened with anyone else. It is not known whether Hong Na is still living at the orphanage.

LIANG JIE (April 1991)
Liang Jie, a mentally normal ten-year-old boy with partially disabled legs, was one of the children responsible for informing Zhang Shuyun about the abuse inflicted on Hong Na. According to Dr. Zhang, when Feng Ya'an discovered this, she

---

[313] As a result of her campaign to improve conditions at the orphanage, Zhang Shuyun had by this time been ordered confined to her office throughout the work day, on penalty of demerits on her work record and loss of salary (see Chapter 6).

retaliated by forcing Liang Jie to swallow a number of small magnets used for attaching notices to blackboards. Feng later induced vomiting in an attempt to retrieve the magnets, but they remained in Liang Jie's stomach.

On August 15, 1992, Liang Jie was taken to the Shanghai Pediatric Hospital[314] suffering from severe abdominal pains. After several days, doctors there scheduled him for an X-ray to check for a possible intestinal blockage, but this was not performed, as Liang Jie passed the last remaining magnet in his stool the evening before the examination.

It is not known whether Liang Jie is still living at the Children's Welfare Institute. Feng Ya'an was not disciplined in connection with Liang Jie's case, and reportedly continues to hold her position as the head child-care worker at the orphanage.

WU LANYIN (July 1991)

Wu Lanyin, a fifteen-year-old retarded girl placed by her parents at the Children's Welfare Institute as a "self-paying" inmate, was subjected to cruel and degrading treatment by an orphanage child-care worker, who was later shielded by the institute's Communist Party secretary, Zhu Qingfang.

On July 11, 1991, during Wu Lanyin's menstrual period, child-care worker Xu Shanzhen, a senior Communist Party member, removed Wu's pants and locked her in a disused toilet, forcing her to sit on a spittoon. After approximately half an hour, a nurse passing by noticed the sound of a child crying and went to investigate. She unlocked the toilet and found Wu inside, hysterical and covered with blood. This nurse was later warned by Zhu Qingfang not to discuss this incident with others.

Xu Shanzhen was ordered to write a "self-criticism" in connection with this case, but was apparently not otherwise disciplined. In April 1995, she was declared a "model worker" and invited to Beijing to receive an award for her services to the Children's Welfare Institute. According to an article which appeared later the same month in the Shanghai newspaper *Labor News*, Xu Shanzhen was the only employee of China's Ministry of Civil Affairs to receive such an honor.[315]

It is not known whether Wu Lanyin is still cared for at the Children's Welfare Institute.

---

[314] *Shanghai Erke Yiyuan*, an affiliate of Shanghai No.1 Medical University.

[315] *Labor News*, the official publication of the Shanghai General Labor Union, had earlier published two articles in 1990 criticizing abuses at the Children's Welfare Institute. A translation of the April 1995 article profiling Xu Shanzhen appears in Appendix Q.

Lu Yi (August 1991)

Lu Yi, a mildly retarded fourteen-year-old boy, was tortured by an orphanage child-care worker in an incident witnessed and ignored by a senior staff member. He was later transferred to a mental hospital without medical justification, in an apparent attempt to conceal the abuse.

On August 25, 1991, a child-care worker asked Lu Yi to steal soap for her from a communal washroom. When this was discovered, another child-care worker, Li Laidi, tied Lu Yi up in a standing position and then stabbed his genitals repeatedly with a *yacha* (a metal fork attached to a bamboo pole, used to hang and remove clothes hangers from a clothesline or drying rack). Li Laidi also ordered other children to pull out Lu Yi's pubic hair, and forced him to jump up and down while tied, causing him to fall over several times.

Vice-director Zhen Weiming came across this incident accidentally while passing by the room where the abuse was taking place. However, he reportedly laughed and passed by, commenting that the children were playing a "game."

The following January, Lu Yi was transferred to the Shanghai No.1 Social Psychiatric Rehabilitation Institute, a mental hospital administered by the municipal Civil Affairs Bureau, despite the fact that he showed no signs of mental illness. His present whereabouts are unknown.[316]

Li Laidi has since retired. She was not subject to any disciplinary action for her abuse of Lu Yi.

In addition to these and other cases, in which children suffered violent physical abuse on the orphanage grounds, Human Rights Watch/Asia has also documented several incidents in which children were forcibly removed from the orphanage and physically abused while being held illegally at other locations (see below, "Illegal Detention").

Rape and Sexual Abuse by Staff

A number of orphan girls at the Shanghai Children's Welfare Institute claim to have been raped or sexually assaulted by various men on the orphanage staff, including former director Han Weicheng. Although details of most individual cases have been difficult to obtain and corroboration is generally not available, Human Rights Watch/Asia believes the reports of rape and sexual abuse, based chiefly on statements by alleged victims, to be credible. Given the reluctance of most victims to come forward and the general climate of impunity prevailing at the orphanage, it

---

[316] Lu Yi's transfer to the mental hospital was apparently an attempt to conceal this incident from investigators who had recently arrived from the Shanghai Bureau of Supervision (see Chapter 6).

seems likely that they represent only a small fraction of the actual number of sexual assaults which have occurred there in recent years.

For example, older girls at the Children's Welfare Institute complained to Zhang Shuyun of frequent sexual harassment by Sun Miaoling, a former staff teacher who has since been promoted to a position in the orphanage's Propaganda Section. Sun reportedly entered the orphanage dormitories at night on a regular basis to fondle girls' breasts and legs. As a result, many girls said they were forced to sleep fully clothed, in some cases under their beds, and attempted to keep dormitory doors and windows shut and locked even in hot summer weather.

Other reports involved more violent incidents of sexual assault. The cases of Chou Hui and Qin Gaoming, two orphan girls who were allegedly raped or sexually abused at the Children's Welfare Institute, are examined in greater detail in the last section of this chapter. The following three cases represent additional incidents in which Human Rights Watch/Asia has been able to identify victims of sexual abuse by name.

FU QING (1985)

Fu Qing, a girl born in February 1975 and brought to the Children's Welfare Institute with a cleft palate, which was later surgically repaired, has alleged that Han Weicheng sexually abused her when she was approximately ten years old. She made this claim after being transferred from the orphanage to the Shanghai No.2 Social Welfare Institute on Chongming Island,[317] where she was secretly interviewed on July 11 and 12, 1992 by delegates to the Shanghai Municipal People's Congress. (Human Rights Watch/Asia has obtained a transcript of these interviews.)

Fu Qing claimed that one summer afternoon at approximately 5:00 p.m., Han Weicheng visited her in her dormitory, tapped her on the shoulder and pulled her forcibly into a dormitory toilet. He then pulled up her dress and pulled her underwear down to her calves, and began fondling her upper body and genitals, inserting one finger into her vagina. This lasted for approximately five minutes, during which Han told her that he would order a child-care worker to beat her if she told anyone else about the incident. Fu Qing told the delegates that she had suffered from painful urination for some time after the attack.

---

[317] The Shanghai No.2 Social Welfare Institute is a general-purpose custodial home run by the municipal Civil Affairs Bureau. Conditions at this institution are described in greater detail in Chapter 7.

XIANG WEN (1987)

Xiang Wen, a mildly retarded girl born in 1973, reportedly told other orphan girls that Han Weicheng had sexually abused her in 1987, fondling her breasts. Her case was one of several investigated by delegates of the Shanghai Municipal People's Congress during a visit to Chongming Island in July 1992. Although Xiang Wen was then living at the Shanghai No.2 Social Welfare Institute, the delegates chose not to interview her directly, fearing that she would be unable to keep the discussion secret and that their investigation would be compromised if she mentioned the interview to institute staff. Another girl of normal intelligence, also a former orphanage inmate held at the No.2 Social Welfare Institute, reported this case during an interview with the delegates.

WANG GUANG (1993)

The case of Wang Guang illustrates that serious cases of sexual abuse, including rape, have continued to occur at the Children's Welfare Institute since Zhang Shuyun's departure in 1993. According to information received by Dr. Zhang from a source within the orphanage, Wang Guang, an abandoned girl without apparent handicaps born in 1979, was found to be pregnant in early 1994, supposedly as a result of having been raped by another orphan. However, many orphanage staff were reportedly skeptical that the boy said to have been responsible was the actual rapist. (Dr. Zhang notes that cases of rape by male orphans had never been reported during her employment at the Children's Welfare Institute, and that all other known cases of sexual assault at the orphanage had been committed by staff members.)

According to the source, Wang Guang was forced to undergo an abortion and then immediately transferred to the Shanghai No.2 Social Welfare Institute, despite the fact that she had not yet reached the age of sixteen, at which such transfers normally take place. As a result of her relocation, no further information on her case has become available.

Lack of Medical Care and Medical Negligence

Visitors to the Shanghai Children's Welfare Institute are frequently given guided tours of its facilities for rehabilitation and medical care. A building dedicated for these purposes, the seven-story Shanghai Municipal Rehabilitation Center for Disabled Children, was completed in June 1989. The fourth floor of this building functions as the orphanage's hospital ward, while other floors contain rooms for massage and physical therapy, particularly for children with cerebral palsy, as well as administrative offices and meeting halls.

However, medical facilities at the orphanage offer much less than meets the eye. Sections of the Rehabilitation Center appear disused and partly abandoned, and the building developed serious structural and hygiene problems shortly after its completion, including sewage leaking from walls and ceilings. These are apparently related to the use of low-quality building materials and to financial irregularities in the center's construction.

In years past, the management of the Children's Welfare Institute went to extreme lengths to preserve the illusion of adequate medical care for orphans. Until a change of institutional policy in mid-1993, which allowed local Shanghai families and expatriate volunteers more or less unrestricted access to the orphanage grounds during daylight hours (see Chapter 7), visits to the Children's Welfare Institute were strictly controlled to prevent outsiders from discovering the deplorable health conditions actually prevailing at the orphanage. Zhang Shuyun reports that during scheduled visits by government officials or foreign delegations, sick or dying infants were removed from the wards and concealed in toilets or other locked rooms, usually laid out on the tiled floor and covered with blankets to prevent the visitors from hearing their cries. Dr. Zhang also notes that until 1991, the Rehabilitation Center's hospital ward was ordinarily empty, with children placed in hospital beds for display only when overseas delegations and other outsiders came to visit.[318] Even after 1991, the hospital ward was used only sporadically, with routine medical care usually provided in children's dormitories. As the medical records in Chapter 4 indicate, even seriously ill and dying children were apparently almost never transferred to the Rehabilitation Center for intensive care.

As was explained in Chapter 4, the quality of medical care actually provided at the orphanage before 1993 was generally very poor, with medical malpractice sometimes resulting in deaths and disabling injuries to children. In addition to the general atmosphere of indifference to children's welfare, this problem was aggravated by the low educational level of the orphanage medical staff, many of whom lacked adequate professional credentials. The lack of adequate staff training extends to non-professional employees as well. Newly employed child-care workers at the Shanghai orphanage receive no formal training whatsoever, instead serving a two-week probationary period during which they learn the necessary work skills by observation.[319] A number of individual incidents illustrate the incompetence and lack of professionalism of many orphanage medical employees. The following cases of staff negligence, some of which resulted in death, have been selected from orphanage medical records and from official reports on conditions at the Children's Welfare Institute.

---

[318] The children asked to play these roles were usually not orphans but paying patients from other provinces whose parents were offered discounts on rent at the orphanage guesthouse to persuade them to cooperate with the ruse.

[319] Author's interview with Han Weicheng, March 1995.

HUO ZHEN (February 1991)

Huo Zhen, a boy of uncertain age with a severe spinal curvature,[320] contracted hepatitis which was originally misdiagnosed as pneumonia. The correct diagnosis was made only after the disease had reached an advanced stage, with jaundice appearing. In February 1991, during the eight-day Spring Festival (lunar new year) holiday, Huo Zhen and two other boys with hepatitis were tied to beds in a disused room and left unattended after 2:00 p.m. each day. The room was locked, and newspaper was taped over its windows to conceal the children from other staff.

However, a child-care worker discovered the boys and notified Zhang Shuyun. Dr. Zhang was unable to gain access to the room but saw the boys through a gap in the newspaper covering the windows. She reports that Huo Zhen was speaking in delirium by this time; he died the same evening and was found to have passed large quantities of blood in his stool. Dr. Zhang believes the other two boys may later have died as well but was unable to continue monitoring the situation, as her movements on the orphanage grounds were, by this time, severely restricted by official order.

GAN RUI (October 1991)

Gan Rui, an girl without apparent handicaps born in 1979, contracted acute nephritis in 1991, which was ignored by orphanage medical staff until it had reached a very advanced stage. On November 24, 1991, after developing serious edema, Gan Rui was finally sent to the Shanghai Pediatric Hospital, where she remained hospitalized for over a year. Gan Rui was not assigned an attendant by the Children's Welfare Institute, and during the first three months of her stay, before Zhang Shuyun learned of her situation, she received no visitors or supplies.[321] Although Dr. Zhang was by this time confined to her office at the orphanage during working hours, she eventually began visiting Gan Rui secretly at the hospital to bring food and other supplies, sometimes bringing other orphans with her.

Gan Rui returned to the orphanage in late 1992, shortly before Dr. Zhang's forced retirement. Although she retained limited kidney functions, Dr. Zhang speculates that she may not have survived for more than a few months after her discharge, as the orphanage refused to pay for dialysis treatment at a local hospital.

---

[320] Huo Zhen was abandoned well past infancy, and was identified by his dialect as a native of Anhui Province. Orphanage staff recorded his estimated age as two years, based on his height, although he appears in fact to have been considerably older.

[321] Inpatient care at Chinese hospitals does not normally include food, linen, or other non-medical services. Patients' families are expected to provide these.

WEI ZHI (June 1992)

Wei Zhi, a mildly retarded boy aged approximately five years, was seriously injured on June 20, 1992, when another retarded girl nearly severed his penis with a pair of scissors left unattended. No adults were in the room at the time. The injury was crudely stitched up, but Wei Zhi's penis developed gangrene and part of it dropped off, requiring the addition of a second set of stitches.

Although an internal investigation was launched into this incident, high-level orphanage staff, including director Han Weicheng and vice-director Zhen Weiming, conspired to suppress the truth and shield those responsible for the accident. A child-care worker named Rong Aizhen was persuaded to give false testimony, stating that Wei Zhi's penis had been "pulled off by stretching" by the retarded girl. Rong Aizhen was later promoted and inducted into the Communist Party by Zhen Weiming. Another child-care worker, Guo Minying, insisted on giving the true version of the accident, however. She was dismissed from the orphanage as a result, despite efforts to intercede on her behalf by Ma Mimi, a delegate to the Shanghai Municipal People's Congress. It is not known whether Wei Zhi is still living at the orphanage.

ZHANG YANSONG (April/May 1989)

Zhang Yansong, a girl born in December 1982 suffering from cerebral palsy, was brought to Shanghai by her parents from her hometown of Benxi, Liaoning Province, in order to receive physical therapy at the Rehabilitation Center in the spring of 1989. On April 12, Ding Yi, a medical employee at the orphanage, accidentally broke Zhang Yansong's leg while administering a "therapeutic" massage. Despite the girl's extreme pain, Ding Yi initially denied that Zhang Yansong's leg was broken, and continued the regimen of massage therapy until May 4. By this time the bone had already fused crookedly, leaving Zhang Yansong with a permanent limp.

Zhang Shuyun and a number of other staff members complained to Han Weicheng after learning of this incident. However, Han successfully intimidated Zhang Yansong's parents into returning to Benxi without filing a formal complaint against the orphanage, offering no compensation other than a waiver of their room rental at the orphanage guesthouse.[322] He later boasted to other orphanage staff of his skill in handling this incident, and accused the concerned employees of acting disloyally towards their work unit by supporting Zhang Yansong's family rather than defending Ding Yi.

---

[322] Families from outside Shanghai normally board at a guesthouse owned by the Children's Welfare Institute during their children's treatment courses at the Rehabilitation Center.

Use of Forced Child Labor

Older orphans at the Shanghai Children's Welfare Institute were normally required to do maintenance chores at the orphanage, such as washing clothes and bed linens, which were nominally the responsibility of low-level child-care workers but which the staff preferred to assign to the children themselves. Ai Ming has stated that he began performing these tasks at the age of approximately seven, and was expected to work for three hours each afternoon.

The orphanage also rented out space on its grounds to a number of privately-owned companies and supplied them with child labor for an additional fee, a practice which apparently dates back to the early 1980s. Ai Ming notes that only somewhat older children, over the age of approximately eleven, were assigned to work in the commercial enterprises, again for three hours each day. The businesses employing orphans included small workshops manufacturing various products, including cosmetics, measuring devices, and game boards for *tiaoqi* ("Chinese checkers"). One of the largest commercial operations at the orphanage, however, consisted of wrapping Chinese-made bicycles, including the major "Phoenix" and "Forever" brands, in protective cotton sheeting for the export market. This activity, in which Ai Ming was formerly employed, was conducted in children's dormitories, rather than in a dedicated building.

The assignment of individual children to particular types of labor apparently took little account of their individual capabilities or handicaps. Wrapping bicycles, for example, required spreading out large sheets on the dormitory floors, a task most orphans performed on their knees. Ai Ming, who is unable to bend his knees completely as a result of polio in infancy, found this work particularly onerous.

Although orphans performing child labor were nominally considered paid employees, receiving a monthly salary of eight yuan (around one U.S. dollar), Zhang Shuyun reports that staff teachers, who were responsible for managing these funds, often succeeded in withholding most of this money by making "deductions" from children's wages on pretexts such as poor workmanship or unexcused absences from work, and by charging them exorbitant prices for items purchased outside the orphanage (the children themselves were not normally allowed to leave the institute grounds). Ai Ming, who left the Children's Welfare Institute at the age of nineteen with accumulated savings of more than one hundred yuan, was one of the few inmates who successfully retained any earnings at all from years of forced labor at the orphanage.

Zhang Weiqiang, a reporter for the Shanghai newspaper *Labor News*, reportedly wrote an article on forced labor at the Children's Welfare Institute and submitted it for publication in May 1991. This article, which was titled "We Want To Study, Not To Perform Child Labor," and reported older orphans' plea to be released from employment, was canceled on orders of the newspaper's deputy editor, Yu Jianmeng.

Illegal Detention

Human Rights Watch/Asia has documented a number of cases in which orphans were removed from the Shanghai Children's Welfare Institute and held illegally at other locations, either as a punishment or to prevent them from revealing information about abusive conditions at the orphanage. Several instances of such unlawful detention, such as the transfer of Lu Yi to the Shanghai No.1 Social Psychiatric Rehabilitation Institute, are discussed elsewhere in this chapter.

In addition to these incidents, at least two children, Ai Ming and Zhu Yan, were also unlawfully detained and ill-treated at institutions run by the Shanghai Civil Affairs Bureau, in both cases at the request of orphanage director Han Weicheng.

AI MING (January 1987)

Ai Ming was born in November 1972 and was brought to the Shanghai orphanage as an abandoned infant, after suffering an attack of polio which left his legs partly disabled. He escaped from China in 1995 and currently lives as a political refugee overseas.

In January 1987, Han Weicheng, at that time the vice-director of the orphanage, ordered Ai Ming transferred to the Shanghai No.1 Social Psychiatric Rehabilitation Institute, without any medical justification. Han had apparently concluded that Ai Ming was mentally disturbed–or decided to treat him as such as a punishment–after he made three attempts to escape from the orphanage to visit a friend who had left to take up an assigned job several months earlier.

Ai Ming has stated that on the day of his transfer, Han Weicheng originally invited him to his office "to talk," but instead walked with him towards the orphanage gate, where a van was waiting. Assisted by two heavily built workers on the orphanage staff, Ni Kongyong and Xu Qianqian, Han Weicheng then seized Ai Ming and forced him into the van. Ni and Xu continued to hold him during the drive to the psychiatric institution. They were accompanied by Wang Xueqing, then the director of the orphanage's Business Department, but not by Han Weicheng himself.

On arrival, Ai Ming was ordered by the hospital's vice-director to undress and change into a set of clothes provided by staff. He refused to do so and was then ordered to submit to what was described as a "test." This consisted of an electric shock lasting approximately five seconds, administered between the thumb and forefinger of both hands. Ai Ming then agreed to change clothes.

Apart from this initial incident, Ai Ming appears to have been treated reasonably well during his stay at the psychiatric hospital, which lasted six months. Indeed, the hospital administration was clearly well aware that he suffered from no mental disorder. Apart from one perfunctory physical examination, during which a doctor tested his leg reflexes, he was largely ignored by hospital staff and was even given a key to let himself into the outer walled compound of the hospital, a privilege not allowed to any other patient.

Shortly before his release and return to the Children's Welfare Institute, staff at the psychiatric hospital asked Ai Ming to write a "guarantee" as a condition of his release, pledging that he would not try to run away from the orphanage again. He initially refused to do so but eventually agreed to sign a guarantee written in his name by another patient.

ZHU YAN (June 1988)

Zhu Yan, a boy with a cleft palate, was brought to the orphanage as an abandoned infant in 1973. The defect was eventually corrected through surgery, but only after a considerable delay, leaving Zhu Yan unable to speak clearly.

In June 1988, Han Weicheng accused Zhu Yan of stealing a teapot and money from the orphanage and ordered him transferred for one week to the Shanghai Municipal Civil Affairs Bureau Deportation Station (*Shanghaishi Minzhengju Qiansongzhan*). This is a temporary detention center used to confine homeless people and rural workers who have migrated to the city without valid residence permits (the so-called *mangliu* or "blind wanderers"), before they are forcibly returned to their place of origin.[323] Zhu Yan was beaten with electric police batons during his detention and was given only steamed white rice to eat.

On March 13, 1991, Zhu Yan was transferred to the Shanghai No.2 Social Welfare Institute along with four other orphans. He has since made two unsuccessful attempts to escape, according to information received by Zhang Shuyun from another inmate at the institute. After each attempt, he was recaptured and punished by institute staff by being tied by the wrists, hung from a high window frame, and severely beaten.

Three Case Studies: Chou Hui, Qiu Zhen, Qin Gaoming

The detailed histories of three former inmates of the Shanghai Children's Welfare Institute, all now young adults, testify to a pattern during the late 1980s and early 1990s of arbitrary and unlawful actions by orphanage staff, including widespread physical and sexual abuse, and extensive complicity in these abuses by other official bodies in Shanghai. In particular, the events surrounding the case of Chou Hui indicate a decision taken at the highest levels of the Shanghai municipal government to shield

---

[323] Beatings, torture and severe ill-treatment of inmates at "deportation stations" in other Chinese cities are reported to be commonplace. Stations in many cities (though apparently not in Shanghai) also employ forced labor, requiring inmates to work off the cost of their transportation before being returned to their home villages.

Han Weicheng and other orphanage staff members from prosecution despite clear evidence of a range of criminal offenses, some of which are punishable by death under Chinese law.

Chou Hui

Chou Hui, born in 1972, was brought to the Shanghai Children's Welfare Institute as an abandoned infant with a congenital malformation of the anus. The defect was successfully corrected by surgery.

Chou Hui has stated that Han Weicheng raped her twice, first in his office in late 1988, and again in her dormitory approximately one month later. She made these allegations first to Zhang Shuyun, more than a year afterward, and later repeated them for the record in interviews with lawyers from the Shanghai No.2 Legal Affairs Agency and with delegates to the Shanghai Municipal People's Congress. (Human Rights Watch/Asia has obtained transcripts of both interviews.)

After the alleged rapes, Han Weicheng was apparently concerned to avoid being discovered. Not long afterward, he entered Chou Hui's dormitory at night and told the other girls in the room to leave, explaining that he wanted to give Chou Hui a "medical examination." He then palpated Chou Hui's uterus to assure himself that she was not pregnant, telling her, "I want to see if you're big." When a child-care worker later reported that Chou Hui had developed a stomachache, Han Weicheng ordered that she be given another medical examination, including a urine test.

Several months later, in April 1989, Chou Hui was transferred to the Shanghai No.3 Social Psychiatric Rehabilitation Institute, a women's psychiatric institution administered by the Civil Affairs Bureau. The transfer took place under bizarre and secretive circumstances. Chou Hui had previously been told that she was about to be assigned employment outside the orphanage and was provided with new clothes and other supplies purchased by a sympathetic child-care worker, Wang Genlin. On the day she was scheduled to leave for her "new job," a squad car driven by officers from the nearby Chengjiaqiao police station arrived at the orphanage and took her to the psychiatric hospital instead.

Wang Genlin soon discovered Chou's whereabouts and went to visit her at the hospital. She later reported that she had found Chou terrified, confined to a room with psychotic patients who had pulled out much of her hair. After returning to the orphanage, Wang reportedly confronted Han Weicheng in his office, demanding to know why he had ordered a mentally normal child sent to a psychiatric hospital. However, Chou Hui remained confined at the hospital for some six months, until she was again transferred, in October 1989, to the Shanghai No.2 Social Welfare Institute on Chongming Island. She remained there against her will for more than two years, even after reaching her eighteenth birthday in 1990. Her signed statements to representatives of the Shanghai No.2 Legal Affairs Agency and the Shanghai

Municipal People's Congress were made during clandestine visits to Chongming Island by these officials in September 1991 and July 1992.

In August 1992, shortly after making her statement to the People's Congress delegates, Chou was removed from the No.2 Social Welfare Institute and confined to the city's No.1 Jail (*Shanghai Diyi Kanshousuo*), a detention center administered by the Shanghai Public Security Bureau (PSB). Her detention followed a visit to the Chongming Island institute by officials of the PSB's Social Order Department (*Zhi'anchu*), during which police officers had interrogated Xin Cao, another young woman held there who had previously lived at the Children's Welfare Institute and had seen Chou Hui shortly before and after the first of the alleged rapes in 1988.

During her detention, Chou Hui was threatened with indefinite imprisonment if any error was found in her accusations against Han Weicheng. Chou later told Zhang Shuyun that Wu Hengjun, the director of the PSB's Social Order Department, had questioned her in her cell while wearing a holstered pistol, in the presence of two female officers, and had warned her that she would be charged with "false accusation" if even minor details, such as her description of what Han Weicheng had been wearing at the time of the alleged rapes, were found to be inaccurate. Wu Hengjun then took Chou to the women's section of the jail and showed her a group of female prisoners, telling her that all of them were serving life terms for "false accusation." After four months in jail, Chou Hui recanted her testimony and was released in December 1992.

Chou was then assigned employment at the Longhua Electrical Appliance Factory (*Longhua Diangong Qicaichang*), a scrap-copper recycling plant in Shanghai's Longhua district.[324] The police officers who delivered her to the plant allegedly warned other workers that she was a "bad woman" who needed to be "punished." Possibly as a result, in 1993 she was raped for a third time by another employee, the younger brother of the plant manager. The manager's brother was forced to leave the plant when the rape was exposed, after an angry reaction from other workers, but was apparently not prosecuted.

Qiu Zhen

Qiu Zhen, a boy born with malformed fingers and abnormally short forearms, was brought to the Child Welfare Institute as an abandoned infant in September 1972.

---

[324] The reprocessing of discarded copper cable and machinery containing copper, chiefly imported from overseas, is fast becoming a major industry in China, where it operates with virtually no regulation to protect workers' health or the environment. Conditions at the Longhua plant, which employs many of the surviving Shanghai orphans born in the early 1970s, are reported to be extremely severe, with employees working long hours exposed to sulfuric acid and other hazardous chemicals. (With the exception of the orphans, all shop-floor workers at this plant are reportedly rural migrants from other provinces.)

In August 1988, Han Weicheng ordered Qiu Zhen transferred for two weeks to the Shanghai Municipal Civil Affairs Bureau Deportation Station (*Shanghaishi Minzhengju Qiansongzhan*). This was apparently a punishment imposed on Qiu for trying to scale the outer wall of the orphanage. Unlike Zhu Yan, who was detained and tortured two months earlier at the same location (see above), Qiu Zhen was not physically abused while held at the station.

On March 12, 1990, Qiu Zhen was accused of breaking into an office at the orphanage and stealing money and grain ration coupons. Two senior staff members, vice-director Zhen Weiming and security chief Li Zhouqing, held a private session to interrogate Qiu for several hours, choking him and beating him with electric police batons. (According to Zhang Shuyun and Ai Ming, they also asked another boy at the orphanage, Fu Qiang, to provide false testimony against Qiu.) Qiu eventually persuaded them to let him leave, promising he would retrieve the "stolen" money, but instead ran away from the orphanage, leaving a note saying he would never return.

Around midnight, however, Qiu telephoned the orphanage to announce that he was coming back, assuming that Zhen and Li would have gone off duty by the time he returned. However, when he arrived back at the institute at around 2:00 a.m. on March 13, both men were still waiting for him in Zhen Weiming's office, with Li Zhouqing in full security uniform. They attempted to intimidate Qiu, pointing out the gun in Li's holster and an electric police baton lying on Zhen's desk. They then tried to convince Qiu to spy on Zhang Shuyun and other critics of the orphanage management, giving him a pen and notebook and asking him to visit the critics' offices secretly and copy down details of any documents he found.

In the afternoon of the same day, however, Qiu was sent to the Chengjiaqiao police station and taken into custody. Chen Dongxian, the orphanage driver, who had been ordered to take Qiu to the police station, notified Zhang Shuyun, who then went to the station with Li Guilan, another medical employee. The two doctors approached the station commander and found him to be sympathetic, apparently unaware of his subordinates' friendly relations with Han Weicheng.

The police found dirt undisturbed on the sill of the window Qiu Zhen was accused of climbing through, and no evidence that the window had been opened. Noting that Qiu Zhen's deformed arms were also too short to have allowed him to climb the wall of the building, the police released Qiu and returned him to the orphanage. The following day, Zhen Weiming and Li Zhouqing confronted Zhang

Shuyun in her office and accused her of "forcing" the police station to release Qiu from custody.[325]

On March 1, 1992, Qiu Zhen asked a teacher, Li Juyun, for written permission to leave the orphanage grounds to participate in a training meet for the Special Olympics, in which he hoped to compete as a runner. Unfortunately, Qiu accidentally knocked against Li with his deformed arm during the conversation, and at this point Li, for some obscure reason, began shouting that her arm was "broken," knocked Qiu to the ground and began beating and kicking him.

Later, Li Juyun publicly offered 200 Chinese yuan to anyone who would help her beat up Qiu Zhen. She also brought her husband and brother to wait at the orphanage gates to attack Qiu as he left for school, but he escaped injury after being warned by other orphans to stay inside.

Qiu was later expelled from the local high school (which he had begun attending) at the request of Lu Rongfang, head of the Children's Department at the orphanage, who told the school authorities he had assaulted Li Juyun.[326] Qiu was barred from training for the Special Olympics and had his gym clothes, satchel, and money confiscated. The Chengjiaqiao police station also placed a criticism in Qiu's personal file, claiming he had "violated Public Security Bureau regulations." As a result of this harassment, Qiu Zhen became severely depressed and was eventually admitted to the Shanghai No.2 People's Hospital. Lu Rongfang had no food or other supplies sent to Qiu at the hospital and arranged only for a retarded orphan to care for him.

Child-care worker Wang Genlin eventually learned of Qiu's whereabouts and went to visit him in the hospital, where she found he had developed a heart complaint requiring surgery. Wang later accompanied two orphanage medical staff, Zhang Shuyun and Yang Yaming, to confront Lu Rongfang, warning her that she would be held responsible if anything happened to Qiu. Lu responded by replacing the retarded child with a child-care worker who allegedly "hated" Qiu. This woman threatened Qiu at the hospital, warning him not to discuss conditions at the orphanage with other patients or hospital staff.

---

[325] A factual report on this incident was published by the Shanghai newspaper *Labor News* on April 12, 1990 (see Appendix C). However, an internal report circulated by the Shanghai Civil Affairs Bureau on August 15, 1990 repeated the orphanage management's previous accusations against Qiu Zhen and Zhang Shuyun (see Appendix D).

[326] Lu Rongfang replaced Tang Youhua as head of the Children's Department after Tang's demotion for criticizing the beating of Yue Yi (see above). She was popularly known as *"Didiwei,"* after a type of insecticide. This nickname was apparently invented by the orphans in her care.

Qiu remained in hospital for one month and was implanted with a Siemens pacemaker costing 20,000 Chinese yuan, which, in an exceptional departure from normal practice and only after sustained pressure from Zhang Shuyun and other critics, the orphanage agreed to pay for. After his return to the orphanage, he was threatened with transfer to the No.2 Social Welfare Institute on Chongming Island. However, he was eventually able to find work as a clerk in a garment factory in the city's Pudong development area.

Qin Gaoming ("Zhong Xiu")

Qin Gaoming was born to a peasant family on Chongming Island in approximately 1977, missing her left hand and forearm. Soon after her birth, her maternal grandmother took her to Wusong (the port town on the south bank of the Yangtze river which links Chongming Island to the mainland of Shanghai Municipality) and abandoned her, without telling her parents. She was discovered and taken to the Shanghai Children's Welfare Institute, where staff assigned her the name "Zhong Xiu."

Shortly before her death in 1986, Qin Gaoming's grandmother confessed to having abandoned the infant in Wusong. She told Qin's parents that she had waited nearby until the child was discovered and had overheard a bystander suggest that she be taken to the orphanage. Qin's mother then wrote to the Children's Welfare Institute, asking if a girl of her daughter's age and description had been brought there. The letter was referred to Zhang Jinnuan, then vice-director of the institute's Business Section (*Yewuke*), which handles the administrative requirements of admissions, adoptions, transfers, and deaths of children at the orphanage.

Zhang Jinnuan failed to answer the letter, however. Four years later, in 1990, Qin Gaoming's father visited the orphanage in person but was told by Zhang Jinnuan that the child was not there.

In March 1991, a relative of Qin Gaoming's mother, an employee at the No.2 Social Welfare Institute, told her that a girl with a missing hand and forearm had recently been transferred to Chongming Island from the orphanage. Qin's parents went to the institute to meet the child, who turned out not to be their daughter but a close friend of hers, Ru Sha. Ru Sha confirmed that a girl matching Qin Gaoming's description was living at the orphanage under the name "Zhong Xiu" and showed the parents a photograph which the two girls had had taken together.

Qin Gaoming's paternal aunt, Gu Ma, the Communist Party secretary of Lühua Township in Chongming County, then asked the director of the county Civil Affairs Department to contact Sun Jinfu, director of the Shanghai Civil Affairs Bureau, and request that Sun look into the case personally. Sun confirmed that "Zhong Xiu" was living at the orphanage but urged the family not to try to take her back to Chongming, as she would lose her urban residency permit (entitling her to live in

Shanghai proper). Sun also assured Qin's relatives that children at the orphanage were "well fed and well dressed" and were given ample opportunities for education and employment.

However, Qin's parents were by then more concerned than ever to remove her from the Children's Welfare Institute, as Ru Sha had told them of the severe abuse suffered by children there. Qin's father returned to the orphanage on June 16, 1991, bringing a photograph of his daughter as an infant, but was turned away at the gate.

On June 26, 1991, Qin Gaoming's parents traveled to the orphanage with eight of their siblings in a van "borrowed" by Gu Ma from the Lühua township government. Posing as an official delegation from the No.2 Social Welfare Institute, they succeeded in driving the van into the orphanage grounds, where they spread out and began asking other children where "Zhong Xiu" was. Qin Gaoming was eventually located and identified by her malformed left arm and by a birthmark on her thigh.

At this point, Zhang Jinnuan told Qin Gaoming's relatives that she had known Qin's true identity ever since receiving her mother's letter in 1986. She then refused to let the van leave the compound until the adults had handed over all the cash in their possession, totaling approximately 4,000 Chinese yuan. After collecting the money, Zhang Jinnuan allowed Qin Gaoming to leave with her family, without completing any paperwork or documentation.

Qin later told her parents that she had been sexually abused in 1986 and 1987 by Ni Kongyong, a carpenter on the orphanage staff. Her father returned to the orphanage on June 30, 1991, to complain to Han Weicheng, but no action was taken at the time.[327]

Qin Gaoming now lives with her family on Chongming Island. Her parents have reportedly been visited by officers of the Shanghai Public Security Bureau, who threatened them in an attempt to prevent them from associating with delegates of the Shanghai Municipal People's Congress and other critics of the orphanage management who had visited their home in the past.

---

[327] Zhang Shuyun has stated that Ni Kongyong stopped reporting to work in 1992, after the arrival of an investigation team from the municipal Supervision Bureau, but another source at the orphanage reports that he returned to work in 1994.

VI. THE COVER-UP IN SHANGHAI

Evidence obtained by Human Rights Watch/Asia has revealed far more than the intentional killing and brutal ill-treatment of orphans at the Shanghai Children's Welfare Institute. During late 1991 and early 1992, conditions at the orphanage were the subject of an extended official inquiry, resulting from a series of complaints filed against the institute's management by several employees. The investigation involved not only the Shanghai Civil Affairs Bureau but a range of other municipal agencies, including the Shanghai Communist Party Committee, the Shanghai Procuracy, and the Shanghai Public Security Bureau, as well as sixteen members of the Shanghai Municipal People's Congress, the city's nominal legislature.

These efforts to end the abuse of Shanghai's orphans and to bring to justice their chief perpetrator, orphanage director Han Weicheng, ended in total failure, as a result of unrelenting hostility from the city's senior political leadership. The most senior municipal official directly responsible for suppressing the results of the inquiry was Wu Bangguo, then the city's Communist Party secretary. In April 1992, Wu personally informed a member of the Municipal People's Congress that conditions at the orphanage involved questions of "human rights," and that it was therefore necessary to prevent any news of the investigation from leaking out. Wu also instructed the director of the Shanghai Municipal Propaganda Department, Jin Binhua, to issue orders to all Shanghai media outlets prohibiting any negative coverage of the Children's Welfare Institute, and requiring local journalists to turn in any material they had gathered on conditions there.[328]

Other top Shanghai officials were also informed of the abuses taking place at the orphanage but took no action to stop them. Apart from Wu Bangguo, these included Huang Ju, the city's then mayor; Xie Lijuan, vice-mayor responsible for health, education, and social welfare; and Sun Jinfu, the director of the municipal Civil Affairs Bureau.[329] Due to deliberate obstruction by these leaders, the campaign to

---

[328] The information on Wu Bangguo's role in this affair comes from a source with direct knowledge of the incident but who cannot be named for reasons of safety.

[329] All of these persons were closely involved in directing the official response to the dissident staff members' petitions on the abuses occurring at the orphanage. One item of documentary evidence which substantiates this very clearly is the internal report submitted on December 9, 1991 by Shi Shengren, legal consultant to the Shanghai General Labor Union, to senior municipal leaders. (A full translation of this document appears below as Appendix F.) Those on the shortlist for distribution of this confidential document were: "Municipal [Communist Party] Secretary, and Deputy Secretary; Standing Committee [of the municipal

reform the Children's Welfare Institute resulted instead in the complete vindication of the inquiry's main target, Han Weicheng, and in professional ruin for many of those who spoke out on the orphans' behalf.

The full story of this episode is already known to hundreds of people in Shanghai, including senior official and journalistic circles and some members of the city's Christian community, but it has been successfully concealed from the vast majority of the population. During 1995, however, two key witnesses to the events of this period succeeded in escaping from China, bringing with them extensive written documentation of the official investigation and subsequent cover-up. The evidence and personal testimony of Dr. Zhang Shuyun, a former employee of the Shanghai Children's Welfare Institute, and Ai Ming, a polio victim raised from early infancy at the Shanghai orphanage, offer proof of the municipal leadership's complicity in concealing the unnatural deaths and abuse of hundreds of children. Based on the evidence of these and other participants, and on extensive documentary evidence in the form of the internal minutes of a series of meetings held between Shanghai Municipal People's Congress delegates and leading city officials in mid-1992, Human Rights Watch/Asia has assembled the following chronology of events.

Early Complaints, September 1988-August 1990

In September 1988, Dr. Zhang Shuyun was appointed to a joint medical and administrative position at the Shanghai Children's Welfare Institute, leaving her previous post as a researcher at the Shanghai Municipal Research Institute for the Prevention and Cure of Occupational Diseases. Her new responsibilities included supervising the completion of the orphanage's seven-story Rehabilitation Center, which was to open in June 1989, as well as performing biomedical tests at the orphanage laboratory. Zhang Shuyun was offered this post partly in an effort to supplement the management staff at the Children's Welfare Institute, as the position of orphanage director had been vacant since the formal retirement in 1988 of the previous director, Qian Pei'e. At the time of Dr. Zhang's arrival, day-to-day management of the institute was largely in the hands of Qian's chosen successor, vice-director Han Weicheng, with tacit support from Qian herself, who retained a salaried position as "consultant" to the orphanage leadership until 1990.[330]

In October 1988, Dr. Zhang was joined at the orphanage by a former colleague from the research institute, Li Guilan, who took up a position as a speech therapist for "self-paying" deaf-mute children. Zhang and Li quickly became aware of

---

Communist Party]; Mayor, and Deputy Mayor."

[330] Han Weicheng formally assumed the position of director in late 1989.

severe management problems at the Children's Welfare Institute, including the high death rate among newly admitted infants and the routine physical abuse of older children, as well as extensive financial improprieties involving work on the Rehabilitation Center project. To the apparent surprise of other senior staff, they failed to accomodate themselves to the existing situation at the orphanage, and in 1989 they began instead to seek out other dissatisfied employees to assist them in exposing these abuses. The most prominent of their eventual allies was Yang Yaming, a physical therapist at the orphanage and a Communist Party member. Yang Yaming, who had worked at the Children's Welfare Institute since 1977, had previously held a senior administrative position but had been demoted in 1985, after she filed an earlier set of unsuccessful complaints against the management of the institute. A fourth employee who played an especially active role in the critics' campaign was Chen Dongxian, the orphanage driver. Other sympathetic staff members who participated in the campaign included doctors, nurses and child-care workers.

Beginning in December 1989, the dissident staff members took their complaints beyond the orphanage itself to successively higher levels of the Shanghai Civil Affairs Bureau, where they met indifference or outright opposition at every stage. Within the Children's Welfare Institute itself, however, the initial response to these criticisms among rank-and-file staff was strongly favorable, suggesting that many ordinary employees shared the critics' concerns without daring to support them openly. Indeed, Zhang Shuyun was elected by a staff ballot in March 1990 to represent the orphanage in the People's Congress of Nanshi District, defeating Han Weicheng in an unexpected contest for the seat previously held by retired director Qian Pei'e. In addition, Zhang Shuyun and Yang Yaming were selected in 1990 as the unit's "model workers" for the previous year.

However, the early sympathy which had greeted the critics was quickly dispelled. Senior staff at the orphanage, led by Han Weicheng, responded to the campaign with an escalating counterattack both inside and outside the orphanage walls. Han and his supporters deployed the entire panoply of tools available to the leaders of a Chinese *danwei* (work unit), including control over bonuses, staff assignments, and housing allocations, to harass his opponents and reward loyal supporters. Zhang Shuyun's seat in the district People's Congress remained vacant, as a result of election fraud carried out by Han Weicheng with the assistance of the institute's then Communist Party secretary, Zhu Qingfang.[331]

More important, however, was the political support which Han Weicheng and his associates were able to obtain from higher authorities, particularly their

---

[331] After two additional ballots failed to reverse the initial outcome, a fourth vote was held under the direct supervision of Han and Zhu, but produced no winning candidate.

immediate superiors in the Shanghai Civil Affairs Bureau. By 1990, the critics had held two meetings with senior bureau officials, including one in December 1989 with the bureau's vice-directors, Feng Guishan and Qian Guanlin, and another in February 1990 with bureau director Sun Jinfu. During these meetings, the leadership of the Civil Affairs Bureau was made fully aware of conditions at the orphanage.[332]

Despite the extensive information made available to Sun Jinfu and his subordinates, the Shanghai Civil Affairs Bureau took no action against Han Weicheng. Indeed, the bureau reportedly provided Han with full details of the accusations made against him in confidence by dissident staff members. On the basis of these reports, the orphanage management began in March 1990 to convene a series of increasingly large staff meetings to organize opposition to the critics' efforts. These meetings were coordinated with the actions of the Civil Affairs Bureau itself, which sent Ye Xinghua, then vice-director of the bureau's Organization Department (*Zuzhichu*) to meet individually with the critics and pressure them to abandon their campaign.[333]

The orphanage management was also able to harness Shanghai's official media in its efforts at self-defense. An article published in the specialized journal *Shanghai Masses Public Health News* (*Shanghai Dazhong Weisheng Bao*), on March 29, 1990, praised the quality of management at the Child Welfare Institute and quoted Han Weicheng as saying that unnamed "comrades who have recently arrived at the institute" were working to undermine the orphanage from within.

The critics were even less successful in avoiding retribution within the orphanage itself. On June 25, 1990, Li Guilan was suspended from her duties as a speech therapist and was transferred to a position cleaning windows and bathrooms; an untrained child-care worker was assigned to continue her work with deaf-mute children. On July 17, Zhang Shuyun was transferred to a minor post performing Chinese massage therapy, for which she has no professional qualifications, and her status was reduced from "specialized technical staff" (*zhuanye jishu zhicheng*) to that of an ordinary worker, with correspondingly lower salary. She was denied all subsidies and bonuses and an effort was made (which she successfully resisted for some time) to take away her private office.

Several days later, on July 28, Sun Jinfu contacted Zhang Shuyun and told her that he approved of the institute's decision to demote her. On August 15, the Shanghai Civil Affairs Bureau published a classified report written by Ye Xinghua, which accused Zhang Shuyun, Li Guilan, and Yang Yaming of conducting a smear campaign against the orphanage leadership. This document, a translation of which

---

[332] The critics also wrote two letters to Sun Jinfu, dated March 31 and April 10, 1990.

[333] Ye Xinghua has since been promoted to director of the Organization Department.

appears in Appendix D, was circulated to Deputy Mayor Xie Lijuan and to a limited number of other senior city officials.

Appeals to Higher Authority, August 1990-December 1991

By this time, recognizing the futility of seeking redress within the Civil Affairs Bureau, the critics had already begun seeking out other municipal agencies for assistance. After being told by Zhang Bangxiang, director of the city's Committee for the Protection of Young People and Children (*Qingshaonian Baohu Weiyuanhui*), that he had no authority to help them, the critics contacted the Shanghai Municipal General Labor Union (*Shanghaishi Zonggonghui*) and began cooperating closely with a staff attorney at the union, Shi Shengren.

The critics also wrote to the editors of several Shanghai newspapers, in an attempt to spur journalistic investigations into conditions at the orphanage. This approach was initially successful, leading to the appearance of two critical articles in *Labor News*, the official publication of the General Labor Union. The first of these articles, published in April 1990, dealt with the false accusation of theft made several weeks earlier against the orphan Qiu Zhen. A second article in May 1990 exposed the routine practice of tying orphans to their beds. (Translations of both articles appear in Appendix C.)

In September 1990, three dissident staff members (Zhang Shuyun, Li Guilan, and Chen Dongxian) contacted the Shanghai No.2 Legal Affairs Agency (*Shanghai Di'er Lüshi Shiwusuo*), a state-owned legal aid agency, for assistance in preparing a defamation lawsuit against Han Weicheng and *Shanghai Masses Public Health News* in response to the newspaper's March 29 article. The resulting judgment was only a partial success; the Jing'an District People's Court held the newspaper liable for the false accusation, but exonerated Han Weicheng, accepting his claim that he had been misquoted.[334] Despite their partial defeat in this case, two attorneys from the No.2 Legal Affairs Agency, Cao Haiyuan and Cui Aidi, continued to cooperate with the critics, making two clandestine visits to Chongming Island in August and September 1991 and interviewing a number of former inmates of the orphanage who had since been transferred to the Shanghai No.2 Social Welfare Institute. During one of the lawyers' visits to Chongming, on September 1, 1991, the orphan Chou Hui testified that she had been repeatedly raped and sexually abused by Han Weicheng.

Beginning in October 1991, the critics also began cooperating with several delegates to the Shanghai Municipal People's Congress (SMPC). Although some

---

[334] The district court's ruling was issued on August 9, 1991; a judgment by the Shanghai Municipal Intermediate People's Court reaffirming the original ruling on appeal was issued on October 29 of the same year.

sixteen delegates to the congress eventually joined the investigation into misconduct by the orphanage management, three who worked particularly closely with the dissident staff were Ma Mimi, the chairwoman of the labor union at the Shanghai Food Products Machinery Factory *(Shanghai Shipin Jixiechang)*; Gao Junzhu, a retired teacher; and Xu Xinyuan, a cadre in the labor union at the Shanghai Photographic Apparatus Research Institute *(Shanghai Zhaoxiang Qicai Yanjiusuo)*.

Shortly afterwards, on December 9, 1991, the Shanghai General Labor Union released a brief but scathing memorandum written by Shi Shengren, which referred to the high rate of unnatural deaths at the institute and accused Han Weicheng of raping orphan girls. This report was classified "intermediate-level secret" *(jimi)* and circulated only to a limited number of senior Shanghai officials, including Communist Party Secretary Wu Bangguo, Mayor Huang Ju, Vice-Mayor Xie Lijuan, and the members of the Standing Committee of the SMPC. (A translation of this report appears in Appendix F.)

The General Labor Union's report, contrasting sharply with earlier efforts by the Civil Affairs Bureau to discredit charges made by the dissident staff, was the first official acknowledgment that problems at the Children's Welfare Institute were severe and rapidly worsening. At the time, its release convinced Zhang Shuyun and her associates that their campaign was well on its way to success.

The Authorities Strike Back, December 1991-March 1992

The initial response to the General Labor Union's report was swift. On orders from Xie Lijuan, a work team from the city's Bureau of Supervision *(Jianchaju)*, an independent agency directly responsible to the Shanghai municipal government and charged with investigating official malfeasance, was dispatched to the Children's Welfare Institute within days of the report's publication. The work team, which was to spend eight months conducting an on-the-spot inquiry on the orphanage grounds, immediately began collecting statements and documentation from the dissident staff members.

Meanwhile, the SMPC began taking decisive action on its own. Based on letters of complaint from the dissident staff, Lu Ming, a former senior procurator in Shanghai and a member of the SMPC's Legal Committee, convened a meeting on January 6, 1992, with a number of senior law enforcement officials in the city, including Ma Ruikang, the deputy director of the Shanghai Public Security Bureau, and Wu Hengjun, the director of the bureau's Public Order Department *(Zhi'anchu)*. At this meeting it was decided to send two officials from the Procuracy into the orphanage to investigate alleged criminal offenses committed by Han Weicheng, particularly "hooliganism" (an apparent reference to charges of sexual harassment made by several female child-care workers) and the assault and illegal detention of the orphan Yue Yi. The Procuracy employees also agreed to report back to a second meeting, scheduled for March 2.

In retrospect, it appears that the consensus reached on January 6 may have represented a tactical error on the part of the SMPC delegates. Efforts to investigate the extremely high ratio of deaths to admissions at the orphanage, although clearly the most serious element of the case, were temporarily set aside, as the delegates sought to build a criminal case against Han Weicheng for relatively minor offenses, such as the beating of Yue Yi. According to Zhang Shuyun, this partly reflected the delegates' belief that proof of orphans' unnatural deaths, even when brought about deliberately through "summary resolution," could expose Han to nothing more serious than administrative penalties for mismanagement. More important, however, was the general assumption that the inquiry would make no substantial progress unless Han Weicheng were arrested and jailed. The delegates hoped that removing Han from the Children's Welfare Institute would eliminate the main obstacle to their investigation, by ending the intimidation of other staff members and allowing the actual conditions at the orphanage to be publicly examined.

However, as earlier chapters have shown and as a number of Western journalists have already documented, institutionalized children throughout China are subject to essentially the same abuses that sparked the dissident staff members' campaign in Shanghai–indeed, the death rate recorded at the Shanghai orphanage in 1989 was slightly lower than the national average. By holding Han Weicheng personally responsible for the conditions at the Shanghai orphanage, therefore, both the dissident employees and the SMPC delegates may have misunderstood the true nature of the problem they were dealing with. Possibly for this reason, the critics eventually confronted an official response which was entirely unexpected: the city's highest leaders united in their determination to defend Han Weicheng from even minor criticism, despite overwhelming evidence implicating him in serious criminal offenses. In January 1992, however, the delegates still had no inkling of the retaliation awaiting them.

In anticipation of what they believed might be Han's imminent arrest, those present at the January 6 meeting agreed that the SMPC's Legal Committee should formally prohibit him from leaving China. This turned out to be a prescient move, for Han and his superiors within the Civil Affairs Bureau apparently panicked at this point. On January 6 (the day of the first meeting called by Lu Ming) and again on February 29, the bureau submitted applications to the city's Foreign Affairs Office for permission for Han to travel abroad. These were turned down after the Public Security Bureau sent a letter to the Foreign Affairs Office–later backed up by an official directive–specifically prohibiting the approval of any overseas travel plans by Han. The Shanghai Public Security Bureau also forwarded this directive to their counterparts in the border city of Shenzhen, in order to ensure that Han did not escape to Hong Kong by land. The last decision was a crucial one: minutes of a subsequent meeting held on March 11, 1992 indicate that Han Weicheng had recently returned from Guangdong Province, apparently after an unsuccessful attempt to flee the country with the encouragement of the Civil Affairs Bureau. Referring to this incident, Lu Ming commented: "He won't be able to escape."

The March 11, 1992 meeting, at which the Bureau of Supervision submitted its first report to the SMPC delegates (and for this reason the meeting is generally referred to by those concerned as having been the "first" in a series of altogether six key sessions held by SMPC delegates after the preliminary discussions of January 6), suggests that the city government's investigation was at this stage still relatively impartial.[335] Ma Mimi, one of the SMPC delegates cooperating most closely with the dissident orphanage staff, was reportedly not satisfied with Vice-Mayor Xie Lijuan's decision to place the inquiry solely in the hands of the Supervision Bureau, as she and other delegates had originally planned a much more extensive official investigation involving several branches of the city government. In its preliminary findings, however, the Supervision Bureau had concluded that the leadership group of the orphanage was implicated in "violations of discipline," and recommended that Han Weicheng be suspended from his duties as of March 20. The bureau also called for the case to be "filed for investigation" (li'an), a first step towards possible criminal charges against Han.

The response of senior officials responsible for overseeing the orphanage was at least superficially cooperative, reflecting the Supervision Bureau's relatively serious attitude towards the case at this stage. Sun Jinfu, the director of the Civil Affairs Bureau, endorsed the Supervision Bureau's findings and even suggested that Han Weicheng be required to "confess" (jiaodai) his wrongdoing to the authorities. This may have reflected Sun's concerns about having to answer for Han's behavior to his own superior, Xie Lijuan. At one meeting with Civil Affairs Bureau vice-director Feng Guishan and Supervision Bureau vice-director Yu Ming, Xie had reportedly criticized the Civil Affairs Bureau for withholding information on conditions at the orphanage, telling Feng, "You said there was nothing wrong!"

Even at this early stage, however, danger signs had already begun to appear. One of the city's three major newspapers, *Liberation Daily*, had published an article on February 4 praising management of the Children's Welfare Institute, along with a photograph of Xie Lijuan standing beside Han Weicheng during one of her visits to the orphanage. The appearance of this article, a translation of which appears in

---

[335] Much of the information that follows concerning, and all the individual quotations from, the series of six meetings between the SMPC delegates and Shanghai government officials has been taken directly from the internal minutes of those meetings, copies of all but the fifth of which have been obtained by Human Rights Watch/Asia.

Appendix H, indicated that Han already had at least tacit support from the deputy mayor's office.

Other departments quickly weighed in on Han's behalf as well. Despite his tactical endorsement of the Supervision Bureau's initial recommendations, Sun Jinfu also requested that Han's suspension as orphanage director be postponed beyond March 20, ostensibly in order to allow time to find a suitable replacement. Given the general indifference of China's civil affairs departments towards the welfare of abandoned children, Sun's support for a beleaguered subordinate under these circumstances is hardly surprising. What was to prove far more devastating to the progress of the inquiry, however, was the increasingly ambivalent attitude of the SMPC leadership, despite the fervent commitment of many rank-and-file delegates to a successful resolution of the matter. The minutes of the delegates' March 11 meeting indicate that concerns about the political implications of the case were beginning to be voiced openly for the first time, often in terms reminiscent of those used by China's official historians of civil affairs work. Lu Ming, for example, stated that it would be crucial to establish that the Shanghai orphanage was better managed by the Communist authorities than by the Catholic Church operating under Nationalist rule, adding that the issue represented a contrast between "two systems and two societies." Moreover, he noted, "The international and domestic impact [of this affair] would be very great."

At the same session, Ma Mimi described the case as the most difficult she had ever handled and suggested that the Civil Affairs Bureau could not be trusted to deal with it correctly. As she and other participants pointed out, forces were already gathering to divert the course of the investigation. Orphanage staff members who supported Han Weicheng had begun sending their own letters of complaint to higher authorities, alleging that the Supervision Bureau's investigation team was interfering with their work and that Han's critics were themselves responsible for abusing orphans. More seriously, the orphanage had by this time begun an organized effort to suppress evidence on the unnatural deaths of hundreds of children. Ma Mimi noted that of 478 deaths recorded during the three-year period 1989-1991, the orphanage had so far handed over medical records for only 346, and these only after long delays during which many records were amended or falsified. She added that Han Weicheng was "carrying out factional maneuvers" and had already won all the institute's mid-level cadres over to his side.

The second of the six main meetings held by SMPC delegates was convened less than three weeks later, on March 30, 1992. By this time, however, it appears that the attitude of the Supervision Bureau had already changed substantially. The bureau's second report dealt with a number of individual allegations of misconduct by Han Weicheng and other staff members. In nearly every case, however, its conclusions were ambiguous or self-contradictory. Despite attempts to minimize several cases of abuse reported by dissident staff, the bureau's report conceded that serious incidents had in fact taken place. For example, it observed that in forty-nine out of the 346 cases of death examined thus far by the investigation team, no causes of death whatsoever had been entered in the children's medical records. But it merely noted, without further comment or display of concern, the fact that "malnutrition" had been recorded as the cause of death in no fewer than ninety-nine of the cases. The question of abnormal or unnatural deaths was evaded entirely.

The report also referred to highly unusual accounting practices at the Children's Welfare Institute. These included the unauthorized use for staff bonuses of funds donated to the orphanage by Master Zhen Chan, the abbot of the city's Jade Buddha Temple, as well as the existence of a personal account opened in Han Weicheng's name at the Nanshi District branch of the Agricultural Bank of China, containing nearly US$80,000 in foreign currency obtained from overseas donations and adoption fees. Asked for a detailed accounting of these practices, the director of the orphanage's Finance Department had told the work team, "The accounts are in my head." Apparently, the Supervision Bureau officials found this response to be acceptable, for they failed to pursue the matter any further.

On other crucial issues, notably the allegations of sexual assaults at the orphanage, the March 30 report was simply inaccurate or evasive. On the case of Chou Hui, who had allegedly been raped twice by Han Weicheng in late 1988, it sought to find inconsistencies in her testimony and claimed that the three-person sofa in Han's office where she said the first rape took place was in fact only a two-person sofa. (According to Ai Ming, Han had later replaced the original sofa with a smaller one.)

The March 30 report asserted that the Shanghai Municipal Communist Party Committee (then chaired by Wu Bangguo) had "paid much attention to this matter," as had the Municipal Procuracy. Despite this high-level interest, however, the report failed to reach any coherent conclusion on the facts of the case. Although the report conceded that the accusations made by the dissident staff members were "basically correct, and not a case of false accusation" it then added, in an apparent effort at even-handedness, that the critics' actions had caused "chaos" and "serious antagonisms" within the orphanage.

The report ended by noting that after consultations with Sun Jinfu, the terms of Han's suspension had been altered from "relieved of duties for investigation" (*tingzhi jiancha*) to "no longer in charge of orphanage work" (*bu zhuchi yuanzhang gongzuo*). This reclassification allowed Han to retain his salary and benefits while suspended. It seems clear, therefore, that the tide had turned decisively in Han Weicheng's favor during the second half of March 1992. Events subsequent to the March 30 session further confirmed that the critics were losing ground. On March 31 and April 6, foreign delegations visited the orphanage on tours led by Han Weicheng, despite his official suspension from duties.

A further private session (the "third" meeting) between SMPC delegates and the dissident staff, held on April 8 without representatives of the Supervision Bureau present, confirmed that a number of other city agencies had been informed of the investigation into the Children's Welfare Institute. Lu Ming referred to a meeting held on April 2 to discuss the issue, which had included, among others, representatives of the Education Bureau, the Discipline and Inspection Committee, and the Letters and Visits Department (*Xinfang Bumen*), an agency responsible for handling citizens' complaints against the authorities. This time making more explicit a theme he had earlier raised, Lu stated: "In late March, I met with Sun Jinfu. [Sun said,] 'We must unify people's thinking on this matter. If the [news of] large-scale deaths got out, it would have an extremely bad influence and the consequences would be severe. This is a political issue, and we must deal with it as a political task.'" Lu himself noted, moreover: "What was the situation like at the KMT's [Nationalist Party] foundling home? There are people looking into this question now....This is precisely a question of human rights."

Still more ominously for the orphanage critics, Lu Ming confirmed at the April 8 meeting that their charges in fact represented the third successive round of criticism since 1986 by employees of the Shanghai Children's Welfare Institute. Similar allegations of misconduct had been submitted in the past to the city's Discipline and Inspection Committee and the Committee for the Protection of Young People and Children, leading to calls for the replacement of the institute's leadership group. However, neither of these earlier appeals had achieved any visible result.[336] Ma Renbing, the chairman of the Shanghai Islamic Association and an SMPC delegate, wondered aloud at this point: "Just how high up do these people's connections reach, that they're able to evade the law and go scot-free like this?" *(You duo da de houtai, keyi xiaoyao fawai?)*

The Investigation Collapses, March-August 1992

There were indications at the April 8, 1992 meeting that a similar fate was already in store for the third series of complaints filed against the orphanage management. Participants in this meeting commented that the Supervision Bureau had not been doing its job properly and that its reports were "not [real] reports." The SMPC delegates also expressed concern over the fact that Han Weicheng's suspension had only been announced to six people, despite an earlier decision to give the case wide

---

[336] One of these campaigns was apparently that led by Yang Yaming in the mid-1980s, which had resulted in her demotion.

publicity in official circles. In addition, Lu Ming's comments on April 8 showed an increasing concern for the political overtones of the case, and for the potential damage to China's international reputation which any adverse publicity might cause. He referred again to the possibility that conditions at the orphanage might be worse than those which prevailed before the Communist takeover. For this reason, he stressed that it would be "inappropriate" to allow the city's newspapers and broadcasting stations to report any news of the investigation.

On the following day, April 9, a bizarre incident took place at the Children's Welfare Institute. A camera crew from China Central Television (CCTV), the Beijing-based national television network, arrived to produce a news report on the orphanage, ostensibly to commemorate the first anniversary (on May 15) of the passage of China's "Law For The Protection Of Disabled Persons." The crew was escorted by Sun Jinfu and by Wang Yinian, then director of the Shanghai Civil Affairs Bureau's Department of Social Welfare. Reporters on the crew, which continued filming until April 10, ignored demands by the dissident staff members to be allowed to speak on camera and instead conducted interviews with Han Weicheng, despite the fact that he had been relieved of his position. When questioned by the critics, the crew explained that they had been asked to produce the news report by both the Shanghai Civil Affairs Bureau and its parent body, the Ministry of Civil Affairs in Beijing.

On April 14, several officers from the nearby Chengjiaqiao police station arrived at the orphanage escorted by staff from the Civil Affairs Bureau. They summoned three of the four leading dissident employees (Li Guilan, Yang Yaming, and Chen Dongxian) to the station for questioning, where they were accused of "persecuting" the CCTV news crew during its visit. Zhang Shuyun was not summoned for questioning until the following day, but was interrogated more intensively, apparently in the belief that she was the ringleader of the critics' group. All four staffers were released after questioning and told to go home to await further action.[337]

The minutes of a fourth meeting of SMPC delegates, held on April 17, indicate in graphic detail the near-collapse of the investigation. Yu Ming, Deputy Director of the Supervision Bureau, opened the meeting by producing two spurious sets of statistics on infant and child mortality at the orphanage between 1989 and 1991, indicating much lower death rates than those earlier calculated by the critics. He also suggested that of the hundreds of children's deaths recorded at the institute during this period, only three (those of Bi Feng, Xi Liang, and Xing Fei) could be considered potentially unnatural. For the remainder of the investigation, the bureau's team was to make no further concessions on this crucial issue. Officials of the Supervision Bureau

---

[337] The news crew returned to the orphanage on April 17 for an additional day of filming, explaining that the critics' interference had spoiled their original effort.

also announced at this meeting that the orphan Chou Hui had retracted her accusations of rape against Han Weicheng, a claim which astonished the SMPC delegates and persuaded several of them to visit Chongming Island in mid-July, at which time Chou Hui repeated her charges during a tape-recorded interview conducted at the No.2 Social Welfare Institute.[338]

During the April 17 meeting, Yu Ming also reported on his efforts one day earlier to deal with the overwhelming opposition of the orphanage staff to any punitive measures against Han Weicheng. On the morning of April 16, Yu Ming, Sun Jinfu, and Xu Jianrong (a member of the Supervision Bureau work team) had met directly with Han to discuss his suspension, and a general meeting of the institute's "cadres of middle rank and above" (*zhongceng yi shang ganbu*) had been convened later the same day to announce Han's suspension formally.

By this time, the Supervision Bureau was aware that it faced organized resistance from senior staff at the orphanage, as some forty-two employees, a sizeable proportion of the total, had already signed petitions on Han Weicheng's behalf. However, it is unlikely that Yu Ming was prepared for the reaction he received at the April 16 session. The meeting erupted in pandemonium at the announcement of Han's suspension, and the institute's "mid-level cadres" threatened to stop reporting to work if further measures were taken, asserting that an attack on Han was equivalent to an attack on the entire staff. Yu Ming described the scene at the meeting, which lasted for several hours, as "somewhat similar to the Cultural Revolution." The session was eventually suspended late in the afternoon. As a result of the day's fiasco, the Supervision Bureau made what was described at the following day's meeting of SMPC delegates as a decision to "postpone" Han's suspension, despite the fact that it had technically taken effect already.

Following Yu Ming's description of these events, Gao Junzhu then presented his own findings, based on a clandestine visit he and other delegates had made to the orphanage on October 20, 1991. He described himself as "deeply shocked" by the visit, during which he had witnessed the bodies of seven children who had been brought to the orphanage morgue, in three separate bundles, within the space of half a day.[339]

Nevertheless, more senior SMPC delegates continued to voice fears at the April 17 meeting about the possible political repercussions of the investigation. Ma Renbing expressed anger at the Supervision Bureau's findings: "How can these

---

[338] An audio tape of this interview has been obtained by Human Rights Watch/Asia.

[339] For extracts from Gao's personal testimony on this incident, see Chapter 4, "An Outline of the Attritional Process."

problems still be emerging, forty years after Liberation?" He added, however, that it was necessary to "protect the image of socialism...of the Party, and of the orphanage." Lu Ming was even more explicit, commenting, "We must not let this news get out .... Imperialism wants to get its hands on this material of ours." At least one delegate, Ma Mimi, seemed to suspect that a decision to suppress the inquiry had already been taken at a higher level: she accused the Supervision Bureau of seeking to "minimize" the problems at the orphanage.

The April 17 meeting ended with a discussion of whether the SMPC should conduct hearings of its own, calling witnesses to testify before the fifteen or so delegates who had expressed greatest concern. Although the participants in the meeting acknowledged that the SMPC had legal authority to call such hearings, both Lu Ming and Wang Chongji (the chairman of the SMPC's Standing Committee) rejected the possibility, on the grounds that the investigation required absolute secrecy. Lu Ming concluded: "The People's Congress will not question people [directly]....We must consider the political implications. I hope none of the delegates will leak the news." Wang Chongji concurred, adding that hearings "would increase the danger of news leaking out."

By this time, it was clear that this view was shared at the highest levels of the municipal government. During a face-to-face conversation in April 1992 which lasted some forty minutes, Wu Bangguo, the city's Communist Party secretary, told one delegate to the SMPC that the issue of the Children's Welfare Institute was one involving "human rights," and would therefore be handled with no publicity. Wu, whose position as municipal Party secretary made him the most powerful official in the city, in practice outranking the mayor and other government leaders, took practical steps to ensure that all publicity was, in fact, suppressed. A directive issued on Wu's personal instruction by the head of the municipal Propaganda Department, Jin Binhua, and circulated to all press and broadcasting outlets in Shanghai, made three stipulations on proper handling of the orphanage issue by the city's official media: no further critical reports were to be published on conditions at the Children's Welfare Institute; all journalists possessing documentary materials on the orphanage were to turn these in immediately to the municipal government; and special care was to be taken to ensure that information about the case did not fall into the hands of foreigners.

By this time, therefore, the dissident staff members and their allies had become increasingly despondent, especially after senior leaders of the SMPC delegates accepted the Supervision Bureau's claim that no more than three deaths at the orphanage in recent years could be considered potentially unnatural. At the suggestion of the orphan Ai Ming, who pointed out that hard evidence of atrocities at the Children's Welfare Institute might attract the attention of more senior officials outside

Shanghai,[340] Zhang Shuyun provided Ai Ming with a small camera which he used to take two rolls of prints depicting conditions at the orphanage. Most of these pictures were of dead or dying children in the morgue and the "waiting-for-death room," although others showed less serious abuses, such as children being required to do laundry and perform other chores for orphanage child-care workers. Some of the latter photographs were taken by another orphan, Zhan Tong.

A third child later left the orphanage secretly and handed over the negatives for development at a privately-owned photography shop in Shanghai. However, Zhan Tong had attracted the attention of several orphanage staff while taking photographs outdoors, and Wang Yinian, then director of the Department of Social Welfare (whose offices are located on the orphanage grounds), ordered him detained overnight on April 19 for questioning in the department's offices. Zhan Tong then revealed the identity of the third child, who was to return to the photography shop later to claim the developed pictures. On April 20, Civil Affairs Bureau director Sun Jinfu arrived at the orphanage along with a number of officers from the Shanghai Public Security Bureau, and the inmates of the Children's Section were all interrogated intensively. Sun and Wang then visited the photography shop accompanied by several police officers and forced the owner to hand over the photographs and negatives.

Pressure on the dissident orphanage employees also continued to intensify after their defeat at the April 16 staff meeting. The campaign of retaliation by staff members loyal to Han Weicheng reached a peak on May 18, when Chen Dongxian, the orphanage driver, was attacked and badly beaten by a group of approximately eleven other employees, led by then vice-director Huang Jiachun.[341] Two days later, on May 20, Zhang Shuyun was visiting Chen Dongxian at his home, where he was recuperating from the assault, when three officers from the Chengjiaqiao police station arrived and tried to take Chen into custody. When Zhang Shuyun intervened, they threatened to beat her. Zhang then telephoned Ma Mimi, who rushed to the headquarters of the Shanghai Public Security Bureau and received a promise that the harassment would be stopped. Although the police had by then called in two additional officers to the standoff at Chen's house, they left after being paged by Wang Yiping, the director of the Nanshi District Public Security Bureau.

In marked contrast to this police harassment of Chen Dongxian himself, no criminal charges were ever brought against any of the orphanage staff members who participated in the May 18 assault. Although Zhang Shuyun and other dissident

---

[340] Dr. Zhang notes that the dissident staffers' original intention was to appeal to Qiao Shi, the chairman of the National People's Congress in Beijing.

[341] A report filed by the Shanghai police on this incident, detailing Chen Dongxian's injuries, has been obtained by Human Rights Watch/Asia.

employees approached an initially sympathetic Wang Yiping and asked him to ensure that action was taken on Chen's case, Wang later told them that he had received orders from his superiors at the municipal level not to assist them.

A fifth meeting between SMPC delegates and Shanghai municipal officials was held on May 22, but Human Rights Watch/Asia has not been able to obtain the minutes of this meeting. On June 8, the sixth and last in the series of meetings to discuss the situation at the Children's Welfare Institute was held. In attendance was Han Kunlin, director of the Shanghai Supervision Bureau and the most senior official to have appeared at the meetings thus far. Yu Ming, his deputy, opened the meeting by stating: "Our investigation work has now basically come to a close." Turning to the question of high death rates at the Shanghai orphanage, he revealed, for the first time, that expert investigators from both the Shanghai Municipal Procuracy and also the city's Bureau of Public Health had been brought in to examine the incomplete medical records of the 478 children who died at the orphanage between 1989 and 1991, and that physicians from the latter bureau had focused on the question of whether the medical records had been tampered with or fabricated. Crucially, however, he failed to report anything at all on what the experts' actual findings on the issue of deaths from unnatural causes had been, instead merely stating: "The Supervision Bureau...is not a medical department, so we cannot reach any conclusions on this matter."

Yu then summarized the mortality statistics, as calculated according to three different methods: first, the annual overall deaths-to-admissions ratios during the three-year period had been "50 percent, 60 percent and 70 percent respectively, averaging 64 percent"; second, the ratios of deaths only from among new admissions to the numbers of new admissions had been "between 40 and 50 percent, averaging 43 percent";[342] and third, the average ratio of deaths to total population over the three-year period had been "24 percent."[343] Ignoring the fact that the great majority of those who died did so within one year of admission to the orphanage, and that the first of the three methods was thus the most relevant and meaningful one, Yu asserted that the figure of 24 percent gave the most accurate picture of the mortality trend. Astoundingly, he then went on to state that a "top-level official" (*buji ganbu*) from the Ministry of Civil Affairs had recently come to Shanghai and informed him that, by

---

[342] In Chapter 3, the first method is termed Method A. In Chapter 4, under "Mortality Statistics; 1960-92", the second method is described. It was put forward by Yu Ming at the fourth key meeting (April 17, 1992). This second method excludes all those children who died in any year other than the one in which they were actually admitted to the orphanage.

[343] This is more or less equivalent to calculations obtained through method B, as described in Chapter 3.

comparison with the situation in orphanages elsewhere in China, "Shanghai's [death rates] cannot be considered to be very high."

Yu Ming then repeated, with some satisfaction, that since Chou Hui had now recanted her previous testimony regarding her alleged rape by Han Weicheng, "The question of the rape does not exist." Another Supervision Bureau official, section chief Zhao Baixing, added: "Judging by her appearance, she's not a child any more. She looks like someone who's already had children. You can even tell from her way of walking that she's had sex before."

Next, with regard to the allegations that Han had embezzled public funds, Yu stated that Han's having placed the money in his own private bank account was of little importance, "since the sum was US $79,000–not very much." He confirmed, however, that orphans as young as thirteen or fourteen had been made to work in factories and workshops associated with the orphanage, and "this violated Shanghai's regulations on the protection of minors." But no disciplinary measures against those responsible were even discussed.

At this point, Hong Dalin, an SMPC delegate and a distinguished economist at the Shanghai Academy of Social Sciences, could take no more. At 10:45 that morning, he revealed, he had met with Wu Bangguo, the city's Communist Party secretary, and shown him the results of the delegates' various investigations, both open and covert, into the orphanage's affairs. Wu had replied: "Just trust us. We will definitely inform the delegates of our decision on how to handle this case." Hong then fired a series of questions at Yu Ming: Why had the investigation team, after examining hundreds of dead orphans' medical records, only come up with the same three cases of unnatural death first pointed out by the staff critics themselves? Had they failed to find even one other case? Was "congenital maldevelopment of brain" even a legitimate cause of death? Why was Hu Qiaomu's grandson doing so well, when so many other children at the orphanage were dying? How many medical records had the investigation team actually been able to obtain? And why was Chou Hui, regardless of the truth or otherwise of her rape accusations, still being held against her will at the No.2 Social Welfare Institute? He then erupted with rage:

> As regards what the senior official from the Ministry of Civil Affairs is supposed to have said, I have major suspicions about this. Why are they trying to lay down this camouflage screen? Are they trying to say that Shanghai's death rates still aren't high enough? If so, it's just like Hitler trying to achieve the superior race. Tell me which ministry official said this. I want to express my views on the matter and take him to court. Surely our other cities and provinces don't also have people like Han!

The June 8 meeting marked the end of any hope for constructive action on the orphanage case by Shanghai city authorities. By this time, it was also clear to the dissident staff members that senior officials in Beijing would be equally unwilling to deal with the problem. Indeed, at least one of China's highest leaders, Chairman Mao Zedong's former secretary Hu Qiaomu, had traveled to Shanghai to intercede personally on Han Weicheng's behalf, apparently out of gratitude for the high quality of care his severely retarded grandson, Hu Fangfang, was receiving at the Children's Welfare Institute.[344] For this reason, a second roll of film taken by Ai Ming in the summer of 1992, which also showed dead or dying children at the orphanage, was never submitted to higher authorities as originally planned, but was held in safekeeping by Zhang Shuyun for nearly two years.

The final blow to the critics' hopes for redress fell in August 1992, when the orphan Chou Hui was forcibly removed from the No.2 Social Welfare Institute and detained for four months, without any apparent legal basis, at the Shanghai No.1 Jail. A letter sent from the jail to Zhang Shuyun, dated September 20 and supposedly written by Chou, suggested that she had already been intimidated into retracting her allegations of rape against Han Weicheng: the letter read, in part, "I know now that I was wrong! I listened to you once..."[345]

Aftermath, August 1992-1994

The pressure on dissident orphanage employees continued to intensify during late 1992 and 1993, until all of Han Weicheng's leading opponents had been transferred or driven out of the Children's Welfare Institute. Zhang Shuyun was refused medical leave to treat heart palpitations which developed after the beating of Chen Dongxian, and was asked to hand in the health card which entitled her to treatment at the institute's expense. Beginning in March 1993, her base salary was suspended. One morning in May of the same year, she arrived at work and found her office door taped shut. This marked the beginning of her dismissal in stages from employment at the orphanage. For the next several weeks, she continued to report to

---

[344] On other occasions in early 1992, Hu Qiaomu, who died in September of the same year, reportedly sent his private secretary and his daughter-in-law to meet with Shanghai municipal officials and lend their support to the orphanage leadership. His grandson, who was assigned a private room with round-the-clock professional nursing care, was apparently still living at the orphanage as of late 1995 (see Chapter 7).

[345] Dr. Zhang's suspicions were later confirmed by a telephone call she received from Chou Hui herself on December 28, 1992, shortly after Chou's release from jail. During this call, Chou Hui admitted to having changed her story under duress and apologized for having let the critics down.

work but was denied meals, showers, and other fringe benefits, and was required to spend each day sitting in another office in the Rehabilitation Center until the end of her shift. Zhang Shuyun resigned her position in June 1993.

Other dissident staffers experienced similar treatment. Chen Dongxian was forced to resign in March 1993 and took up a job as a driver for a foreign joint venture. Yang Yaming resigned her position in 1994; she now works in the medical clinic of a sewing machine factory in Shanghai's Luwan District. Li Guilan, the last of the prominent critics to leave the orphanage, was forced to take early retirement in late 1994. By this time, all other employees who had publicly supported the four main critics had also been forced out, although a small number of staff members who had remained silent during the investigation of 1991-1992 retained their positions and have provided sporadic reports on conditions at the orphanage since Zhang Shuyun's departure (see Chapter 7).

In October 1992, fourteen delegates to the Shanghai Municipal People's Congress signed a one-page letter to the members of the SMPC Standing Committee, attacking Vice-Mayor Xie Lijuan and the leadership of the SMPC for their failure to halt the abuse of orphans and to protect the staff critics from retaliation. The delegates' willingness to sign this letter, which is reproduced and translated in Appendix I, was largely an act of symbolic defiance, since by then the inquiry into the Children's Welfare Institute had been regarded as officially closed for several months.

In April 1993, new elections were held for delegates to the Shanghai Municipal People's Congress. In accordance with the relevant provisions of China's "Election Law," candidates for these seats are nominated by members of the public and then submit their names to the SMPC Standing Committee for prior screening. This screening process normally produces extremely predictable results: elections are usually uncontested, and turnover among delegates is very low. In the elections of spring 1993, however, none of the fourteen SMPC delegates who had signed the October 1992 letter were re-selected by the Standing Committee. Given the prestige enjoyed by People's Congress delegates and the security of their seats under ordinary circumstances, the Shanghai delegates' failure to win re-selection was tantamount to outright dismissal from the congress. Since the protest letter was directed against the very people who controlled the screening of candidates, however, the results of the selection process were more or less inevitable, and might also be considered an indirect form of voluntary resignation by the delegates themselves, all of whom were distinguished members of Shanghai's political elite whose combined length of membership in the Chinese Communist Party totaled several hundred years.

VII. DEVELOPMENTS IN SHANGHAI, 1993-1995

Dramatic changes have taken place within Shanghai's custodial welfare system since 1993, when the Children's Welfare Institute launched a wide-ranging new policy of "openness" towards the outside world. The orphanage now receives considerable financial support from external sources, including the Shanghai Charitable Fund (*Shanghai Cishan Jijinhui*), recently established by the city's Civil Affairs Bureau to solicit contributions for orphans' welfare, and a U.S.-based charity, Hope Worldwide Limited, which has financed the hiring of a speech therapist and a physical therapist from Hong Kong.[346] Expatriate volunteers are now an everyday presence at the orphanage, feeding and playing with infants and small children, and both Chinese and Western families often "sponsor" children for excursions and home visits. As a result of the regular contact promoted by this program, an increasing number of foreign residents has recently begun adopting orphans from the Children's Welfare Institute. The institute's gates now stand open throughout the day, and visitors are permitted to come and go without prior appointments--an arrangement almost unheard of among Chinese work units of any description, much less one with such a lurid recent history. As a result of these reforms, the Shanghai orphanage has been repeatedly praised in the local and national media as a model of humanitarianism in its treatment of abandoned and disabled children.

Meanwhile, the officials responsible for crushing earlier efforts to end abuses at the orphanage have fared considerably better than those who appealed for their assistance in protecting children's lives during 1991 and 1992. Wu Bangguo, the former chairman of Shanghai's Communist Party Committee, was promoted into the Politburo in 1994, becoming China's vice-premier for industry. Zhu Rongji, the city's mayor until 1992, is now a Politburo member and vice-premier responsible for economic affairs. Huang Ju has also been elevated to a seat on the Politburo. Xie Lijuan and Sun Jinfu have retained their posts as deputy mayor of Shanghai and director of the Shanghai Civil Affairs Bureau, respectively.

Perhaps most significantly, the orphanage's former director, Han Weicheng, was promoted in 1994 to deputy director of the Civil Affairs Bureau's Department of Social Welfare, which is responsible for the administration of custodial welfare institutions. As of early 1995, he had also assumed the concurrent position of acting department director, following the retirement of his superior, Wang Yinian. From this position, he now controls the operation of all welfare institutions run by the Shanghai

---

[346] These employees perform tasks similar to those for which the dissident staff members Li Guilan and Yang Yaming were formerly responsible.

Civil Affairs Bureau–including the Children's Welfare Institute, which is located within the same walled compound as the department's offices.

However, a closer examination shows that the vaunted improvements in the city's child welfare system have been almost entirely illusory. Human Rights Watch/Asia has concluded that in 1993, following the collapse of the official inquiry into Han Weicheng's conduct and at roughly the same time that dissident staff members at the orphanage were being transferred or forced into early retirement, the Shanghai Civil Affairs Bureau began a wholesale "reform" of its child welfare system which may in fact have reduced most abandoned children's chances for survival. Since then, the Children's Welfare Institute has been converted into a quasi-commercial establishment, operated almost exclusively to generate income for the bureau by soliciting charitable donations and by operating a promotional scheme for foreign adoptions. Evidence gathered during repeated visits to the orphanage in 1995 suggests that this policy of commercialization has accelerated drastically in the past year, following Wang Yinian's replacement by Han Weicheng as director of the Social Welfare Department.

Meanwhile, the population of the Children's Welfare Institute appears to have fallen sharply in recent years. The majority of abandoned children arriving at the orphanage are now quickly shifted to another location, under a new policy kept secret from the public.. Since early 1993, at around the same time as the last of the dissident staff were driven out of the orphanage and the institution opened itself up to foreign visitors, the Shanghai No.2 Social Welfare Institute on Chongming Island has begun accepting infants and young children transferred from the Children's Welfare Institute, in addition to its stated function of caring for severely retarded adults. Human Rights Watch/Asia has obtained evidence of grossly inhumane conditions for both juveniles and adult inmates at the No.2 Social Welfare.

Much of the information that follows was obtained directly by one of the authors of this report in a series of interviews conducted in Shanghai in 1995 with several eyewitness sources who visit the Shanghai Children's Welfare Institute regularly and are closely familiar with the orphanage's current situation. For a variety of different reasons, ranging from the risk to certain sources of direct retaliation or punishment by the authorities to other sources' fears for the well-being of children at the orphanage if their identities become known, it has been necessary for us to maintain confidentiality of attribution for the information provided by them. In the following account, these various individuals are referred to as "Source A," "Source B," and so on.

Potemkin Orphanage: The Children's Welfare Institute Since 1993

General Trends, 1993-1995

The unusual degree of openness which now greets visitors to the Children's Welfare Institute, particularly foreigners, suggests that the Shanghai Civil Affairs Bureau now intends to make the orphanage a showcase for its supposedly advanced policies. Although Human Rights Watch/Asia has confirmed that some of the abusive practices which prevailed before 1993 have continued unchanged since then, conditions for children living at the orphanage appear to have improved.

Recent daytime visitors report that orphans are no longer tied to their beds or cribs, except for a very small number of children who show signs of hyperactivity. The problem of improper feeding practices has also diminished, due to the regular presence of expatriate volunteers who assist the paid child-care staff with feedings during the day. However, it is not known if the same feeding techniques continue to be used at night, when foreigners are not present. One regular visitor to the orphanage, Source A, notes that infants with cleft palates invariably disappear within two to three months of arrival, and believes the mortality rate among these children is still close to 100 percent due to inappropriate feeding practices.

Other abusive practices appear to have continued since Zhang Shuyun's departure in 1993. The negligent use of tranquilizers, for example, has caused at least one death in recent years. According to another informant, Source B, a retarded girl aged approximately ten died of an overdose of sleeping pills on her first night at the institute, late in 1994. The girl, whose parents are living in the United States, had been sent back to Shanghai and entrusted to the care of her maternal grandparents, who then decided to place her in the orphanage as a "self-paying" patient. The source reports that the child had not been given dinner on the night of her arrival, and so ate a number of pills left unattended. On learning of the child's death, her grandparents threatened to expose the staff's negligence to the press but were reportedly paid to keep silent by orphanage management.[347]

As of early 1995, regular visitors to the orphanage claimed that conditions there were much worse than publicly acknowledged, despite substantial improvements over the previous two years, and that deaths from inadequate medical care were relatively common. Source A, for example, reported that foreigners who took children out for home visits were instructed to return them immediately to the orphanage if they showed any signs of illness, and were prohibited from taking them to see local doctors. Some expatriates who ignored these instructions and took orphans to the Shanghai

---

[347] Source A has also reported that older children are normally put to bed at 5:00 p.m. each day, suggesting that the use of sedatives may still be a fairly common practice at the orphanage

Pediatric Hospital for medical checkups were told that the children were seriously undernourished. There is also evidence that physical abuse of children has not entirely ceased: Source A knows one young child who shields his head with his forearm whenever adults approach, a defensive reflex which was reportedly much more common in previous years.

The most vital question, of course, is whether the deliberate killing of children by starvation has continued since 1993. Although this possibility cannot be ruled out altogether, since some areas of the orphanage remain off-limits to visitors, it seems unlikely that the orphanage has continued its previous practice of "summary resolution," which allowed infants and children targeted for death by starvation to waste away gradually on the ordinary wards, with transfer to the "critical ward" or a specialized "waiting for death room" postponed until a few days before death was expected.

These practices were not difficult to conceal before the summer of 1993, when outside visits were scheduled well in advance and sick or dying children could be hidden in locked rooms before visitors arrived. A change of policy in mid-1993, however, allowed expatriate residents unrestricted access to the Infants' Section on an unscheduled basis. When one of the earliest visitors under the new policy, Source C, asked orphanage staff about a number of infants who were visibly malnourished, she was told that these children suffered from "intestinal problems" which made it difficult for them to absorb food. More recently, however, such signs of severe malnutrition have reportedly not been seen on the infants' wards. As noted above, however, large numbers of infants and young children are now being secretly transferred from the orphanage to the Shanghai Civil Affairs Bureau's restricted-access custodial facility on Chongming Island, giving rise to serious grounds for suspicion and concern as to their fate. According to Source A, such transfer is in many cases "equivalent to a death sentence."

Eyewitness Accounts from 1995
In early 1995, one author of this report interviewed a number of people in Shanghai familiar with conditions at the Children's Welfare Institute, including both foreigners and local residents, and made two visits to the orphanage. In late September 1995, the orphanage was visited by two Hong Kong residents not affiliated with Human Rights Watch/Asia, in the course of an independent investigation they were conducting into current conditions there. The evidence obtained during these various visits is outlined below.

The author's initial visit to the Children's Welfare Institute began with a brief interview with Zhou Zhuqing, Han Weicheng's successor as orphanage director. Zhou, who is reportedly a former officer of the People's Liberation Army,[348] was reluctant to discuss certain issues: when asked what the orphanage's annual death rate was, she replied that this was "not a good question to ask." She did, however, provide statistics on the number of children at the orphanage and their distribution by age, claiming that of a total of 650 orphans, some 180 were under the age of three and the remaining 470 between the ages of three and sixteen. Zhou also stated categorically that children below the age of sixteen were not transferred from the orphanage to other state institutions under any circumstances.[349]

The author then pointed out that these figures, if correct, implied that the number of older children at the orphanage was very small in proportion to the number of children under age three, confirming the impression produced by an earlier guided tour. When asked how this could be the case, given that children under sixteen supposedly left the orphanage only through death or occasional adoptions, Zhou Zhuqing was unable to give an intelligible answer.

Later the same day, Han Weicheng gave the first of two interviews in his office at the Social Welfare Department, adjacent to the orphanage grounds. Han was considerably more forthcoming than Zhou Zhuqing on the question of children's deaths, stating that the mortality rate for new arrivals at the orphanage was "very high–almost, sometimes, half." Han's explanation for this was that infants were frequently brought to the orphanage suffering from incurable diseases such as leukemia, or after lying exposed to the elements for several hours.[350] This issue was clearly of little interest to Han, who instead went on to speak at great length about his nationwide reputation as an expert on childhood cerebral palsy.[351]

Han Weicheng initially repeated Zhou Zhuqing's assertion that orphans were never transferred to other institutions until the age of sixteen, in particular not to the No.2 Social Welfare Institute. This claim was inconsistent with reports from several

---

[348] Author's interview with anonymous source, March 1995.

[349] Author's interview with Zhou Zhuqing, March 1995.

[350] Author's interview with Han Weicheng, March 1995. Other staff members have contradicted this claim, however. A Chinese woman who telephoned the Children's Welfare Institute posing as a potential adoptive parent, shortly after this interview, was told that abandoned children with serious health problems were never accepted by the orphanage but were instead sent to local hospitals for treatment–or, in the case of incurable conditions, until death.

[351] For details on Han's medical qualifications, see Chapter 4, "Medical Staff and Standards of Treatment."

other well-informed people, who confirmed that such transfers were a common practice at the orphanage.[352] During a second interview some days later, however, Han Weicheng made an unexpected admission. When asked about two apparently disused buildings on the orphanage grounds, he explained that these were dormitories under renovation, and that "more than one hundred" older children previously housed there had been sent "temporarily" to the Chongming Island institute pending completion of the repair work.[353] Han also acknowledged that the No.2 Social Welfare Institute offered no facilities for rehabilitation and virtually no medical care of any kind, despite the fact that its stated function was to care for the most severe cases of mental disability. He described the institute's purpose as providing lifelong maintenance to patients with "no hope."

During this visit, the author also requested a tour of the physical therapy room at the Rehabilitation Center, which is primarily intended for the treatment of children with cerebral palsy and has featured prominently in press coverage of the orphanage.[354] On the day of the visit, the room was being used exclusively by mothers and grandmothers of disabled children from Shanghai, who told the author that they had been trained by orphanage staff to perform the necessary exercises and were charged ten yuan per day for the use of the center's facilities.

This suggested that the room was still reserved for the use of "self-paying" patients, an impression later confirmed by Source A, thus reinforcing earlier accounts by Zhang Shuyun and Ai Ming. Nevertheless, Han Weicheng claimed that orphans and abandoned children suffering from cerebral palsy normally also received physical therapy sessions, but that these had been canceled for the day to allow the orphanage medical staff to attend a lecture by a prominent specialist. The author then accompanied Han to the orphanage lecture hall, where dozens of employees were intently taking notes on the speaker's presentation. Han explained that such lectures

---

[352] Author's interviews with four separate sources, March 1995.

[353] This implies that only about 500 children were actually living at the orphanage in early 1995, contrary to Zhou Zhuqing's claim. Some weeks earlier, after considerable reluctance, the orphanage management had reportedly given the same figure to members of the Shanghai Expatriate Association, who were seeking to arrange a donation of vitamin supplements to the orphanage by a foreign joint venture in Shanghai. An October 1994 article in the official newspaper *China Daily* (see Appendix Q) also stated that the Shanghai Children's Welfare Institute had a population of some 500 orphans.

[354] See, for example, the article "Showing Concern for Orphans Becomes New Common Practice in Shanghai," *People's Daily*, May 10, 1995, p. 3.

were extremely popular, as they offered the medical staff an opportunity to upgrade their professional qualifications and move on to better jobs.

Han Weicheng was visibly ill at ease during his second interview, in marked contrast to his earlier enthusiasm at the prospect of speaking to a foreign journalist. He ended the author's guided tour with a request to be allowed to read any forthcoming "article" on the Children's Welfare Institute before it was submitted for publication, and then returned to his office to work.

The author then made a lengthy unescorted tour of the orphanage grounds. After searching for more than an hour, he was unable to locate more than a handful of the hundreds of older children supposedly living at the institute. This appeared to confirm that the orphanage population was much smaller than officially acknowledged, even allowing for Han Weicheng's admission that many children had been sent "temporarily" to Chongming Island.

The two buildings where many of these children had previously lived had been stripped of all furniture, but they showed no signs of any renovation in progress. Moreover, the uses to which other orphanage buildings had been put raised serious questions about plans for the empty dormitories' future use: a room in one building had been rented out as the Shanghai sales office of a consumer-products company, and a small brick building towards the back of the orphanage compound (also a former children's dormitory, as Zhang Shuyun and Ai Ming later confirmed) had been converted into an automobile repair shop. Although a sign on this building identified it as a "taxi repair station," the vehicles parked behind it were in fact police cars belonging to the Shanghai Public Security Bureau. The sixth floor of the Rehabilitation Center, though not in use at the time, had been set aside as a training center for municipal firefighters, who also serve under Public Security Bureau discipline.

This unauthorized tour came to the attention of the orphanage leadership shortly after the author's departure, reportedly producing a somewhat hysterical reaction. The author was informed of this development by two previously cooperative sources, who expressed personal fears about the possible consequences and recommended that he make no further visits to the orphanage.

Human Rights Watch/Asia has also received important information from two Hong Kong residents who visited the Shanghai Children's Welfare Institute in late September 1995. The informants had been told earlier by sources in Shanghai that the orphanage was very well managed and was successfully promoting adoptions and "sponsorships" of children by foreign residents.

They arrived at the orphanage for a brief introductory visit, posing as a married couple, and explained that they were interested in sponsoring one or more children. As explained to them by Zhang Qinying, the director of the orphanage's Business Department and the staff member in charge of the sponsorship program, this entails making a monthly payment of 300 yuan for an infant or 500 yuan for a child over the age of approximately three. Individuals or families who sponsor an orphan are entitled to take the child out for unsupervised home visits.[355]

Zhang Qinying, although eager to arrange such a sponsorship for the informants when they returned for a second visit, urged them vigorously to adopt an orphan on a permanent basis instead. When one of the visitors pointed out that they were ineligible to adopt a healthy child under the terms of China's Adoption Law, as they were both under the age of thirty-five, Zhang explained that she had "connections" which she could use to circumvent this rule, and that if they wanted to adopt an infant with no disabilities, "we can make up a certificate to prove the child is handicapped."[356] Zhang quoted a standard price of US$3,000 for adopting a child from the orphanage; when told that this seemed rather expensive, however, she added that the fee was negotiable.[357].

The two informants were given a tour of the orphanage facilities and were struck by the relatively large size of the Infants' Section, which contained approximately 200 infants. The number of orphans between the ages of three and eleven was much smaller, however. The informants described these children as "good-looking," extremely polite, and apparently healthy, suffering from only minor disabilities. When asked, Zhang Qinying was unable to show the visitors any seriously handicapped children over the age of three. Older children were even harder to find, and the informants concluded that there were fewer than ten teenagers at the orphanage.[358]

---

[355] The Children's Welfare Institute began allowing home visits for orphans in early 1994, during the Spring Festival (lunar new year) holiday. However, the policy of charging fees for such visits, and of reserving specific children for each outside sponsor, is apparently a more recent development. It is not known whether these fees are charged only to foreign sponsors; they would be prohibitive for all but a small minority of Shanghai families.

[356] Such deceptive practices have been reported from other Chinese orphanages as well. See "Babies for Sale Business Thriving," *Eastern Express* (Hong Kong), November 9, 1995.

[357] On hearing that her visitors were looking for business opportunities in Shanghai, Zhang Qinying suggested that they rent office space inside the orphanage compound, and quoted a very attractive rate. After checking with the staff member in charge of these rentals, however, she discovered that there were no vacant units available.

[358] Nevertheless, they apparently succeeded in locating Hu Fangfang, the severely retarded teenaged grandson of the late Hu Qiaomu (see Chapter 4, "Recorded Causes of Death", and Chapter 6, "The Investigation Collapses, March–August 1992").

Conditions in the Infants' Section appeared to be reasonably good, although the child-care workers on duty seemed indifferent to their charges and paid no attention to crying children. However, the informants noted that the frames of many cribs were fitted with long strips of cotton cloth. These resembled the bonds used to tie down the eleven-year-old deaf-mute child Jian Xun, as shown in photographs taken shortly before his death in the summer of 1992. The informants speculated that these strips, which the child-care workers described as "play strings," were used to tie infants to their cribs at night after the expatriate volunteers had left for the day.[359]

The two visitors from Hong Kong paid 500 yuan for a one-month sponsorship, and were then offered a selection of young children to take out for the afternoon. They chose a slightly handicapped boy aged approximately seven. During their conversations outside the orphanage with this child, who was normal in intelligence but apparently illiterate, they discovered that he had been "sponsored" already. This contradicted claims by the orphanage staff that each child was only assigned a single financial sponsor, and tended to confirm the visitors' general impression that the Children's Welfare Institute was run primarily as a commercial enterprise.

Behind the Scenes: The No. 2 Social Welfare Institute Since 1993

General Trends, 1993-1995

The Shanghai No.2 Social Welfare Institute, located just outside Gangyan Village on the Yangtze delta island of Chongming, is the largest general-purpose welfare institution under the jurisdiction of the Shanghai Civil Affairs Bureau.[360] Its stated function is to care for adults with disabling neurological conditions, such as severe mental retardation, epilepsy, cerebral palsy, and brain damage caused by stroke.[361]

Unlike the Children's Welfare Institute, which is located in a densely populated residential neighborhood in downtown Shanghai and is now largely open

---

[359] A later attempt to visit the Infants' Section after dark was not successful.

[360] Chongming, an oblong island lying along the north bank of the Yangtze River, is Shanghai's poorest and most isolated suburban county. Roughly fifteen kilometers in width and over seventy kilometers in length, it is the second largest island in the People's Republic of China.

[361] According to Zhang Shuyun, the institute is intended to care for "idiots, imbeciles, and morons" (*baichi, daizi, shagua*). As noted in Chapter 4, the Shanghai Civil Affairs Bureau makes few efforts to diagnose severe mental disabilities with greater subtlety.

to the public, the No.2 Social Welfare Institute is a remote and heavily secured facility, which admits outside visitors only on rare occasions. Moreover, even this limited access was significantly curtailed during 1995, reportedly reflecting the Civil Affairs Bureau's perception that information on the city's welfare institutions was being collected for release outside China.

Evidence obtained by Human Rights Watch/Asia indicates that since 1993, the Chongming Island institution has become the main component of Shanghai's institutional child welfare system: a dumping ground not only for mentally handicapped adults but for inmates of the Children's Welfare Institute considered superfluous to its new profit-making functions. Orphans sent to Chongming Island in recent years include infants and children under age sixteen, as well as a group of young adults without mental disabilities who have been transferred to the No.2 Social Welfare Institute and are presently held there against their will, after failing to find employment outside the orphanage.

Despite repeated claims by officials at the Children's Welfare Institute that all children not adopted remain at the orphanage until the age of sixteen, a number of sources confirm that large numbers of infants and young children have, in fact, been transferred to the No.2 Social Welfare Institute under a new policy which took effect in early 1993. This practice was first reported in a letter received by Zhang Shuyun in March 1993 from a mentally normal inmate at the Chongming Island institute who had previously lived at the orphanage. This letter, a translation of which appears in Appendix K, claimed that a number of older "self-paying" children with severe disabilities had arrived at the institute in February 1993. Shortly afterwards, the orphanage apparently began sending even younger children to Chongming Island, including abandoned infants as well as children with families in Shanghai. Another letter sent to Zhang Shuyun by the same inmate later in 1993 states that many of these infants were not being cared for at the institute itself, but were boarded with the families of institute employees and other local residents.

Several sources confirmed that this practice was continuing in early 1995. Source A reported that at least forty infants had been transferred to Chongming Island in the first two months of the year. Another informant, Source D, was told by a close relative who works at the Shanghai No.2 Social Welfare Institute, and whose family is boarding several infants under the institution's private fostering scheme, that such families received a monthly stipend of 105 yuan for each fostered infant.[362]

The Children's Welfare Institute apparently uses very vague criteria to select orphans for transfer. Although one source reported that the selection process seemed

---

[362] The source reports that the infants fostered out under this scheme are invariably "retarded," but as noted in Chapter 4, such diagnoses are highly unreliable.

to target the most seriously handicapped infants, another two informants, Sources E and F, disagreed, claiming that most of the transferred children had been no different from those who remained behind, and had often showed no abnormalities other than those produced by understimulation.

Infants and children are not the only inmates at the No.2 Social Welfare Institute whose existence remains a closely guarded secret. Many of the adults confined on Chongming Island have also been transferred there from the Children's Welfare Institute after reaching young adulthood–and contrary to official claims, not all of them are mentally handicapped. In recent years, in fact, it has become fairly common for orphans of normal or near-normal intelligence to be sent to Chongming Island after reaching the age of sixteen, and then detained there indefinitely against their will. A partial list of eighteen such adults presently confined to the No.2 Social Welfare Institute, compiled by Ai Ming, appears in Appendix J.

The stated policy of the Shanghai Civil Affairs Bureau is to arrange employment at the age of sixteen for orphans at the Children's Welfare Institute capable of living independently, and to transfer the remainder to the No.2 Social Welfare Institute for lifelong custodial care.[363] In practice, however, mentally normal teenagers sometimes linger at the orphanage well beyond the age of sixteen, because of lengthy delays in assigning jobs. The transfer of such orphans to Chongming Island may simply reflect official indifference and an inability to arrange appropriate employment for them elsewhere in Shanghai.[364]

However, the cases of Fu Qing, Zhu Yan and Chou Hui, discussed in Chapter 5, suggest that such transfers may also target teenagers who have suffered physical or sexual abuse at the orphanage or who have antagonized senior staff. Ai Ming concurs in this analysis, noting that Ba Shou, the first classmate of his to be sent to Chongming Island against her will, was transferred in early 1990 after arguing with Lu Rongfang, the head of the Children's Department at the orphanage.

Although inmates at the No.2 Social Welfare Institute are not allowed to receive telephone calls and their correspondence is censored by institute staff, some information about conditions for mentally normal adults there has been received

---

[363] Author's interview with Han Weicheng, March 1995.

[364] Zhang Shuyun has stated that until the mid-1980s, most mentally normal orphans reaching adulthood were assigned employment at a Civil Affairs Bureau workshop for the handicapped in Shanghai's Baoshan District, which manufactures steel screws and washers from metal supplied by the nearby Baoshan Iron and Steel Works. This practice has since been discontinued, reportedly because of a shortage of workers' housing at the Baoshan plant. The majority of the surviving Shanghai orphans in their early twenties are now either confined to the No.2 Social Welfare Institute or employed at the Longhua Electrical Appliance Factory.

through letters mailed from outside the institute grounds. Some former orphans are apparently compelled to perform staff duties by caring for other severely disabled inmates; one reported in a letter to Zhang Shuyun that she was paid three yuan per month to look after self-paying retarded children held at the institution.

Adults held at the Chongming Island institute are allowed to leave the institute grounds for brief periods, for example two or three hours at the weekends, in order to purchase articles for daily use in nearby Gangyan Village. However, unauthorized absences for longer periods are severely dealt with, and the inmates' lack of access to more than very small sums of money makes escape almost impossible. As noted in Chapter 5, the former orphanage inmate Zhu Yan was recaptured and severely beaten after each of two attempts to flee the No.2 Social Welfare Institute, the first of which took place only days after his transfer. Letters received by Zhang Shuyun in recent years also reveal that inmates at the No.2 Social Welfare Institute are frequently subjected to a form of restraint referred to as "pressure bondage" (*yasuodai*), in which the victim is forced to stand bent at the waist with his or her hands bound tightly behind the back and tied to a high window with strips of cloth, so that the bonds become tighter as the victim's weight pulls on the knot. This commonly used disciplinary measure, moreover, is reportedly sometimes enhanced by injecting tranquillizers into the victim's back to induce hours of unconsciousness in a hanging position, leaving the victim's arms partly paralyzed for long periods afterwards.

Even such gross mistreatment is not the most serious abuse reported from the No.2 Social Welfare Institute in recent years. According to an internal Civil Affairs Bureau report shown to Zhang Shuyun in 1992, a twenty-nine-year-old epileptic inmate, Guang Zi, was murdered on October 14, 1991 by Li Deming, a senior Communist Party cadre and the vice-director of the institute's Business Department. The report stated that Li Deming had confessed to raping Guang Zi, strangling her unconscious, and throwing her into a small stream on the institute grounds, where she drowned. It is not known whether any criminal proceedings were eventually undertaken against Li.

Eyewitness Accounts from 1995

In the spring of 1995, one author of this report made arrangements to accompany members of the Shanghai Expatriate Association on their third annual tour of the No.2 Social Welfare Institute, scheduled for April 29. This proved to be impossible, as the Social Welfare Department announced shortly before the trip that advance ticketing would be required for all participants, ostensibly because of short staffing at the institute over Labor Day weekend.

Members of the Shanghai Expatriate Association who did participate in the tour later refused to discuss their impressions with the author. One participant, Source

G, predicted that foreigners' volunteer work at the Children's Welfare Institute would be shut down if conditions in Shanghai's welfare institutions were publicized overseas.

In late September 1995, the two Hong Kong residents who had earlier investigated conditions at the Shanghai orphanage traveled to Chongming Island in an attempt to visit the No.2 Social Welfare Institute. They were told by local residents that all inmates at the institute were mentally disabled, including a number of "self-paying" cases, and that older inmates were generally free to come and go in the village nearby.

The two informants arrived at the gates of the institute, claiming to be Buddhists who had come to donate money and other items. After speaking initially with a female staff member, they were introduced to the institute's director, Mr. Shen. The director was suspicious, asking them: "How did you find out about this place? You shouldn't know about it, even Shanghai people don't know." Nevertheless, the visitors were allowed into an office near the compound gate. When they asked to be allowed to see children at the institute, the director refused on the grounds that "according to policy, we do not admit foreigners." Instead, five or six female inmates, all in their late teens or early twenties and clearly mentally retarded, were called to the office to collect the gifts of candy and cookies which the visitors had brought.

The visitors were told that the institute housed 526 inmates, and saw several hundred tags hanging on the walls of the office, each with the name and age of a single inmate. Only five or six of these tags were for inmates under the age of five. The director explained that these were "self-paying" retarded children, and repeated the standard claim that orphans from the Children's Welfare Institute were not transferred to Chongming Island unless they had reached the age of sixteen and were unable to care for themselves.

However, the visitors from Hong Kong saw two forms headed "Death Report" lying on a desk in the reception office. The forms were on stationery belonging to the Shanghai Children's Welfare Institute; the form on top recorded the death from illness of a nine-year-old boy.

APPENDICES[365]

Appendix A.   Glossary of Names[366]

Ai Ming (M)   Abandoned child brought up at the Shanghai Children's
                              Welfare Institute. Sent to psychiatric hospital in 1987
                              without medical justification. Assisted Zhang Shuyun in
                              gathering evidence on abuses at the orphanage, by
                              photographing bodies of dead children in June–July
                              1992. Escaped from China in March 1995.

Ba Shou (F)   Abandoned child brought up at the Shanghai Children's
                              Welfare Institute. Transferred to the Shanghai No.2
                              Social Welfare Institute in 1990, after arguing with Lu
                              Rongfang.

Bao Wei (F)   Blind child at the Shanghai Children's Welfare Institute.
                              Took overdose of chlorpromazine in late 1992.

Cao Haiyuan (M)   Attorney with Shanghai No.2 Legal Affairs Agency.
                              Interviewed Chou Hui on Chongming Island in August
                              and September 1991.

Chen Dongxian (M)   Driver at the Shanghai Children's Welfare
                              Institute. Participated in campaign to improve
                              conditions at the orphanage. Assaulted by
                              Huang Jiachun and other staff members on May
                              18, 1992. Forced to resign in March 1993.

Cheng Zihua (M)   China's first Minister of Civil Affairs, appointed in 1978
                              after the end of the Cultural Revolution.

Chou Hui (F)   Abandoned child brought up at the Shanghai Children's
                              Welfare Institute. Allegedly raped twice by Han
                              Weicheng in late 1988. Transferred to psychiatric
                              hospital without medical justification in April 1989; later
                              transferred to Shanghai No.2 Social Welfare Institute on

---

[366] Excluding infants and children whose names appear only in Chapter 4 and persons
whose names appear only in footnotes or appendices to the main text.

Chongming Island. Transferred to Shanghai No.1 Jail in August 1992, during the official investigation into conditions at the Shanghai orphanage, and threatened with indefinite detention by Wu Hengjun until she retracted her allegations. Released in December 1992.

Cui Aidi (M) Attorney with Shanghai No.2 Legal Affairs Agency. Interviewed Chou Hui on Chongming Island in August and September 1991.

Cui Naifu (M) Minister of Civil Affairs, 1982-1993.

Ding Yi (M) Head of the General Medical Ward at the Shanghai Children's Welfare Institute. A "worker-peasant-soldier" medical graduate.

Dorje Tsering (M) Former governor of the Tibet Autonomous Region, 1985-1990. Minister of Civil Affairs since 1993.

Feng Guishan (M) Vice-director of the Shanghai Civil Affairs Bureau. Met with Zhang Shuyun and other critics in December 1989 to discuss conditions at the Children's Welfare Institute.

Feng Ya'an (F) Head child-care worker at the Shanghai Children's Welfare Institute. Shielded by the orphanage management after abusing Hong Na and Liang Jie.

Fu Qiang (M) Abandoned child brought up at the Shanghai Children's Welfare Institute. Forced to give false testimony against Qiu Zhen, March 1990. Later sent to the Shanghai No.2 Social Welfare Institute.

Fu Qing (F) Abandoned child brought up at the Shanghai Children's Welfare Institute. Allegedly molested by Han Weicheng. Later sent to the Shanghai No.2 Social Welfare Institute.

Gan Rui (F) Abandoned child brought up at the Shanghai Children's Welfare Institute. Denied medical treatment for nephritis.

Gao Junzhu (M)   Delegate to the Shanghai Municipal People's Congress. Denied reappointment in April 1993, after supporting critics of the Children's Welfare Institute.

Gu Ma (F)   Paternal aunt of Qin Gaoming. Senior Communist Party cadre on Chongming Island.

Guang Zi (F)   Epileptic patient at the Shanghai No.2 Social Welfare Institute. Reportedly raped and murdered in August 1991 by Li Deming, a cadre at the institute.

Guo Minying (F)   Child-care worker at the Shanghai Children's Welfare Institute. Dismissed for testifying to staff negligence in the case of Wei Zhi.

Han Weicheng (M)   Director of the Shanghai Children's Welfare Institute, 1989-1994. Chief target of the official investigation of 1991-1992. Promoted in 1994 to deputy director of the Social Welfare Department of the Shanghai Civil Affairs Bureau. Assumed position of acting director after the subsequent retirement of Wang Yinian.

Hong Na (F)   Abandoned child brought up at the Shanghai Children's Welfare Institute. Abused by Feng Ya'an, April 30-May 1, 1991.

Hu Fangfang (M)   Severely retarded teenage grandson of Hu Qiaomu. Now cared for at the Shanghai Children's Welfare Institute.

Hu Qiaomu (M)   Former private secretary to Mao Zedong. A leading "hard-liner" within the Chinese Politburo during the 1980s. Shortly before his death in September 1992, he flew from Beijing to Shanghai to intervene personally on behalf of Han Weicheng and other senior officials at the Shanghai Children's Welfare Institute.

Huang Jiachun (M)   Vice-director of the Shanghai Children's Welfare Institute. Led other employees in attack on Chen Dongxian on May 18, 1992. Since promoted to concurrent post of orphanage Communist Party secretary, replacing Zhu Meijun.

Huang Ju (M)   Mayor of Shanghai until 1994. Informed of conditions at the Children's Welfare Institute in late 1991, but failed to act on staff members' complaints. Promoted in 1994 to a seat on the Politburo.

Huo Zhen (M)   Abandoned child brought up at the Shanghai Children's Welfare Institute. Died of untreated hepatitis, February 1991.

Jiang Huifang (F)   Doctor in the Infants' Department (*Ying'erbu*) of the Shanghai Children's Welfare Institute. A "worker-peasant-soldier" medical graduate.

Jin Binhua (M)   Director of Shanghai municipal Propaganda Department (*Xuanchuanbu*). On instructions from Wu Bangguo, issued order to local media prohibiting negative reporting on the Shanghai Children's Welfare Institute.

Li Deming (M)   Staff member and senior Communist Party cadre at the Shanghai No.2 Social Welfare Institute. Allegedly raped and murdered Guang Zi in late 1991.

Li Guilan (F)   Speech therapist at the Shanghai Children's Welfare Institute. Participated in campaign to improve conditions at the orphanage. Forced to take early retirement, late 1994.

Li Juyun (F)   Teacher at the Shanghai Children's Welfare Institute. Beat Qiu Zhen, March 1, 1992.

Li Laidi (F)   Child-care worker at the Shanghai Children's Welfare Institute. Tortured Lu Yi, August 25, 1991. Now retired.

Li Zhouqing (M)   Head of the Security Section (*Baoweike*) at the Shanghai Children's Welfare Institute. Threatened Qiu Zhen, March 12, 1990.

Liang Jie (M)

Abandoned child brought up at the Shanghai Children's Welfare Institute. Forced to eat magnets by Feng Ya'an, April 1991.

Lu Hongyan (F)

Doctor on the General Medical Ward of the Shanghai Children's Welfare Institute. A university graduate of medicine.

Lu Jingdi (F)

Paramedic responsible for X-ray work at the Shanghai Children's Welfare Institute.

Lu Ming (M)

A former senior procurator of Shanghai municipality. Vice-chairman of the Legal Subcommittee of the Shanghai Municipal People's Congress Standing Committee.

Lu Rongfang (F)

Head of the Children's Department (*Ertongbu*) at the Shanghai Children's Welfare Institute. Replaced Tang Youhua.

Lu Yi (M)

Abandoned child brought up at the Shanghai Children's Welfare Institute (allegedly retarded). Tortured by Li Laidi, August 25, 1991. Transferred to psychiatric hospital in January 1992, during official investigation into conditions at the orphanage.

Lu Yin (F)

Paramedic in Infants' Department of the Shanghai Children's Welfare Institute. *Zhongzhuan* graduate from public health school (high school equivalent).

Luo Xiaoling (F)

Vice-director of Medical Department (*Yiwuke*) of the Shanghai Children's Welfare Institute; promoted to full director in 1992. Nursing school graduate. Continued to work at the orphanage as a paid "consultant" after formally retiring in 1994.

Luo Zhan (F)

Abandoned girl brought to Shanghai Children's Welfare Institute with malformed nose bridge, later corrected through surgery. Won three gold medals in table tennis at International Paralympics (Madrid, 1992) after being fraudulently registered for competition as "mentally retarded."

Ma Mimi (F)   Delegate to the Shanghai Municipal People's Congress. Denied reappointment in April 1993, after supporting critics of the Children's Welfare Institute.

Ma Renbing (M)   Delegate to the Shanghai Municipal People's Congress and chairman of the Shanghai Islamic Association. Supported critics of the Children's Welfare Institute, but did not sign protest letter submitted to the Shanghai Municipal People's Congress (SMPC) Standing Committee by 14 other delegates in October 1992.

Ma Ruikang (M)   Deputy director of the Shanghai Public Security Bureau. Participated in meetings with delegates to the Shanghai Municipal People's Congress and representatives of the Shanghai Supervision Bureau, early 1992.

Ni Kongyong (M)   Carpenter at the Shanghai Children's Welfare Institute. Helped Han Weicheng abduct Ai Ming from the orphanage for transfer to psychiatric hospital, January 1987. Alleged to have sexually abused Qin Gaoming ("Zhong Xiu"), 1986-1987.

Sister Odile [?][367] (F)   French Catholic nun. Director of the Shanghai New Puyu Home, predecessor of the Shanghai Children's Welfare Institute. Fled China after the 1949 revolution.

Qian Guanlin (M)   Vice-director of the Shanghai Civil Affairs Bureau. Met with Zhang Shuyun and other critics in December 1989 to discuss conditions at the Children's Welfare Institute. Now a senior staff member at the Shanghai branch of the China Disabled Federation.[368]

---

[367] The Chinese transliteration is "Aodila."

[368] This organization is headed by Deng Pufang, the paraplegic son of Deng Xiaoping.

Qian Pei'e (F)

Director of the Shanghai Children's Welfare Institute, 1982-1988. Seized *de facto* power at the orphanage during the early stages of the Cultural Revolution, overthrowing her predecessor, Yang Jiezeng. Selected Han Weicheng as her eventual successor.

Qin Gaoming (F)

Abandoned child brought up at the Shanghai Children's Welfare Institute under the name "Zhong Xiu." Alleged to have been sexually abused by orphanage employee, Ni Kongyong. Reclaimed by her parents, June 1991. Now living on Chongming Island.

Qiu Zhen (M)

Abandoned child brought up at the Shanghai Children's Welfare Institute. Detained for two weeks in municipal "deportation station," August 1988. Threatened by Zhen Weiming and Li Zhouqing after false accusation of theft, March 12-13, 1990. Illegally expelled from Puyu Middle School in 1992.

Rong Aizhen (F)

Child-care worker at the Shanghai Children's Welfare Institute. Promoted and inducted into the Communist Party for giving false testimony in the case of Wei Zhi.

Ru Sha (F)

Abandoned child brought up at the Shanghai Children's Welfare Institute. Later transferred to the Shanghai No.2 Social Welfare Institute, although mentally normal.

Ru Wang (M)

Abandoned child brought up at the Shanghai Children's Welfare Institute. Brought photographs taken by Ai Ming to shop outside the orphanage for development, but was prevented from retrieving them afterwards.

Sheng Xiaowei (F)

Paramedic at the Shanghai Children's Welfare Institute and Head of the Infants' Department. *Zhongzhuan* graduate from public health school (high school equivalent).

Shi Shengren (M)

Legal consultant to the Shanghai General Labor Union. Wrote December 9, 1991 report which led to official investigation of the Shanghai Children's Welfare Institute.

Sun Jinfu (M)   Director of the Shanghai Civil Affairs Bureau. Authorized retribution against Zhang Shuyun and other dissident employees of the Children's Welfare Institute. Assisted Han Weicheng by arranging for favorable television coverage of the orphanage and by confiscating photographs taken by Ai Ming.

Sun Miaoling (M)   Former teacher at the Shanghai Children's Welfare Institute, later promoted to administrative post in the orphanage's Propaganda Department. Accused of sexually harassing orphan girls.

Tang Yizhi (M)   Head of Urban Welfare Office (*Chengfusi*) of the Ministry of Civil Affairs during the 1980s.

Tang Youhua (F)   Head of the Children's Department (*Ertongbu*) at the Shanghai Children's Welfare Institute. Demoted in 1990 after refusing to deny beating of Yue Yi by Han Weicheng.

Tao Xinzhong (M)   Former vice-director of the Shanghai Children's Welfare Institute.

Wang Chongji (M)   Vice-chairman of the Shanghai Municipal People's Congress.

Wang Genlin (F)   Child-care worker at the Shanghai Children's Welfare Institute. Now retired.

Wang Guang (F)   Abandoned child brought up at the Shanghai Children's Welfare Institute. Found to be pregnant in early 1994, supposedly after rape by another orphan. Forced to undergo abortion and transferred to the Shanghai No.2 Social Welfare Institute.

Wang Xueqing (F)   Former director of the Business Department (*Yewuke*) at the Shanghai Children's Welfare Institute. Replaced by Zhang Jinnuan.

Wang Yinian (M)   Former director of the Social Welfare Department of the Shanghai Civil Affairs Bureau. Now retired.

Wang Yiping (M)   Nanshi District director of the Shanghai Public Security Bureau.

Wei Zhi (M)   Abandoned child brought up at the Shanghai Children's Welfare Institute. Penis injured by retarded girl playing with scissors on June 20, 1992; later developed gangrene due to lack of proper medical treatment. Orphanage leadership, including Han Weicheng and Zhen Weiming, later tried to conceal staff negligence in this case.

Wu Bangguo (M)   Former Shanghai Communist Party secretary, 1991-1994. Issued order to the municipal Propaganda Department prohibiting negative coverage of the Shanghai Children's Welfare Institute and ordering local journalists to hand over all materials on the case. Promoted into China's Politburo as vice-premier for industry in 1994.

Wu Hengjun (M)   Director of the Social Order Department (*Zhi'anchu*) of the Shanghai Public Security Bureau. Threatened Chou Hui with indefinite imprisonment if she failed to recant her accusation of rape against Han Weicheng.

Wu Junfeng (M)   Deputy head of the Medical Department of the Shanghai Children's Welfare Institute. A "worker-peasant-soldier" medical graduate.

Wu Lanyin (F)   Retarded girl boarded as a "self-paying" patient at the Shanghai Children's Welfare Institute. Locked in disused toilet by Xu Shanzhen, July 11, 1991.

Xiang Wen (F)   Abandoned child brought up at the Shanghai Children's Welfare Institute (mildly retarded). Reportedly raped by

Han Weicheng. Later transferred to the Shanghai No.2 Social Welfare Institute.

Xie Lijuan (F)

Deputy mayor of Shanghai for health, education, and social welfare (formerly a practicing physician in Shanghai's Luwan District). Lent support to Han Weicheng through a public appearance at the Children's Welfare Institute in early 1992. When confronted with forged orphanage medical records by Zhang Shuyun and other dissident staff, denied that any falsification had taken place.

Xin Cao (F)

Abandoned child brought up at the Shanghai Children's Welfare Institute. Questioned by Public Security Bureau over her possible corroboration of Chou Hui's charge of rape against Han Weicheng.

Xu Jianrong

Member of the investigation team sent to the Shanghai Children's Welfare Institute in December 1991 by the municipal Supervision Bureau.

Xu Qianqian (M)

Employee of the Shanghai Children's Welfare Institute. Helped Han Weicheng abduct Ai Ming from the orphanage for transfer to psychiatric hospital, January 1987.

Xu Shanzhen (F)

Child-care worker at the Shanghai Children's Welfare Institute. Locked Wu Lanyin in toilet, July 11, 1991. Awarded "model worker" status in April 1995.

Xu Weihe (M)

Vice-director of the Shanghai Children's Welfare Institute since 1993. A classmate of Han Weicheng's at Shanghai No.1 Medical University, he worked as an ear-nose-throat doctor in rural Fujian Province until Han arranged his transfer to the orphanage in 1989, claiming that Xu was an "eminent surgeon."

Xu Xinyuan (M)

Delegate to the Shanghai Municipal People's Congress. Denied reappointment in April 1993, after supporting critics of the Children's Welfare Institute.

Yang Jiezeng (F)   Former director of the Shanghai Children's Welfare Institute. Overthrown by her subordinate, vice-director Qian Pei'e, shortly after the outbreak of the Cultural Revolution. Partly crippled after unsuccessful attempt to escape from the orphanage, where she was confined after Qian's takeover. Unable to recover effective authority after the Cultural Revolution's end. Accepted formal retirement in 1982.

Yang Yaming (F)   Welfare Institute. Demoted from senior administrative position in 1985, after filing complaints about the management of the orphanage. Joined Zhang Shuyun and other critics in campaign to end abuses at the institute, 1989-1992. Resigned from the orphanage in 1994.

Ye Xinghua (M)   Vice-director of the Organization Department (*Zuzhichu*) of the Shanghai Civil Affairs Bureau. Wrote August 1990 report attacking dissident staff members at the Children's Welfare Institute. Later promoted to director of the Organization Department.

Yu Feng (F)   Blind child at the Shanghai Children's Welfare Institute. Took overdose of chlorpromazine in late 1992.

Yu Ming (M)   Vice-director of the Shanghai Supervision Bureau. Participated closely in the bureau's investigation of conditions at the Children's Welfare Institute in early 1992; attended meetings with dissident orphanage staff members and delegates to the Shanghai Municipal People's Congress.

Yue Yi (M)   Abandoned child brought up at the Shanghai Children's Welfare Institute. Beaten and locked up by Han Weicheng, August 1988.

Zeng Shan (M)   Minister of the Interior, 1960-1968.

Zhang Jinnuan (F)   Director of the Business Department, Shanghai Children's Welfare Institute. Refused to reveal Qin

Gaoming's whereabouts to her parents, then extorted cash from Qin's family members in exchange for allowing her to leave the orphanage.

Zhang Shuyun (F)   Medical and administrative staff member of the Shanghai Children's Welfare Institute, 1988-1993. Led campaign to improve conditions at the orphanage. Forced to resign, June 1993. Escaped from China in March 1995.

Zhang Yansong (F)   Girl with cerebral palsy (native of Benxi, Liaoning Province). Permanently disabled in 1989 after negligent medical care administered by Ding Yi at the Shanghai Children's Welfare Institute, and later covered up by Han Weicheng.

Zhao Wanhua (F)   Luo Xiaoling's predecessor as head of Medical Department, Shanghai Children's Welfare Institute. Promoted in 1992 to an administrative position in the Social Welfare Department of the Shanghai Civil Affairs Bureau.

Zhen Weiming (M)   Director of the Personnel Department at the Shanghai Children's Welfare Institute. Later promoted to vice-director of the orphanage.

"Zhong Xiu" (F)   (See Qin Gaoming)

Zhou Zhuqing (F)   Director of the Shanghai Children's Welfare Institute since 1994.

Zhu Meijun (F)   Former Communist Party secretary of the Shanghai Children's Welfare Institute. Described symptoms of frostbite on children dying of hypothermia in December 1991 as result of a "platelet disorder."

Zhu Qingfang (F)   Former Communist Party secretary of the Shanghai Children's Welfare Institute. Replaced by Zhu Meijun in 1991.

Zhu Yan (M) Abandoned child brought up at the Shanghai Children's Welfare Institute. Sent to municipal "deportation station" for one week and beaten with electric police batons on instructions from Han Weicheng, after being accused of theft. Later sent to Shanghai No.2 Social Welfare Institute, where he was recaptured and beaten after each of two unsuccessful escape attempts.

Appendix B.   Excerpts from *Historical Manuscripts on Civil Affairs in China*[369]

Operating Social Welfare Facilities

After the liberation of the whole country, the people's government took over and reformed the old society's "relief organizations" throughout the nation, and at the same time established some [new] facilities. The units handed down from the old society were of three main types:

1. The "relief institutions" (*jiujiyuan*), "labor training centers" (*laodong xiyisuo*), and so forth, run by the Nationalists. According to 1951 statistics from the Southwestern Sector, there were 163 such "relief institutions." Although they operated under the name of "relief," their true function was exploitation. If a person sought shelter at the labor training center behind Beijing's Yonghe Temple or the relief institution on the site of the Capital Theater, he was made to work for more than 10 hours a day and eat cornmeal buns, while most of the funds went into the pockets of the bureaucratic capitalist class.

2. The "benevolence halls" (*citang*) in feudal areas. The names of these varied, and some were called "widows' halls," others "moral education halls," and so forth... Nominally, the benevolence halls operated primary schools, which were not only outrageously managed, but did not even have many students. They maintained funeral bureaus which issued coffins, but these were very few and basically of no use.[370] They did provide medical care, but they had virtually no good doctors, and in reality there was corruption which enriched warlords and the ruffians and hooligans of feudal associations. Thus these were places which operated under the name of "benevolence" while actually practicing extortion and racketeering.

3. The "charitable organizations" and "charitable institutes" established by imperialism....[The] relief institutions established [by foreign churches and charities] were in fact places of atrocity (*zui'e changsuo*) for China's disabled children. According to 1953 statistics, there were 451 "charitable organizations" established by imperialism, of which 247 were American, and 204 belonged to countries such as Great Britain, France, Italy, and Spain. One hundred ninety-eight of these belonged to the Protestant churches and 208 to the Catholic Church. Some "relief organizations"

---

[369] Meng Zhaohua and Wang Minghuan, *Zhongguo Minzheng Shigao* (Harbin: Heilongjiang Renmin Chubanshe, January 1987), pp.299-300.

[370] The Ministry of Civil Affairs is now responsible for operating funeral homes and crematoria in China. One of its aims is to encourage cremation over earth burial, as a means of conserving scarce farmland.

were also established in large and medium-sized cities. In the "House of Mercy Foundling Home" established by the French Catholic Church in Hangzhou, children of seven and eight were made to work and to wait on the nuns, while orphan girls of 11 and 12 were made to do heavy work and those blind in both eyes had to stitch the soles on cloth shoes. What the orphan girls ate was gruel and raw greens, and when they became dangerously ill, six or seven of them would be given the same prescription. The work there was so hard and the nutrition so poor that orphan girls of 13 or 14 were as short and small as children of five or six. In the Huayuanshan Foundling Home in the city of Wuhan, there was a "ten-thousand-man pit" (*wan ren keng*), where weak and crippled children suffered to a degree the eye could not bear to witness, and where those not yet dead were thrown in while still alive. The Catholic orphanage in Xi'an, the Catholic foundling home in Zhaoqing, Guangdong [Province], the "Kindly Affection Foundling Home" in Nanjing, and so on....The truth about the crimes in all these places is unspeakably shocking.

Appendix C.   Official Press Reports On Conditions At The Shanghai Children's Welfare Institute, 1990-1992

1. Letter to the Editors of Labor News, With Accompanying Article (April 12, 1990)

"The Truth About Some Cadres' Methods at the Orphanage is Cause for Concern: Disabled Young People Particularly Need Care and Love"

Comrade Editor:

We are medical and special-education staff at the Shanghai Children's Welfare Institute. Recently, many people at the institute have beaten and abused disabled orphans such as Qiu Zhen, infringing their personal rights and interests and harming their physical and mental health. We demand that disabled children be protected, so as to avoid further persecutions, and that this [matter] be dealt with severely.

A Group of Shanghai Orphanage Staff

Reporter's Investigation:

When this reporter entered the orphanage to conduct interviews, the orphanage director[371] explained that on March 8, an employee at the Zhenfu Meter Factory, located inside the orphanage, had had 44 yuan and some grain [ration] tickets stolen. Another disabled child had said that Qiu Zhen, from the Children's Department, was responsible. On the morning of March 12, a cadre from the institute's Security Section[372] questioned Qiu Zhen. Qiu Zhen at first denied [the theft], but later admitted it. He also produced a deposit receipt for 40 yuan (however, the date of deposit on the receipt was February of this year). Some time after one o'clock that afternoon, Qiu Zhen ran away, leaving behind a note saying he would never return to the orphanage. After seven that evening, [however,] he suddenly telephoned the orphanage and announced that he wanted to come back, and he returned at around 9:30. When the Security Section cadre resumed his interrogation of Qiu Zhen, he absolutely denied having stolen the money.

---

[371] Han Weicheng.

[372] Li Zhouqing.

This reporter found Qiu Zhen as he was working. His fingers are severely malformed as a result of a congenital bone abnormality. As soon as the reporter touched on the incident of March 8, his first words were: "I didn't do it!" He told the reporter: "I was playing with friends all that evening. My friends and the staff can all confirm this. The man from the Security Section decided I was responsible without any investigation. He manhandled and choked me, and in the evening he also threatened me with an electric police baton, until one o'clock in the morning." He hung his head and said softly: "I knew it wouldn't be any use to keep telling the truth, so I decided to admit it and get a chance to run away from the orphanage."

Afterwards, this reporter saw the boy who had "exposed" Qiu Zhen's theft of the money.[373] He told the reporter: "I was forced to testify."

The orphanage director and the Security Section cadre believed that Qiu Zhen was the prime suspect in the theft from the Zhenfu factory, but they produced no conclusive evidence, even after spending two hours on "interrogation [to find] the facts (*xunwen shikuang*)"! The head of the Security Section admitted that on that occasion he had twice shoved Qiu Zhen into a chair, with the electric police baton already laid out on the table. He also said that the interrogation had ended at well after 11 p.m.

The leadership of the orphanage appeared to be extremely impatient with this reporter's interviews and investigations. They considered that it was interfering with their normal operations, and that a section of the orphanage staff was intentionally "making trouble."

Disabled children need care and affection. Even when they make mistakes, this should be [dealt with] starting with love and education, with their lawful rights protected.

Cai Hui, Trainee, Fudan University Department of Journalism

2. Article in **Labor News** *(May 31, 1990):*

"The Whole Of Society Should Care About the Healthy Growth of Young People: Don't Forget the Unfortunate Children"

Tomorrow is June first, International Children's Day. On that day, our heads of households, holding the hands of their pure and innocent "treasures" or carrying them in their arms, will arrive to play in a park echoing with the sounds of laughter, or to satisfy the desires of the "next generation" in well-stocked department stores.

---

[373] Fu Qiang.

This reporter, specializing in mass work, wants to tell them: You are very lucky....We have witnessed the following grave sights:

At a certain unit for the rehabilitation of children, a large number of orphans, who have been abandoned by their irresponsible parents, are longing for their own fathers and mothers. Even though they enjoy the devoted attention of child-care staff, some physically and mentally disabled children face many difficulties in their lives. We saw close to 200 infants and young children lying in bed with their hands tied to the bed frames with gauze. According to the person concerned,[374] this was to prevent the retarded children from eating the cotton wadding [of their bedding] or hurting themselves by gouging their own eyes out. We were deeply saddened and shocked...

Cai Hui, trainee, Fudan University Department of Journalism
Zhang Weiqiang, reporter

*3. Excerpts From Article In "Internal Reference" (**Neibu Cankao**) Edition Of* ***Guangming Ribao** (July 21, 1992):*

"Brutal Abuse Of Disabled Children At Shanghai Municipal Orphanage Causes Outrage"

(By Shanghai correspondent Yu Chuanshi)

Delegates to the Shanghai Ninth People's Congress, including Xu Xinyuan, Ma Mimi, Gao Junzhu, Xu Feng, Li Weiyi and other comrades, recently informed this reporter that in recent years, the Shanghai Municipal Children's Welfare Insitute has suffered from chaotic management. [The problem of] unnatural deaths among disabled orphans and infants is very serious, disabled children suffer maltreatment and abuse, and there have been repeated cases of [children] being beaten and unlawfully locked up without cause. Illegal acts and crimes have also occurred at this institute, such as public funds being misappropriated for personal use and disabled orphan girls being molested and sexually abused.

It is understood that since 1989, a number of staff members at the Shanghai Children's Welfare Institute have been submitting letters of complaint to the city [authorities] regarding these matters. On October 14 of last year, after Xu Xinyuan, Ma Mimi and other delegates to the Shanghai Municipal People's Congress received these letters, they repeatedly undertook investigations of the Shanghai orphanage and

---

[374] I.e., Han Weicheng.

employees involved, both openly and covertly. They confirmed that the conditions reported by the complainants were genuine. The main problems at the orphanage are as follows:

1. The High Rate Of Unnatural Deaths Among Disabled Infants And Orphans.

In the three years 1989, 1990, and 1991, there were a total of 478 deaths at the institute. In 1989, there were 235 intakes and 141 deaths;[375] in 1990, 224 intakes and 126 deaths; and in 1991, 272 intakes and 211 deaths....Xi Liang, male, aged eight months, suffered from pneumonia for a month. [His treatment] was under doctor's orders from the beginning. The doctor prescribed six doses of penicillin, but the nurse only administered one injection (there was only one needle puncture on the buttocks), and he died on December 30, 1991.

Bi Feng, female, who entered the orphanage at the age of seven, died in her dormitory at age 14, on January 2, 1991. She was sallow and emaciated, only skin and bones (pibao gutou). No medical records had been entered for this girl for four years. But after this was exposed, the current leadership immediately arranged for a false medical record to be written, saying that [the cause of death] was diarrhea and that she had been given anti-diarrheal medication. But the prescriptions [for these drugs] could not be found, as the laboratory test records and medical record showed. According to investigations, the altering and falsification of medical records of infants and children who die unnaturally at the institute has already occurred in more than 10 cases.

In the seven months between December 1991 and June 1992, a total of one hundred [orphans] died, and at least 57 of these died unnaturally.[376] Most of these deaths were from causes such as cold, hunger, inaccurate diagnosis or no diagnosis at all, and medical accidents. On December 19 [sic] of last year, the weather was very cold, but some orphans were still wearing only a single layer of clothing. In the space of two days, one died of illness and nine froze to death.

---

[375] According to the official figures cited in Table 4.1, above, there were 146 deaths in 1989; slight statistical variations such as this can be found in several of the different source documents from the Shanghai orphanage consulted by Human Rights Watch/Asia.

[376] According to the mortality data presented in Table 4.6, altogether 102 children died during the period December 1991–June 1992.

2. The Wanton Maltreament, Abuse, Beating And Unlawful Detention Of Disabled Orphans.

In the course of their clandestine investigations, the People's Congress delegates came across disabled orphans such as Yue Yi and Qiu Zhen, who had been beaten and kicked by the institute's director, Han Weicheng. Yue Yi, now aged 18, is disabled in his fingers and feet, but his intelligence is normal. One day in August 1988, he did not get up at the appointed time because he was tired. A teacher came to wake him, and while he was still dreamily asleep, he swung his arm out. The teacher, caught unawares by the impact, fell over. In the afternoon, Han Weicheng called him into his office, and proceeded to beat and kick him all over. He also locked him up on his own for three days. Qiu Zhen, now aged 19, has abnormally formed hands and fingers, but is normal in intelligence. One day in the summer of 1988, he was slow getting up in the morning because he had stayed up late reading. When Han Weicheng saw him, without asking the reason, he pulled him out of bed by his ears, and shoved him into a wall four or five meters away. With the director taking the lead, the child-care workers followed the example of their superior (*shangxing xiaxiao*). On April 30 of last year, the orphan Hong Na, now six years old, because she had taken a packet of candy placed on a table by a child-care worker, was beaten on her ears, head, and both hands by the child-care worker, using a mop pole and a plastic shoe. A 10-year-old boy, Liang Jie, was forced to eat magnets because he had told the truth about Hong Na's being beaten, and they didn't come out. The child-care worker also forced him and another orphan, Ru Xiu, to hurt themselves, beating their hands against a radiator until they bled...

Appendix D.   Excerpts From Report By The Shanghai Civil Affairs Bureau On Its Investigation Of Complaints By Orphanage Staff (August 15, 1990)

Chinese Communist Party Committee, Shanghai Civil Affairs Bureau
Circular No. 33 (1990)
Classification: Intermediate-level Secret (*jimi*)
Main recipient: Deputy Mayor Xie Lijuan
Copies to: Deputy Party Secretary Ni Hongfu; Municipal Discipline Inspection Committee: Comrades Zhang Dinghong and Sun Weiguo; Municipal Government Letters and Visists Department; Ministry of Civil Affairs' Urban Welfare Section

Number of Copies: 20

Report on An Investigation Into the Situation of A Small Number
of Employees At the Children's Welfare Institute Who Are
Alleging Various Problems with the Institute's Leadership

Since the end of last year, several employees from the municipal Children's Welfare Institute under our Bureau, including Zhang Shuyun, Yang Yaming, and Li Guilan, have repeatedly appealed to the Bureau about so-called "serious" problems with the institute's leadership. The leaders of the Bureau and of the departments involved have been very concerned, and the relevant Bureau leaders and comrades responsible for the departments involved have given personal interviews to these employees, patiently listening to their detailed reports.

In order to bring the facts to light, on February 7 of this year we assigned four directors and vice-directors and two cadres from two branches of the Department of Social Welfare to thoroughly look into the Children's Welfare Institute, taking nearly a month altogether. They sought out 35 comrades, and undertook to obtain information from them by holding individual discussions. (Prior to this, we had already sent staffers there to do some investigation.) These 35 comrades constitute 10 percent of the entire staff.[377] They include middle-level cadres, work team leaders, and ordinary employees, as well as Party cadres. They also included the comrades who had made

---

[377] This implies that the orphanage had a total staff of approximately 350, and is consistent with the 1990 *China Civil Affairs Statistical Yearbook*, which gives the number of employees at the end of 1989 as 348. But see Chapter 6, footnote 8.

the complaints and [other] parties involved. Moreover, we also talked to comrades in relevant departments of the Bureau in order to verify certain information. What follows are the results of our investigation into the situation and conditions at the orphanage at present, as well as our own views.

A. Major Problems Alleged by Comrade Zhang Shuyun and Others

1. Regarding lifestyle problems of the orphanage director, Han Weicheng.
It is alleged, first, that one afternoon last summer, Comrade Han Weicheng was working alone in his office on the sixth floor of the Rehabilitation Center building. Some people outside then knocked several times, but no one opened the door. It is suspected that Han Weicheng was having inappropriate relations with a female employee, Zhu Meiping. Second, that Han was seen several times on the street with Zhu after work. Third, that one early morning in the summer of 1988, Han watched a female employee undressing.

2. Regarding orphanage leaders' arbitrarily beating and abusing disabled children, damaging their physical and mental health.
Among these is the question of Han Weicheng's having beaten and abused Yue Yi. Zhang Shuyun, Yang Yaming, and other comrades have alleged that the leaders behaved viciously towards several disabled children, Qiu Zhen, Zhan Tong, Chou Hui, and Yue Yi, physically punishing them, locking them up, and so forth, and in particular that Han Weicheng himself beat Yue Yi.

3. Regarding questions of fraud and deception.
Most importantly, it is alleged that when [staff] from the Bureau came to the orphanage in 1989 to conduct a work inspection, infants with symptoms of diaper rash were hidden in the morgue, and that whenever outsiders came to visit, emaciated children were hidden in the storage rooms.

4. Regarding the question of orphanage leaders' exacting retribution against dissidents (*yiji*).
In particular, Zhang Shuyun and other comrades believe that the transfer of staff such as Zhan Qinyi and Li Weifang[378] was aimed at expelling dissidents, and that measures taken with regard to Zhang Shuyun's employment subsidies and public

---

[378] Zhan Qinyi, a former employee of the Personnel Department at the Shanghai Children's Welfare Institute, was transferred to the orphanage barbershop after criticizing Han Weicheng's management of the institute. Li Weifang, a teacher in the Children's Department, was assigned a position washing diapers after a dispute with Lu Rongfang, the department head.

transportation allowance, as well as Zhang's not being upgraded to the level of "advanced worker," were a form of retribution.

5. Regarding financial questions about the leadership.

First, it is alleged that not long after the six-floor Rehabilitation Center was completed, rain began leaking into the building, and it is suspected that there were financial problems with the leadership in connection with this...

On February 13, just as our organization's staff were undertaking this investigation, comrades including Zhang Shuyun, Yang Yaming, and Li Guilan made a series of additional allegations, orally and in writing, to bodies such as the municipal Committee for the Protection of Children and Youth, the municipal Discipline Committee, the municipal Bureau of Supervision, and the editorial offices of various newspapers, as well as the Nanshi District Elections Office and the Nanshi District Procuracy. In addition to the abovementioned problems, they also raised additional questions about Han Weicheng's using his authority for private gain, as well as his falsely posing as an "expert on cerebral palsy" and claiming credit for scientific achievements.

B.   Results of the Investigation and Circumstances of Our Work.

In light of the allegations from comrades Zhang Shuyun, Yang Yaming, Li Guilan and others, and with a sense of responsibility to the undertakings of the Party and to the masses, we dispatched four directors and vice-directors and two cadres to undertake an in-depth investigation for one month, and listened in detail to the views of all sides. We repeatedly verified some questions of a serious nature, and afterwards analyzed one by one the various problems mentioned above. In the course of our investigation [we have drawn the following conclusions]:

1. On the question of Han Weicheng's lifestyle:

i) Because Han was working on the sixth floor of the Rehabilitation Center one day last summer, and some people knocked at the door for a long time but got no answer, a few staff members at the institute said that Han and Zhu had been having improper relations. Having looked into this, [we found that] those who spread this rumor and filed the complaint were not the ones [present] at the time. After we repeatedly sought information from those who were present, they all denied having seen Han and Zhu together in the room.

ii) Although Han did walk in the street with Zhu after work, it cannot be concluded that their relationship was inappropriate.

iii) As for Han's having watched a female employee undressing, it was in fact the female employee who violated the institute's rules on changing clothes. Not only did she do so during working hours, but also in a work room. Han was conducting an inspection, and did not intentionally watch the employee undress.

It is inappropriate for the complainants to claim that Han has problems with his lifestyle.

2. The problem of orphanage leaders' beating and abusing disabled children, and harming their physical and mental health, does not exist. The fact is that the orphanage has to impose strict education and necessary protective measures on some incorrigible disabled children (some of whom are in fact already young adults). For example, the children mentioned by the complainants, such as Qiu Zhen and Zhan Tong, are all in fact fully grown adults (15 to 18 years old). One of these, Qiu Zhen (aged 18), has had contacts with society and has received unhealthy influences. He frequently steals money and property from other people, and has also behaved indecently with a few retarded girls at the orphanage itself. The educational measures to which he was subjected at the orphanage were approved by the Bureau...and there is a huge gap between the circumstances alleged and the facts.

As for the question of Han Weicheng's having personally beaten and abused Yue Yi, it was in fact comrades such as Zhang Shuyun and Yang Yaming who exploited the fact that Yue Yi had once been severely criticized and educated by Han. Taking advantage of Yue Yi's naivety and lack of social experience, they repeatedly coached him to tell untrue stories. Yue Yi, Qiu Zhen and others have explained the situation to our organization and said that Han Weicheng did not beat them.

3. With respect to the question of fraud and deception, this is a misunderstanding arising from the complaining comrades' reliance on hearsay and their lack of understanding of the policy on dealing with foreigners (*duiwai shi gongzuo zhengce*). There were some specific circumstances in the complaints which were not accurate. The orphanage never arranged for infants with symptoms of diaper rash to be transferred to the morgue during work inspections. As for the times when foreign guests came to visit the orphanage who did not fully understand the socialist system or who held different views, in order to prevent misunderstandings from arising, a few disabled children whose physical appearance was very bad were temporarily transferred to other wards which the foreign guests had not arranged to visit. This cannot be described as "fraud and deception."

4. The orphanage leadership's personnel policies are consistent with the Party's principle of collective decisionmaking. The transfer of staffers such as Zhan Qinyi and Li Weifang has been collectively considered and decided by the institute's Party administrative group. The reasons were legitimate, and there has been no question of retribution or expulsion of dissidents. As for making deductions from

Zhang Shuyun's employment subsidies and public transportation allowance, this is a decision in accordance with policy. Of course, the orphanage could have been more creative and skillful in dealing with conflicts with individual employees. For example, Han gave a speech at a committee meeting to select "advanced individuals" within the Medical Department, in which he hoped to clarify these matters somewhat, but in fact the results were not good, and misunderstandings easily arose.

5. Financial questions about the orphanage leadership. Upon investigating, we found a gap between the alleged circumstances and the facts. Regarding the dispute over whether the construction quality of the Rehabilitation Center was good or bad, this had no direct connection with the orphanage leaders. It was a conflict between the architects and the construction team [sic]. Those comrades who complained about the situation did not know the true circumstances. Based only on superficial appearances and the loose talk of certain persons, their suspicion that there were financial questions about the orphanage leadership cannot be supported...

C.   A Summary of the Backgrounds of Zhang Shuyun and Others, and Some of Their Inappropriate Ways of Behaving.

Zhang Shuyun, female, aged 47, graduated from the medical department of Beijing Medical University in July 1967. She formerly worked as a doctor at the Luodian Health Center in Baoshan County, [Shanghai,] and later transferred to the Shanghai Municipal Research Institute for the Prevention and Cure of Occupational. Because she was dissatisfied with her job and felt that she had no prospects for advancement, she transferred in September 1988 to the Children's Welfare Institute, where she is now engaged in biochemical work in the medical laboratory.

Li Guilan, female, aged 50, graduated from the department of biology of Fudan University in 1967. She formerly worked as a doctor at the clinic of the Haigong Industrial Salt Factory, and later transferred to the Shanghai Municipal Research Institute for the Prevention and Cure of Occupational Diseases, where she was engaged in research on noise. Because her former unit rated her technical skills as below average, her relations with the director of the research institute were very tense, and she arranged a transfer to the Children's Welfare Institute in October 1988, taking on a position as a speech therapist for deaf children.

Yang Yaming, female, aged 39, joined the Party in September 1973. A "worker-peasant-soldier" university student in the medical department of the Shanghai Institute of Chinese Medicine (class of 1976), she was assigned to the Shanghai Children's Welfare Institute in January 1977, and was formerly the deputy head of the Medical Department and vice-director of the Business Department. She was demoted in March 1985, and is now engaged in rehabilitation and physical therapy with disabled children. Her base of support among the masses is rather weak.

Zhang Shuyun and Li Guilan have not been working at the Children's Welfare Institute for very long. In order to take advantage of their efforts, they were assigned important responsibilities at the orphanage, but their organizational discipline was rather weak, and they did not often ask for instructions or report to their superiors. In some instances they relied on their own judgment, and were criticized by the orphanage [leadership]. Afterwards, this gradually produced divisions of opinion on various work matters. These should have been resolved through consultation and frank discussion, but they took the initiative in seeking out these employees for discussions. By expressing their concerns and ingratiating themselves with these employees, they thereby obtained so-called "materials" on the leadership, which they used as the basis for their campaign. Yang Yaming was an especially important person in this role. Their main methods with respect to collecting the so-called "materials" submitted by Zhang Shuyun included the following:

1. In order to prove that Han Weicheng had lifestyle problems, on several occasions Zhang Shuyun shadowed Han's movements, following him on her bicycle.

2. In order to demonstrate that the orphanage leadership was practicing fraud and deception, Yang Yaming and others secretly took a large number of photographs, and intentionally created false appearances.[379]

Comrade Zhang [Bangxiang], of the office of the municipal Committee for the Protection of Children and Youth, pointed out upon receiving an application for a hearing from Zhang Shuyun, Yang Yaming, and other comrades, that although they could complain to higher-level authorities if they had opinions about the leadership, using such methods was quite wrong, and more importantly could be considered illegal.

3. They frequently gathered together at work and discussed ways of dealing with the leadership.

4. They incited Yue Yi and Qiu Zhen to make false statements.

---

[379] These photographs illustrated, among other things, the decrepit condition of the Rehabilitation Center shortly after its completion.

5. They encouraged Qiu Zhen to file complaints, provided him with funding, and drew a map for him showing the route [*sic*].[380]

6. They interfered with the normal operations of a police station. In March of this year, an incident of theft occurred at the orphanage. According to analysis, this was [done by] a disabled child.[381] The local police station cooperated with the orphanage to summon the suspect for investigation, but Zhang Shuyun and others went to the police station unexpectedly to complain about so-called "problems" with the orphanage leadership. They forced the police station to release the suspect by bailing him out. They also added to the difficulties of the orphanage in disciplining the disabled child.

D.   Our Views.

We have shown to comrades such as Zhang Shuyun and Yang Yaming the inappropriateness of their methods, and sternly pointed out to them that their ways of doing things are mistaken. Many upstanding cadres and employees at the orphanage are thoroughly disgusted with them, and have demanded that the institute take steps to deal with them immediately. In order for the problems at the Children's Welfare Institute to be resolved properly, we have consistently deferred to the judgment of the municipal Discipline Committee. At the same time we have worked hard on the attitudes of the broad mass of cadres and employees, repeatedly and unstintingly trying to persuade them to remain calm and reasonable. But with "bitter tongues and shrewish hearts" (*kukou-poxin*), [the critics] have turned a deaf ear to this education, causing even more trouble within the unit and making it impossible to resolve the problem for a long time. This has seriously affected the progress of routine work at the orphanage. In order to preserve the morale of cadres and employees at the institute, and to ensure the normal progress of work on the rehabilitation of children, we plan [the following]:

1. We will once again undertake to educate comrades such as Zhang Shuyun and Yang Yaming. We hope that they will put their energies into their work and not continue collecting and disseminating false information, thereby affecting the normal progress of work at the orphanage, and that they will [gain] a basis of understanding

---

[380] This refers to Zhang Shuyun's providing Qiu Zhen with a map showing the location of the main office of the Shanghai Civil Affairs Bureau, in order for him to seek protection there if he suffered further abuse at the orphanage.

[381] I.e., Qiu Zhen.

on some important questions. The orphanage leaders should sit down and talk frankly with them, develop criticisms and self-criticisms, and by these means gradually attain mutual understanding.

2. If comrades such as Zhang Shuyun and Yang Yaming still refuse to accept help from the organization, and continue to make a fuss about Han Weicheng's so-called "problems," then in order to show responsibility for the institute and respect for the facts, we will publicize the facts of the situation to the entire institute, allowing all its employees to make a clear distinction between truth and falsehood. At the same time, it will be necessary to take administrative action against Zhang Shuyun and Yang Yaming.

3. We will undertake internal Party criticism and assistance for Comrade Yang Yaming, a Party member who participated in these activities and played a key role in them. If she still does not listen to this advice, Party disciplinary action will be taken against her.

4. The orphanage is now undergoing its annual assignment and appointment process for cadres. With regard to the appointments of comrades Zhang Shuyun and Li Guilan, we will respect the views of the institute.

5. In view of the fact that there are presently only three people in the leadership of the orphanage's Party administration, although the task is very heavy, the leadership must be augmented as soon as possible. (Two people have already been added, one in the Party administration.) This will also be useful in moderating all sorts of conflicts.

6. As always, we will show concern and support for the work of rehabilitating children. We will also provide some collective assistance and leadership. When these conflicts have been moderated, we will continue helping the Party and administrative leaders of the orphanage to review and seriously reflect on this experience, in order to draw lessons from it. Please indicate whether this is acceptable.

> (Seal Affixed)
> China Communist Party Committee, Shanghai Civil Affairs Bureau
> August 15, 1990

Appendix E.   **Proposal Submitted By Three Delegates To The Shanghai Municipal People's Congress (October 21, 1991)**

A Sincere Proposal To The Municipal People's Congress And The Municipal People's Government, To Send Investigators To Look Deeply Into The Ways In Which The Shanghai Children's Welfare Institute Has Violated The Law And Discipline

To the Municipal People's Congress and the Municipal People's Government:

We are delegates to the Shanghai Ninth People's Congress. Some time ago, deputy Ma Mimi received a large quantity of materials denouncing and exposing the Shanghai Children's Welfare Institute, as well as a number of letters. These materials and letters were sent to Ma by a group of staff members at the institute, including Tang Youhua, Yang Yaming, Dai Changhai, Zhang Shuyun, Li Guilan, Chen Dongxian, and Zhan Qinyi. Having read these materials, we find a huge discrepancy between the actual situation and the praise that has been heaped on the institute. For this reason, we have discussed among ourselves how best to deal with these letters. As a result of these discussions, we now believe that:

1. If the allegations are true or basically true, there are serious problems at the Shanghai Children's Welfare Institute, and the leadership there should be replaced immediately. We shall first raise this matter when we attend the meeting of the SMPC Standing Committee as non-voting delegates, so as to attract the attention of the leadership. (Sun Guizhang, the deputy head of the Standing Committee, has already indicated that the matter should be thoroughly investigated. It would not do simply to write a comment on the report and send it down to the unit concerned.)

2. We shall conduct investigations both openly and covertly, so as to check and verify the allegations with cadres, teachers, and children at the institute. We decided to conduct a covert investigation on October 20. (As a result of that investigation, we found that the allegations were true or basically true. There are indeed many problems and questionable points that need to be further examined.)

3. [We shall] submit the results of our covert investigation, together with the materials and letters we have received, to the Municipal People's Congress and the Municipal People's Government, so as to bring them to the attention of the responsible departments concerned...

Please do not forward this proposal or related materials to the municipal Civil Affairs Bureau. When organizing the investigation, please consider including reporters from the *Shanghai People's Congress Gazette.*

To summarize, the [orphanage] staff members reported problems and questionable points in the following areas:

1. Certain cadres at the Shanghai Children's Welfare Institute are suspected of corruption.

....There are many indications that some cadres, on the pretext of constructing the Rehabilitation Center, have squandered state funds, sought private gain at public expense, and sold their power and influence for money, thus committing economic crimes.

The building reportedly cost 5.6 million yuan. It has a total floor space of 5,000 square meters, averaging more than 1,000 yuan per square meter. But what about the quality? It was opened for use in June 1989. Within two months, during a moderate rain, water leaked from the foreign visitors' reception room on the sixth floor all the way down to the ground floor. On some floors, slight pressure on the ceilings caused water to pour down. Water had accumulated 10 centimeters deep on the floors....Comrade Chen Wenzhu, of the municipal Civil Construction Design Institute, advised from the very beginning against using poor-quality building materials and shoddy workmanship, but to no avail. He was furious, and planned to appeal to the municipal government and the media. To this day, he has refused to approve the document certifying that the building had been examined and authorized.[382] No one knows why (and this is something that calls for special investigation) the institute paid the construction team the huge sum of 5.6 million yuan in cash and in a lump sum. According to our on-the-spot inspection, there are many cracks and faults in the building. It was truly "ruined before use." Quite a few lampshades, glazed tiles, and ceiling fans had been stolen. The rate of utilization of the building has been extremely low. It is practically unusable...

2. The management of the institute is a mess, and the leadership's workstyle is evil.

There are many accidents, and Han Weicheng and certain teachers and nursing staff are totally negligent. They have knowingly violated the law, beating and abusing children at will and meting out corporal punishments such as tying up disabled children and locking them up. Moreover, these things have occurred frequently...

---

[382] By proceeding with work on the Rehabilitation Center without official authorization from the Civil Construction Design Institute, the orphanage management therefore acted illegally.

Director Han also arbitrarily sent the perfectly normal orphan boy Ai Ming and orphan girl Chou Hui to mental hospitals, where they languished for four to six months. The Civil Affairs Bureau even admits that they authorized this.

The institute has used disabled children under the age of 16 as child laborers. The shortest period worked [by the orphans we interviewed] was two years. Some had worked as long as four years. Many children were forced to drop out of school to become child laborers. Their pay was very low, ranging from a few yuan to 20 yuan [per month]...

According to some staff members, the institute performed its own autopsies to cover up medical malpractice. Comrade Li Guilan and others reported to higher authorities in August that the institute's masseur [Ding Yi] had broken the bones of a child patient [Zhang Yansong]. He continued the massage therapy for another 15 days. When director Han found out what had happened, he had a false case history prepared while threatening the child's family members. He also abused those staff members who tried to tell the truth as being disloyal...

During out covert investigation, we were told by the disabled children that five or six deaths a week were nothing out of the ordinary. That very day [October 20, 1991] there were three deaths, and the day before, two. They also showed us the morgue. The doors and windows had been left open, and dead bodies lay in a pile, making it difficult to count the number...

3. Factionalism, poor workstyles, stifling democracy, and excluding outsiders.

Clothing donated by Chinese people is strewn everywhere, to be picked up by whoever is interested or sold to junk dealers for money to be squandered on food [for the leadership]. Donations from foreigners and high-quality toys are divided up among the cadres, who pay a nominal price of 50 fen or one yuan for each item. Some are given to trusted followers in exchange for their loyalty.

We were informed that director Han forms factions and runs the institute like an independent kingdom, by offering his trusted followers foreign travel, better housing, promotions, jobs, and bonuses...

Last year, during the [Nanshi District] People's Congress elections, Han and the Communist Party secretary Zhu [Qingfang] tried to stifle democracy. At meetings, they did their best to win votes for Han [as the orphanage's delegate to the district People's Congress], declaring that all ballots not for Han would be null and void. This created nervousness among all the employees at the institute. Han lost, and he blamed his defeat on those who dared to inform on him. He called those who reported on him to higher organs "troublemakers" engaging in "anti-organization" activities. For example, Comrade Tang Youhua was not hired as a middle-rank cadre and was transferred to an administrative [postion] because she dared to speak the truth [about

Han Weicheng's beating of Yue Yi]. She went to see the director of the Civil Affairs Bureau, asking for just two minutes of the director's time. Director Sun [Jinfu] refused to see her, saying, "You have to have an appointment to see me. If you demanded that [Mayor] Zhu Rongji see you, would the mayor do so?" Tang begged him again and again, but in vain. She told all the employees of the institute her story at a meeting. The hall was absolutely quiet. Party secretary Zhu Qingfang denounced Tang, declaring that no one was scheduled to speak at the meeting. Zhu said that Tang was disrupting the meeting and should be punished according to the institute's regulations.

We prepared the above report in a hurry. It probably suffers from incompleteness and lack of depth. We hope the Municipal People's Congress and the Municipal People's Government will attach great importance to it and handle the matter very seriously.

With best wishes,

(signed:)   Xu Xinyuan
                   Gao Junzhu
                   Ma Mimi

                   October 21, 1991

Appendix F.   Report Submitted To Shanghai Municipal Authorities By Shi Shengren, Legal Consultant To The Shanghai General Labor Union (December 9, 1991)

[Classification level:] Intermediate-Level Secret (*jimi*)

LABOR UNION BRIEFING
Supplement #3

Compiled by the office of the Shanghai Municipal General Labor Union
December 9, 1991

Disabled Children Suffer Repeated Abuse;
Number Of Deaths Increases Year By Year

Problems at the Shanghai Children's Welfare Institute Demand Prompt Resolution

The Shanghai Children's Welfare Institute is a specialized welfare unit for the shelter and foster care of disabled children and orphans. As the name implies, the disabled orphans at the Welfare Institute ought to be leading happy lives, in order to compensate for the misfortune of the physical and mental disabilities with which they arrive. But repeated appeals to higher authority by employees of this institute and a thorough investigation by delegates of the municipal People's Congress, as well as an investigation by lawyers [from the Shanghai No.2 Legal Affairs Office], have revealed that the Shanghai Children's Welfare Institute has serious problems. Disabled children are being abused, and the number of children dying has increased each year.

Disabled orphans suffer brutal abuse. Cases have occurred of disabled children at the institute being wantonly beaten and abused, physically punished, tied up, and locked up. On the morning of April 30 of this year, the six-year-old disabled orphan Hong Na (female) was beaten on her ears, head, and both hands by a child-care worker using a mop pole and the sole of a plastic shoe, because she had taken a packet of candy from her teacher, Feng Ya'an. Hong could not bear this, and tried unsuccessfully to jump off the building by climbing over an iron railing. On the afternoon of August 25, two children, including a retarded 14-year-old child named Lu Yi (male), were instigated by a child-care worker to steal items such as soap and shampoo. After this happened, Lu told the truth about the incident. The child-care worker took brutal reprisals against the two orphans: she used cloth diapers to tie Lu Yi's hands and feet to a wooden pole, and then struck his mouth and lower body with a ruler.[383] The other orphan was also hit until his lips were bleeding. On hearing these accusations from staff, the institute's leadership had no choice but to convene a hasty meeting ten days later to "look at the injuries." The orphanage director, Han Weicheng, also frequently beats and abuses children: he once viciously kicked Yue Yi's two disabled legs while wearing leather shoes, used an electric police baton to beat the disabled orphan Zhu Yan on his upper arms,[384] and forcibly committed the mentally normal orphans Ai Ming and Chou Hui to psychiatric hospitals, "placing them in care" so that they could "improve their attitudes."

Management is chaotic, and the number of children's deaths has increased year after year. The management of the orphanage is chaotic, and accidents occur all the time. In January of this year, a member of the nursing staff broke a thermometer inside the rectum of a 13-month-old baby, and then actually used [metal] tweezers to remove the glass and mercury in the rectum, causing this child to lose a great deal of blood. Towards the end of this year, when several orphans showed symptoms of hepatitis, the orphanage tied the patients' hands and feet to their beds, locked the door [of the sickroom] and did not arrange for nursing care during the afternoon and night shifts. This went on for more than three months, and one of the orphans died at the institute. The 15-year-old orphan Du Bei (female) received no medical care after becoming ill, and one day in May 1990, she suddenly fell to the floor and died. By the time she was discovered, the body was already stiff. In the past few years, the institute's medical equipment has been refurbished, and nursing and medical staff are also being constantly added, but the incidence of common and contagious diseases among children at the orphanage has been seen to increase, and the number of deaths among disabled orphans has also increased each year. In 1985, there were 49 deaths, or 49.5 percent of the number admitted; in 1987, there were 95 deaths, or 58.6 percent; in 1989, there were 141 deaths, or 60 percent.

Practicing fraud, falsification and deception on leaders and on the trust of society. Meals and snacks at the Children's Welfare Institute are normally very monotonous, but when senior leaders visit, [the orphanage management] puts a wide range of food on the menus and so forth. When other units or senior staff come to visit, the orphans are all dressed in new clothes for the time of inspection and every child

---

[383] According to Zhang Shuyun, this is incorrect; the child-care worker who inflicted the abuse, Li Laidi, was not the one originally responsible for asking Lu Yi to steal the soap.

[384] In fact, this beating was carried out by employees of a "deportation station" run by the Shanghai Civil Affairs Bureau. Han Weicheng was responsible both for transferring Zhu Yan to the center and for asking the station staff to inflict the beating.

has a piece of candy in its hand. The rule is that only when the visitors have arrived for the inspection are they permitted to eat it, and the orphans are all ordered to recite, "Eat well, dress well, live well." But when [medical] accidents happen, Han Weicheng assigns staff to write up false medical records, and if anyone reports this to higher authorities, the low-level staff are condemned as "living off one person while secretly helping another (*chili pawai*)," while the senior staff are faced with retribution.

Moreover, employees at the institute have reported that there are financial questions about personnel responsible during the construction of the new [Rehabilitation Center] tower, and problems with orphanage director Han Weicheng, such as his having raped orphan girls. In order to safeguard the reputation of the state and the lawful rights and interests of disabled children, a part of the staff at the institute, delegates to the municipal People's Congress, and legal workers have called for [the following measures]:

1. Bodies such as the municipal [Communist Party] Committee, the municipal government, and the Legal Committee of the [municipal] People's Congress should immediately organize a special group to thoroughly investigate the Children's Welfare Institute;

2. The institute's leadership group must be completely turned over, to end its obstruction of the investigation;

3. The Public Security organs should register the case for investigation, and, in accordance with the law, seek to hold relevant personnel legally responsible.

Shi Shengren

Circulate To: Municipal [Communist Party] Committee Secretary, Deputy Secretary; Standing Committee [Of The Municipal Communist Party]; Mayor, Deputy Mayor

Editor: Ma Jihong

Appendix G.   Letter To Lu Ming From Three Delegates To The Shanghai Municipal People's Congress (January 22, 1992)

Vice-Chairman Lu:[385]

Greetings. We have received a letter from Yue Yi and four other disabled children at the Shanghai Children's Welfare Institute, informing us that they did not receive a proper education during their school-age years. Now, even though they have reached the age of 17 or 18, their attainment is only equivalent to that of a primary-school graduate. They want very much to study more and to become better prepared to serve society as useful persons. But the institute is to send them away soon to work. They are unwilling to accept this arrangement.

Vice-Chairman Lu, we three delegates are forwarding this letter to you. We sincerely request that you take some time out of your very busy schedule to deal with this matter, and help them complete their nine years of compulsory education in accordance with the "Shanghai Municipal Regulations on Compulsory Education" and the "Compulsory Education Law of the People's Republic of China." We believe their cases are not the exception at the Shanghai Children's Welfare Institute. Some of the children, although physically handicapped, are no less intelligent than normal people. Why can't they enjoy the right to education just like normal children? It might be said that in implementing Shanghai's compulsory education regulations, there is a forgotten corner—the Shanghai Children's Welfare Institute.

Vice-Chairman Lu, please help these children! To do so is to uphold the dignity of the law, and also to protect the right of the children to a proper education. Finally, allow us to suggest that the Civil Affairs Bureau should be told that as the Children's Welfare Institute is currently under investigation, the children should not be sent away, at least for the time being. And efforts should be made to arrange for them to go to school, so that they may enjoy the right to complete their nine years of compulsory education. We look forward to hearing from you.

Yours truly,
(signed:)   Gao Junzhu
                   Xu Xinyuan
                   Ma Mimi
                          (Delegates to the Municipal People's Congress)

---

[385] Lu Ming was deputy head of the Shanghai Municipal People's Congress's Legal Affairs Committee.

Appendix H.   Article From *Liberation Daily* (February 4, 1992)

Toys Carry Deep Feelings: Wishing Orphans
Happiness In The Year Of The Monkey

Liberation Daily and Shanghai No. 7 Toy Factory Get Together With LittleFriends
From The Children's Welfare Institute; Xie Lijuan Thanks Supporters Of Child
Welfare Work On Behalf Of The Municipal Government

(Reporter: Zheng Xinao)

On the afternoon of Lunar New Year's Eve, the auditorium of the Shanghai
Children's Welfare Institute was decorated with lanterns and colored streamers. It was
filled with happy chit-chat and laughter. Some 400 orphans living in the big warm
family of socialism were gathered joyfully together in their holiday best. Xie Lijuan,
deputy mayor of Shanghai; Zhou Ruijin and Ding Ximan, [Communist] Party secretary
and deputy secretary of Liberation Daily; Sun Jinfu, director of the municipal Civil
Affairs Bureau; Xu Xikang, director of the Shanghai No. 7 Toy Factory; and members
of the Shanghai People's Comedy Theater got together with their little friends for
Lunar New Year celebrations. In a joyous atmosphere, *Liberation Daily* and the
Shanghai No. 7 Toy Factory gave each of the 400 orphans a New Year present–a
"Whale" brand plush toy.

Deputy mayor Xie Lijuan spoke at the gathering. On behalf of the Shanghai
Municipal People's Government, she thanked people from all walks of life, who have
shown solicitude and supported child welfare work. She expressed the hope that they
would give greater support in the coming year, and that the Children's Welfare
Institute would be more successful in its work.

Disabled children from the Children's Welfare Institute performed songs and
dances and exhibited their drawings and calligraphy that they had worked very hard
to produce. Lin Xibiao, Li Feisong, and Mao Mengda, well-known performers with
the Shanghai People's Comedy Theater, put on an excellent show.

Han Weicheng, the director of the Shanghai Children's Welfare Institute,
conveyed heartfelt thanks to *Liberation Daily*, the Shanghai No. 7 Toy Factory, and
the Shanghai People's Comedy Theater for their solicitude and support for child
welfare work. He issued each of them with a certificate of honor.

Appendix I.   Appeal Signed By Fourteen Delegates Of The Shanghai Municipal People's Congress (October 14, 1992)

To the Standing Committee of the Shanghai Municipal People's Congress:

On September 30 of this year, Wang Chongji, vice-chairman of the municipal People's Congress, and vice-mayor Xie Lijuan met with [People's Congress] delegates on the issue of the Children's Welfare Institute, and the municipal Bureau of Supervision reported to them on the circumstances of the case. The delegates felt very dissatisfied after listening to them, and at the same time felt deeply concerned about thoroughly resolving the problems at the orphanage. Why did they confound black and white, and confuse truth and falsehood, further complicating the orphanage question and making it even more difficult to deal with? Why did they tolerate the orphanage leadership's continuing to alter medical records during the course of the investigation? Why couldn't they protect the lawful rights and interests of disabled children? Why did they tolerate the retribution and persecution against those who filed complaints? Why have they tried until this day to cover up the facts about unnatural deaths of disabled children? Why did they allow criminal elements to get off scot-free (*xiaoyao fawai*)?

In order to thoroughly look into the problems at the orphanage, we propose that the 37th Session of the Standing Committee organize a committee to investigate the question of the Children's Welfare Institute, in accordance with Article 26 of the "Representatives Law," and appoint delegates to participate in it. [This committee should] lawfully investigate and verify the relevant circumstances, and pursue the [criminal] responsibility of the leaders concerned. The criminals who abused, maltreated and molested disabled children absolutely must not be allowed to escape. The retribution and persecution against those who filed complaints absolutely must not be allowed to continue.

Further establish the socialist image of child welfare work, and save the children!

We earnestly ask that the 37th Session of the Standing Committee of the Municipal People's Congress provide a satisfactory reply to these requests as soon as possible.

(Signed:)   Municipal People's Congress Delegates:

Ma Mimi, Li Weiyi, Xue Chengyou, Gao Junzhu, Da Shikui, Hu Limei, Jun Lansheng, Shen Xianzhong, Fei Zhenyu, Xu Xinyuan, Hong Dalin, Xu Feng, Zhang Genggeng, Dai Mu

Appendix J. **Orphans of Normal or Near-normal Intelligence Presently Confined to the Shanghai No. 2 Social Welfare Institute (Partial List)**

Name	Sex	Date of Transfer
Ba Shou	F	1990
Cao Cheng	M	Before 1990
Cao Qiang	M	1994
Fu Qiang	M	March 13, 1991
Fu Qing	F	March 13, 1991
Guang Juan	F	Before 1990
Ji Cheng	M	March 13, 1991
Liu Wen*	M	March 13, 1991
Peng Yu	M	Before 1990
Ru Sha	F	July 1990
Shen Qi	F	1990 or earlier
Tang Xin	M	Before 1990
Xi Zi	F	Before 1990
Xiang Wen*	F	1992?
Yu Bin	F	1990
Yuan Yun	F	1992?
Zhu Yan	M	March 13, 1991

[* Mildly retarded.]

**Appendix K.   Letters Written To Zhang Shuyun By Orphans Brought
Up In The Shanghai Children's Welfare Institute**

*1. Letter Sent from the Shanghai No.2 Social Welfare Institute (Dated March 18,
1991)*

Doctor Zhang:

Greetings! How is your health? Is your work going smoothly? Let me tell you
about our situation here. When we first arrived at the No.2 Social Welfare Institute,
many people came to greet us. I was very happy. Yet I was also very scared. Because
Zhu Yan, who came with us last time, ran away. He was caught and brought back. The
aunties and uncles [i.e., institute staff] beat him and abused him. I was so scared and
I cried. But don't you worry about me. Our aunties and uncles treat me very well.
Things are all right here.

Doctor Zhang, I miss you very much. I hope you will write me a reply.
Finally, I wish you good health and success.

(signed by letter writer)

*2. Letter From Chou Hui, Sent From The Shanghai No.2 Social Welfare Institute
(Dated September 15, 1991)*

Doctor Zhang:

Greetings! I was very happy to get your letter. But something has come up
here. Let me give you the details of the situation. The day after Yu Bin arrived [at the
institute], someone claimed that some money had been stolen [and] accused me of
stealing the money. I was puzzled, and denied that I took any money. One of the
aunties said she saw me buying snacks every day and got suspicious of me. The
leadership asked me where I hid the money. I was very scared, so I admitted that I
stole the money. But in fact, I did not steal the money. Some of the leadership and the
aunties tied me up with "pressure bonds" (*yasuodai*) and locked me up. They insisted
that I confess to stealing.

Doctor Zhang, I swear to you I did not steal the money. The real thief got off
scot-free and felt good about it. Please tell me what to do. I have been labeled a thief
and no one will believe me any more. How am I going to live as a decent person!

Doctor Zhang, I really don't want to stay here any longer. Please get me out of here quickly. I want freedom. I don't want to be like a bird in a cage. I can no longer stand the way they bully me.

Doctor Zhang, I don't know when you will come and see me again. Please do not forget about it. It would be better for us to talk about this matter when we get to Zhong Xiu's house. So I will stop here.

Wishing you good health and success,

(signed) Chou Hui

3. Letter Sent From The Shanghai No.2 Social Welfare Institute (Dated March 15, 1992)

Doctor Zhang:

Greetings, and thank you for [sending] the things [I] received.

Doctor Zhang, for the last two days, four people have been here to investigate things connected with the Children's Welfare Institute. They're from the Bureau of Supervision. They wanted to know when a birthday party was in progress at Zhong Xiu's house, and whether some strangers were there. They did not disclose anything. Another matter concerns you. They asked Chou Hui whether some people had come looking for you. She kept quiet and said nothing. She did so because I told her to keep quiet no matter who asked about you.

They also questioned me. Tell me if I should talk about it. I had a hard time making up my mind. I hate those people in the leadership. So I wanted to talk. Then again, I did not want to talk. Tell me if I should talk. Please answer me, will you?

Finally, wishing you good health and success.

(signed by letter writer)

4. Letter Ostensibly From Chou Hui, Sent From The Shanghai No.1 Jail (Dated September 20, 1992)[386]

Doctor Zhang:

Greetings. I have read your letter, which Wu Hengjun[387] gave to me. Thank you all for your concern. I am fine, your concern [*sic*], I miss you all. Thank you all for the things you sent me.

Doctor Zhang, please let [another orphan at the No.2 Social Welfare Institute] know that I am thinking of her, and also tell the kids at Chongming not to worry. I am now in the Public Security Bureau. I can say of my own situation that I must obey them. The staff here, the uncles and aunties, care for you and love you just like relatives.

Teacher Tang [Youhua], Doctor Li [Guilan], Uncle Chen [Dongxian], and Teacher Zhan [Qinyi], thank you all for your concern. Thanks to everyone for the money you gave me. I'm happy. I'm very happy. Thank you all for your concern. Send my regards to everyone, and write back to me. I'm telling you I'm in the Public Security Bureau [crossed out, illegible]

I know now that I was wrong! I listened to you once [crossed out, illegible]
Please don't come to see me, okay? [crossed out, illegible]
Wishing you happiness and success in all things.

(signed) Chou Hui

5. Letter Sent From The Shanghai No.2 Social Welfare Institute (Dated March 16, 1993)

Doctor Zhang:

Greetings. I haven't written for such a long time. Since Chou Hui left, the administration has tightened its grip. On February 24, 1993, many children between

---

[386] This letter is not in Chou Hui's handwriting. In a conversation between Chou Hui and another orphan which took place after her release from jail, Chou Hui claimed that she had originally written a much shorter note to Zhang Shuyun, which was apparently never sent. (A tape recording of this conversation is in the possession of Human Rights Watch/Asia.)

[387] Chief of the Public Order Department of the Shanghai Public Security Bureau.

the ages of nine and thirteen years[388] who have families came to our institution. They are unable to take care of themselves; they can't eat or go to the bathroom by themselves. Every day, we have to take care of feeding them, dressing them, and putting them to sleep. They are so troublesome that we have all become nursemaids.

Doctor Zhang, I really want to leave this place now. I don't want to behave like a fool all day, and get bored when there is nothing to do. I am already twenty-five, I don't want to live this kind of life forever. When I learned that Chou Hui had left the mental hospital and started working, I was happy for her.[389] But what about myself?

Doctor Zhang, Luo Zhan, Zhu Cao, Yao Qing, and Yue Yi have either been adopted or found work. They are so happy. We have all grown up together in the Children's Welfare Institute. We're so close to each other that we're like sisters. Now I have no one here to confide in. You may be impatient, but I need your help just the way you helped them. I have my own ideals. I don't want to spend all my life here. Doctor Zhang, I'm begging you.

I wish you good health and success.

(signed by letter writer)

6.   *Letter Sent From The Shanghai No.2 Social Welfare Institute (Dated September 10, 1992)*

On August 1, 1990, just a few days after I got here, I saw Shen Qi tied up with "pressure bonds." She was being punished because she reported on the aunties who played cards and washed their clothes during working hours. So the aunties told the district chief that Shen Qi had fought with her boyfriend. That was why she was tied up.

The way she was bound, the district chief tied her hands behind her back, pulled her pants halfway down, had her sit on the toilet seat and then gave her a shot to put her to sleep. She was hanging there for a day and a half. She went without food for noontime, evening, and the following morning. Afterwards I saw her wrists were swollen and blue.

---

[388] The ages are given in *sui* (the Chinese method of calculation), and thus correspond to between eight and to twelve Western years.

[389] This is apparently a reference to Chou Hui's four-month detention in late 1992. In fact, she was held at the Shanghai No.1 Jail, not at the women's mental hospital from which she had originally been sent to Chongming Island.

The second time was just like the first. Only it started at 8:30, and she was not released until 5:30. She had neither lunch nor supper.

(signed by letter writer)

Appendix L.   Text Of "Applicable Explanation Of The Regulations On The Specific Range Of State Secrets In Civil Affairs Work And Their Classification Level" (Circulated August 6, 1991)[390]

On July 27, 1989, our Bureau and the State Secrets Bureau jointly promulgated, in Issue #32 (1989) of [XXX], the *Regulations on the Specific Range of State Secrets in Civil Affairs Work and Their Classification Level* (hereinafter abbreviated as *Range of Secrets*).

These regulations were formulated in accordance with legal procedure, and have the force of law. They are specific criteria for determining whether or not particular matters in civil affairs work constitute state secrets, and if so, of what classification level (*miji*). They are also a basis for civil affairs departments at all levels to supervise and inspect secrecy. On this basis, civil affairs departments at all levels can directly determine the classification level of matters in civil affairs work which constitute state secrets, without needing to define the range of secrecy at every level.

To understand accurately and implement precisely the *Regulations on the Specific Range of State Secrets in Civil Affairs Work and Their Classification Level*, and with the approval of the State Secrets Bureau, [we have prepared the following] explanations of the relevant provisions:

a)   Item #1 among the "top secret" (*juemiji*) items in Article 2 of the *Range of Secrets*, "[figures] possessed by the Ministry of Civil Affairs on numbers of wounded, disabled, and losses by our armed forces in wartime," refers to [figures on] numbers of dead and wounded suffered by our armed forces in the course of war or of undertaking military tasks, which have not yet been made public by the responsible state or military authorities.

b)   Item #3 among the "top secret" items in Article 2 of the *Range of Secrets*, "major military operations," refers to unusual troop maneuvers, such as battles, exercises, redeployments, and military transports for defense preparedness.

---

[390] Reprinted in *Selective Compilation of Documents on Civil Affairs Work (Minzheng Gongzuo Wenjian Xuanbian)*, 1991 edition ed. Ministry of Civil Affairs Policy and Regulations Office (Beijing: Zhongguo Shehui Chubanshe, November 1992), pp.45-46.

c)   Item #6 among the "top secret" items in Article 2 of the *Range of Secrets*, "material results and data from scientific research of major economic value," refers to social welfare enterprises reaching or passing advanced international standards, scientific research of great economic value, and other relevant materials or data.

d)   The provisions of the *Range of Secrets* relating to "national statistical data" include provincial-level statistical data.

Appendix M.   Laws and Regulations Relating to the Treatment of Chinese Orphans

1. Excerpts from the "People's Republic of China Law for the Protection of Disabled Persons" (Enacted May 15, 1991)

Section I.   General Principles

> Article 1. To safeguard the lawful rights and interests of disabled persons, to develop facilities for the disabled, and to ensure that disabled persons participate equally in the abundance of social life and share in the material and cultural products of society, this Law is enacted in accordance with the Constitution...

> Article 3. Disabled persons enjoy equal rights with other citizens in such areas as political, economic, cultural, social, and family life. The citizens' rights, dignity, and honor of disabled persons shall receive the protection of law. It is forbidden to discriminate against, humiliate, or harm disabled persons.

> Article 4. The state shall take supplementary measures and undertake programs of assistance to give special help to disabled persons, to alleviate or eliminate the effects of their disabilities and of obstacles in the outside world, and to realize the guarantees of disabled persons' rights and interests.

> Article 5. The state and society shall implement special guarantees for disabled soldiers, [official] personnel disabled while on duty, and other personnel disabled in the course of safeguarding the rights and interests of the state and the people, and give them preferential treatment and compensation...

Section II.   Rehabilitation

> Article 13. The state and society shall adopt measures for rehabilitation, in order to help disabled persons recover or compensate [for the loss of] their functions, and to enhance their ability to participate in social life...

> Article 15. [...] Educational institutions for disabled persons, welfare enterprises and organizational units, and other institutions serving the

disabled, shall create conditions for the development of rehabilitation and training activities...

Section III.   Education

Article 18. The state guarantees the right of disabled persons to receive education...
The state, society, schools, and families must implement compulsory education for disabled children and young people...

Article 22. Ordinary educational institutions shall educate disabled persons who are capable of receiving ordinary education.

Ordinary schools at the primary and junior middle school level must enroll disabled children and young people who can adapt to a life of study. Ordinary senior middle schools, technical and vocational schools, and higher-level educational institutions must enroll disabled candidates who meet the state's admission standards, and may not refuse to enroll them because of their disabilities; if they refuse to enroll [a disabled person], the [affected] party or his relatives or guardians may demand that the relevant departments take action, and the relevant departments must order the school to enroll him...

Section IV.   Labor and Employment

Article 27. The state guarantees the right of disabled persons to labor.
The people's governments at all levels must make comprehensive plans for the labor and employment of disabled persons, and create conditions for labor and employment of the disabled...

Section VI.   Welfare

Article 43. Local people's governments at all levels and society should establish welfare institutes and other organs for settlement and fostering, to settle and foster disabled persons in accordance with regulations, and to gradually improve their lives.

Section VIII.   Legal Responsibility

Article 47. When the lawful rights and interests of a disabled person are violated, the victim or his proxy has the right to demand that the responsible departments involved take action, or to bring suit in a people's court in accordance with the law.

Article 48. When a state employee infringes the lawful rights and interests of a disabled person through violation of the rules or dereliction of duty, his work unit or a higher-level organ shall order him to make restitution or shall take administrative measures against him...

2. Excerpts from the "People's Republic of China Law for the Protection of Minors" (Enacted September 4, 1991)

Section I.   General Principles

Article 1. To protect the physical and mental health of minors, to guarantee their lawful rights and interests, and to advance the comprehensive development of minors' moral character, intelligence, and constitution, and to bring them up as inheritors of the tasks of socialism, with ideals, moral principles, culture, and discipline, this Law is enacted in accordance with the Constitution.

Article 2. For the purposes of this Law, minors are citizens who have not reached the age of 18...

Article 5. The state guarantees that the personal, financial, and other lawful rights and interests of minors shall not be infringed...All organizations and individuals have the right to discourage, prohibit, or report to relevant authorities actions which infringe the lawful rights and interests of minors...

Article 6. Central and regional state bodies at all levels should work well for the protection of minors within their respective fields of authority...

The Communist Youth League, the Women's Federation, the General Labor Union, the Youth Federation, the Students' Union, the Youth Vanguard, and other social groups should assist the people's governments at all levels in working for the protection of minors, and in safeguarding the lawful rights and interests of minors...

Section III.   Protection in School

Article 14. Schools should respect the right of minors to receive education, and should not arbitrarily expel minor students.

Article 15. Education workers in schools and kindergartens (*you'eryuan*) should respect the individual dignity of minors, and should not practice corporal punishment, disguised forms of corporal punishment (*bianxiang ticheng*) or other actions which humiliate individual dignity...

Section IV.   Protection in Society

Article 28. No organization or individual may employ minors under the age of 16, except in accordance with other state regulations...

Article 29. The civil affairs departments or other relevant departments should be responsible for returning vagrant and runaway minors to their parents or other guardians. If there is no way to identify their parents or other guardians for the time being, they should be fostered and cared for at child welfare organs (*ertong fuli jigou*) established by the civil affairs departments...

Article 31. No organization or individual may confiscate or destroy the correspondence of minors, except when the public security organs or the procuracy is conducting an investigation in accordance with laws and regulations, necessary to solve a crime...

Article 32. The public health departments and the schools should implement necessary health protection measures for minors, and work well for the prevention of disease...

Article 34. The public health departments should implement the vaccination certificate system, actively prevent common and widespread diseases, strengthen the supervision and management of the prevention of contagious diseases, and guide the health protection work of day-care centers and kindergartens...

Article 37. For minors who have reached the stipulated age limit for compulsory education and who do not enter a higher school, the relevant government departments and social groups, enterprises, and organizational units should undertake employment and technical training, and should create conditions for their labor and employment, in accordance with the actual situation...

Section V.   Administrative Protection

Article 41. The public security bodies, the people's procuracy, and the people's courts should hold minors awaiting trial or those in detention separately from detained adults...

3. Excerpts from the "Adoption Law of the People's Republic of China" (Enacted December 29, 1991)

Section I.   General Principles

Article 1. To protect lawful adoption relationships, and to safeguard the rights and interests of those in adoption relationships, this Law is enacted.

Article 2. Adoption should be for the benefit of the adopted minor's support and upbringing, adhering to the principles of equality and voluntarism, and should not violate public morals.

Article 3. Adoption should not violate laws and regulations on family planning.

Section II.   Establishment of the Adoption Relationship

Article 4. The following [categories of] minors under the age of 14 may be adopted:

a)   orphans who have lost their parents;
b)   abandoned infants and children whose parents cannot be found after investigation;
c)   children whose birth parents are in especially difficult circumstances and have no way of supporting them.

Article 5. The following [categories of] citizens and organizations may give up [children] for adoption (*zuo songyang ren*):

a)   guardians of orphans;
b)   social welfare organs;
c)   birth parents in especially difficult circumstances, who have no way of supporting their children.

Article 6. Adoptive [parents] must meet the following criteria at the time [of adoption]:

a)   [They must] be childless;
b)   [They must] have the ability to support and educate the adopted [child];
c)   [They must] have reached the age of 35...

Article 8. Adoptive [parents] may only adopt one child.

Those who adopt orphans or disabled children need not be childless or have reached the age of 35, nor need they observe the limit of adopting one [child].

Article 9. When an unmarried male adopts a female, the ages of the adoptive [parent] and the adopted [child] must differ by more than 40 years...

Article 15. Adoptions of abandoned infants and children whose parents cannot be found after investigation, as well as of orphans cared for by social welfare organs, must be in accordance with the regulations of the civil affairs departments...

Article 16. Orphans and children whose birth parents cannot support them may be fostered (*fuyang*) by relatives or friends of their birth parents.

The relationship of a fostering [adult] and fostered [child] does not constitute an adoption relationship (*shouyang guanxi*)...

Article 18. Persons giving up [children] for adoption may not do so with the aim of having more children in violation of the family planning regulations.

Article 19. It is strictly forbidden to buy and sell children, or to buy and sell children under the guise of adoption.

Article 20. Foreigners may adopt children in the People's Republic of China in accordance with this Law.

Foreigners who adopt children in the People's Republic of China must submit documentation proving the circumstances of the adoptive [parents], such as age, marital status, occupation, assets, health, and absence of a criminal record. This documentation must go through a state notary body or notary public in the locality, and must also be certified by a People's Republic of China consulate in the country [concerned]. The adoptive [parent] must conclude a written agreement with the person giving up [the child] for adoption,[391] must personally register with the civil affairs department, and must have the adoption notarized at an appointed notary office. The adoption relationship takes effect on the day the notarization is certified...

Section V.   Legal Responsibility

Article 30. Criminal responsibility shall be sought for those who traffic in children under the guise of adoption, in accordance with the "Decision of the Standing Committee of the National People's Congress on Severely Punishing Criminal Elements Who Traffic and Kidnap Women and Children."

Those who abandon infants and children shall be fined not more than 1,000 yuan by the public security authorities. When the circumstances are especially grave, this constitutes a crime, and responsibility shall be sought in accordance with Article 183 of the "Criminal Law of the People's Republic of China"[392]...

---

[391] As specified in Article 5, the term *songyang ren*, "person giving up [a child] for adoption," includes orphanages and other social welfare institutions as well as natural persons.

[392] "Anyone who bears the responsibility of caring for an aged person, small child, sick person, or anyone else unable to live independently, and who refuses to do so, shall, if the circumstances are especially grave, be subject to not more than five years' imprisonment, detention, or surveillance." *The Criminal Law and the Criminal Procedure Law of China* (Beijing: Foreign Languages Press, 1984), p. 61.

4. Excerpts from "Notice of the People's Republic of China Ministry of Civil Affairs On Strictly Distinguishing, In the Handling of Adoption Registrations, Between Orphans and Abandoned Infants Whose Birth Parents Cannot Be Found After Investigation" (Promulgated August 11, 1992)[393]

To the civil affairs offices and bureaus of every province, autonomous region, and directly-administered city...

Since the enactment of the "Adoption Law of the People's Republic of China," adoption registration work has already begun developing in every region. It has now been discovered that in the course of registering adoptions, various regions have differing viewpoints and policies towards orphans (*gu 'er*) and abandoned infants whose birth parents cannot be found after investigation (*cha zhaobudao sheng fumu de qiying*), and that some errors have emerged. In order to strictly implement the "Adoption Law," to safeguard the lawful rights and interests of the parties, and to [deal with] the present problem, the following special notice [is issued]:

1) Those referred to as orphans (*gu 'er*) in our country's "Adoption Law" are minors under the age of 14 whose parents are proved to have died or whose parents are declared dead by a people's court.

2) [Persons] offering orphans for adoption must submit to the relevant authorities the death certificates produced for the orphans' parents (certificates of natural death to be produced by medical or public health units, and certificates of unnatural death to be produced by public security authorities at or above the county level), or a finding by a people's court declaring them dead.

3) Adoption registrars should strictly investigate evidence of the deaths of orphans' parents submitted by the parties, undertake necessary checks, and archive the records of their investigations. The adoption registry body should refuse to perform registrations for parties who practice fraud and deception. If a registrar investigates inadequately or is negligent, his supervisory body should cancel his qualifications to register adoptions or administer other necessary administrative penalties...

---

[393] *Selective Compilation of Documents on Civil Affairs Work (Minzheng Gongzuo Wenjian Xuanbian)*, 1992 edition ed. Ministry of Civil Affairs Policy and Regulations Office (Beijing: Zhongguo Shehui Chubanshe, October 1993), p. 354.

Appendix N. Unpublished Letter To The Editors of *China Youth Daily*[394]

Should Adopting An Abandoned Baby Be Punished?

On June 14 of last year, my husband and I went to the city of Hanzhong on business, and we stayed at my younger brother's place. As we were chatting, he said: "The police station on Nanda Street brought in a baby girl last night, not yet a month old. She's being kept temporarily at the home of an old woman. It's been more than ten days now, and still nobody wants her. It's awfully sad." I felt sympathy for this abandoned infant and hatred for the immoral action of her natural parents. In addition, I was influenced by a report in the fourth issue of *Women of China* of 1981, on the exemplary act of the woman Party member Liu Manli, who adopted four orphans.

I was determined to adopt this abandoned baby, with the aim of fulfilling my duty to society. After we had made the decision and had brought her home, we were then censured by the family planning office at the factory, which stubbornly insisted that this constituted having a second child in defiance [of the rules] (*qiangxing sheng de di'er tai*), and wanted us to send the baby back where she came from. Otherwise, we would be dealt with according to the family planning regulations of Shaanxi Province. We said that since the police station had agreed to give us the baby, and had issued us a certificate, we had therefore acted responsibly towards the [government] organization and the baby, and it would be wrong for us to send her back. Although we explained this many times, it was no use.

Since then, the factory's family planning office has not only withdrawn our single-child certificate and cancelled only-child treatment for my son,[395] but at the same time has fined us both 20 percent of our wages every month, greatly affecting the livelihood of our entire family. If we are to enjoy the status of a single-child [family], must we then not do such a good deed? I really can't understand it.

(Signed:)   Liu Yu
                 Hanzhong City, Shaanxi Province

---

[394] Reprinted in the internal periodical *Digest Of Letters From Youth (Qingnian Laixin Zhaibian)*, issue 365 (December 15, 1982).

[395] Single-child families in urban China are entitled to preferential treatment in areas such as housing and school assignment.

Appendix O. **Excerpts From Press Report On The Provisions Of China's "Draft Law On Eugenics And Health Protection" (December 20, 1993)**[396]

State Plans Laws To Prevent 'Inferior' Births

Beijing, December 20 (Xinhua): China is to use legal means to avoid new births of inferior quality and heighten the standards of the whole population.

The measures include deferring the date of marriage, terminating pregnancies and sterilization, according to a draft law on eugenics and health protection, which was presented to the current session of the Eighth National People's Congress (NPC) Standing Committee.

Explaining the law to participants at an NPC session that opened here today, Minister of Public Health Chen Minzhang said that the measures will help prevent infections and heredity diseases [*sic*] and protect the health of mothers and children.

Under the draft law, those having such ailments as hepatitis, venereal disease or mental illness, which can be passed on through birth, will be banned from marrying while carrying the disease.

Pregnant women who have been diagnosed as having certain infectious diseases or an abnormal fetus will be advised to halt the pregnancy. Couples in the category [*sic*] should have themselves sterilized, the draft says.

China is in urgent need of adopting such a law to put a stop to the prevalence of abnormal births, Minister Chen explained. Statistics show that China now has more than 10 million disabled persons who could have been prevented through better controls...

The draft does not state whether China will adopt euthanasia to eliminate congenitally abnormal children, saying that the international community has not come to a conclusion on that issue...

---

[396] English translation from *Foreign Broadcast Information Service* (FBIS-CHI-93-242), December 20, 1993, p. 16.

Appendix P.   Article From *Der Spiegel*, No. 37 (September 11, 1995)[397]

The Children's Gulag of Harbin

(Jürgen Kremb on the Gruesome Consequences of the One-child Policy)

A second knock is not necessary. The crying begins at once. "Shush, shush," call shrill little voices, wildly confused. Behind the thick metal-plated door a heavy iron bolt is pushed to the side, and with a loud rasp the greasy gate swings open. The noisy confusion could indicate relaxed warmth, but a glance shows that it is horribly otherwise. Children like discarded, abandoned human garbage, their hands raven-black with dirt, their faces smeared with leftover food, snot, and excrement, their small bodies strangely twisted.

A bloated young boy with hair loss who looks like a shrunken old man stares with a dull look at the foreigners. He turns around, shuffles in his urine-soaked cloth shoes to the whitewashed walls, and swings his upper body back and forth. Again and again his forehead hits the wall.

"*Shazi*" (blockhead), says the overseer harshly. Waving her hands in the air, she herds the children into the inside of the barracks and points to the pupil: "That one, he can't be helped, he's always doing the same nonsense."

What is stupid is this rash diagnosis: every educated caretaker would recognize this behavior as hospitalitis. Children show such behavior when they've been locked up for months and years. The little Junjun, who answers slowly and with a smile when one asks him something, tries to attract attention, obviously longs for a little tenderness and closeness.

But that is not the aim of the overseer. She minces around on black high-heeled shoes, frazzled, among her pupils, and threatens them imperiously to silence. She is alone in the department, with no other care personnel. It is Children's Day in China, on which happy children kiss the top Communist cadres on state television and Young Pioneers parade with red neck-scarves and starched white shirts in Tiananmen Square. And most employees of the state orphanages in northeast China's Harbin have the weekend off.

But on normal workdays there is also a dramatic lack of care-workers. Mentally retarded women, who themselves are confined here for life, must take care of three-year-old foundlings as well as babies with harelips. Children in China, especially girls, are abandoned for quite minor defects, such as birthmarks.

---

[397] English translation by Carol Rigsby.

The overseer rapidly barricades the entrance door behind the foreigner and thrusts her pointed chin forward: "Over there, there they all are." She quickly stamps into the care-room. Her boyfriend is visiting today. Who doesn't want to have his rest? In her absence Guo Ying is to look after the proprieties.

Guo Ying is 14 years old. At least that's what it says on the yellowed slip of paper attached to her bed. She's just 4 feet 2 inches tall and thin as a rake. Her father is a drunkard, and her mother landed in an insane asylum. That brought her the stigma of mental illness. She has never attended a school; she can only leave the orphanage with the consent of her parents. But where are they? Guo Ying shrugs her shoulders. She has a life sentence. Yet of all people, this half-grown girl is the "Mother of the Station." Running past, she takes from the autistic boy the sticky cornbread he has just soaked in the waste water from the toilet. She takes out of the hands of an eight-year-old boy the tin bowl with which he is hammering a handicapped girl on the skull.

Then, where the care-worker had pointed with her arrogant movement, Guo Ying goes along a long hall. The plaster is crumbling from the wall. In a dim room, as big as a dance hall, babies and small children are lying–no, they are not lying, they are laid out, in cribs: handicapped small bodies, some just skin and bones.

Kicking and thrashing, they doze in their own urine, some naked, some dressed in a dirty little jacket. About 30 infants and small children are here, together with 20 mostly mongoloid women, shut off from the outside world....This room that's grave-cool even in summer is a madhouse and dying wing at the same time. The children's gulag of Harbin.

With a contorted face, an old, mentally handicapped woman staggers, shaken by howling cramps. In an eating room smeared with filth, two girls, perhaps eight years old, have been sitting for hours on the pot–with thick, suppurating wounds on their arms and legs. Now and then they emit a guttural howling sound. But mostly they stare with wide-open eyes into the void. Sometimes, when one of the older children splashes the unidentifiable fodder from a tin pail into an enamel bowl, they again stuff something into their mouths with excrement-smeared fingers.

The windows have not been cleaned in a long time. Dirt clings to the glass and the frames; outside there are iron bars. It stinks of excrement and decay.

Under a bed in the next room: a small bundle of rags. "Dead," says the graceful Guo Ying, motionless. Last night, the infant, whose name no one knows, died. "While feeding, he couldn't take in any more air." He apparently suffocated, she guesses, shrugging her shoulders. The older children have wrapped the body in a couple of dirty cloths, which serve as a shroud. Then they shoved the dead baby under the bed, where it stays until the staff get around to removing the corpse. On weekends that can take two or three days. That's normal here. On the holiday, on "Children's Day," the children played undertaker.

Taiping District, where the "welfare institute" (*fuliyuan*) stands on a street lined with plane trees, is not one of the better addresses in Harbin. An asphalt path damaged by frost leads from the suburbs of the capital of Heilongjiang Province through an ugly industrial landscape.

Up here, in the former Manchuria, is China's Siberia. For generations, governments have banished men to the pitiless border province. In the Sixties, the Communists furnished the landscape along the Amur and Ussuri with garrison towns, settled with young Red Guards from the big cities or with convicts. They were supposed to drain the swamps and make the fields tillable.

Revolutionary dreams end here in despair. Like exhausted monsters, the industrial giants of the trash-can economy disfigure the anti-human landscape.

The street to the orphanage leads past a cookshop and an auto-repair shop. Two prisons with big watchtowers line the horizon, in front of which uniformed men with big searchlights cut a path through the landscape at night.

The exterior of the institute is not especially striking. Behind a grate, which keeps the children from the street, lives the administration of the home. Ding Changkui, the leader of the establishment, is a former soldier. In the main building are housed those inhabitants who, after an unfathomable selection process, have been found worthy to live.

Deng Pufang, son of the Communist Party patriarch Deng Xiaoping, visited this section of the establishment in 1987. Yellowed color pictures in a display case give information about it. Deng Pufang, who has been paralyzed from the waist down since a torture session during the Cultural Revolution, leads China's association for the handicapped. "Since he was here, conditions have improved," says a nurse. The children no longer have to spend the night together on a wooden bed.

Among the children, girls are in the majority here as well. Still, only a very few are true orphans; most were abandoned by their parents because they prefer male descendants and because they want to be free of their daughters on account of the state-ordered one-child policy. Besides, most could not pay for the treatment of chronic illnesses.

But the showcase station is only one part of the orphanage. Block Three, the terrible death house for handicapped infants and small children, normally remains forbidden to visitors. It lies hidden behind shrubs. "When I set foot in here for the first time," says the Canadian teacher Peter Costello, "I thought to myself, 'I've entered Hell.'"

The lecturer came to China with his wife Melanie in the fall of 1993. He heard about the establishment from a social worker he had befriended. He visited it and then came back almost every weekend. "I soon came to terms with the dirt and the filth, the almost medieval hygiene in which the children vegetate," the lanky young man reports. But then he discovered: again and again, babies disappeared from Block Three. He began to take notes for himself.

At the beginning of this year, the younger residents, separated between boys and girls, received a number–followed by the date on which they were first delivered. Under "status," Costello noted "died," or only "gone" when he couldn't confirm the exact cause of the departure. Under "details," he listed the reconstructed cause of death. As the most common single cause there stood: "starved, died of thirst."

The list grew into a gruesome accounting, comprehensive proof of the existence, denied by the Chinese government, of dying rooms in the country's orphanages. "We've seen about 100 babies die here in the last two years," says the Canadian. Of the 50 children he has put down on his list since the beginning of January, 36 are certainly dead, possibly 40.

"There's no lack of reinforcements for the death houses," says an American, who for fear of being expelled does not want to be named, and who tries, along with other foreigners, to arrange for the adoption of orphaned children overseas. In the past year, such projects have earned about 22 million marks [US $15,600,000] in income for the Chinese government–at least a tenth of the skimpy state budget for orphans and the handicapped.[398]

Yet the hardliners of the central Party are opposing this policy. They fear loss of face for China if it comes out that neglected and handicapped children are being pushed out to foreign lands. "I would rather have seen all the children die in our country," the American overheard from Zhang Xiaoping in Beijing's Ministry of Civil Affairs, "than have them destroy our image abroad." The functionary Zhang heads the Bureau for Foreign Adoptions.

There are no reliable statistics on how many children vegetate in China's orphanages. In the central Chinese province of Jiangxi alone, where nearly 40 million of the 1.24 billion Chinese live, 50,000 babies were abandoned in 1993, according to United Nations figures.

From this one can conclude that in the whole of China, around a million children are abandoned each year by their parents, in train stations, department stores, or even hospitals. "We must assume from these numbers that in the well-managed orphanages, 50 percent of the children die," says Gale Johnson, one of the USA's leading Sinologists. "In the average ones, it's 80 percent. In the poorly-run

---

[398] In fact, the total budget for all of China's "child welfare institutes" in 1992, the latest year for which Human Rights Watch/Asia has obtained official financial statistics, was only 25,009,000 Chinese yuan. At exchange rates prevailing on October 31, 1995, this was equivalent to roughly US$3,000,000. The sum Kremb cites for revenue from overseas adoptions is therefore more than five times the state's own budget for orphanage care in 1992. Figures from *China Civil Affairs Statistical Yearbook* (1993 edition), p. 326.

institutions, scarcely anyone survives," says Johnson, whose grown daughter herself has three adopted Chinese children. This death rate, he knows, is without parallel even among Asian developing nations.

The blame for the fact that children in socialist China are abandoned and die wretchedly is assigned by the American expert to the official one-child policy. As long as only inadequate social insurance exists for China's 800 million rural dwellers, many poor farmers will see no other alternative than simply to throw away handicapped children–and often healthy girls as well. It's true that in the countryside the Party often turns a blind eye when one child too many is born, especially to parents who can afford to bribe the local cadre. Yet occasionally the Party bigwigs strip the farmers of house and home as a punishment.

The "Gathering Place for Social Problem Cases" is located at Harbin's Number 7 Long Summer Lane. The houses here are somewhat more charming than the comfortless socialist mass-produced buildings of other large Chinese cities. White Russian immigrants built these buildings in the Twenties.

Two slovenly-dressed policemen in sweat-soaked undershirts are building an entrance to the office. "No admittance for foreigners," they bark at the visitor, but then a friendly old official invites us into her office on the second floor. Yang Fan is responsible for foundlings. "We find them most often in railway stations and in department stores, or they are left behind in the hospitals after the mother has delivered."

Don't you find it strange that in a so-called socialist state, of all places, parents throw away their handicapped children–and above all their daughters–like used tissue paper? "We know there are certain problems with the one-child policy," she finally says with an uninterested shrug of her shoulders. "Besides, many children are already frozen when they are brought to us. In northern China it gets very cold in the winter."

During the past fall, lecturer Costello met with the American Brent Johnson, who also knows of the inhuman conditions in the orphanages and wants to change something. Together with the Nebraska doctor, Costello developed an ambitious plan to found an adoption agency himself.

The idea is simple. Childless couples from the USA pay between five and ten thousand dollars for an adoption. The orphanage, so they offer, will receive three thousand of that; the rest is needed for fees, plane tickets, and certifications.

That this is more difficult in practice Costello and Johnson have already learned with their first case, the tiny Ku Cong from Block Three of the Harbin orphanage. The seven-month-old girl with a large birthmark on her face is gravely ill. After a long stay in the poorly-heated dying wing, her body is covered with chilblains. It is questionable how long she will last.

Orphans in Harbin: The Official Story

Not all visitors to the Harbin Social Welfare Institute were shown the same conditions witnessed by German journalist Jürgen Kremb. On May 31, 1995, one day before Kremb's visit, the institute hosted a large official delegation to commemorate International Children's Day. An official local newspaper reported the event as follows:

> *On the eve of June first, there were many visitors to the Harbin Social Welfare Institute. Yesterday afternoon, friends from the municipal People's Congress, the municipal People's Political Consultative Congress, the Foreign Investment Bureau, the municipal committee of the Communist Youth League, the Civil Affairs Bureau, and the Office of Spiritual Civilization came to visit and show their solicitude to the 70 orphans and handicapped children. Today, the Youth League committee of the municipal Administration Bureau took the children to the playground for the [Children's Day] festival.*
> *For several days, the welfare institute has been filled with happiness and friendship. Zhang Fan, general manager of the Japanese-owned Tiancan Food Company, sent the children 1,000 bags of potato chips in four different varieties. The "Looking for Kin Group" organized by Youth League cadres of the Civil Affairs Bureau came here, held the orphans they had become familiar with in their arms, and engaged in small talk. A Christian church from Nangang gave the children 140 suits of new clothing. Pupils from the Dongxin Primary School in Taiping District came to hold hands with the children here under the sun.*
> *According to the welfare institute's leadership, some 300 people from 30 units have come to visit the children in the last few days.*
>
> (From: *Heilongjiang Daily*, June 1, 1995)

Although the two lecturers at a Chinese university earn only 1,500 yuan (266 marks) per month, they have advanced money to the hospital. They have also found foster parents, who for about 100 marks will feed the girl until she can leave the country.

Nevertheless, institute director Ding at first refuses: he sniffs business. Let Ku Cong leave? Only in return for a "transfer fee" of 10,000 yuan (1,775 marks), says the ex-soldier. Normally, one counts on 10 marks a month for [support of] a child in an orphanage.

Ku Cong threatens to fall into a coma. Costello wraps the infant in his loose quilted army jacket. He storms out with her. And takes her to the hospital. Ku Cong survives. A doctor declares himself ready to remove her birthmark for 1,000 yuan. Soon the little girl, long since fat and chubby-cheeked, will be brought to her adoptive parents in the USA.

Johnson, himself the father of a blond two-year-old, has taken a dying girl to the hospital. Guo Fengtian looks like the victim of an African famine. "Third-degree malnutrition," the doctors in Harbin's No.1 Hospital certify. Her bottom is chafed with wounds and shows open suppurating holes. A deep wound stretches across her lower leg, as if someone had tried to amputate the already lifeless little leg with a wire.

The girl, who in the orphanage was considered mentally disturbed, reveals herself after a few weeks of care with bottled milk and fruit pulp as a normally developed infant. In the meantime, Johnson has found a new home for Guo Fengtian in the USA.

Now the orphanage must produce the little one's files, so that the authorities and the US Embassy in Beijing can arrange the departure. In the notebook is found a letter on thin rice paper. It was attached to the foundling, whom a watchman discovered in a stairwell of Harbin's Qiulin Department Store. The sentences are in clumsy handwriting, written with large characters.

"Kind-hearted people, we are abandoning our child not because we cannot care for her, but because of the official one-child policy. Dear daughter, we do not have bad hearts. We couldn't keep you. Friendly people who take her up, we cannot repay the debt in this life. But perhaps in the next life."

Appendix Q. Recent Official Commentary On China's Child Welfare System

1. Excerpts from Article in China Daily (October 1, 1994)[399]

"Fostering Parental Ties For The Orphans"

(By Chen Liang)

Xi Jie sits in bed and peers at the door of the nursery every Saturday after lunch, anxious and restless. The 7-year-old orphan can hardly wait for Ma Jia and her husband, Sun Shenpin, to pick her up.

To her, Ma and Sun are "mother and father." Ma, a worker in a State-owned factory, and Sun, who works in a joint-venture with overseas investment, have taken in Xi as their "foster" daughter. Every Saturday they bring her to their home for the weekend, leaving behind the lonely confines of the Shanghai Children's Welfare Institute...

Xi does not know who her real parents are. She has lived in the orphanage for seven years. But now the girl with the pigeon-toed, or knock-kneed, left foot has found parental hugs and family warmth in Ma and Sun.

The yard in the Children's Welfare Institute is clean and shaded, hidden in a back-alley of Shanghai. It has provided a quiet and secure life for Xi and 500 other orphans.

"Food and clothing alone are not enough for the children's development," said Huang Jiachun, vice-director of the orphanage. "They need emotional ties, family care and body contact with their dear ones. Especially since 98 per cent of the kids suffer from various disabilities [sic]."

Nurses at the institute have tried their best. "We make it a rule that nurses should spend some time holding children in their arms," Huang said. But for every two nurses, there are 27 children to take care of. They must clean the rooms, feed the children, change their diapers and otherwise help them with their problems in turn. "The nurses don't have time for individual attention," Huang said.

So the institute had to turn to the public for help. "Good people, take orphans in your arms please" glared the front pages of the *Shanghai Youth News* and *Xinmin Evening News* in late January. The stories announced that on three days during the Lunar New Year celebration, the orphanage would hold three open houses; volunteers were invited to spend time with the orphans or bring one home for eight hours.

---

[399] Original document in English.

The community's response was beyond Huang's expectation. More than 700 people repied, from the vice-mayor,[400] to a 72-year-old retired teacher, to a 16-year-old student, saying they would attend the open house. "We checked with the applicants who wanted to bring an orphan back home and made sure that they have a harmonious family and no infectious diseases," Huang explained.

So on February 9, the Eve of the Lunar New Year, the first volunteers visited and had supper with orphans. The next day and on the 13th, another two groups enlivened the usually quiet nurseries, and most of the orphans got a hug from warm-hearted strangers. Of the 700 volunteers, 100 were allowed to bring home an orphan who was fit to leave the orphanage temporarily...

Following the trend, the institute in March formally launched its new programme. Those who volunteer for the new programme become "foster" parents, giving orphans a chance to live with a family on weekends. "We just hope that our children can enjoy more warmth with a family," Huang explained...

But Huang and other nurses are not so worried about Xi and the children who have "foster" parents. It is the more than 400 other orphans who have no family or friends outside the institute that have Huang concerned. Some of them suffer from serious heart or mental diseases. And since March, the institute has taken in more than 60 new orphans.

"Some people asked me whether we should invite more volunteers to be foster-parents to the orphans," Huang said, his voice turning bitter. "And I said I hoped it wouldn't be necessary.

"But now, I think we should continue this programme."

2. Excerpt From Front-page Article In **Shanghai Legal News** *(April 5, 1995)*

"The Predicament Of 'Kind-Hearted People'"
(By Staff Reporter Wang Kangmei)

The activity of "kind-hearted people taking orphans in their arms" (*haoxin ren bao-yi-bao gu'er*) and showing them a loving heart has now affected the hearts of all residents of the city. But in the course of recent interviews, this reporter learned of the following matter: many kind-hearted people have developed real affection while taking in orphans, and the orphans and their "families" have developed feelings of deep regret at parting from their loved ones. As a result, some kind-hearted people

---

[400] Xie Lijuan.

have submitted requests for the lawful adoption of orphans, but have unexpectedly run into legal obstacles, leaving these kind-hearted people troubled and perplexed.

According to comrades at the city's Adoption Registration Department, the adoption of orphans must conform to the "Adoption Law" and the "Family Planning Law" [*sic*]. The "Adoption Law" expressly stipulates that persons who adopt must be childless and must have reached the age of 35; if an unmarried man wishes to adopt an orphan girl, the difference in their ages must be at least 40 years. But for the most part, the kind-hearted people who seek to adopt orphans do not meet the criteria mentioned above. If kind-hearted people who already had children were allowed to adopt an orphan, this would also violate the "Family Planning Law."[401] The kind-hearted people who formerly treated [orphans] like their own sons and daughters are affected by this, and cannot but feel regret.

The relevant comrades at the Children's Welfare Institute, although they express concern about this, are willing to help but unable to do so. They told this reporter that for the institute to rear an orphan to the age of 16, the state's contribution for basic living expenses is only 100,000 yuan per capita [sic]. Orphans past the age of 16, when they walk out of the institute's gates, face a set of problems in such [areas] as schooling, employment, marriage and housing. The civil affairs departments expend tremendous efforts on these, and "kind-hearted people" have gladly lent a hand to lighten this burden on the state. Moreover, the loving concern of the "kind-hearted people" for orphans' upbringing is also extremely beneficial. Under the institute's authorized [staffing] limits, there are normally two employees to look after more than 20 orphans.[402] Although the spirit is willing, this is obviously not enough to give them more "stimulation" in language and activity. Originally, the orphans taken home by these kind-hearted people, although not considered to be disabled children, were all noticeably slow in their intellectual and physical development. After bathing in the warmth of a family, these orphans are now changed beyond comparison from before, and some of them are already approaching the condition of normal children...

---

[401] There is, in fact, no nationwide law on family planning in China. The reference here is apparently to an ambiguous provision in the "Shanghai Municipal Family Planning Regulations" (see Chapter 3).

[402] I.e., on each ward.

*3. Article in **Labor News** (April 30, 1995)*

> "Giving Complete Mother's Love To 'Defective' Children: Interview With Xu Shanzhen, A Child-Care Worker At The Children's Welfare Institute"
>
> (Reporter: Ren Chun)

On the morning of April 28, a gong and drum sounded at the Shanghai Children's Welfare Institute, and there was great rejoicing. Leaders such as Wang Fumao, the deputy [Communist] Party secretary of the municipal Civil Affairs Bureau, had made a special trip to the orphanage, to send off the nation's only Model Worker within the civil affairs system–child-care worker Xu Shanzhen, who was going to Beijing to receive her award. When Xu Shanzhen, who has quietly put in fourteen springs and autumns in her humble position, was "packed off" for the first time by all her co-workers, from the highest to the lowest, she became visibly far more youthful in appearance. Xu Shanzhen accepted some brightly-colored flowers offered up to her by the children, and her eyes became slightly moist.

Since Xu Shanzhen, now aged fifty, was transferred to work at the Children's Welfare Institute in 1981, she has steadfastly persisted in her exceedingly difficult and exhausting task as a child-care worker. For the past decade and more, she has cared for newborn infants, totally paralyzed children, "big simpletons" of thirteen or fourteen. However great their difficulties, once in her hands, children are inevitably neatly dressed and clean. Keeping infants' bodies free from the smell of urine is not easy at the orphanage, because these pitiful abandoned children suffer, for the most part, from various mental or physical deficiencies, and are unable to control their own behavior. Moreover, as Xu Shanzhen does not shrink from filth or fear hardship, not only does she wipe and change the sick children when needed, she even dresses them up most attractively, because she feels that every person has the right to be beautiful. At times, some children become angry with child-care workers and suddenly launch "surprise attacks" against them, spitting and flinging food in their faces. Xu Shanzhen has had her face scratched and her hair pulled more than once, but she has never once lost her temper with these stupid children (*sha haizi*). She often says, "The children have enough misfortune already, and will never be loved. How can one become angry with them?"

When she sees the children into whom she has poured the love of her entire heart gradually grow up and then leave one by one, she cannot but feel a deep sense of loss in addition to her happiness. When Fang Xiu arrived at the institute afflicted with suppurative meningitis, she had only just reached the age of one, and her illness left her unable to walk or stand. One look at the child's two pleading eyes, and Xu Shanzhen's heart began to ache. She often brought Fang Xiu fish soup and marrow stock prepared in her home to improve her nutrition; she asked a doctor specially to train her in massage techniques, and undertook rehabilitation exercises for Fang Xiu every day; she took great pains to teach her to speak. One year later, Fang Xiu's physical condition and mental ability were obviously strengthened, and on catching sight of Xu Shanzhen, she would call out "Mama!" with affection. At night she would clutch at her, begging her to tell a story, and only afterwards would she finally go to sleep. Two years on, the pair had settled into a deep affection, as of mother and daughter. Not long ago, a childless couple adopted Fang Xiu. Though the "daughter" now had a home to go to, her "mother" wept hot tears.

Xu Shanzhen not only shows loving solicitude for the defective children in every possible way, but has cared unstintingly for some dangerously ill infants. Last autumn, an abandoned infant not yet two months old, Su Xiaoqi, was struck with vomiting, diarrhea, and a persistent high fever. Xu Shanzhen kept watch over her for three days and three nights. Pounding medicine with a pestle and pouring it down the child's throat with water, she finally pulled Xiaoqi back from death's door.

The stature she possesses has come from her own ordinariness. Owing to Xu Shanzhen's outstanding performance in her humble post, her organization has several times awarded her various honors. In the face of the aura [conferred by] these awards, Xu Shanzhen still adheres to her original intentions: "I'm just a good child-care worker." For that one word, "good," she has made efforts far beyond the norm.

4. Excerpts from Article in **People's Daily** *(May 10, 1995)*[403]

"Showing Concern For Orphans Becomes New Common Practice
In Shanghai"

(By Staff Reporter Lu Wangda)

. Since Shanghai launched the activity of "kind-hearted people taking orphans in their arms" during the 1994 Lunar New Year festival, the issue of orphans has become one that attracts growing concern in society with each passing day. As a result, showing concern for orphans has now become a new common practice in the city. As social organizations and people of all walks of life are stretching out their warm hands one after another to donate cash and goods, a batch of orphans deprived of household warmth now find themselves soaked in the warmth of society. Being the only government-funded charitable welfare nursery in the city, the Shanghai Children's

---

[403] English translation from *BBC Monitoring: Summary of World Broadcasts*, May 26, 1995 (text slightly edited for style by Human Rights Watch/Asia).

Welfare Institute now takes care of more than 600 orphans [sic]. This reporter visited the school the other day, and found that it is as clean and tidy as any other kindergarten or school in the city. In the classrooms, this reporter saw children dancing to music and playing games under the direction of their teachers. In an infants' room, this reporter saw child-care workers walking between cribs, feeding infants and changing their diapers. In order to meet children's diverse needs, the school's kitchen prepares such staple foods as liquid formula, nutritious porridge, fried dishes, rice, steamed buns and so on...

For years, the Shanghai Children's Welfare Institute has adhered to the principle of integrating the raising, medical treatment, and education of orphans....For instance, it sends those who are mentally sound but physically handicapped to the city's big hospitals to undergo surgical operations, and provides on-campus rehabilitative treatment combining Western and traditional Chinese medicines to those with difficulties in movement. The school has a Rehabilitation Center open to society, providing comprehensive medical treatment to thousands of handicapped children every year. As a result, a large number of handicapped children has received proper treatment over the past few years. Insofar as the education of orphans is concerned, the school teaches different types of orphans in different ways. For instance, it sends school-aged blind, deaf and dumb orphans to special schools, but still takes care of their daily life and academic learning. Within the institute, there is also a "Master Zhen Chan School"[404] where handicapped children who are incapable of going to normal schools can learn in tutorial classes, nursery classes or elementary classes. The school also teaches children daily life management schools and professional skills, and provides them with vocational training...

The municipal government all along has attached great importance to and shown concern for orphans' welfare undertakings, which have also received warm support and subsidies from a growing number of organizations and individuals. While working in Shanghai, Comrade Jiang Zemin once donated 1,500 yuan, payment for a book he had translated, to the Shanghai Children's Welfare Institute. Master Zhen Chan, a member of the National Committee of the Chinese People's Political Consultative Conference and vice-president of the China Buddhist Association, has donated a total of one million yuan to the school in recent years. Deng Pufang, president of the China Disabled Federation, has also visited the school and met with both handicapped children and also staff members and workers.

---

[404] The orphanage school was renamed in 1993 in honor of Master Zhen Chan, the abbot of Shanghai's Jade Buddha Temple. Master Zhen Chan, who is the vice-president of the state-sponsored China Buddhist Association and president of its Shanghai branch, is a major financial donor to the Children's Welfare Institute (see below).

*[The same issue of **People's Daily** carried a commentary entitled
"Devote More Love," which reads in part:]*

A report carried in this paper today says that Shanghai has successfully run a children's welfare institute, and that people from all walks of life in society are profoundly concerned with the issue of orphans. The report urges party committees and governments at all levels to become more concerned about the issue of orphans, and calls on people from all walks of life in society to show more concern for the growth of orphans.

The issue of orphans is a social issue, as well as a common issue in the world. Orphans can be found in any country, any place and any region. According to statistics, there are now about 100,000 orphans in China, most of whom are young children who are sick in one way or another or are even handicapped....The Party and government all along have attached great importance to and provided protection for orphans' survival, as well as their subsistence rights and interests, and have also properly handled the issue of orphans, including those orphaned by wars, by natural calamities and by birth....There are now more than 1,200 government-funded orphanages and social welfare institutions in the country, taking care of nearly 20,000 orphans. In addition, people from all walks of life in society have stretched out their warm hands to orphans by taking part in building social welfare institutions, and by donating either cash or goods to these institutions. In April 1994, party and state leaders, including Jiang Zemin, Li Peng and Qiao Shi, wrote inscriptions especially for a nationwide campaign called "Program for Assisting Orphans," which was organized and launched by social welfare institutes across the country....To answer the call of the Party and government, the whole country now is indeed showing more concern for the growth of orphans than in the past...

Dear readers, when you and your children have a good time in a park on a holiday, or when you light candles on a birthday cake for your children and sing "Happy Birthday" with your family, do you ever think of orphans, who are deprived of parental love, or of children without homes? Let us carry forward revolutionary humanism and devote more love to them!

*5. Excerpts From "Briefing By The Chinese Embassy On China's Orphanage,"
Issued By The People's Republic Of China Embassy In London In Response To The
Impending Broadcast Of The British Television Documentary* **The Dying Rooms**
(June 1995)[405]

China has all along attached great importance to the healthy development of children, and committed to the substantial protection of the rights of children, orphans in particular, by legislative, judicial and administrative means. The rights of children, including those of orphans, are protected by the Constitution of the People's Republic of China. Chinese laws prohibit the abuse of orphans and anybody who violates the relevant laws will be brought to justice...

The Chinese Government has set up and supported a great number of child welfare establishments....At present, there are 40,000 welfare institutions, including orphanages, in China's rural area, and 100 orphanages in urban area [sic]...

The welfare facilities in China provide orphans with adequate adopting, medical, rehabilitation and educational services until they reach adult age, when they are even helped with employment and marriage. Retarded and seriously disabled orphans are guaranteed life-time care...

The so-called "dying rooms" do not exist in China at all. Our investigations confirm that those reports are vicious fabrications out of ulterior motives. The contemptible lie about China's welfare work in orphanages cannot but arouse the indignation of the Chinese people, especially a great number of social workers who are working hard for children's welfare...

The Chinese government and the whole society have been making tremendous efforts to attain the noble aim of protecting children's rights and giving love and care to the healthy development of orphans. The living conditions of orphans have been improving continuously. This is a fact which can not be misrepresented, nor denied.

---

[405] Original document in English.

Appendix R.   International Standards for Medical Treatment, Including Care of the Disabled and Terminally Ill

1. United Nations and World Medical Association Standards

An extensive body of international standards on medical ethics and physician behavior has been drafted and approved by organizations such as the United Nations and the World Medical Association over the past few decades. A selection of some of the most important and relevant of these is included below for purposes of reference.

*   The core right is that set forth in the Universal Declaration of Human Rights:

    > Article 3.   Everyone has the right to life, liberty and security of the person.

*   According to the International Code of Medical Ethics, adopted by the World Medical Association in 1949 and amended in 1968 and 1983:

    > A physician shall always maintain the highest standards of professional conduct....A physician shall act only in the patient's interests when providing medical care which might have the effect of weakening the physical and medical condition of the patient....A physician shall always bear in mind the obligation of preserving human life...

    > A physician shall owe his patient complete loyalty and all the resources of his science. Whenever an examination or treatment is beyond the physician's capacity he should summon another physician who has the necessary ability.

*   Additional minimal standards of patient care are specified in the Declaration of Lisbon on The Rights of the Patient, adopted by the 34th World Medical Assembly in September/October 1981:

    > ....b) The patient has the right to be cared for by a physician who is free to make clinical and ethical judgements without any outside interference...

e) The patient has the right to die in dignity.

• Moreover, according to the Declaration of Venice on Terminal Illness, adopted by the 35th World Medical Assembly in October 1983:

> 1. The duty of the physician is to heal and, where possible, relieve suffering and act to protect the best interests of his patients.
>
> 2. There shall be no exception to this principle even in the case of incurable disease or malformation.
>
> 3. This principle does not preclude application of the following rules:
>
> 3.1 The physician may relieve suffering of a terminally ill patient by withholding treatment with the consent of the patient or his immediate family if unable to express his will.
>
> Withholding of treatment does not free the physician from his obligation to assist the dying person and give him the necessary medicaments to mitigate the terminal phase of his illness.
>
> 3.2 The physician shall refrain from employing any extraordinary means which would prove of no benefit for the patient...

• At its 36th Assembly, held in Singapore in October 1984, the same body adopted a Statement on Child Abuse and Neglect, which reads in part:

> The World Medical Association recognizes that child maltreatment is a world health problem and recommends that national medical associations adopt the following guidelines for physicians:
>
> 1. Physicians have a special role in identifying and helping abused children and their troubled families...

4. The physician should be alert to the classic features of abuse and neglect...

6. It is the physician's responsibility to do all that he can to protect the child from further harm. This may require promptly contacting the appropriate agency that handles child protection matters, and in some cases, admitting the child to a hospital...

8. During the evaluation process, it is essential that the physician record the findings in the medical chart, since the medical record may provide pivotal evidence in court proceedings.

- According to the Declaration on the Rights of Mentally Retarded Persons, adopted by the U.N. General Assembly in December 20, 1971:

Article 1.   The mentally retarded person has, to the maximum degree of feasibility, the same rights as other human beings.

Article 2.   The mentally retarded person has a right to proper medical care and physical therapy and to such education, training, rehabilitation and guidance as will enable him to develop his ability and maximum potential...

Article 4.   [...] If care in an institution becomes necessary, it should be provided in surroundings and other circumstances as close as possible to those of normal life...

Article 6.   The mentally retarded person has a right to protection from exploitation, abuse and degrading treatment...

- Finally, the United Nations' Convention on the Rights of the Child, which came into force in September 1990 and was ratified by China in December 1991, contains the following wide-ranging protections for the physical and medical well-being of all children, especially those placed in state institutional care:

Article 6.   States Parties recognize that every child has the inherent right to life...

Article 19.   States Parties shall take all appropriate legislative, administrative, social and educational measures to protect the child from all forms of phyical and mental violence, injury or abuse, neglect or negligent treatment, maltreatment or exploitation, including sexual abuse, while in the care of parent(s), legal guardian(s) or any other person who has the care of the child.

Article 20:   A child temporarily or permanently deprived of his or her family environment, or in whose own best interests cannot be allowed to remain in that environment, shall be entitled to special protection and assistance provided by the State.

Article 23:   1. States Parties recognize that a mentally or physically disabled child should enjoy a full and decent life, in conditions which ensure dignity, promote self-reliance and facilitate the child's active participation in the community.

                  2. States Parties recognize the rights of the disabled child to special care and shall encourage the extension, subject to available resources, to the eligible child and those responsible for his or her care, of assistance for which application is made and which is appropriate to the child's condition and to the circumstances of the parents or others caring for the child.

                  3. Recognizing the special needs of a disabled child, assistance extended in accordance with

paragraph 2 of the present article shall be provided free of charge, whenever possible, taking into account the financial resources of the parents or others caring for the child...

Article 24:   1. States Parties recognize the right of the child to the enjoyment of the highest attainable standard of health and to facilities for the treatment of illness and rehabilitation of health. States Parties shall strive to ensure that no child is deprived of his or her right of access to such health care services.

2. States Parties shall pursue full implementation of this right and, in particular, shall take appropriate measures:

(a) To diminish infant and child mortality;

(b) To ensure the provision of necessary medical assistance and health care to all children with emphasis on the development of primary health care;

(c) To combat disease and malnutrition, including within the framework of primary health care, through, *inter alia*, the application of readily available technology and through the provision of adequate nutritious foods and clean drinking-water...

Article 25:   States Parties shall recognize for every child who has been placed by the competent authorities for the purpose of care, protection or treatment of his or her physical or mental health, to a periodic review of the treatment provided to the child and all other circumstances relevant to his or her placement.

2. Standards for Treatment of Seriously Ill Newborns (German and U.S. Medical Professions)

A)   Limits on The Duty To Provide Medical Care For Seriously Defective Newborns[406]

> (Recommendations of the German Society for Medical Law, developed at the First Conference of Experts, held at Einbeck, Germany, June 27-29, 1986.)

I

1. Human life is a value of the highest order within our legal and moral framework. Its protection is a public duty (Article 2, Section 2, Basic Law of the Federal Republic), its maintenance is a primary medical task.

2. To rank the importance of protecting life according to social value, usefulness, bodily condition, or mental capacity violates the moral law and the Constitution.

II

Death is defined, according to both medical and judicial opinion, as the irreversible cessation of brain function (brain death).

The duty to treat ends with the determination of the death of the newborn.

III

The intentional shortening of a newborn's life by means of active intervention violates the commitments of the medical and judicial professions.

IV

1. The physician is required to do that which is best and most effective in maintaining life and mitigating or eliminating existing deficiencies.

---

[406] Translated version taken from *Euthanasia And The Newborn: Conflicts Regarding Saving Lives*, edited by Richard C. McMillan and Tristram Engelhardt, Jr. (Dordrecht: D. Reidel Publishing Company), pp.303-305; translated by S.G.M. Engelhardt.

2. The physician's duty to treat is not determined solely by what is medically possible. It is also to be determined by taking into consideration human-ethical criteria of judgment and the physician's mandate to heal.

3. Therefore, there are cases in which the physician must not employ all means of medical treatment, especially the establishment and maintenance of vital functions and/or massive surgical intervention.

V

These conditions apply whenever, from the standpoint of actual medical experience,

1. Life cannot be maintained for any length of time, but rather certain death will be postponed, e.g. in the case of severe dysrhaphia-syndrome [incomplete closure of the primary neural tube] or inoperable heart defects.

2. In spite of treatment it it is determined that the newborn will never have the possibility of communicating with his environment, e.g. breathing difficulties without possibility of correction, loss of kidney function without possibility of correction.

VI

1. Treatment falls within the realm of the physician's judgment whenever the treatment of a newborn would only afford a life with the most severe, non-remediable deficiencies, e.g. the most severe brain damage or Potter-syndrome [bilateral renal agenesis], with which the duty to treat does not already cease under V.

When determining whether to initiate or discontinue treatment, the physician should be guided by the duty to treat as it pertains to adults with similar probable outcomes.

2. The same holds true with multiple defects, which in their aggregate are just as severe as those individual defects in 1.

A conclusive enumeration of all conceivable case descriptions and their legal evaluation is not possible.

3. The need for the consent of the parents/guardians remains unaffected by these considerations.

VII

The fact that the newborn would have life with disabilities, e.g. caudal dysplasia, mongoloidism, which do not conform to the levels of impairment listed above, does not justify omitting or terminating life-sustaining treatment.

VIII

1. Even if a duty to employ life-sustaining treatment does not exist, the physician must maintain basic care of the newborn.

2. Interventions to mitigate the defects must be carried out, if they are in due proportion to the expected decrease in suffering.

IX

1. The parents/guardian are to be informed about the newborn's affliction and the possibilities for treatment.

They should be included in the decision process from the beginning through the provision of counseling and information.

2. The rights and duties of the parents/guardian to approve of the medical intervention depend on judicial determination.

This means: If the parents/guardian refuse to agree to medically advised treatment, or if they cannot agree, then the court dealing with guardianship [Vormundschaftgericht] must make the decision. If this is not possible, the physician may carry out urgently indicated medical treatment (emergency measures).

X

The above-mentioned findings, the measures adopted, as well as the bases for refusal of life-sustaining treatment, should be documented in an explicit and conclusive form.

B)   Treatment Decisions For Seriously Ill Newborns[407]

(Report #43 of the Council on Ethical And Judicial Affairs of the American Medical Association, June 1992)

[...] IV. Recommendations:

The Council recommends that physicians should play an active role in advocating for change in the Child Abuse Prevention Act as well as state laws that require physicians to violate the following ethical guidelines:[408]

1. The primary consideration for decisions regarding life-sustaining treatment for seriously ill newborns should be what is best for the newborn. Factors that should be weighed are: 1) the chance that therapy will succeed, 2) the risks involved with treatment and non-treatment, 3) the degree to which the therapy, if successful, will extend life, 4) thepain and discomfort associated with the therapy, and 5) the anticipated quality of life for the newborn with and without treatment.

2. Care must be taken to anticipate the newborn's expected quality of life from the child's perspective. Life-sustaining treatment may be withheld or withdrawn from a newborn upon the parents' request when the pain and suffering expected to be endured by the child will overwhelm any potential joy for life during his or her life. When an infant suffers extreme neurologic damage, and is consequently not capable of experiencing either suffering or joy a decision may be made to withhold or withdraw life-sustaining treatment upon the parents' request. When life-sustaining treatment is withheld or withdrawn, comfort care must not be discontinued.

---

[407] *July 1992 Code of Medical Ethics Reports,* Council on Ethical and Judicial Affairs of the American Medical Association, Volume III, Number 2, pp.66-75; the "Recommendations" comprise the final part of this policy statement.

[408] In 1984, the U.S. Congress passed an amendment to the Child Abuse Prevention and Treatment Act that defined withholding medically indicated treatment from disabled infants as medical neglect (42 U.S.C. S 5102 [1984].) The American Medical Association opposed the amendment on the grounds that certain of the criteria for judgment of these issues that the amendment laid down were medically unsound and inaccurate.

3. When an infant's prognosis is largely uncertain, as is often the case with extremely premature newborns, all life-sustaining and life-enhancing treatment should be initiated. Decisions about life-sustaining treatment should be made once the prognosis becomes more certain. It is not necessary to attain absolute or near absolute prognostic certainty before life-sustaining treatment is withdrawn, since this goal is often unattainable and risks unnecessarily prolonging the infant's suffering.

4. Physicians must provide full information to parents of seriously ill newborns regarding the nature of treatments, therapeutic options and expected prognosis with and without therapy, so that parents can make informed decisions for their children about life-sustaining treatment. Counseling services and an opportunity to talk with persons who have had to make similar decisions should be available to parents. Ethics committees or infant review committees should also be utilized to facilitate parental decisionmaking for these decisions. These committees should help mediate resolutions of conflicts that may arise among parents, physicians and others involved in the care of the infant. These committees should also be responsible for referring cases to the appropriate public agencies when it is concluded that the parents' decision is not a decision that could reasonably be judged to be in the best interests of the infant.

C)   Quality of Life[409]

(From "Opinions on Social Policy Issues," prepared by the Council on Ethical and Judicial Affairs of the American Medical Association, 1992)

In the making of decisions for the treatment of seriously deformed newborns or persons who are severely deteriorated victims of injury, illness or advanced age, the primary consideraton should be what is best for the individual patient and not the avoidance of a burden to the family or society. Quality of life is a factor to be considered in determining what is best for the individual. Life should be cherished despite disabilities and handicaps, except when the prolongation would be inhumane and unconscionable.

---

[409] *1992 Code of Medical Ethics Current Opinions*, Council on Ethical and Judicial Affairs of the American Medical Association, Item #2.17.

Under these circumstances, withholding or removing life supporting means is ethical provided that the normal care given an individual who is ill is not discontinued.